NARRATIVES OF DRUNKENNESS: BELGIUM, 1830–1914

Perspectives in Economic and Social History

Series Editors: *Andrew August*
Jari Eloranta

Titles in this Series

1 Migrants and Urban Change: Newcomers to Antwerp, 1760–1860
Anne Winter

2 Female Entrepreneurs in Nineteenth-Century Russia
Galina Ulianova

3 Barriers to Competition: The Evolution of the Debate
Ana Rosado Cubero

4 Rural Unwed Mothers: An American Experience, 1870–1950
Mazie Hough

5 English Catholics and the Education of the Poor, 1847–1902
Eric G. Tenbus

6 The World of Carolus Clusius: Natural History in the Making, 1550–1610
Florike Egmond

7 The Determinants of Entrepreneurship: Leadership, Culture, Institutions
José L. García-Ruiz and Pier Angelo Toninelli (eds)

8 London Clerical Workers, 1880–1914: Development of the Labour Market
Michael Heller

9 The Decline of Jute: Managing Industrial Change
Jim Tomlinson, Carlo Morelli and Valerie Wright

10 Mining and the State in Brazilian Development
Gail D. Triner

11 Global Trade and Commercial Networks: Eighteenth-Century Diamond Merchants
Tijl Vanneste

12 The Clothing Trade in Provincial England, 1800–1850
Alison Toplis

13 Sex in Japan's Globalization, 1870–1930: Prostitutes, Emigration and Nation-Building
Bill Mihalopoulos

14 Financing India's Imperial Railways, 1875–1914
Stuart Sweeney

15 Energy, Trade and Finance in Asia: A Political and Economic Analysis
Justin Dargin and Tai Wei Lim

16 Violence and Racism in Football: Politics and Cultural Conflict in British Society, 1968–1998
Brett Bebber

17 The Economies of Latin America: New Cliometric Data
César Yáñez and Albert Carreras (eds)

18 Meat, Commerce and the City: The London Food Market, 1800–1855
Robyn S. Metcalfe

19 Merchant Colonies in the Early Modern Period
Victor N. Zakharov, Gelina Harlaftis and Olga Katisiardi-Hering (eds)

20 Markets and Growth in Early Modern Europe
Victoria N. Bateman

21 Welfare and Old Age in Europe and North America: The Development of Social Insurance
Bernard Harris (ed.)

22 Female Economic Strategies in the Modern World
Beatrice Moring (ed.)

23 Crime and Community in Reformation Scotland: Negotiating Power in a Burgh Society
J. R. D. Falconer

24 Policing Prostitution, 1856–1886: Deviance, Surveillance and Morality
Catherine Lee

Forthcoming Titles

Respectability and the London Poor, 1780–1870: The Value of Virtue
Lynn MacKay

Mercantilism and Economic Underdevelopment in Scotland, 1600–1783
Philipp Robinson Rössner

Residential Institutions in Britain, 1725–1950: Inmates and Environments
Jane Hamlett, Lesley Hoskins and Rebecca Preston (eds)

Conflict, Commerce and Franco-Scottish Relations, 1560–1713
Siobhan Talbott

Consuls and the Institutions of Global Capitalism, 1783–1914
Ferry de Goey

13 Sex in Japan's Globalization, 1870–1930: Prostitutes, Emigration and Nation-Building
Bill Mihalopoulos

14 Financing India's Imperial Railways, 1875–1914
Stuart Sweeney

15 Energy, Trade and Finance in Asia: A Political and Economic Analysis
Justin Dargin and Tai Wei Lim

16 Violence and Racism in Football: Politics and Cultural Conflict in British Society, 1968–1998
Brett Bebber

17 The Economies of Latin America: New Cliometric Data
César Yáñez and Albert Carreras (eds)

18 Meat, Commerce and the City: The London Food Market, 1800–1855
Robyn S. Metcalfe

19 Merchant Colonies in the Early Modern Period
Victor N. Zakharov, Gelina Harlaftis and Olga Katisiardi-Hering (eds)

20 Markets and Growth in Early Modern Europe
Victoria N. Bateman

21 Welfare and Old Age in Europe and North America: The Development of Social Insurance
Bernard Harris (ed.)

22 Female Economic Strategies in the Modern World
Beatrice Moring (ed.)

23 Crime and Community in Reformation Scotland: Negotiating Power in a Burgh Society
J. R. D. Falconer

24 Policing Prostitution, 1856–1886: Deviance, Surveillance and Morality
Catherine Lee

Forthcoming Titles

Respectability and the London Poor, 1780–1870: The Value of Virtue
Lynn MacKay

Mercantilism and Economic Underdevelopment in Scotland, 1600–1783
Philipp Robinson Rössner

Residential Institutions in Britain, 1725–1950: Inmates and Environments
Jane Hamlett, Lesley Hoskins and Rebecca Preston (eds)

Conflict, Commerce and Franco-Scottish Relations, 1560–1713

Siobhan Talbott

Consuls and the Institutions of Global Capitalism, 1783–1914
Ferry de Goey

NARRATIVES OF DRUNKENNESS: BELGIUM, 1830–1914

BY

An Vleugels

Routledge
Taylor & Francis Group
LONDON AND NEW YORK

First published 2013 by Pickering & Chatto (Publishers) Limited

Published 2016 by Routledge
2 Park Square, Milton Park, Abingdon, Oxfordshire OX14 4RN
711 Third Avenue, New York, NY 10017, USA

First issued in paperback 2015

Routledge is an imprint of the Taylor & Francis Group, an informa business

BRITISH LIBRARY CATALOGUING IN PUBLICATION DATA

Vleugels, An.
Narratives of drunkenness: Belgium, 1830–1914. – (Perspectives in economic and social history)
1. Alcoholism – Social aspects – Belgium – History – 19th century. 2. Alcoholism – Social aspects – Belgium – History – 20th century.
I. Title II. Series
362.2'92'09493'09034-dc23

ISBN-13: 978-1-138-66201-8 (pbk)
ISBN-13: 978-1-8489-3332-3 (hbk)

Typeset by Pickering & Chatto (Publishers) Limited

CONTENTS

ACKNOWLEDGEMENTS

This book took many years to write. I wish to thank Ruth Ireland and Daire Carr at Pickering & Chatto for believing in the work and supporting me to make it finally happen. Special thanks to Stephina Clarke for her invaluable copy-editing work. Many thanks go to the Wellcome Trust for funding the PhD research on which this book is based and to my supportive supervisors and trusted mentors Stephen Jacyna and Michael Neve. My colleagues at the Wellcome Trust Centre for the History of Medicine at UCL made me feel at home. I want to thank my teachers Kaat Wils in Leuven and Catherine Hall in London for their inspiration and for opening my eyes. Many librarians, archivists and curators helped me in my quest for drunkards: Erna Mannaert's help with the government publications from the KUL library has been formidable. I would also like to thank Annemie Cailliau, Frederik de Preester en Alexander Couckhuyt at the Museum, Dr Guislain in Gent, Prof. Emile Kesteman in the Musée Camille Lemonnier in Brussels and An Sijsmans at the Koninklijk Museum voor Schone Kunsten in Antwerpen. I could never have done this without help from colleagues, friends and family who have commented on drafts of the book: Becky Taylor, Ben Slater, Geertje Cools, Anita Kamat and Valerie Brown. I want to thank Pieter Scholliers and Liesbet Nys for encouraging me all those years ago to focus my research and for their helpful suggestions. I also wish to thank all those amazing students who I have had the pleasure to know and who with their questions and observations shaped many of the enquiries in this book. Finally, infinite thanks to Sue Weddell for taking over the most important task, to Evy Van Beurden for her meticulous drive, to Jan Vleugels for his quiet reassurance and for his work behind the scenes, to Bernadette Van Deun for her unfailing belief. And to Igor Pancaldi who always keeps me going.

LIST OF FIGURES

INTRODUCTION

There are many different ways of approaching history. 'Our memory of yesterday', the editors of the *Nouvelle histoire de Belgique* or *Nieuwe Geschiedenis van België* wrote, 'has today many faces'.[1] There are indeed many ways a history of drunkenness in Belgium can be written and this book is one of many such possible stories.

It will explore shifting ideas of deviant behaviour in the making of culture and attempts to understand the role of the drunkard in society. It aims to discover how the preoccupation with excessive drinking and its shifting interpretations revealed wider social and political concerns in a period of profound social change in Belgium from the mid-nineteenth century towards the First World War.

Drink and the Making of Identities

In the stories of drunkenness this book will tell, drinking was a social force whereby identities were formed.[2] It follows hereby the lead offered by anthropologist Mary Douglas when she claimed that 'drink constructs the world'.[3] Within the narratives, I want to discover what drunkenness meant, as it was lived and experienced by different people. I will try to understand the making of certain groups in society through their different opinions of when and how and especially for whom drinking became 'too much' and unacceptable. Social drinking and convivial drunkenness confirmed belonging to a certain group, but at some point drunkenness would become a negative expression of identity; then it belonged to the 'other': the drunkard.[4]

As drunkenness and attitudes towards it are culturally and historically specific, its understanding has changed over time. Getting drunk can be considered as both social and anti-social behaviour, normal and abnormal. Where excess begins and when drunkenness becomes unacceptable or 'habitual' is not clear and depends on who drinks, where, how one behaves and how this behaviour is perceived. At different times social circumstances, biological constitution or moral failure have been considered, to various degrees, responsible for alcoholic excess.

In Belgium, like in the rest of Western Europe, drunkenness became a major concern in the last quarter of the century. Doctors set up temperance movements, law makers legislated against public drunkenness and drunken characters featured in realist and naturalist art and literature. At the same time ideas of decadence, biological decay and national decline made their way into the vocabulary of doctors, politicians and artists. Tracing how drunkenness came to be seen as so worrying is the main question this book tries to answer.

Historians have located a broad shift in the understanding of drunkenness in the second half of the nineteenth century that took place in Europe: from an explanation of intemperance as a vice that could eventually damage the health of individuals and society habitual drunkenness, and more specifically alcoholism, became perceived as directly related to biological disorder.[5] Influenced by the work of Michel Foucault, this shift has been attributed to the redefinition of deviance within 'modern capitalist society' in which drunkards were unproductive and therefore unwanted members of society.

Based on both medical as well as government publications, Pieter Scholliers concluded that in insisting on picturing the drunkard as an 'ill' person rather than as a 'bad' person, bourgeois doctors reinforced not only their influence and prestige, but also contributed to a 'common sense' condemnation of excessive alcohol-drinking. The process of medicalization of drinking was for Scholliers part of a wider project of the bourgeois to directly discipline working-class behaviour.[6] It was the hegemonic bourgeois idea of normality that was being constructed through establishing the difference between acceptable and unacceptable drunkenness.

In 2001, University of Leuven historian Liesbeth Nys wrote about medical disciplinary discourses on alcoholism and venereal disease in the army related to concerns of national efficiency.[7] Nys also addressed the social construction of the medical language about the three 'socials scourges': 'tuberculosis, syphilis and alcoholism'.[8] I wanted in addition to understand the importance of particular medical specializations, especially that of psychiatry and criminal anthropology, following new, interesting routes Belgian historians have taken in the fields of criminology and the study of degeneration as ideologies that were enthusiastically taken up in Belgium in the last quarter of the nineteenth century.[9]

In a last and most stimulating article on absinthe in the fin de siècle in Belgium, Nys explored the complex reality and multiple assumptions related to this particular drink. Here, she investigated the stories on absinthe as multifarious in which various discourses, medical, political, economic, social and national, overlapped.[10] Inspired by this approach I want to further explore the ways in which drunkenness was constructed as undesirable behaviour and how hegemony was established through complex negotiations. I will argue that drunkenness was linked to fears of degeneration to forge a particular shape of modernity. Roger Cooter explained how ideas of degeneration: 'Dialectically ... cut new social paths in medical thinking at the same time as they established new medicalized ways of thinking about society and individual identity'.[11] This book aims to lay bare the directions in which those paths were drawn through a negotiation of difference.

Cultural dichotomies between, for example, normal and abnormal, civilized and savage, culture and nature, healthy and sick, men and women, lower and upper classes and here, essentially, drunk and sober, work at two levels: the use of separate terms highlights their difference, whilst pairing them evokes their kinship.[12] As Foucault has pointed out, such relations are also uneven. While some differences were stressed, other were hushed in order to thereby 'discursively construct "the other"'.[13] Unearthing such constructed differences can provide knowledge about what Raymond Williams has called a 'structure of feeling': a particular way of life producing a distinct organization.[14] Studying multiform narratives of drunkenness can allow access not only to what it meant in the nineteenth and early twentieth century to be drunk but also 'offer insight in the historical processes that brought them about', into the organizing systems underlying Belgian society at this particular historical moment.[15]

Knowledge, Foucault also insisted, is never stable and self-coherent, and one discursive system does not simply reflect another. Drunkenness was a slippery, cultural construct, within which issues of ideology, biology, social environment and morality were constantly intertwined. Contemporary understanding of social formations of gender and social class allowed for overlapping, paradoxical and ambiguous interpretations of the nature of drink, of the nature of free will and of responsibility. Drunkenness as a lived experience affected all classes of society and it elicited different meanings and accordingly needed an explicatory model that could be equally flexible. Drunkenness was constantly reshaped as different historical agents contributed to its meaning, negotiated and re-thought it. The shift in the understandings of drunkenness was therefore a complex cultural event and the relationship between excessive drinking, morality and biology was always ambiguous and multi-layered. The place of drunkenness within complex cultural frameworks is never fixed and meanings always overlap and contradict. Shifts in meaning occur often in parallel with social change but can also reflect a conservative reaction. Contradictory concepts may be used side by side.[16] This shift formed part of larger changes that took place in the second half of the nineteenth century, a period of profound transformation in Belgium in which power structures were redefined and the established social order was severely challenged. The different narratives of drunkenness and stereotypes of the drunkard always carried with them normative assumptions, making them historically complex subjects. They 'powerfully ordered people's experiences and their own self-representations' and so contributed to the making of social categories such as gender, class and race.[17]

In this interpretation, discursive processes that construct the meaning of drunkenness become practices that also systematically form the object of which they talk.[18] They are therefore also firmly linked to social experience, embedded in a network of material practices, to being drunk or having to deal with drunkards. The historian's task should be to 'explain cultural expressions' in their historically situated authorial consciousness.[19] As a historian raised in the empirical tradition of social history, my allegiance is certainly with real past experiences, relationships and actions. Without question alcohol lined the throats of the workers in the pub singing revolutionary songs; it had an impact on the health of the middle-class lady who needed her pick-me-up every day and contributed to the high spirits of her husband celebrating a promotion. Alcoholism most certainly profoundly affected families, then as it does now. However, I also believe that we can only know about the past through representations and that language both constructs and reflects meaning.[20]

The justified criticism by more economically minded and more traditional social historians, that such understanding necessarily has to remain vague, had already been anticipated by the great J. Huizinga so many years ago. He summarized his historical approach in his monumental history of late Middle Ages in the Low Countries as follows: 'Shapes of life and thought it are, whose description is attempted here'. It was not misplaced modesty that made him explain the outcome of his historical work as such, but instead a preoccupation with the limits of the possibilities of historical knowledge. And so he asked, rhetorically – 'To reach the essential content, that has rested in those shapes, will it ever be the work of historical research?'[21]

And so, while ontologically the gap between materiality and representation, between the real and the symbolic is impossible to bridge, recent historical work shows that overcoming the polemic can offer richer, more layered insights in the past as an alternative for a cultural history hijacked by a linguistic turn from one hand or a social history reduced to stratifying and classifying from the other. And so I do not want to think about drunkenness in terms of myth and reality, whereby the social becomes reality and the cultural, the representation becomes myth. In such an analysis the exaggerated grievances about the problem of drunkenness in the writings of the temperance organizations becomes myth, compared to a more 'authentic' historical reality to be found out by other, more traditional social historical work, such as a statistical analysis. Profoundly influenced by the French Annales-School most Belgian social historians showed and often still continue to do so, a partiality to the recording, stratifying and classifying of data. Historical demography, surveys of wages and studies on the standard of living of the working classes, sometimes mention alcohol consumption.[22] I would argue that statistical evidence, often difficult to interpret, is equally vague when it comes to understanding shifting patterns in drinking behaviour and the social role of alcohol. And of course, the specific symbolic values of drinking are not necessarily directly related to the actual amount of alcohol consumed.[23] One analytical approach should not be treated as more legitimate than another.[24]

Hence, throughout this volume I have tried to combine different traditions of historical analysis when exploring past drinking habits.

In this interpretation, all texts circulate together and in combining political, social, cultural and medical histories of drunkenness, I attempt to lay bare the discourses, always rooted in social reality and experiences, that shaped their understanding. And thus, when charting changing concerns with alcoholism I have cast my nets widely, combining a wide variety of sources. All form part of the way both writer and reader understood their lived reality and the representations that they offer are founded in materiality. Any text can give us 'the evidence of witnesses in spite of themselves' and beyond that, reveal the categories through which reality was perceived and uncover cultural frameworks 'given for granted'.[25] Popular songs and visual representations therefore can give away as much about the history of drunkenness as medical texts and contemporary statistics on consumption. Carefully reading the texts against the grain, comparing them with each other and questioning their underlying assumptions, this book will trace social meanings of drunkenness within the 'structure of feeling' of Belgian society at the end of the nineteenth century.

Case Study: Belgium

> To be always thirsty, everywhere, and under all circumstances, seems to be the national characteristic of the Belgian. For him every occasion justifies a drink: he drinks in the morning to awaken himself and to 'pull himself together', before dinner to get up an appetite, and after dinner to aid digestion; after working hours to restore his energy, and before retiring to make him sleepy. He drinks on Saturday because it is payday, on Sunday because it is rest-day, and on Monday because it is the 'morrow of yesterday'. He drinks for consolation and for enjoyment, because his affairs go well, or because they go badly, because he has inherited from an uncle, or because an aunt has left him nothing.[26]

Drinking a lot of alcohol was part of daily life in Belgium in the nineteenth century. Surely this much drinking brought with it a certain amount of drunkenness. Visitors to Belgium communicated, alarmed, that the Belgians consumed more gin than anyone else in Europe and that they drank almost twice as much as the English.[27] We will never know whether Belgium was indeed in a league of its own when it came to drunkenness, but what is clear is that it was a problem that worried contemporaries. Why this was so, this book will attempt to answer.

But there is more that makes Belgium an intriguing case to explore drunkenness. After its inception in 1830, the new, small triangular-shaped country was embedded between the physical borders and political interests of France, the Netherlands, Germany and Great Britain. Central in and to Europe, with an internationalist outlook and even colonial ambitions, Belgians continued to find inspiration abroad when creating the problem of drunkenness and formulating answers to it. Therefore, this study always harks back to a wider story and tells us about larger European interests and concerns.

It is not only its wide European influences that make Belgium such an interesting case for students of society. Studying the way Belgium was made up, an imagined community combining different 'nations', can perhaps also offer a blueprint for study of the history of Europe.[28] In the nineteenth century, foreigners who visited Belgium were – indeed visitors still are – always fascinated by the coming together of different languages or what was then called the co-existence of different 'races' in one country. Roughly an always – and still – contested 'language frontier' splits the country in two. The Flemish north was poor, very Catholic and mostly rural while the extraordinary wealth of the country was generated in industrialized, francophone south, whose labour population went on to support new socialist ideologies. In both parts of the country rich people, supporting mostly liberal but also Catholic ideologies spoke French and in the north poor people spoke their local Flemish dialect, while in the cities typically Catholic but also liberal middle-class groups started campaigning for Flemish as an official language.

This reductive sketch belies of course a very complex constant negotiation of positions and ideologies and the idea of what it meant to be drunk as held by different groups in this complex society contributed to the making of social, cultural and linguistic differences.

Purposely insisting on studying the whole of Belgium was not a straightforward choice and there are still very few examples of social and cultural history that take in the whole of the country. Firstly there is the problem of what one frustrated American historian of Belgium has called: the 'dismal condition of the country's archives'.[29] The chaotic organization of libraries, universities and archives in Belgium and the ensuing difficulties for scholarship can not only be blamed on haphazard librarianship or German fires. In fact the condition of its archives and the dividedness of its historiography are some of the far-reaching consequences of a strong division in Belgian society along language and ideological lines as established in the nineteenth century. Historians have called this particular organization of society 'pillarization'.[30] Even today, like so many other things in Belgian society, such as saving, insuring, educating and so on, the conservation of its historical documents and the study of its past is done within linguistic and ideological frameworks. This means that there are French-speaking and Flemish-speaking places where documents are kept that are in their turn also politically divided. For example, looking for information of the socialist point of view on drunkenness, I had to visit the 'socialist' archive in Ghent, while when finding out about the Catholic viewpoint, I had to travel to Leuven to the Catholic archive. But those archives then only held Flemish documents, and so for the Francophone stand, I needed to travel south of the language barriers where, again archives are separated along the lines of political ideologies.[31] And thus if records indeed seem 'dauntingly random'[32] this in itself is also the result of the perplexity that is Belgium.[33] In fact, most social and political history has been written by historians that are linked to archives associated with political movements or connected to politically inclined Flemish or Walloon universities and written mainly within the history of 'their movement in their language'.[34]

But because drunkenness in the nineteenth century was of course neither uniquely Catholic, socialist or liberal, nor exclusively Flemish or French, it made for a perfect subject to explore the differences that were and are at the heart of the Belgian experience.

I excavated a wide and composite selection of primary sources dealing with the drunkard: temperance material, government writings, medical tracts, travellers' diaries, stories, songs, films, countless novels and images. A lot of information about how drunkenness was understood and about the personal experience of problem drinkers came out of a detailed study of the patient registers of two asylums in Ghent for male patients for the period 1830–1914, one public and one for paying patients.[35] I then tried to interpret the sources placing them back in their social and cultural context. Inspired by Clifford Geertz's proposition of using 'thick description', which emphasizes the role of context when studying culture, I placed the unearthed stories within interdependent connections and mapped their relationships.[36]

This volume is organized into three parts, each presenting different sites to tell the stories of change in the experience of drunkenness in Belgium from 1830 to 1914 by different groups in society.

Part I: Drunkenness and the People

The first part looks at the formation of class, gender and ethnic relationships through the lens of drunkenness. What it meant to be working class, bourgeois, male, female, Flemish, Walloon or Congolese was shaped by one's own experiences of drunkenness combined with an understanding of other people's drinking.[37] Although there is a rich tradition of social history in Belgian historiography, class as 'essentially a relationship'[38] or the cultural formation of class has only been very partially studied.[39] Like most Belgian social historians, I too understand nineteenth century Belgium as a fundamentally segregated society with strict economic and cultural boundaries between the 'lower class' – those who only possess their labour – and the 'bourgeoisie' – the group that owns the means of production. Such old-fashioned, reductionist and crude Marxist binary division of society based on ownership of property is here used as a starting point for thinking about the construction of different registers of class and as the basis for a more complex cultural explanation of the formation of society and the study of the processes whereby the dominant culture maintains its leading position. Most of the narratives of drunkenness in the second half of the nineteenth century were composed by the bourgeoisie and included lower-class males as protagonists, but I also have traced stories of drinking among other groups in society. I looked at drunkenness among five groups: farmers, workers, middle class, upper class and those in the colony. Class was always intertwined with that other 'useful category of historical analysis': gender, which in its turn fundamentally influenced the meaning of drunkenness.[40] Sidsel Erikson's research in the Danish temperance movement indicates how sobriety was linked to femininity and morality and how drunkenness was considered manly. Drinking women from the other hand were seen as immodest and lustful.[41] In Belgium, class and gender were furthermore very closely connected with language and in its turn with geography. Ideas of what was then called 'race' intersperse the understanding of drunkenness: Flemings were seen as a different type of drinkers to Walloons. This racial understanding was paramount in the colonial context: both Belgian administrators and native Congolese drank, but with different meanings attached to it.

The analysis in these chapters is based on a very wide selection of sources talking about drunkenness: temperance writings, visitor's travel impressions, medical case studies, with specific literary and artistic representations at the heart of each section. The protean and unpredictable character of 'the drunkard' and his or her difficult reception in society inspired artists and novelists to create captivating characters in conflict-laden settings. Those texts took on ongoing concerns in broader society and at the same time confronted them and thus recast what the drunkard stood for.[42]

Nineteenth-century realist and naturalist art was based on an experienced reality and writers such as Cyriel Buysse and Camille Lemonnier insisted that their inspiration was rooted within what they saw happen around them. The latter famously encouraged artists to become 'the historians of their times'.[43] But Buysse also said that 'the description of reality is different than that reality'.[44] This reminds us of the historians' task to assess the text never as a direct representation, but as mediated expression of reality.[45] From the literary critics and specifically the 'Cultural Materialists' I have learned that literature actively participates in the making of history and that literary and non-literary texts always inform each other. When analysing fictional and artistic representation of drunkenness I have intended to loosely follow the approaches proposed by Mary Poovey, who made a case for doing historical research based on literature.[46] While the artist or writer created his work immersed within his own 'social character', revealing its meanings and values to the world, it was there in its turn publicly contested and reconstructed.[47] After placing the 'text', its author and its audience in its historical background the text is repositioned 'in the historically specific discussions in which it participated'.[48]

The organization of this part of *Narratives of Drunkenness* along crude lines of 'class' based on wealth and space is artificial and generalizing. The language used to talk about social class, gender and ethnicity is equally vague and ambiguous. Many narratives told in Chapter 1 on farmers could also be told with relation to the workers in Chapter 2. Division between lower middle classes and working classes was never clear and neither were distinctions between upper middle classes and lower upper classes.[49] Such differences were significantly and notoriously slim and negotiable and I will argue that attitudes towards drunkenness contributed to people's belonging to particular social groups. Even Congo played on the minds of those who stayed at home and therefore treating it as a separate space is an artificial classification. I also assumed that farmers were mostly Flemish and workers mostly Walloon, but of course the wealth of evidence from the workers in Ghent contradicts this and there were certainly also large farms and smallholdings in Wallonia.

The result of this part is a kaleidoscopic and rather out-of-focus overview of drunkenness in Belgium that sets the scene to analyse the subject in different arenas in the next two parts of the book.

Part II: The Politics of Drunkenness

With the explorations into class, gender and ethnicity of Part I in mind, Part II looks at the political discourses on drunkenness. It attempts to understand how the shift from vice to disease and the developments from 1830 to 1914 were played out in the ideological arena. I agree with James Nicholls that 'ideas about drink provide an insight into the wider culture' and so I will look for wider underlying ideological tensions that the discussions on drunkenness exposed.[50] Issues of freedom and liberty became central to the political understanding of drunkenness, but it also became a key theme in social reform more generally. I am interested in finding out how drunkenness became a vehicle in the discussion about who should have the right to partake politically in society and who should not. I followed parliamentary debates, looked at political tracts and read government publications and discussions on legislation in order to understand how the subject of drunkenness was interconnected with ideology. This made me think about the role of drunkenness in the construction of political consciousness and look at how the theme of drunkenness was used as a propaganda tool for different political ideologies. The arguments and discussions for or against legislation to curb what was perceived as 'the growing plague of drunkenness' will show how drunkenness was understood and constructed ideologically.

Part III: Drunkenness and its Specialists

In the final part *Narratives of Drunkenness* explores stories of the 'medicalization' of a social problem. It locates the drunk in the discussions of those who considered themselves experts on the topic: medical practitioners, especially hygienists, alienists, magistrates and specifically criminal anthropologists. In Belgium, medical specialists initiated the first temperance movements and the narratives they presented incorporated and at the same time influenced and contested accepted ideas of drunkenness that also circulated in wider culture. When studying medical and criminological writings on the subject I realized immediately how many of the specialists' text go on relentlessly about drunkenness as a case of madness. This made me go and look for drunkards among asylum patients and so I explored patient registers of two mental hospitals in Ghent that cared for those whose 'abnormal' behaviour was understood to be related to excessive drinking. Also here, as elsewhere in society, what drunkenness meant was constantly negotiated by the specialists, by the drunkards themselves and their families. I tried to understand how medical theory of drunkenness informed medical practice and vice versa.

Drunkenness inhabited that space where the social met the medical and biological, and where the battles over nurture and nature were fought. I am interested in learning about the causes for drunkenness proposed by doctors and the solutions they wished for. In this examination I hope to demonstrate how different 'specializations' became involved with the construction of drunkenness and claimed expertise over the subject.

At first sight the three parts of this book may look like separate entities. Based on very different types of sources, they cover completely different aspects of society. On reflection, hopefully, it will become clear that the three seemingly divergent episodes in fact all tell the same story of the making of modern society through the establishing of difference between acceptable and unacceptable drinking and of the shifts and changes of this understanding in the nineteenth century as part of the making of modernity. While telling the stories of drunkenness, in three very different settings, I suggest that the character of the drunkard was experienced and negotiated in divergent spaces. I want to locate complex relationships between the various narratives to understand how the figure of 'the drunk' circulated in wider culture.[51]

And so the final work offers an incomplete, broad map of different narratives of drunkenness in culture and society. Perhaps I have been too ambitious: Geertz's 'thick description' often remained inevitably just description. But hopefully, despite its flaws, these Belgian narratives of drunkenness can inspire further historical research on drunkenness in a wider European context.

PART I: DRUNKENNESS AND THE PEOPLE

Drinking alcohol was very much part of Belgian life, especially at key moments when there was a cause for celebration. Drunkenness was often the unavoidable result. Foreigners visiting the country recorded the particularities they observed in Belgium and a widespread habit of excessive drinking was part of it. This section looks at the organization of Belgian society in the second half of the nineteenth and the beginning of the twentieth century through the lens of drunkenness. At times condoned behaviour, in other situations no longer so, drunkenness and attitudes towards it were always socially specific. Tracing where the limits of acceptability were drawn can indicate ways in which social relations took shape. Affecting traditional habits of the countryside and adding to the confusion within rapidly transforming city encounters, drinking could become transgressive behaviour that both constructed and worked within social boundaries as a classed, gendered and national experience.

While the drunkard fascinated foreign visitors he, or indeed she, also inspired artists and writers. In fact, Belgian art and literature saw an important renaissance in the 1880s and 1890s. For eminent Belgian historian Henri Pirenne it was no coincidence that this artistic revival coincided with the social upheavals of the 1880s.[1] The drunkard was equally prevalent in 'popular' fiction like folk stories and songs. In addition, the stories recorded in the patient registers of the Ghent asylum offer us an exceptional insight into the experience of the drunkard himself and his family. The texts and images thus produced about drunkenness were established within a series of associations relating the subject back to the social world in which it participated. They took on debates that were ongoing in other areas of society, but also confronted them and thus re-cast what the drunkard stood for.

With their observant pens or paintbrushes, writers, artists and travellers depicted not only rural celebrations but also the rituals of exploited workers who found solace in drink. They denounced the lavish drunken extravagances of the bourgeoisie and the disasters alcohol caused in the colonial context, while film and theatre makers chose to chronicle the drunkard's demise in melodramatic scenarios. Those narratives incorporated and contributed to the complex dynamics of language, class, gender and ethnic relationships, staging the drunkard against a backdrop of upheaval and change. And so, from the apparently unchanging religious countryside to the modern cities, where women worked alongside men and exploited workers shared space with wealthy bourgeoisie, to the remote African colonial experience, overlapping and contradictory narratives of drunkenness emerged.

1 DRUNKEN FARMERS

Though Belgium was one of the most urban developed and industrialized nations of Europe, by the end of the nineteenth century, one third of the population in Flanders still 'lived of the soil'.[1] In the villages, the church stayed at the centre of community life, literally and certainly symbolically: what the priest preached in the pulpit on Sundays was law as religion dominated life in the nineteenth-century Flemish countryside. Drunkenness always meant a moment of dissonance, sometimes condoned and considered part of sociability, but it could also push the limits of acceptability and therefore be considered anti-social. The framework in which drunkenness was understood shifted over the course of the century.

Getting Drunk in the Countryside

A few times a year the ordered society of the Flemish countryside was overturned dramatically when important life events or dates in the agricultural or religious calendar demanded celebration. The highlight of the farmer's festival calendar had always been the fair of kermis, a high point in his otherwise bleak life of hard labour on the land. While for some this was sanctioned as a cheerful festival that belonged to the farmers' traditional culture, for others it was to be denounced as an uncivilized event of sexual, violent and alcoholic excess. Charles Baudelaire, for example, wrote 'What I used to think about as the fancies of the imagination of some painters', referring to paintings like those of Brueghel, 'is in fact a representation of the customs'.[2] Having moved to Brussels in an attempt to evade his creditors, while he himself was hopelessly lost in drink and drugs, Baudelaire viciously attacked all aspects of Belgian habits and customs. In his feverish notes he expressed more than once his outrage about 'the terrible drunkenness among the people' of his guest country he had come to hate.[3]

Since the Middle Ages authorities had tried to cut back on these events, considered rude and uncivilized. Their attempts at regulation were almost always met with disregard or sometimes opposition.[4] Farmers and their families would unwind at such feasts in their own and neighbouring villages. Emigrated farmers who worked in neighbouring cities would return to their old villages for days of overindulgence of food and drink.[5] And, as in Brueghel's time, processions devoted to the Virgin Mary or a locally worshipped saint often accompanied the kermis, while the traveling theatre still entertained with coarse burlesques.[6] Drink and becoming drunk were essential features of the celebration of the kermis, a moment of dissonance, where the farmers felt for once they could subvert the traditional order of things. The drinking farmers, for example, recited 'Our Lord's Prayer of the Drunkard'. This mock prayer repeated the formulas of the 'official' prayer, known by all, but in this version parts of the text were replaced by references to drinking and getting drunk. 'Our lord, who is in all public houses', prayed the farmers with much laughter, 'holy is the bitter and the gin'.[7] The 'uncrowning' of Our Lord's Prayer, the de-sacralization of a prayer so central to the established religion, 'the subversion and penetration of "high" culture by "low"' during the celebrations of Kermess illustrates the power of drink to invert order and hierarchies.[8]

It was surely because kermises threatened authority and social hierarchy that they were so often denounced by the elites. The fever of the event filled the bourgeoisie with fear, and such festivities were described as gratuitous and out of control. Calls for regulation of kermises continued to be heard throughout the nineteenth century. According to many morality campaigners – the clergy but also medical authorities – excessive drinking at these occasions too often led to 'scenes of barbarity': sexual promiscuity, fighting and violence.[9] Henri Chariaut, who was sent on a mission by the French government to find out more about Belgium, wrote in 1910:

> When he is glutted with food and gin, the Fleming, dominated by his brutal instinct, shows the need to become rowdy to affirm his force with great scenes. It is rare that a Sunday passes by without there having been, a 'red kermis' in one or another village.[10]

Some Belgian fin-de-siècle writers like the poet Emile Verhaeren and novelists Georges Eekhout and Camille Lemonnier used the celebration of the kermis as a main theme in their work. The drunkenness and the festive atmosphere which allowed for social conventions to be thrown overboard inspired poetry that celebrated strong emotions with violence as its central sentiment. Many fin-de-siècle artists were fascinated by what were presumed to be the unbridled passions of the farmers, which according to many expressed themselves in the ample opportunity for getting drunk 'With rage and with distress ... the kermis grinds' (*avec colère, avec détresse ... moud la kermesse*). Verhaeren's famous poem commenced.[11] In George Eekhoud's work, the tension between his characters was released in extreme violence or sexual excesses. The kermis and its drunken brawls provided ideal backgrounds for his radical plots.[12]

Another occasion to celebrate and get drunk for Flemish farmers and often part of the kermis was the celebration of a local saint in a religious procession. Socialist journalist August de Winne described the state in which he witnessed farmers on their way back home from the yearly Holy Blood Procession in Bruges: 'in the carriage where I can find a place already 5 women are seated. They carry paternosters and blessed medallions, four among them are scandalously drunk. They sing bawdy bar songs and talk dirty talk'.[13] De Winne criticized here the thin layer of religiosity on top of what he saw as essentially brute Flemish mores of which not just drunkenness but a much more disagreeable female drunkenness formed part.[14] Drunkenness sometimes also occurred as a side effect on pilgrimages: gin was drunk to keep people walking and used to care for blisters on feet.[15]

More generally, excessive drinking formed part of the farmers' lives at celebrations of life changing events, always within a religious framework. For example, when a child was born, after the church ceremony of a christening, godparents of the child bought drinks for the midwife, friends and neighbours in the local bar, while the mother stayed at home to recover. Midwives were often represented as drinking too much and there were plenty of stories told of midwives forgetting the baby in a bar or of holding it upside down.

Another important date, which was always accompanied with much drinking, was the day of the drawing of lots for the military conscription to decide who was to be enlisted for a year of obligatory military service. Whereas rich young men who drew a bad lot mostly sold theirs for money to a substitute, for the poor eighteen-year old this was not an option. When he drew a bad lot he had to enter military service, which was often disastrous for himself and his family, as he could no longer help on the farm. It was custom that, when going for the draw one was to get drunk in his town. For those with a good number, festivities and drinking would go on for days, in case of a bad number, the future soldier and his family drank to forget their problems for the moment. The celebrations or frustrations of the appointment of the military service by lot were also a sort of passage rite for young men into adulthood. From this day onwards he was allowed to visit bars, dance, find girlfriends and have an adult opinion. The *Bulletin de la Société médicale belge de tempérance* called the scenes in the 'cabarets' on days of drawing lots 'orgies by a delirious mass'.[16]

Drinking was unavoidable on wedding days in all social classes. Among the lower classes, after the civil marriage, the groom would invite the company, the witnesses and the civil servant who conducted the ceremony to the bar for gin for the men and 'anis or menthe liqueurs' for the women.[17] Next, after the church service the family, friends and neighbours were also invited for gin and beer. The married couple invited some friends into town, to party and to drink and when they returned the neighbours had organized another party with more drink, which went on deep into the night, with no sober soul left.[18]

At the end of life, drink was equally important. When a person died it was the custom that neighbours came to the house of the deceased for a wake. Plenty of gin and coffee were consumed as they were deemed indispensable to stay awake. Regularly those night wakes were represented as turning into drinking sprees.[19] After the funeral ceremony, again it was customary to drink with the bereaved family in the town cabaret and while they reminisced about the life of the diseased, friends and family members would easily get drunk.[20]

A portion of alcohol was always needed to add weight to an event. The sale of cattle was settled with a glass of gin for example and the owner of a newly built house had to offer a dram to the builders when the roof went on it. Drinking was also an important way to show hospitality: 'borrels' or 'dreupels': a little glass of gin or a pint of beer were always offered to visitors. The English social researcher Seebohm Rowntree was shocked to find out that everywhere he came to call in Belgium, hospitality was offered in the shape of a glass of liquor, 'no matter what the time of day may be, even if it is eight o'clock in the morning'.[21] When the neighbours welcomed a family in a new home, they would offer the new inhabitants gin to celebrate.[22]

Such traditional countryside practices were described by reformers with an almost anthropological interest in the mores and customs of a foreign tribe and they often displayed an almost missionary zeal at changing and improving them.[23]

The rural tavern was a place where the village community felt at home. It served gin and beer, often home-distilled or brewed. Gin was served in small glasses called *borrels* or *dreupels* (drips) and beer came in large pitchers.[24] Beer was so integral to the way of life that it had become considered a 'necessary element for the entertainment of the masses'.[25] Beer was much safer to drink than water and Belgians drank vast amounts of it.[26] The village tavern was the principal meeting place, where men exchanged news and where gossip was told in the evening or on Sunday before and after the mass. As part of the Sunday ritual, after the mass, while their wives would go to the neighbouring town to market to sell butter or eggs, the farmers would return to the bar and drink a few beers or *borrels* more, many would get drunk, others would go home after only a few beers to play cards with friends or games such as sack races and bowls.[27] Some would attend meetings of one or another society to which they belonged, as the centre of society life in a village took place in the pubs. The local brass band for example practised in the room upstairs or adjacent to the pub.

During the week alcohol was also part of daily life. When negotiating a heavy job such as harvesting, agricultural workers demanded their share of gin from their employers.[28] Alcohol was thought to be needed for strength here as the work was very tough indeed. One English visitor wrote: 'The conditions of life among the agricultural classes of Flanders would be considered intolerably hard by the agricultural labourer in England'.[29] After a major exertion such as giving birth, alcohol was given to the mother for strength and dark beer was drunk 'to let the milk flow'.[30] Such customs could but mostly would not necessarily lead to extreme drunkenness. After finishing work in the evening, most weekdays, families would not go to the cabaret. They stayed in, came together to play cards with a glass of beer or gin or just to *buurten* (to chat). And while the Flemish farmers were not reading much 'literature' in the conventional way, their own cultural expression consisted in the telling of stories, passed on orally from generation to generation. Storytelling around the fire during long winter evenings was a typical pastime in the rural villages in Flanders in the middle of the nineteenth century.[31] The stories often explored aspects of the supernatural alongside religiosity. The content of these stories always related immediately back to the context that generated them and incorporated contemporary concerns and themes. The stories therefore present valuable patterns of culture and an insight into the mental universes of peasants.[32] Alcohol featured regularly in these stories mostly in instances of someone seeing an appearance of the Virgin Mary or a ghost while under the influence of too much drink. In rural Limburg, many stories were told about *alvermannetjes*. These were a type of dwarf who would come to help farmers with their work on the field or housewives with the housework during the night, in return for some food of drink. One of these stories related the end of the positive relationship between farmers and dwarves: once people had started to offer them gin as reward, they had stopped appearing, for the dwarves had become drunk and did not want to work any longer.[33] This story of the demise of the *alvermannetjes* was a metaphor for the end of an era of magic and storytelling. It embodied a sentiment of regret for the passing of an old way of life. Gin was perceived as a creation of modernity, a by-product of industrialization, irreversibly transforming the long-standing structures of ordered society.

The Drunkard in the mid-Nineteenth-Century Countryside: A Moral Struggle

Author Hendrik Conscience, the most influential literary figure in the movement to promote the Flemish language and culture, told similar stories about what he saw as the traditional Flemish countryside. His works were based on the major themes of fatherland, family and church. Later, his novels were sometimes criticized as being reactionary and his opponents claimed his writings exuded 'opium smoke'.[34] Conscience most certainly had a very direct agenda with his writing: he wanted to influence the life of the country people and to educate them in matters of religion, morality and the value of their Flemish background. While the audience for Flemish literature in the mid-nineteenth century was very limited, Conscience's novels were among the few books that did reach their audience effectively. They were also popular abroad and many of his books were translated immediately into English, French and German. Most of the works were adapted into plays, which could also be understood by the illiterate country people. In primary schools his literature was on the reading lists and it was frequently the only literature, apart from religious tracts, that was available in towns in the sparse libraries controlled by the church. People like Hendrik Conscience, and a generation later Stijn Streuvels, 'forged' with their literature a language and thereby a culture. Conscience presented himself as close to the people and was inspired by events that took place in the Flemish countryside he knew very well. In 1855 he situated the problem of habitual drunkenness at the heart of a countryside community, in the novel *De plaeg der dorpen* (*The Curse of the Villages*). Initially the writer had been reluctant to address drunkenness, because he would have to depict 'a picture which could excite no emotion but disgust'.[35] But his friend, a priest, had told how in his village a farmer had ruined himself and his family with his drunkenness and this had persuaded the Conscience to write this story, to teach an important moral lesson. The story was not only inspired by the life of the farmers, but the farmers who read it would take on or equally revise the moral principles Conscience presented to contain their own social practices.

The drunkard was no longer only described as an affirmative figure, celebrating life, but he became ever more disapprovingly depicted as a habitual drunkard, drinking 'out of place', a negative figure soliciting pity as a dramatic fallen character. Drink could indeed destroy much of what Conscience loved so much about Flemish village life. In his idea of what was mid-nineteenth-century Flanders, position in society was defined by material wealth and moral strength and the influence of drink was disastrous for both. In *De plaeg der dorpen*, the romanticized vision of an organic society where everybody knew his or her place fell into disarray by the presence of the marginal figure of the drunkard, never able to conform.

The drunkard in the story, Jan Staers, is a tortured man who when sober is aware of his weakness and realizes the consequences of it for himself but also for his daughter Clara. Yet one glass of gin is enough to transform him into a cold and aggressive, jealous and proud man.[36] Torfs, Staer's neighbour, is hard working and never drunk. Both rent a cottage from the same landlord, but ruined by drink Staers receives a visit from the bailiff as he can no longer afford the rent.[37] By depicting the drunkard Jan Staers as originating from a wealthy background, Conscience evaded one of the main concerns within the broader discussion on drunkenness: its recurring provenance in poverty and misery. In Staers's case, drinking is not the result but the cause of his financial ruin. The neighbour Torfs, who has been poorer but morally superior, has saved money through 'twenty years of hard work and thrift' and 'a good landlord', and is even in a position to lend money to Staers. Staers on the other hand defiantly calls his landlord 'a blood-sucker'. By introducing the unlikely story of the economic success of the virtuous farmer Conscience lays the blame for Staers's poverty with the farmer himself, not with that of an unfair system of exploitation by capitalist landlords.

This accusation was indeed heard here and there in the mid-nineteenth century, especially during the difficult recovery of the Flemish countryside from a devastating famine.[38] The tenant farmers' position was always precarious, dependent of the whims of the proprietors and on environmental factors. The vulnerable system of subservience with its roots in the *ancien régime* in the Belgian countryside entailed a constant threat to a farmer's livelihood. Unable to pay the high fees to the landlord as a result of natural adversity or economic crises, the farmer would often have no other choice left than to give up their rented cottage and lands.[39] Conscience wrote of how 'in the Campine, there are plenty of men who make their wives and children unhappy and soon will need to go out begging'. This was not the only time the Campine was mentioned as a region where drunkenness reached worrying proportions and in some towns of the region there was allegedly one bar for every four houses.[40] It was the plague of drunkenness of the inhabitants of the villages that was blamed for causing their poverty, however, we know that the Campine was also one of the poorest regions of the country.[41] So poverty and drunkenness were related to each other in different ways. The possibility that impoverished villagers would perhaps find solace in alcohol did not form part of Concience's conservative Catholic understanding of the problem.

The house, central to the story, symbolized material prosperity maintained by sobriety. The keeper of the house, the wife and mother, was the custodian of that sobriety. Widower Staers has easily drifted into his present debased state because he lacks the elevating presence of a wife, while farmer Torfs is supported by his helpmeet Mother Beth. Conscience agreed with so many other middle-class commentators that it was part of the wife's responsibility to keep her husband away from the temptations of drink. The wife was not only better protected against temptations within the cottage walls, she was also considered morally stronger and less prone to fall under their spell. In the Belgian countryside, however, women did not only do all the housework, they also worked the fields alongside the men. But there is no evidence of this hard toil in *De plaeg der dorpen* and Beth only passes on those skills that came with her role as moral protector of her husband's sobriety onto Clara, her future daughter-in-law:

> What you must take care of especially is that you never – never, do you hear? – allow him to remain a quarter of an hour in a public house from the time of your marriage. As soon as you notice anything of that kind, then begin to be vexed, look sour, and scold, and so on, without easing. Men can't stand out against that, and they will do anything we like to be quit of our everlasting seesawing on one thing, (eeuwigen zaeg), as they call it.[42]

The wife's campaign to keep her husband from drinking, as promoted here by Mother Beth, was not aimed at his own moral feelings or responsibilities, but instead at his need of self-preservation in a marriage with a harassing wife. In some comical pub songs, husbands were depicted as always drunk and not interested in the household, while nagging wives were to convince their husbands to stop drinking and to hand them over the money for the household instead. Songs like *Huwelijkstwist* ('Marriage Dispute') and *De dronkaard en zijne vrouw* ('The Drunkard and his Wife') were comical duets where one singer would sing the part of the drunkard who made fun of his wife when she came to the pub in search for him, while the other singer would answer back with begging pleas. In both songs the arguing partners make up at the end of the story, with the husband's promise to drink less.[43]

In these songs women were not left without a voice; on the contrary, they defended their rights and duties as protector of the household. Like Beth, they called for action by means that were within their power as they no longer wished to remain resigned to suffering and instead demanded change.[44] Remarkably it is exactly this type of empowering strategy, the pestering of drinking husbands, that feminists advised against in their advise on the role of the woman in the struggle against drunkenness. Marie Parent, for example, believed it would have exactly the opposite result. Paradoxically, this makes female characters in arch-conservative Hendrik Conscience's work in the mid-nineteenth century voice their concerns loudly compared to the quiet action proposed towards the end of the century by bourgeois liberal feminists who needed their radical message to be as inoffensive as possible to men.[45]

Like so many other inveterate drinkers, farmer Staers cannot keep his promise to refrain from it. One Sunday, while his daughter goes to church, his old drinking companion the sand-farmer (*den zandboer*), comes to see him and presents him with a bottle of gin and an invitation to go drinking. Contemporary readers knew very well that those peddling sand to cover the cottage floors from door to door would often have a reputation as being drunkards, as they were habitually offered glasses of liquor by their customers. This particular sand-digger had hopelessly succumbed to too much drink and now tries to win over the struggling Staers. The Christian idea of temptation is very powerful here: with his 'brutal and repulsive face ... which grinned behind the flask', the sand-digger embodies the devil, dragging the fraught drunkard into temptation.[46] Under the influence of the rhetoric of the church, gin was often represented as belonging to the devil, also in some of the stories the farmers told to each other in the evenings. One story that was told by the Flemish farmers and passed on in many variations, told of a group of friends who played cards in the evening. When one of them expressed the wish to have a glass of gin and complained about the lack of a bottle in the house, one of the other players – a man who was suspected to have relations with the devil – said that he would 'send the jack of spades to get a bottle' and he threw that particular card out of the window. A few minutes later the men saw a bottle appear in the window with a jack of spades attached to it.[47]

Unable to resist the temptation offered by the devilish sand-seller, Staers is next discovered by a neighbour, seemingly dead along the side of the road. His family finds him in a terrifying state, 'his eyes open and glassy, his lips blue' after apparently being 'seized with cramps or convulsions', and they have to wheel him home in a wheelbarrow.[48] This public display was the drunkard's ultimate humiliation and the family members sigh with relief when they arrive home, 'fortunate enough ... without meeting anyone'.[49] When realizing his downfall, Staers is extremely worried about the response of his neighbours who he fears will use his story as an example to their children and that he would be 'dying of shame and spite'.[50] The drunkard as the mocked and fallen figure, excluded from the village and stripped from all his respectability was a persistent image in the Belgium narratives of drunkenness. The cart or wheelbarrow with the mad, glazed-eyed and convulsive drunkard was a reoccurring image symbolizing loss of respectability that was also taken on regularly by the temperance movement. For example, more than fifty years later the Ligue Pattriotique depicted on one of their didactic postcards a delirious woman being tied to a cart and wheeled away accompannied by villagers.[51] The need for discretion during the operation of carting away the mad drunkard as described in *De plaeg der dorpen* contrasted with the very public display of the same action as depicted half a century later, made more outrageous by the fact that the mad drunkard performing in public was a woman, all of which would have contributed to the shock value of the temperance message.

While the cart in 1910 was supposedly being carried away to the madhouse, the family members take Staers back to the privacy of their home. Nobody in the story suggests calling a doctor to help care for the sick Staers. In fact people were remedying their health themselves as doctors in the Belgian countryside were far and few between and not at the disposition of ordinary villagers.[52] And with medical expertise mostly powerless in the face of habitual drunkenness, people had reason enough to take to folk remedies and religion to cure their drunkenness. Drinking gin in which an eel had died or from a bottle that had accompanied a corpse until its funeral would be some of the solutions proposed to remedy problem drinking in the countryside.[53]

Conscience did use contemporary medical metaphors of contagion to refer to the problem of drunkenness. In the title itself, drunkenness is a *plaag*, literary translated as 'plague' or 'pest' and in the novel Clara talks about the possibility of her father being 'cured'.[54] When Mother Torfs complains about the growth of drunkenness in the countryside, she exclaims 'the vile habit of gin – is gaining ground in our villages like a contagious disease'.[55] In a medical model of contagion, drunkenness remained always a moral issue and the drunkard as a sinner carried a responsibility not to pass his problem onto other people. Jan Staer's parents' moral inheritance was to be held accountable for his actual state and we are told how in his upbringing the seeds were sown for his drinking problem in adult life. Staers had originally come from a family of wealthy farmers, but his parents had made an unforgivable mistake in the eyes of the writer and the corresponding Flemish Catholic world view: 'they lived too high and gave themselves more airs than are becoming in country people'.[56] They had higher ambitions for their son than for him to be a farmer and they had sent him to a school 'where lawyers and doctors are made'. But after a few years Jan had enough of the studies and wanted to be a farmer after all, because he – wrongly of course – believed it would be easier. Then his parents made a second mistake: instead of adjusting their son to the heavy labour on the farm, they had spoiled him. It was certainly no surprise to the villagers and to those reading Conscience's novel that Staers had landed up in pubs and bars, drinking ever more.

Pride and laziness were always closely linked with drunkenness and it ultimately would be punished, while sobriety accompanied by modesty and thrift would lead to life improvement. In this story too, the hero, old farmer Torfs is victorious and in an extremely unlikely ending becomes mayor of the village. However, for the drunkard there is a disastrous end in store: Jan Staers dies a horrible and painful death, conclusing the moral lesson of the book.

Conscience's disapproving portrait of the drunkard and the strong moral condemnation of his behaviour by the morally superior sober characters surrounding him introduces us to an idealized world of neatly ordered moral hierarchies as well as the marginalized and marginalizing, but extremely menacing, threat of drunkenness to this moral order.

The Drunkard in the Fin-de-Siècle Countryside: Resignation

Fifty years later the framework in which drunkenness was construed had changed. From a condition that was presented as a moral choice it had now become an unavoidable part of an individual's biological and hereditary make-up. This was also so for farmer Jan Vindevogel, a drinker born from the imagination of Stijn Streuvels, pseudonym of Frank Lateur in 1902 in his first full length novel *Langs the wegen* (*The Long Road*).[57] Streuvels became one of Flanders' most celebrated writers and his work was deemed to embody exactly what was a desirable national identity; his stories tell of hard work and resignation with one's fate. Although there has been no research into who exactly read his works, his books were written in a simple language that would make them available to 'even the simplest of man'.[58]

His farmer Vindeveughel was a stereotype of a 'typical' Flemish farmer, which appeared in so many other texts of the fin de siècle, when ever more 'racial' motives were given to explain people's drinking habits. Commentators noticed that although the amount of alcohol drunk was less in Flanders than in Wallonia, 'ignorance and crime [were] more conspicuous [in Flanders] than in other parts of Belgium'.[59] Explanations put forward for this incongruity were that that the beer was of better quality in Flanders or that the Flemish farmers were simply too poor to get drunk on a regular basis, whereas their slightly wealthier counterparts in the industrial south could more readily afford to get drunk. But many, such as British visitor Cyril Scudamore thought there was more:

> To my mind the radical character of the two races have much to do with these differences. The Flamand [*sic*] is gross, stolid and phlegmatic and prefers to get drunk (to use an Irishism, in a quiet and sober manner); the Walloon, on the other hand, is excitable and volatile and finds spirits more speedily exhilarating than ordinary beer.[60]

The racial differences observers keenly noted can equally be interpreted as social. Getting drunk for the Flemish-speaking farmers in the Catholic acquiescent countryside took place in a different social framework than when it occurred among indignant socialist Walloon factory workers and miners. French diplomat Henri Charriaut concluded that there was among all Flemish

> the same serenity of life, the same anxiety about the interior existence, jealously hidden from indiscreet looks, the same impenetrable placidity and at the same time the same aggressive mood lightly asleep under the surface for which little bit of alcohol is enough to wake it up.[61]

And all this was true for Streuvels's Jan Vindeveughel: he was sturdy, submissive and introverted, but always threatened by the inborn passion for drink. Similar to Conscience, Streuvels used much religious imagery of the fight between good and evil and of the devil as the incarnation of temptation. However, for Jan Staers, the devil is no longer an outside tempter, like the sand-seller had been, but part of the drunkard's own make-up, in line with contemporary ideas about the subconscious:

> that tyrant demon that rode on his shoulder, violently and unexpectedly jerking him away from his work, carrying him away like a whirlwind, while he, clumsy and defenceless, yielded to a force he did not understand. It simply overcame him, giving him no time to reflect that he was behaving badly, squandering his earnings, and running open-eyed in his ruin.[62]

Streuvels represented Vindeveughel's drunkenness as seated deep inside his body and soul, as part of what Taine had called 'race', coming to the surface as a result of outside forces of the 'milieu'. At special occasions when drink and drunkenness part of agreed sociability for example, Jan was always on his guard and Streuvels offered his readers insight into his drunkard's internal struggles against the backdrop of conformist social life in a rural community. At his own wedding, for example, everyone in the company gets drunk but Jan is terrified that he may not be able to 'keep hold of his senses'.[63]

Therefore for Streuvels writing half a century later than Conscience, drunkenness could no longer be kept easily under control by personal strength and resistance to temptation. Drunkenness had become part of a larger force of nature; it was constituted within the human condition, internalized into the very workings of body and mind as part of the particular racial make-up of the Flemish farmer.

However much Vindeveughel toils on the land to provide for his family he does not succeed in being self-sufficient, while his unremitting desire for drink always looms as an imminent calamity over his household. One day, 'it came'.[64]

Like Staers, Vindevogel also takes money from the household fund protected by his wife, goes on a spree and returns home drunk and violent:

> It was all over now, and there was no mending matters; the devil had entered his soul and must rage unrestrained ... He beat the children to hear them howl and kicked his wife to test her patience. And when everything was completely wrecked he ran out waving his arms in the air and rushed off, no matter where, never to return.[65]

In *Langs de wegen*, the wife's moral authority is supplemented with that of the village priest, who convinces the penitent drunkard to return home, 'with head bowed in shame'. In Streuvels's religious universe, the urge for drink became an 'inborn sin', like an original sin, in the same way Catholic medical writers had connected drunkenness with racial degeneration.[66] While repentance and humility could perhaps not make the inborn tendency go away, they could at least soften and cover up the immoral behaviour that it would unavoidably cause. And so when his wife Vina, exhausted, passes away, Jan's life disintegrates. Without his moral beacon he cannot manage to stay sober.

Another theme that re-emerges time and again in narratives of drunkenness, and still here in 1902, was the matter of respectability and the loss of it through repeated excessive drinking outside the framework of sociability. When Jan wakes up the morning after a binge he is mocked by passers-by and realizes with great shame that he is lying in the rubbish dump next to the bar, without trousers. Here the drunkard is depicted as an infamous character, known in the village, who is ridiculed and marginalized. And as had been the faith of Conscience's drunkard half a century earlier, also in Streuvels's novel the drunkard loses his house and is eventually left with nothing. Hence drunkenness still leads to loss of respectability and property, those two essential components of successful living, according to the hegemonic bourgeoisie.

It seems that Jan's character was completely determined by nature. In much the same way as nature's whims were in control of his field, it also dictated Jan's behaviour. In the battle between man and nature in Streuvels's work, nature always won and drink was understood as one of those forces of nature influencing man directly in his social interactions. Only when the farmer could be one with nature, when he toiled on the land did he feel comfortable, as nature was as unpredictable as his own self. Culture, however, and contact with society confounded Vindeveughel and his passion for drink was unleashed as a response to his inability to cope with the emotional idiom of social interaction. There is no moral judgement in this interpretation of the drunkard as there had been so manifestly in the work of Conscience. In fact, in Streuvels's universe, although the drunkard tries hard, a moral battle here is useless from the onset, all that is left is resignation. In an article written in a nationalistic historical work on Flanders, Streuvels explained why Flemish farmers' reputations so rough. The farmers are known, according to Streuvels, as drunkard and 'animal-like in their core' (*beestig van aanleg*) because they do not know 'like any other people that finds itself on a lower level of civilization' how to deal with wealth, he can only waste it on drink. 'And when the last cent is spent, they become calm again and fold willingly their necks into the harness again'. But he also blamed the influence of the environment: 'How many national "vices" would belonged to the Fleming if he would grow up and live in more beneficial circumstances? ... Who can begrudge the land man who has slaved the whole week when he gets drunk on Sunday and airs his heart with aggressive snorting, (*baldadig briesen*) when he is denied or ignorant of all other pleasure?'[67] In his defence of the farmers drinking behaviour, Streuvels still resorts to an evolutionary language in which he equates the farmer to the animals he takes care off.

Three years earlier, Eugene Laermans, one of Belgians foremost naturalist painters depicted what could have been Jan Vindeveughel 'with head bowed in shame', on canvas in a painting called *The Drunkard* (see Figure 1.1). This drunkard has to leave the security of his community on a cold winter's day and the presence of martyr wife and children, who still depend on his support and who support him still add to the melodrama. In Laerman's dramatic scenario the drunkard was irreversibly cast out and he dragged his family with him in his downfall.[68] Mid-century artists like Charles Degroux (see Figure 2.2, p. 43) and writers like Hendrik Conscience had shown their drunkards within a social and moral setting, in the village, in a bar with gossiping patrons, or at home, with friends – bad or good – who all want to influence his choices and change his behaviour. But in the naturalistic harsh world of Streuvels and Laermans at the change of the century, the drunkard is fundamentally a lonely figure, even when together with his close family. He has to struggle alone with his own organic 'embodied' problem and there is no place in society for him.

This illustrates a process of what Tollebeek has called 'subjectivation' in the context of degeneration.[69] The emphasis shifted from drunkenness to the drunkard as an individual as the story of the drunkard became one of degeneration: not only the drunkard but also his children were hopelessly heading downwards. Streuvels

Figure 1.1: Eugène Laermans, *L'Ivrogne* (*The Drunkard*), 1898 © Royal Museums of Fine Arts of Belgium, Brussels.

describes in evolutionary language the arrested development of Jan's sick baby whereby 'the glimmering spark of life was threatened constantly with extinction'.[70] Streuvels also explains how Jan's sons when they had grown-up – like their father – always needed drink to soften the physical and emotional bleakness of their lives. They grew up to become cruel, cold-blooded villains: criminal drunkards. They had not wanted to continue to farm to survive as their father had done and decided to try their luck in the north of France. Many youths in Flanders in the nineteenth century had left the ungrateful work on the land that seemed to hold no future and had emigrated. Many of those emigrants were attracted to the farms and factories of Wallonia or the north of France where there were working opportunities not existing in Flanders.[71] During the second half of the nineteenth century about half a million Belgians were working in France.[72] Those emigrated Flemish farmers, who were often received with hostility by locals for bringing down wages, were given a bad reputation for being drunkards and troublemakers. They were known as rough men and heavy drinkers, preferring gin over wine.[73] Contemporary socialists explained how when those farmhands emigrated to the towns to work as labourers, alcohol would become an affordable item and it was easy to fall for its attraction.[74] Many others blamed their roughness and drunkenness simply as part of their Flemish racial make-up. In *Langs de wegen*, Jan's sons go to work in the brick-making works, an industry whereby 'alcohol causes so much devastation'.[75] The extremely hard work with blasting ovens, far away from home, was linked to a rough lifestyle.[76] The director of a brick factory of Boom was nevertheless satisfied with the performance of his employees, who in accordance with the stereotype of their Flemish race, meekly put up with the hard work in calm resignation. He told the Commission du Travail about his Flemish worker: 'Alcohol and the excitement of mental brains [*des cerveaux mentales*] seldom override the calmness of his reflections.'[77]

Léopold Serigiers, the manager of a brick-making factory in Beerse, in the very poor rural Campine region believed that drunkenness could never be cured. He urged the Commission to take action to solve this problem, since new-born children among his workers who were almost all conceived in a state of drunkenness, he supposed, would necessarily show the symptoms of *un mal héréditaire*. For the brick-factory manager, hereditary evil as a result of heavy drinking would manifest itself once more in an irresistible tendency towards alcoholic drinks, as the only possible agent to wake up 'their nervous centres atrophied by several generations of drunkards'. He believed that drunkenness was an inborn tendency and that all activities proposed to contribute to sobriety, like music bands, would serve exactly the opposite purpose, to provide an opportunity to drink a first glass, which would mean the beginning of the end.[78]

When the sons of Jan in *Langs de wegen* return to the town after their first season as brick makers their first stop is the village pub where they become terribly drunk. They take their father with them, and with the wine they have brought back from France they make him drunk too. Here the sons have lost all sense of deference and moral feeling. According to the scientific laws of heredity and environment they had become criminals, a version of the criminal drunkard, the pathological type discussed in the contemporary criminal anthropological societies.

This character of the primitive inborn criminal drunkard amidst the depression of the Flemish countryside was also a key figure in the naturalist stories of Cyriel Buysse. Buysse forged the theme of inborn Flemish degeneration and alcoholic heredity much further, indeed too far for Catholic Flanders, where his books were banned by the church. Buysse himself defended his first novella *De biezenstekker*, which had scandalized the Flemish literary world in 1890: 'I believe I have taken it a bit too far and even so, such histories and even more miserable I have known to happen'.[79]

The new socialist movement, however, did appreciate Buysse's work. In 1899 Buysse adapted *De biezenstekker* for the theatre and four years later a socialist amateur theatre group of factory workers in Ghent presented the work for the first time on stage.[80] The story of the poor and degraded farmer's family suffering under the hand of an aggressive alcoholic father on his return from prison was now understood as an indictment of the poverty and social injustices as experienced by a broad section of the lower classes.[81]

While for Streuvels, the moral power of a wife could still somewhat control the husband's inborn drives,[82] here the wife was no longer cast in the role of redeeming character. Instead, here she was in fact the more prominent drunkard, which made her even more morally debased than her violent husband. Very occasionally anti-alcohol campaigners mentioned as the ultimate downfall of the alcoholic family the final fall of the wife of the drinker into the abyss of despair. For example, Catholic teetotaller and campaigner Emile Calewyen wrote

> the mother, to silence her crippling heartache somewhat, also finally looked for solace in the gin bottle. And she drinks, she drinks more and more every day, neglecting everything, selling everything, up until the honour of her children; she drinks with all the tempestuous passion, that strong liquor can kindle in a woman's body.[83]

Also Buysse's drunken wife Cloet 'in the degree of moral degradation she had reached … forgotten to care about the neglect of her duties'.[84] The much more disconcerting drinking of the mother would remain equally more secret than her husband's and it did in Buysse's story: the bottle was 'hidden' and only the writer, as all-powerful observer knows and imparts to the reader the extent of the mother's tippling. The drinking mother abandons her role as mother and wife. She is cruel and hard-hearted and loses all her female features. Her illegitimate child Julken, ill and always weaker embodies both the character of the *enfant martyr*, terrified by a violent, alcoholic father and that of the degenerate offspring of a drinking mother.[85]

Even staunch naturalist Buysse still resorts to moral language to describe Julken's condition: he is 'an outcast of nature, a child of sin'. Following contemporary medical ideas Julken suffers from nervous attacks, as a result of his alcoholic heredity, which make him shudder 'crying and mad [*verwilderd*], with trembling hands and rolling eyes and scarily distorted face'.[86] It had since long been an accepted truth that 'drunken parents beget drunken children'. Epileptic or mentally retarded children were often called 'Sunday children' (*les enfants de dimanche*), said to have been conceived by a father under the influence after a weekend of alcoholic excess.

The climax of the story of *De biezenstekker* is muddled in alcohol, as Julken's mother needs her portion of Dutch courage to prepare for the terrible act she is about to perform: the degraded, drunken mother tries to suffocate her sick child in his bed, but at the last moment loses the nerve to do so. During the act, she finds herself in a state of insanity suffering from 'a continuous fever, caused by drink and nerves'.[87] And then, after this key moment, the story takes a turn from harsh naturalism to melodrama, when instead the mother kills Julken's little dog after which Julken dies from misery. In a final paragraph, that is breathtakingly shocking even by today's standards, Buysse describes how afterwards the parents sleep together for the first time since his return, with the bastard son's dead body lying in the next room. The elimination of the weak, unwanted child is the moment of the return to 'normality' and the end of the story.

In the disordered family life of the rough farmers in *De biezenstekker* drinking is the norm. Unlike what was to be expected in a 'normal moral universe' as Conscience's or Streuvels's had envisaged, here it is not the drunkard who becomes the outsider. What makes this such a cruel story is that in the end against all moral odds the debased drunkards survive and even more shockingly, they procreate. In the brute naturalism of Buysse, in a spiral of degeneration, the drunkards will beget even more morally and physically deteriorated offspring; and this was the nightmarish scenario contemporary specialists, like psychiatrists and criminal anthropologist warned about.

Buysse's characters did not consider their drinking as a weakness or something that needed resisting. The idea of awareness of one's moral responsibility so strongly present in Conscience and constantly negotiated with much struggle in Streuvels, was essential within the Catholic faith, which was practised by both writers and which governed the Flemish countryside. Buysse's agnosticism allowed nature – Darwin's nature, not God's – to take central stage and his characters showed no sense of civilized morality.

Historian Jo Tollebeek has explained how decadent artists at the turn of the century in this sense 'glorify that what in degeneration thinking was constructed as horrifying'.[88] It was mostly the depiction of the female drunkard, so coldly and crudely, that made this novel so shocking and radical. But Cyriel Buysse was not the only avant-garde controversial artist who shamelessly represented a drunken farm-

Figure 1.2 : Félicien Rops, *Dimanche ou griserie flamande*, 1883 © Provincial Museum Félicien Rops, Namur.

er's wife. The image another dissenter of the Belgian art world, Félicien Rops, drew of her could be a fitting illustration for the story of *De biezenstekker* (see Figure 1.2).

Rops became known as a painter of sexually perverse scenes and his drawing of the drunken woman farmer was interpreted exactly so.[89] The avant-garde artist and friend of Camille Lemonnier, was always keen to shock and had already in 1866 represented an absinthe-drinking prostitute, a subject he would repeatedly paint throughout career.[90] This small drawing of the drunken woman farmer was interpreted as scandalous and pornographic. Rops dressed her in traditional costume with a bonnet, wooden clogs and full-length black dress. But he perverted tradition: her breasts are completely bare and visible. They protrude out of the contrasting white frame of her opened blouse. She lies dead-drunk on a table-top with a pitcher of beer and a mug next to her, supporting her head on her arms, just as Charles Degroux had depicted his male drunkards. This time the roles are reversed, but there is no dependent and supportive man standing behind the slumped drunken woman. Instead Rops's figure is all alone. And unlike Degroux's male character, the woman here was not shown within the setting of a public place like in a cabaret, where the drunkard was surrounded by other characters. The other gossiping patrons and his tormented wife nearby located Degroux's drunkard within an intelligible social and moral framework, somehow still within normality. Rops's drunken farmer's wife on the other hand is represented against a neutral, black background and thus becomes a lone outcast character. The pitcher, the wooden solid furniture and her clogs situate her within the Flemish countryside. By calling the work *Dimanche ou griserie flamande* (*Sunday or Flemish Intoxication*) Rops tells the story of the farmer's wife illegitimate drinking.

Instead of frugally tending the household budget, this dissident character has spent the money brought back from the market on beer. This was always a looming possibility and a worrying scenario which returned elsewhere as well. In Raymond Stijns's early twentieth-century novel, *Hard labeur* for example, the main character farmer Speeltie, shadows his wife Mie, suspecting her of such behaviour. He sees her enter a 'spices shop' and his suspicion grows: 'What did she want to go in that house for, where there were bottles in front of the window, bottles with drink!'[91]

Rops depicted Mie or Wife Cloet alone in a bar or even more likely in the privacy of her home, while her husband was drinking in the bar with his male companions. The black background accentuates her loneliness: this is a secret impudent private scene made shockingly public in Rops's etching.

There are many similarities between this print and a famous seventeenth-century Dutch genre-painting by Jan Steen, called *Het verlopen huishuiden* (*The Dissolute Household*), that Rops must have known.[92] In this painting there are two women. One is a sleeping, perhaps drunken mother ignoring her children. She is dressed in a similar outfit as Rops's figure and is placed in the same position, slumped on the table. The other is a prostitute, with a very low-cut dress and much breast on show, holding a glass of liquor. Rops's farmer's wife merged those two emblematic characters into one in the context of his own late nineteenth-century countryside. His etching is the opposite of a morality tale. While in the Dutch genre painting subtle metaphors and symbols are used within the image to indicate forlorn sexual mores, there is nothing subtle about Rops's image. Apart from the naked breasts also the bare upper arms and plump lips of the drunk farmer's wife suggest sex and linked with the empty pitcher, it offers a clue as to the debauched nature of what might have happened here before the woman fell asleep.

The drunken, sexually corrupted female farmer perverted tradition and the right order of things on Sunday morning. These scenarios mocked morality and conventional ideas about drinking and female sexuality, and directly and deliberately affected those bourgeois viewers and readers who harboured anxieties about decadent artists and female drunkards alike. For eminent Belgian historian Henri Pirenne it was no coincidence that the country's important artistic revival coincided with its social upheavals of the 1880s.[93]

Visitors to Belgium and also contemporary writers and artists understood drunkenness as belonging to the environment, the village life in the nineteenth century, where drink was part and parcel of sociability. They also identified an inclination to drink as part of the Flemish race, and this inborn need to drink offered excellent material for understanding the workings of the human condition. In doing so these narratives of drunkenness in the countryside laid bare and helped to construct a desirable Flemish identity and an enduring image of the Flemish farmer.

2 DRUNKENNESS AND THE WORKING CLASSES

By 1900, textile industry, heavy metal works, coalmines and the exploitation of the Belgian king's African territory had provided extraordinary wealth for Belgium, which would rank it in second place together with the United States, within the hierarchy of industrial powers, to be topped only by Great Britain.[1] But this was not the only league table the new, small country dominated. According to the British alcohol-specialist, Norman Kerr, Belgian exhibited at the end of the nineteenth century, together with Denmark and Russia, the 'greatest proportional extent of inebriety'.[2]

In fact, the Belgian industry owed its economic success in part to the fact that workers' wages were kept extremely low which meant that in the beginning of the twentieth century, Belgian workers were 'among the most miserable of Europe',[3] earning a third to half less than the British, while their working hours were 10 to 20 per cent higher.[4]

The Way of the Worker

Almost the entire nineteenth-century public discourse on drunkenness was centred on male working-class drinking habits. We know much more about the drinking habits of workers than any other groups in society, but almost all we know was written by those who tried to purge these habits. Temperance campaigners presented endless worrying evidence that the consumption of gin was on the rise.[5] After 1900 and the introduction of a higher tax on strong liquors, people started to drink less gin and more beer instead. Also here Belgium seemed to top the tables: consumption of beer was two times higher than in Germany and Belgians drank six times more of it than the French.[6] Both gin and beer were of course the drinks of choice of the working classes. Non-anti-alcohol sources, such as the comments of foreign visitors, literature and art, give us a more nuanced picture, and in fact fin-de-siècle artists and writers bring their interpretation of the female working-class drunk onto the table. In the first half of the nineteenth century middle-class commentators talked in patronizing tones about the 'ways of the worker' and the idea that he was morally lacking in the way he spent his money. In the second half of the nineteenth century emphasis shifted more towards the 'nature of the worker' with a particular focus on their inborn uncultivated nature, their 'natural temperament' that was just not equipped to resist the temptations of alcohol.

Most bourgeois commentators agreed that drunkenness was endemic among Belgian miners and factory workers. For example, British visitor Demetrius Charles de Kavanagh Boulger observed: 'The only amusement known to these people is to drink and to get drunk. There are no abstainers or half abstainers among them. The only distinction lies between beer-drinkers and spirit-drinkers'.[7] Most were also convinced that immorality and poverty went hand in hand with the drinking habits of the Belgian working classes. In the later years of the nineteenth century, notions of disobedience and revolution were also linked to excessive alcohol use. It was less clear what came first.

In the mid-nineteenth century many argued that the miserable circumstances to which the workers were subject triggered their alcohol abuse. However, in the later part of the century, especially after 1886, bourgeois commentators became increasingly convinced that the workers were poor, dirty, immoral and most worryingly insubordinate, *because* they overindulged in drink. Linked to topical ideas of degeneration, this would then lead to a terrible downward spiral to ever more misery and drunkenness. For Swiss psychiatrist and anti-alcohol campaigner Auguste Forel, the drunkenness he found in 'certain mining districts in Belgium' was the worst he had ever seen, even compared to what he considered to be the awful situation in large English towns, such as Liverpool. He wrote in 1905: 'Modesty, morality and health are destroyed in this swarming human mass – dirty anemic, tuberculous, rickety, imbecile or hysterical ... What can we expect from a population so completely degenerate?'[8]

However, not all believed that Belgian workers were inveterate boozers. For example, an ex-miner from Herstal told the Commission du Travail in 1886 that the workers seldom drank gin, if only, he continued, because they simply could not afford it.[9] The delegate to the Commission du Travail of la Groupe du Fond-des-Loups, a working men's organization in Verviers believed there to be intemperance in all classes of society. People from the higher classes drank because they liked it, he thought, or as a result of their decadent lifestyle, while in the lower classes drink was often a result of misery and a means to forget about it.[10] This was also the argument of contemporary socialists. Journalist Auguste de Winne was told by the workers in Flanders whom he interviewed that they never ate meat and drank 'less than ten glasses of beer a year'.[11]

Historian Peter Scholliers researched the correlation between workers' wages and the amount of alcohol consumed and concluded that alcoholic drink only became part of the family budget if it could be afforded. Mostly, however, workers simply did not earn enough to spend anything whatsoever in the 'cabaret'.[12] Salaries were often paid out in pubs and some historians and contemporary commentators concluded that as soon as the workers received their wages they would spend much of it on drink.[13] This was often accompanied by violence. In the northern French towns with many Flemish immigrants, for example, racist riots broke out around pubs on payday.[14] Novelist Paul Heusy, sympathetic to the plight of the workers, wrote how after this first initiation to the drinking ritual every two weeks on payday workers would feel 'the taste for gin arise'.[15] He addressed his bourgeois readership directly and rhetorically: 'How many, between the preachers of sobriety, with a quiet stomach and a contented throat, would resist, if they had to go through a similar period of abstinence?'[16] The workers themselves sang in pubs: 'Happiness was in the glass' and 'drink makes hurt and pains disappear'. Their song continued: 'we won't bother when it's said the times are bad, we prefer to drown that complaint in our glass, until the landlord wants his debts'.[17] Many drank in their local pub on a running tab bill to be settled at the end of the week.[18] That this practice of running a tab in the bar was curbed as part of the law on public drunkenness indicates that this was indeed considered a problem, perhaps rather more from the perspective of the part of the bar owner who did not get paid.[19]

The Good Sober Worker

In Eugene Zetternam's early socialist novels the workers were never drunkards. Instead, they are represented as idealized and morally strong characters. At the end of the story of their oppression by the tyrant capitalist Mr Luchtervelde, for example, they are ultimately victorious. In Zetternam's mild socialist view this meant that they had climbed up the social ladder – Zetternam's revolution of 1848 was a petit-bourgeois one. The carpenter Louis, for example, becomes a *patron* himself with apprentices. He is determined to give them an honest wage and to teach them to 'take care they do not drink it'.[20] Whereas the villainous bourgeois owner Luchtervelde represents an old system of authoritarianism, in which a man's position of society was dependent only on property and not on demeanour or high moral standards, the character of Louis embodies a new paternalistic system, advocating social flexibility through the assumption of 'modern' bourgeois values like moderation.[21] This ideology was in need of a 'good sober worker', to confirm that the wages were sufficient and that the real cause of the workers' misery was spending the money on drink instead of using it wisely.

When the workers started to voice protest in the last quarter of the nineteenth century, drunkenness became ever more recognized as a typical behaviour of factory workers, as part of their way of life and also of their biological make-up. The story of the sober prudent worker for whom the wages were sufficient was still being told, if only because it supported the idea that workers' protest against unfair distribution of wealth was not legitimate. In the naturalist novel *Happe-chair* from 1886, by the 'maréchal' of Belgian literature, Camille Lemonnier, the main character is an idealized model worker who also completely abstains from alcohol. When writing *Happe-chair* Lemonnier acted upon contemporary events as the book tells the story of a strike in an imaginary iron works community called 'le Culot' situated in the Borinage close to Liège, in the Belgian 'Black Country'. To prepare for his work, like any self-respecting naturalist writer, Lemonnier had conducted extensive research: he had visited, pen in hand, the industrial towns to study the people he met and the places where they worked and lived.[22] Jacques Huriaux, the model worker, shows that free will and rationality can overcome misery, in accordance with progressive liberal and socialist ideas. He decides sensibly that he does not *want* to drink and his sobriety and ambition eventually lead to his emancipation. But Huriaux was also 'gifted' by Lemonnier with a good heredity and a solid education. This was unusual as primary school in Belgium was only made compulsory in 1914 and in 1900 still almost one in five of the Belgian population could not read or write. Among women this was one in four.[83] So while in *Happe-chair*, the uneducated, angry workers drink away their troubles in gin, Jacques does not participate: 'drink did not for him have the natural attraction it had for the others, he would have to violate himself to defy, by drinking, the black ghost of his pain'.[23] Hurieux's mother is Flemish, like the writer's own, and she is presented as a silent, serious matron. Lemonnier admired the Flemish farmers, ascribing to them the usual attributes of stubbornness, strength and perseverance. Huriaux's family background is thus helpful, with an encouraging education to crown it.[24]

Huriaux is of course a utopian character. During the workers' dispute, he argues for dialogue with the employers rather than for strikes. He reads newspapers, is ambitious and his allegiance is ultimately rewarded when the enlightened factory owners offer him a new career as overseer, which allows him to pay off his wife's debts.

The socialist press was never particularly keen to print *Happe-chair* for serialization, although they would publish other works by Lemonnier, like *La fin des bourgeois*. The more radical wing of the socialist movement could not agree with the ideology put forward in the novel: Lemonnier sympathized with liberal paternalistic ideas rather than with socialist reform.[25] However, the reformist orthodoxy of the Belgian Worker's Party equally had at its heart the paternalistic idea of betterment of the workers through education and sobriety. The motto of Vandervelde's Ligue Socialiste contre l'Alcoolisme founded within the Party in 1898, was '[fight] against alcohol by means of the book'. While praising the Belgian workers' remarkable organizational and political strength, socialist foreman and anti-alcohol campaigner Emile Vandevelde denounced their lack of literacy and reading skills together with their excessive drinking habits. The narrative of the 'good worker' as reasonable, obedient and abstaining from excess was reproduced and repeated endlessly in the repertoire of the bourgeois and it was at the heart of both liberal as socialist temperance efforts.[26]

Making Strong Men

In the middle of the century there were few who doubted that alcohol formed part of a healthy diet, that it provided strength and prevented disease. As late as 1906 the temperance movement found it necessary to produce a poster counteracting these 'false beliefs' in relation to drink. During the cholera epidemic of 1866 in Ghent, the working-class population drank large amounts of gin, which they regarded as an antiseptic and prophylactic. Drunkenness became an unavoidable side effect. Those who were employed to go around the houses to pick up the dead victims of the disease were offered a glass of gin in every house they visited, and consequently were more often than not terribly drunk.[27]

Alcohol use was linked with tough factory work. The workers themselves claimed they needed the alcohol to perform their work properly,[28] and many foremen in factories or mines offered their workmen a glass of gin before starting the day.[29] Those who worked in exceptionally physically demanding jobs like construction or as dock labourers in the harbour insisted on their dram. This has been interpreted as a remainder of 'artizanal drinking habits' of a pre-modern work environment that continued to persist in the new fully mechanized modern circumstances of the factory workplace.[30] As long as workers did their duties and their drunkenness did not affect their performance, such drinking was considered unproblematic. Equally, as part of these traditional drinking habits, the employers, who were sometimes also café owners, paid part of the wages in kind at their bar.[31] It is not clear how widely spread this custom was, but it was a practice which the temperance movement fought against and it was abolished in 1887 as a result of the suggestions of the Commission of Work.

Drinking was part of daily life for male workers and getting drunk at weekends or on payday contributed to the making of a group identity. It would be hard to resist the pressure to drink on with fellow workers. Miner Antoine Mathieu admitted that he had drunk for the first time because he wanted to imitate his peers and 'act like a man'.[32] But however much drinking and getting drunk was part of traditional workers' way of life, in practice drunkenness was never an option in the modern factories of the nineteenth century. Labourers were made to work under a strict regime and being drunk on the job was severely punished.[33] Many factory owners expressed their frustration about the phenomenon of the lost Monday, when some of their employees did not show up for work because they had drunk too much at the weekend. The repercussions for a worker who failed to attend the workplace because he was nursing a hangover were severe – not only for him, but also for his family. Anti-alcohol activists placed this issue at the forefront of their campaign, making combatting work negligence a central theme.

The opportunities for getting drunk were clearly manifold. Théophile Gautier who travelled in the 1830s with Gerard de Nerval to Belgium in search of blonde women and booze, wrote excitedly in his journal: 'In Vallencienne I saw for the first time on the wall that formidable description, which is reproduced invariably every 10 houses, until the end of this marvellous odyssey: *Verkoopt men drunken.* This means in true Flemish "Here drink for sale"'.[34] A picture taken in Antwerp in 1894 of an antiques shop reveals that sixty years later not much had changed. Next to the sign with the name of the shop, one can perceive a smaller sign announcing that apart from antiques the shop also sells drinks and 'fine liquors'.[35]

The Home of Socialism

It was the drinking that took place in bars that was considered most problematic. Bourgeois temperance campaigners complained relentlessly about the amount of drinking places in Belgium. In industrial centres like the mining district of the Borinage visitors counted one bar for five adult men.[36] Most agreed that the situation with regard to unlicensed and unlimited alcohol sales could only encourage drinking habits,[37] although there were others who did not really consider this the problem. Some determined defenders of free enterprise concluded that the situation was 'not so bad as statistics might lead us to infer'. English visitor Cyril Scudamore explained that the common practice of powerful brewers buying up small houses which they would let to the workers in return for selling their beer alone was a good way for the workers to 'secure a cheap house'. According to Scudamore, this monopolizing of property by brewers for their own interests had 'a rather beneficial effect in lessening the evils of intemperance'. When there had been only one or two pubs in a town, workers would crowd together and 'encourage one another to drink'. Now that there were so many different places to buy a drink 'the men ... only meet in groups of two or three, and avoiding undue excess, depart quietly home to bed'.[38] So what was ultimately problematic was not the amount of drinking places or the amount of drink that was consumed, but the sociability of the event.

Indeed, for the working classes in the cities, as in the countryside, the pub was at the centre of social life and often the only entertainment available. It encompassed many more social functions than just drinking and getting drunk together. In the industrial regions of Wallonia, where the socialist movement found its adherents, the bar slowly replaced the church as the place for socializing.[39] Pubs became important places for political meetings and in the absence of government provisions for workers' relief, saving funds and societies for mutual relief often had their seat in the local pub.[40] The strong ideological function of the pub that historians have pointed out for other European countries was perhaps even more pronounced in Belgium, where party politics started at the basic level of social gathering.[41] Workers joined in at the top of their voice with Karel Waeri when he sang:

'I don't like the drink of Spain, that wine which one drinks with water, I don't feel at all like champagne, that drink heats up the blood too fast, I drink with much pleasure the double beer of Ghent'.[42] These lyrics affirmed working class and local identity: the ceremony of drinking constructs an ideal world. As workers they were proud of the affordable local beer which was better than those so-called superior drinks of the bourgeoisie. A subversive message was hidden between the lines. For the workers getting drunk together in their pubs was a way to construct an ideal world.[43] 'Since we cannot show off with a velvet hat, we drink in our clogs, it tastes equally good', sang the cotton labourers together. Such beliefs worried the bourgeoisie. The workers' drunkenness was an expression of dissent, always political and ideological.

The Revolutionary Drunken Worker

As in France, police in Belgium observed the activities of pub-goers closely, a fact which patrons did not always appreciate.[44] The secret police was always on the lookout for prospective insurgents and had already warned that drink would influence possible uprisings, years before the onset of mass socialist action. Their prejudices about the innate drunkenness and irrationality of socialists were obvious in the reports they wrote. A policeman who in the autumn of 1880 attended a meeting organized by a radical socialist organization Les Circles Réunis, in a bar owned by a worker-joiner in the metal industry around Liège, reported:

> A group of louts [*voyoux*] all in rags, seemingly drunk, came into the room, with a red flag (a red handkerchief, tied to a stick). They started to sing *La Carmagnole*, gesticulating, dancing and vowing that the police would never rip their flag. The individual that carried the rag, balanced it on top of my head.[45]

When the informer realized that a 'proper' meeting was not going to take place after all and that the patrons had found out who he was, he left. The undercover agent described the meeting as trivial and unorganized and its participants as irrational and drunk. Underneath the policeman's disdain for the socialist workers shown in his description of their pathetic red flag and the place of meeting, described as 'a hovel', the language of the report gives a sense of his feeling threatened and subject to an unarticulated fear of uncontrollable, revolutionary passion. The group that had entered the bar had seemed drunk (*paraissant être ivres*), but the informer had not been quite sure, he had just assumed it. A revolutionary fever could, like madness, become confused with mass-drunkenness. And drunkenness, as essentially loss of control, was spontaneously linked to revolution.

Drunkenness stood for violent anarchy. The song the drunken workers in the pub had sung, la Carmagnole, was the preferred song for the anarchist wing of the socialist movement between 1880 and 1890.[46] The danger associated with drunkenness eventually led the government to intervene with laws regulating public drinking. Towards the end of the century, the temperance press eagerly took up the topic of dangerous criminal drunkards. Also in the local press in the last decades of the century and the beginning of the twentieth, many sensational articles were printed of men who had committed hideous crimes under the influence of too much alcohol. This violence would manifest itself as political violence as in the spring of 1886.[47] Localized and spontaneous strikes had taken place previously and were immediately and violently repressed, but this time it was different. The workers marched from pit to factory and sparked a protest such as Belgium had never known before. A haunting prospect was painted by those with most to fear and lose from violent attacks by drunken revolutionaries. Temperance writers and doctors warned that: 'a people that spends all it has in order to become numb and to get over-exited, will turn its insanity [*démence*] against you!'[48]

Strikes were organized in bars in which during work stoppages, the workers gathered to discuss subsequent actions. Pubs would do very good business during the strikes and workers were accused of idling and getting drunk in pubs instead of going to work. Strikes were explained not as a means by which the workers put pressure on their patrons, but as the outcome of the workers' innate laziness. The workers' lack of desire to work was caused by the same diseased and weakened willpower as their urge for the bottle. And so, according to this logic, drunkards were always strikers. Docter Barella who was familiar with striking miners in the Borinage where he worked wrote:

> One of the first symptoms one remarks with the drunkard, is the loss of taste for work, the loss of necessary energy to dedicate himself to it. In all the strikes it is always the drunks [*les alcoolisés*] who dislike the work and who look for all the pretexts to free themselves from it, who put themselves at the head of the movement. Work honors man, but it demands willpower and willpower is weakened among drunkards.[49]

One of the most memorable chapters of the spring of 1886 was the story of a group of revolutionaries who, after destroying the glass factory of Baudoux in Charleroi, marched to the owner's sumptuous castle. There they threw furniture out of windows and dressed up in the owner's clothes. They also raided Baudoux's vast wine cellar and finally set fire to the building. Eyewitness Gustave Houdez told the court of terrible scenes he observed of a mob of drunken revolutionaries, dancing around the flames of a fire, dressed in expensive finery whilst drinking bottle after bottle of expensive champagne. Historian Gita Deneckere called this scene a 'revival of the saturnalia'.[50] Although this had been a very isolated event, this image caught the bourgeois' imagination and it became an enduring image of workers' revolution. This grotesque reversal of roles, a bacchanal of unbridled drunkenness and violence directed towards their possessions and way of life, encapsulated the worst fears of the wealthy. The images of drunken workers dressed up like their patrons, acting out a lavish, decadent party, was too close for comfort.

Additionally, in France this same narrative of drunkenness fuelling revolution had become prominent. Much of the violence of the Commune for example had been blamed on drunkenness.[51] However, the French sociologist and criminologist Henry Joly who was in search of specific national traits in criminal behaviour concluded that Belgians were more violent than the French, that both men and women were more brutal, and that this was mostly the result of a greater abuse of alcoholic drinks.[52]

The Victim Wife

The drunkard's potentially violent behaviour was always a great concern and it affected his family members directly. Many stories in the Ghent mental asylums testify to this. Many drunkards there were brought in by the police on the demand of close family members, because they were violent. In many cases it was the wife who initially applied for the committal; however, it was often the case that she would come to retrieve her husband after a few days when he had calmed down, because the family needed the income from the main breadwinner.[53] This meant that however proactive the wife of the drunkard was in protecting herself and her family from a drunken partner, her social and material oppression would always seem to cast her back into the role of the role of suffering victim. Left to beg to her husband to give up drinking, her plight made for excellent melodrama. The narrative of the martyr wife, who suffered her husband's violent drunkenness and tirelessly protected her children was central everywhere in the stories told about drunkenness in the mid-nineteenth century. Both wives and children were depicted as the innocent victims of the careless drunk.

When Degroux's painting *L'Ivrogne* (see Figure 2.2), which depicts a woman trying in vain to revive her dead-drunken husband in a bar, was put on show on the Brussels Salon in 1870 it immediately became a great success. This specific narrative of the martyr wife or child coming to fetch husband or father from the pub proved so enduring that a hundred years later Louis Paul Boon could still use it convincingly in his historical novel about the struggle of the workers in the factory city of Aalst:

> Thus one could see on the Sunday night around the pubs always the same scenes: men who would drink their little bit of wages, women with a throng of whining children stuck to their skirts, who tried to drag the sloshed home[54]

In pubs people would sing along with heart-rending ballads on the melodramatic theme of suffering children. One very well-known song told the story of a child pleading unsuccessfully with his father in the pub to come home where there is no fire left. Every hour the child returns with a worse scenario: at home his mother is weeping over his dying baby brother. When the brother ultimately dies, with the father still in the pub, the child tells the father that his little brother's last words had been 'kiss father farewell from me'.[55] This story was repeated in endless versions, by Charles Degroux again, for example in a painting called *Scène de Cabaret*, from 1855, today in the Musée d'Orsay. In *L'Ivrogne* (*The Drunkard*) from 1853 (see Figure 2.1), he portrayed children leading a tottering drunken father into a room towards a bed in which their mother has just died, with a baby still at her breast. Degroux's images were immensely popular and prints were reproduced and widely distributed. The interest in these stories crossed class boundaries and were present in both countryside and city. The casting of the wife and children of the drunkard as central figures confirmed and reinforced the emotional involvement of the public in their plight and their awareness and appreciation of such scenarios.

Figure 2.1: Charles de Groux, *L'Ivrogne*, 1853 © Royal Museums of Fine Arts of Belgium, Brussels.

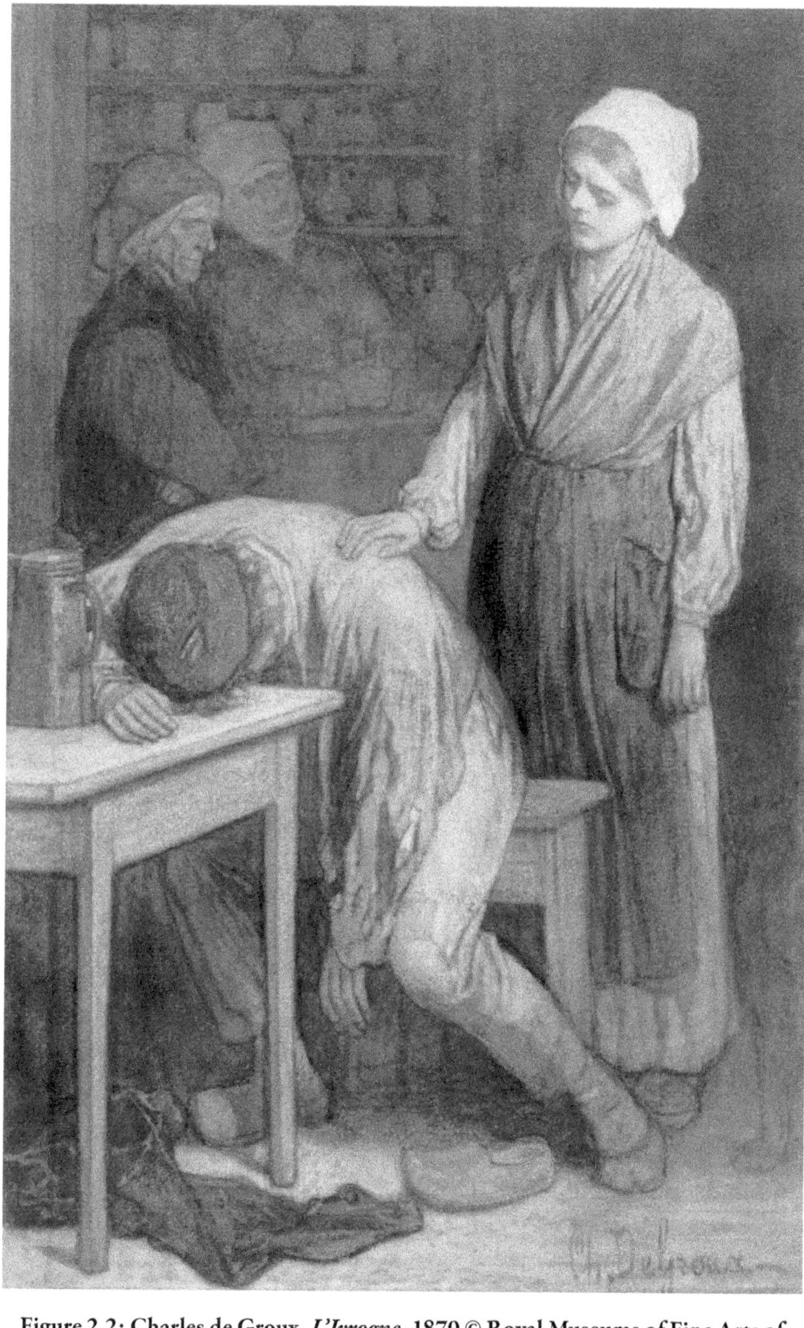

Figure 2.2: Charles de Groux, *L'Ivrogne*, 1870 © Royal Museums of Fine Arts of Belgium, Brussels.

The omnipresence and popularity of such cultural expressions indicates that anyone could recognize this image as steeped in reality and make it their own in many ways. Critics sometimes accused Degroux of socialist sympathies, but his work, wavering between moralizing and melodrama, would also have solicited compassion and pity.[56] One commentator addressed his bourgeois readers about Degroux's *Scène de Cabaret*:

> you all, favoured by fortune, who sees with a weary eye the misery of the people around you, you will feel, if only for a moment, a generous thought coming up, for the sufferings of your wretched brothers, when De Groux with his artistic eloquence exhibits it before your eyes.[57]

It served to provoke a moral stance condemning both the drunkard as well as the poverty he finds himself in. On the other hand, such stories as were told on the paintings served to bring into focus the woman's role in the struggle against drunkenness. In a context of heredity their role became twofold. As educators of children and helpmeets of men they needed to create the right environment to direct whatever inborn tendencies in her family away from drinking. Secondly, in preventing her husband from drinking, the wife helped to protect the future of the race she was to procreate.

Worries were voiced about women not living up to those responsibilities and we read reproachful comments towards women driving men to the bar by not fulfilling their responsibilities. Hygienist Dr Kuborn wrote in 1909:

> the attraction of the bar is often due to the negligence and the ignorance of the housewife. At the end of the working day, the worker returns to a dirty untidy home. Instead of a meal with a tempting aroma, served on a table covered in a nice white tablecloth, he only sees in front of him coarse dishes, badly prepared: the cook does not even know how to put together a soup. So while he does not find at home the slightest comfort, he goes looking for it in a bar.[58]

By the end of the nineteenth century anti-alcohol campaigners ceaselessly depicted this image of the deficient housewife. They based their narrative on what they saw at home, but such comparisons were hardly appropriate: with a good family income the wives of the bourgeois could afford nutritious food, a cook to prepare it and servants to wash and iron white tablecloths. The absurdity of claiming this ideal as a possibility for workers' wives shows a lack of insight into the way the other half lived, and a complete ignorance of the backstage politics of the kitchen: part of their wives' remit. The leading feminist voice in Belgium in the late nineteenth century, Marie Parent, also insisted in her anti-alcohol campaign directed at women on the urgent need to cook tasty and nutritious food and to keep the house clean in order to prevent husbands to escape to the pub.[59] The education of the housewife was considered part of the political feminist project.

Dr Barella wanted the state to organize special schools to educate girls for their task as future wives and importantly for their emancipation, to allow women to open their own savings account to prevent husbands drinking the money needed for the household.[60] The idea that women were to be master of their 'own' money was taken directly from the programme of the bourgeois feminist campaign. Among rich women, those who took family wealth into a marriage could possibly see it disappear when managed by a drinking and squandering husband. Among the working classes, however, women were mostly in charge of the purse strings and in stories of working-class drunkenness we read about husbands having to 'steal' money from their wives in order to spend it on drink.

The nervousness about the lack of household care by wives was related to a broader discomfort about working women within the debates on the conditions of workers. In the mines and metal factories, women were indeed working alongside men as they did in the countryside and Belgium was the only country where women were still doing underground work in the mines in the late nineteenth century.[61] Working women were considered the cause of the problem of male drinking and hence an indirect cause of the political unrest.[62]

Women, Work and Drink

In fact, women were not only working in factories and mines together with men, in nineteenth-century Belgium most of the drink consumed by the working classes would be sold by women who often supplemented their husband's factory earnings with the income from a modest bar in the front-room of their house.[63] These women who served drink in male-dominated spaces created uncomfortable feelings among the bourgeoisie and much potential drama for novelists. Indeed, it was a barmaid who became the principal female character in *Happe-chair* by Camille Lemonnier.

In *Happe-chair*, Clarinette is the wife of the moral and sober Jacques Hurieux, who earned enough money to let his wife stay at home to take care of their baby. Lemonnier clearly considered this an ideal situation, which many women working in factories could only dream of. However, Clarinette is not satisfied, after having worked her entire youth she now feels trapped indoors. Instead of taking care of the household and her child, she gets drunk with her girlfriends, whom she invites over to gossip over cake and many glasses of anisette. She then convinces Jacques to open a bar to provide her with some distraction from the housework while earning a bit extra when he was in the factory.[64] Her bar, called *Les fanfares* becomes the meeting place for the town's music societies and the centre of community life.

The reason morality campaigners fumed against those modest bars run by women, and about women in bars in general, was because of the confusion about social space and social class this generated. While it was acceptable for working-class women to work underground, wearing trousers and doing men's work in the mines: at home in their appointed sphere they were to be only wives and mothers, like their middle-class counterparts. By making the privacy of their homes public, women would cast glimpses of their private world into the public. 'It is there' one appalled opponent of workers' bars wrote, 'that mothers, without any shame, give the breast to newborns'.[65] Such a muddling up of boundaries between the public and private sphere made it difficult for women running a pub to maintain their respectability, certainly in the eyes of the bourgeois observers, but also within her own class. In a bar song, one working-class women insulted another by calling her 'ye old barmaid': a woman behind a pub counter was easily seen as a less respectable member of the working-class community.[66] In the cities, towards the latter part of the century, in new spaces for drinking and entertainment like vaudeville theatres, *café-cabarets* or *café-chantants*, working women became ubiquitous: there were female waitresses and also singers and dancers. In a number of infamous establishments, indeed barmaids would sometimes offer more to the customers than just drink.[67] But where was the distinction between a bar and a brothel? And how could you tell the difference between a barmaid and a prostitute?

In Belgium brothels were legal as controlled 'maisons de tolerance' and their link with excess drinking was for the participants in the debate obvious. 'We all know', wrote one medical writer addressing his colleagues on the topic, 'that prostitutes are receptacles for pox and gonorrhea, friends above all of drinking places. A brothel girl who does not drink and who does not make her clients drink is not kept by the owner, because she doesn't bring any money in'.[68]

Overall, the girl in the pub exposed to the male sexual gaze was seen as 'available' and she became an easy victim of sexual harassment.[69] Therefore it was very important for female workers in drinking places to stay sober at all times and to safeguard their respectability while approaching male visitors and potential suitors. More than one self-respecting female character working in bars in Buysse's oeuvre insisted on 'good intentions' from admirers and a prospect of marriage.[70] However, behind her bar subversive Clarinette relishes the male interest she receives and she sends out mixed signals to her customers. Always flirtatious, she starts drinking now and then a glass offered by a customer, eventually she is emptying entire bottles behind her counter.[71] Readers were shocked by the realistic representations of female drinking in the novel and this work greatly contributed to Lemonnier's reputation as an artist with decadent tastes and subversive morals.[72]

Historian Penny Penn Hilden argued that because the situation of the Belgian working-class women was extraordinary in that they did generally the same factory and mining jobs as men, they consequently also drunk together with the men in the pub. Patricia Prestwich concluded for the French situation that although many bars were presided over by a woman behind the counter, the clientele would predominately be male and female presence in ordinary bars at weekdays would be irregular.[73] Perhaps this was different for Belgium, as French visitor Henri Charriaut was shocked to see some wives of workers in Belgium accompany their husbands to the cabaret.[74]

While we find very little evidence of female presence in bars, even fewer examples are found that can shed light on female drinking habits. The Commission of Work of 1886 was concerned that female drinking habits were on the rise. One of the few working-class witnesses, when asked about female drinking, explained that the women indeed sometimes drank a glass, but not commonly.[75] Jean Coppin, a policeman in Roux close to Charleroi, on the other hand was very concerned about female working-class drinking. He found that there was much drinking among the women in his town but that they would usually not go to the cabaret. Those women would drink at home gin bought at the grocer's or in the pub taking advantage of the time when their husband was at work to engage in such excesses. The women sometimes met in groups, Coppin knew, for what he called 'gin-parties'. Other witnesses expressed similar fears about secret female drinking. They explained how since rules of respectability prevented women from buying their alcohol overtly, they would for example carry alcohol from the greengrocer in bottles equipped with a wick, to make it look as if they were buying petroleum.[76] This particular anxiety and the clarification that drinking women need to hide what they were up to, shows how female drinking was most certainly not within the norm. And this is why a drunken female protagonist in naturalist decadent literature could raise a good deal of dust.

The Excessive Woman

In *Happe-chair* the *estaminet*, badly ran by Clarinette, does not bring in the expected extra money for the household. Like a working-class Emma Bovary, Clarinette's spendthrift ways and desire for luxury ruins the couple further as she shamelessly runs up debts with all the shopkeepers in town. For women, the urge for living beyond one's means and a lack of modesty was outwardly signalled by inappropriate dress. Lemonnier ridiculed the very ostentatious way Clarinette and her friend are dressed when they go out shopping.[77] Workers themselves made a connection between showing off with dress and the equally inappropriate behaviour of visiting bars as well, when they sang for example the song about wayward neighbour Lange Trien, who would come into the bar showing off a new dress and boots.[78]

Modesty was the backbone of respectability among the working and middle classes and abandoning it was a first step towards more and graver transgression. Clarinette and her friend's exuberantly dressed outing to the corrupting city sets the scene for more alcoholic and also sexual indulgence. The women meet the travelling salesman Giginet who takes them to various drinking places and to a bar with dancing girls where they drink punch which, 'added to all their [excesses] of the day, caused their heads to turn and made them mischievous'.[79] At the end of the evening Giginet whispers an indecent proposal into Clarinette's ear which she readily accepts – her fall from grace now complete. The 'cult of the excessive woman', easily lured into temptation of all kinds of which drink was one, while flaunting her sexuality and dragging man down with her in her degradation was at the heart of much naturalist art.[80]

Unsettling female drunkenness was always coupled with potentially dangerous sexuality. The shock impact the combination of female public drunkenness, sexual availability and their luring of men with them, had on polite society became equally evident when the sculptor Jef Lambeaux presented the work *L'Ivresse* (*The Drunkenness*) (see Figure 2.3) at the Brussels Salon in 1893.[81]

This life-size plaster sculpture represents two drunken women, this time not inappropriately dressed but much worse: not dressed at all. They are dancing, tottering and laughing and underneath them, slumped, lies a dead-drunk male figure. Lambeaux called his naked inebriated threesome simply *Drunkenness (Ivresse)* which was hardly considered an appropriate theme for a classical-type sculpture. Subsequently a contemporary art review called the women two nymphs, and then perhaps the sleeping man could have been Bacchus.[82] This renaming took the shocking subject indeed a bit further from home, into the realm of myth, which was much safer. But nevertheless, dismayed viewers at the Salon could not help but wonder what had preceded the scene and what was to come next? What had the 'nymphs' done to the slumped man? Lambeaux already had a tarnished reputation when he presented the plaster; he was a controversial figure, a free mind from a lower middle-class background. He never shied away from themes of sexuality and he was furthermore known as a veteran pub-crawler and a 'slave of his passions', both in his work as in his life.[83] One critic wrote that the sculptor was 'drunk of life'.[84] In 1886 he had already started a controversy with his interpretation of the *Human Passions*, a bas-relief of writhing human flesh, of men and women intertwined in sexually explicit positions. When the final work was eventually put on display in 1900, it was immediately boarded up again after only three days on public view amidst outcries of indecency. Francophone critics found his expressive work either frightfully 'Flemish' or delightfully so, describing it as 'the magnificent outcome of the rude race of Flanders'.[85] His sculptures were accused of being too naked and too rough, and now there were these two drunken dancing prostitutes, because everybody knew that that was of course what the nymphs really were. The commotion surrounding this particular statue reached its peak when it became known that the prostitutes the artist had used as models had been authentically drunk when posing. The debauched artist Lambeaux had presumably made these women drunk, on purpose, so that he could better study and represent the effect of alcohol on the muscles and on their posture.[86] What was also shocking was that nothing in

Figure 2.2: Jef Lambeauxe, *L'Ivresse*, 1893 © Laboratorio delle arti visive, Pisa.

the scene presupposed any guilt or punishment for such behaviour; instead the nymphs were behaving carefree, laughing and having fun.

In Lemonnier's scandalous novel and Lambeaux's shocking art sexual passion was entwined with explicit drunkenness. For Clarinette in *Happe-chair*, once she had seduced her first lover, as for the drunkard with his first glass of gin, there was no way back. Lemonnier described how she was taken over by an atavistic animal-like desire and when seducing a shy and innocent young boy for example he wrote: 'She depraved him, she deranged him with her large hunger of female animal [*une femelle*] feverish with alcohol, with lustful ferociousness'.[87] Psychiatrist Auguste Forel wrote in his signature abrasive style how in the mining towns of the south of Belgium 'there was no distinction between the factory girl and the prostitute'.[88] So far was the race of Belgian miners degenerated by drunkenness he found, that all the female workers were necessarily sexually immoral. Also Clarinette's behaviour was predestined by birth by negative heredity and a miserable childhood.[89] Her mother had not merely been a drunkard, but also like her daughter, an adulteress and there were even rumours that she had even murdered one of her lovers. Clarinette's father had been a violent alcoholic who used to beat his daughter.[90]

The subversive subject of female drunkenness symbolized turmoil, unpredictability and dangerous change, and a dramatic combination of anarchy, drink and sex came to a climax in the novel in a scene of revolutionary violence that takes place in Clarinette's bar. She becomes the leader of a furious crowd and throws glasses from behind her bar at the police. Lemonnier describes how Clarinette exudes a 'feral' attraction to the mob and how she is almost raped in her own bar. The mores of the workers, intemperate and depraved, were generally commented upon by aghast bourgeois commentators in terms that were comparable to the way they would describe the natives in the far away colony in Africa. Like the Flemish countryside, in the middle-class imagination the miners' and factory workers' communities were as far removed from their own lives as those exotic African savages, and their morals seemed very similar: 'In certain Belgian districts which are prey to alcoholism, one sometimes sees human beings copulating in the street like animals, or like the drunken Kaffirs in South Africa.[91]

Clarinette, as a thoroughly subversive character, announced social revolution in much more subtle ways as well. Her drinking corrupts cultural conventions of what was feminine and masculine behaviour. Neglecting her household and her child, her entire attitude is described as 'male'. With her equally debased friends she would go from bar to bar 'drinking while standing upright at the counter, among the men, buying rounds of strong drinks for each other, laughing together ... patting each other loudly on the back'.[92] In the meantime, Jacques took over the role of caring figure, but without ever straying from his role as male provider.

Because ultimately *Happe-chair*, shocking as it was, remained always conformist: in Lemonnier's account, subversive action did not endure: the strike dies out when the proprietors promise changes and drunken Clarinette is cast out of society. Jacques chases his adulterous wife out of the house and onto the street. To escape her neighbours mocking and chasing her, she hides in a communal toilet 'with an enormous black hole, from which a stench of fetid fermentation rose up'.[93] Then, Clarinette disappears from the village and no one knows what happens to her. One can guess she is swallowed up in the black hole of society's underworld. But the insecurity of where she has gone continues to preoccupy Jacques: 'especially the great silence of *la Rinette* worried him like a threat; he felt her around him, lurking in the shadow of the house'.[94] In this way, lurking in the shadows of nineteenth-century society after the violent strikes had been repressed, haunting the bourgeois dreams, was always the possibility that social unrest could re-emerge. In the calm after the storm of 1886, Dr Charles Petithan warned his readers not be lulled into a false sense of security:

> The actual calmness in which we live should not encourage us in our illusions ... A people weakened by misery, ignorance and alcohol is a permanent danger. A similar density of population moves fatally closer to the elements of social decomposition and at every instant a fire might rise up, which, kindled by the popular poison, will soon devour our national edifice.[95]

3 DRUNKENNESS AND THE MIDDLE CLASSES

The city, with its new structures and rapidly adapting cultural formations, symbolized an environment in which drunkenness became more readily presented as a problem threatening the smooth running of society, a 'modern' problem in need of a suitable solution. The inhabitants of the cities – men and women, rich and poor – were obliged to share its space. Bourgeois observers complained relentlessly about the annoying presence of unruly and drunk lower-class people, who were to be found now literally on their doorsteps. Unlike the almost completely segregated reality of the countryside where the bourgeois family in its country house would only glimpse the farmers far away working in the fields, and sometimes drink a polite glass in a respectable pub in the village, in the city there was no avoiding the confrontation with 'how the other half lived'. From the middle-class perspective these encounters generated fears and intolerance, and resulted in moralizing efforts to change the ways of the workers. Artist James Ensor caught this feeling in an ironic print from 1888 (see Figure 3.1).

This image depicts a scene of Ensor's hometown, the Ostend seaside. A bourgeois couple sit on a bench on the promenade. Instead of breathing in the fresh air the seaside promises they are surrounded by clouds of horrible smell.[1] The bad odour originates from a whole crowd of people surrounding the apprehensive couple on and around the bench. The hot sun depicted above seems to be throwing up her warm rays over the scene, the heat making the smells only more unbearable. There is a beggar woman in rags who seems to be spitting, with an unhealthy looking child with sweaty feet. There are two fish sellers carrying stinking fish, one with a runny nose, there is dog faeces under the bench and a man smoking a cigar puffing smoke in the couple's faces. Next to the lady sits a woman of dubious reputation. With a little bottle of liquor in her hand and flushed cheeks and an inebriated, dazed look, this woman is clearly drunk. The lady looks at her with an expression of unease. Smell had a very important influence on social relationships, but it is usually untraceable in our sources.[2] Ensor here makes it visible by drawing it in the air as thick white clouds. The smell of alcohol on one's breath would trigger a whole array of cultural associations and conclusions. And this drunken woman does not only invade the perturbed lady's nostrils with her smell, but almost falls over towards her and therefore literally threatens to invade her space as well.

Figure 3.1: James Ensor, *Peste dessous, peste dessus, peste partout* © Lukas – Art in Flanders VZW / Koninklijk Museum voor Schone Kunsten Antwerpen, foto Hugo Maertens.

In Ensor's print the bourgeois couple is surrounded by dirty and stinking lower-class people. One trusted way for the bourgeoisie to keep the boundaries clear between themselves and the lower orders had always been the idea of cleanliness, implied by orderly appearance.[3] The gentleman wears a clean white buttoned-up shirt; the lady is simply but elegantly dressed in black and wears a hat. The drunken woman next to her by contrast wears no hat, is dressed in a dishevelled way with a dirty apron suggesting her working background. Her hair falls untidily over her forehead.

The clouds of smell drawn in the air over the scene convey the idea of contamination. Ensor titled the work explicitly *Peste dessous, Peste dessus, peste partout!*, which he wrote in the sky above the scene. *Peste* means bad smell but also plague, i.e. contagious disease. The stinking characters are all depicted as spreading disease: they are sneezing, coughing, spitting, smoking and drinking. In the cities, the smells of the unclean, drunken masses entered, like a miasma, into the clean life sphere of the wealthy.

Those middle classes who praised cleanliness insisted on respectable dress and fervently condemned lower-class drunkenness, were not the haute-bourgeoisie – the traditional elites – those old wealthy families that had been at the basis of Belgium's economic success and who had merged with and almost supplanted the waning aristocracy. Instead, they represent a growing urban bourgeoisie, of educated professionals: academics, doctors and lawyers, called by Georges-Henri Dumont, based on economic grounds, the *moyenne bourgeoisie*.[4] It was among this group that concerns about the drinking habits of the lower classes were first voiced and that the first temperance organizations were organized. It was their system of values, of reform liberalism, that would provide the dominant voice in the discourse on alcoholism in the second half of the nineteenth century.

Together with this professional, liberal middle class and central to the life in the city was a large but quiet lower middle class that occupied the shifting ground between proletariat and bourgeoisie. Known as 'petite bourgeoisie', this group was much taken for granted and often disregarded by contemporaries and consequently by historians. The capitalist enterprise was kept running by the paperwork of countless clerks, and essential to the social and economic interactions in the city were small shopkeepers and their wives. Furthermore there were artisans like cobblers and printers, proud of their trade. Ideologically, the formation of the petite bourgeoisie in Belgium was linked closely to the success of the Catholic Party.[5]

These middle classes, whose boundaries were difficult to define, shared the self-consciousness that they were different from a higher, 'consuming class'. They would, for instance, criticize those of their own class who would 'drink champagne on other occasions than at family dinners'.[6] They presented themselves as respectable and productive, an attitude that did not sanction drunkenness.

Marking Respectability

The middle classes fought a tenacious struggle to establish themselves as 'respectable' and different from the large crowds of working-class people, perceived as dirty, dishonest, loud and heavy drinking.[7] By implicit contrast, they felt they themselves represented the 'reverse of those vices'.[8] It was important for this middle class to distinguish itself from the lower classes through behaviour and performance, because financially, their situation as wage-earners could be just as precarious. Therefore, while the petite bourgeoisie could not afford to travel second class on trains, for example, they felt very uncomfortable having to share a compartment with members of the class beneath them. In third class, someone complained: 'one comes in contact with drunkards, with disheveled people without any education, who make vulgar comments in the presence of young children and who smoke, sing and spit'.[9]

In the cities where class distinctions were much more fluid and precarious, in the drinking places artisan or middle-class men frequented, often euphemistically called coffee houses, unambiguous efforts were made to distinguish them from the noisy bars the workers frequented. In those 'estaminets' respectable men came to read their newspaper, to play cards or to chat about politics behind a glass of local beer like Faro or Gueuze. As a rule they would not get loud, drunk or rowdy. Camille Lemonnier wrote how those 'quiet sanctuaries, well stocked with bourgeois clients, enemies of noise, enforce a ban on singing. An infraction to this rule will result in an invitation to leave'.[10] Correct behaviour and the right environment were central to the idea of respectability that was the heart of the bourgeois identity.

For example, the reputation of the family of the painter James Ensor was seriously damaged by his father's drunkenness in the small bourgeois shopkeeping circle of Ostend. According to James, who always respected his father, a wealthy educated Englishman, it was the shallow life of the Belgian bourgeois circles and their unavoidable drinking culture that had led to his problems: 'The bourgeois used to enjoy getting him drunk; we have suffered greatly for it'.[11]

Masks came to represent hypocrisy in Ensor's work, and his *Scandalised Masks* painting from 1883 has been interpreted as a representation of his own family situation. Ensor's father, through his drinking, went bankrupt and had left the family dependent on his wife's fortunes. The painting shows a masked character stooped behind a table with a half empty bottle being startled and discovered by a masked female figure entering the room, carrying a stick – perhaps this duo represent Ensor's weary father menaced by the painter's formidable mother-in-law?[12] In the same year the painter again caught the desperate mood of loss of respectability and desperation caused by drunkenness in a painting depicting drunken farmers. In *Les Pochards* (*The Boozers*) two drunken farmers are sitting at either end of a table. On the wall behind them, a poster is pinned informing the customers of the pub of the availability of a farm for rent. The defeated drunken peasants evoked the precariousness of the situation of the Belgian rural population, as their excessive drinking habits were possibly linked to their economic misfortune. But Ensor here possibly also hinted at the real situation of so many bourgeois families as well, of his own family, suffering loss of property as a result of drink. And like the farmers, Ensor's own father was marginalized, mocked and vilified by the townspeople and his family with it. Once private drunkenness became known, the reputation of the drunkard would be shattered. An outcast in society, James Ensor senior would die from his habit in 1887: a scandalous and public death from drink and exposure in an Ostend doorway.

This idea of respectability and scandal was even more important when it came to female drinking habits. Middle-class women, like working-class wives, certainly would accompany their husbands on days of *fête* or on Sundays, when the whole family would go for an excursion to a restaurant or tavern out of the city to eat waffles and to dance and women would join in with a glass of alcohol. On special occasions, equally, women would drink sweet liqueur with the men to celebrate. In the beginning of the new century for them 'to enter in a café was not a complete ignominy'.[13] But women would never get drunk in public.

Lynda Nead has argued how the differentiation of women between 'the fallen' and the 'virtuous' depended on sustaining visible differences between them.[14] Therefore some cafés found it necessary to set rules to differentiate between 'respectable' and 'not-respectable' women. In the famous café Milles Colonnes in Brussels the admission of women was only tolerated if they were accompanied by their husbands and wearing a hat.[15] Such rules were obviously very easily subverted or broken and confusion about identity would certainly occur.[16] The only and ultimate way to delineate between respectable and non-respectable behaviour was the attitude towards drinking. Respectable women from all classes would most certainly not want to be seen drunk in public. While this attitude was encouraged by the anti-alcohol leagues and the message of the hygienists of what was the appropriate place of a woman, it was also enforced by the application of social control within women's own circle.

Flemish Melodrama in the Theatre

In Flanders, the petite bourgeoisie aimed to speak a standardized Flemish, different from the Dutch spoken in Holland, and most certainly different from the working classes who spoke the local dialect. On 6 October 1853, in the Théâtre des Variétés in Antwerp, Flemish-speaking middle-class audiences enjoyed for the very first time professional theatre in their own language with a performance by the new Nationael Toneel staging a drama in three acts by Pieter Frans Van Kerckhoven, called *de Dronkaerd* (*The Drunk*). The play tells once more a story of decline and fall through drink, but this time of a respectable man. The particular choice of play for such a momentous occasion for this social group is meaningful as it contributed to the forging of the identities of those who felt part of the new Flemish cultural movement. Van Kerckhoven was Conscience's anticlerical counterpart, a failed doctor who had turned author of Flemish popular dramas.[17] The guidance notes for the set design of the play gave away the social universe the audience had to think of: 'a ramshackle bourgeois interior with expensive but run down furniture'. We are introduced to hard-working clerk Frans, who is the son of the drunkard. A focus on the family of the drunkard was always interesting for audiences who perhaps felt they could relate to it, and casting the virtuous son as hero in opposition to a fallen drunkard was fashionable in this type of moralizing Flemish literature of those middle years of the century. Conscience would invent righteous Lucas, the son of the drunkard his *Langs de Wegen* two years later and Aldemar Camillo van der Cruyssen introduced the honest son Bernard in his equally moralistic novella *De zoon des dronkaerds* (*The Son of the Drunkard*) in 1856. But in other aspects the story falls within the template of similar stories belonging to this first output of Flemish literature. An ill and long-suffering wife and daughter are the drunkard's victims and the play features a sexually predatory, obviously French-speaking, upper-class man who the imprudent drunkard wants to match with his own daughter.[18]

In Van Kerckhoven's play, the drunkard Baptist wastes all the painstakingly gathered family fortune on drink. His ill and long-suffering wife reminds her son and the audience that a few years earlier the family 'could be called respectable, when your father employed around fifty workers and when his affairs were still successful'.[19] He did not drink cheap beer or gin as ordinary workers did: when the proprietor of his local bar came to call with the family to collect the father's debts, on the list of drinks to be paid for there are all sorts of upmarket liquors. *Maagbitter, Elixir d'Anvers*, a popular local drink and *Menthe* were drinks generally known and promoted as healthy and fortifying *apéritifs* or *digestifs*. Among the middle and wealthy classes the habit of taking liquors as *apéritifs* and *digestifs* was regarded as a necessary part of any meal, since alcohol would stimulate appetite and help digestion after heavy dining.[20]

When business slackens, Baptist refuses to take up a job as an ordinary worker after having been in charge. And thus it is the dreaded vice of pride that directly causes his demise as slowly but surely unemployment and money worries lead to desperation and the bottle. 'First only occasionally', Frans explains, 'because one does not fall at once into the deep abyss, but gradually he gave himself more and more ... to drunkenness and it had become a habit'.[21]

However, the real drama starts when son Frans, the only remaining breadwinner of the family, loses his job as well. His boss dismisses him because 'he desired no longer to keep the son of a drunkard, a scandal of the streets, in his office'.[22]

The event of Frans's dismissal and his demure acceptance of it demonstrate how much the respectability of the petite bourgeoisie was felt to be dependent on their and their families' public performance. In fact, Belgian offices had strict rules and regulations to control the behaviour of their employees, which included articles on the consumption of alcohol. For example, article 6 of one such *règlement de bureaux* read:

> It is prohibited to speak during office hours. An employee who smokes cigarettes, takes alcoholic drinks, and frequents billiard rooms or political environments [*milieux politiques*] is considered dubious as for his honour, his honesty and his accuracy.[23]

The story of *The Drunkard* continues along familiar lines: after more of the drunkard's atrocious acts, his wife dies from misery and in a final melodramatic scene the drunkard admits all his crimes and he jumps out of the window to his death. His son Frans becomes a teacher (one step up the social ladder from being an office clerk), and he and his wife live happily, soberly and modestly, ever after.

An Occupational Hazard

While drinking *digestifs* and *aperitifs* was part of social ritual for middle-class men, some would find it harder to reject an offer of drink than others. This was especially so for men whose work was closely linked to the sociability of drink and for some drunkenness could become an occupational hazard. For example, the Ghent asylum's records offer many examples of people who had fallen victim to an environment where alcohol was ubiquitous and who had become alcoholics because of a professional life in which drinking was deeply imbedded. Many were pub landlords and a striking number of alcoholic brewers or brewer assistants. Jacqueline Lalouette showed that alcoholics locked up in French asylums had often professions related to the wine industry. This happened in Belgium as well, but in a country where beer was the national drink, many more alcoholics in the asylums in Ghent were active in the brewing industry or were café-workers.[24]

Other professions were also linked to excessive drinking: those who would sell or deliver from door to door, like postmen, would often have a penchant for strong drink. Hospitality would dictate the offering of a shot of gin and social customs and good business sense would prevent the salesperson from declining such offers. Salesmen were also often represented as tempters not only into buying their product but also into joining them for a drink. The sand-seller in Conscience's work represents the devil and in Lemonnier's *Happe-chair*, Giginet the wicked travelling salesman seduced Clarinette with the help of drink.

One profession notorious for its connection with heavy drinking was that of 'electoral agents'. Electoral agents or 'electoral runners' (*kiesdravers*) were often members of local government who were responsible for the running of the campaign of a candidate MP. During election time this involved much drinking with potential voters. Elections and drunkenness were intimately linked in nineteenth-century Belgium. Apart from the political meetings called to harness voters, which according to observers were fuelled with drink, on election day – a free day for all – drink would flow freely. Before the introduction of general franchise voting had to take place in the capital of the *arrondissent* and therefore the candidate organized and paid for an excursion of countryside voters to the polling station. The voters were collected and accompanied by the agent by train or by cart. On the way they were offered food and drink and after the voting they received a meal ending in a drinking spree that could last until late. The accounts of the election campaign of Félix de Béthune, the mayor of Kortijk, who ran for the senate in 1847 for example, show that more than half of the campaign budget was spent on food, cigars and 'wine, beer, liquor and alcoholic drinks' offered to the voters. A detailed bill shows that one of the electoral agents spent more than 400 fr. on drink for the voters he took along to the polling station. Eighty-six men drank 9 litre genever, plus forty separate shots, one bottle of 'puns' (punch?), one bottle of 'curaseau', one bottle of 'menthe', probably before leaving. Then they drank one barrel of beer and sixty-two bottles of wine with lunch and dinner and in the evening at the bar each voter drank another ten shots.[25] Surely at the end of election day there were not many sober souls left. These voters and drinkers were decidedly middle class: they would be shopkeepers, businessmen and rich farmers, part of the 2 per cent of the population that paid enough taxes to be allowed to vote before 1892. The habit of drinking on election day was widespread. When in Antwerp the announcement of election results in 1880 caused street riots, the civil guard that was called up especially because of the event of the elections proved incompetent as they had been drinking most of the day. [26]

Many contemporary commentators were shocked by the scenes of drunkenness that accompanied election time and they disapproved of the practice of buying votes with food and drink. When in the last decade of the nineteenth century suffrage was extended to all male voters, the practice of bribing with food and drink became ever more widespread. Before the election, votes were being recruited in bars with numerous free rounds. After casting their vote, the agent would hand out vouchers for a meal or for ten pints of beer and *borrels*.[27] Sometimes the excessive drinking during election times led to the downfall of those who were organizing the campaign and the pressures of the job would become too heavy for those acting as agents. An insurance broker of Mont-St Amand was such an 'electoral agent' who during election succumbed to drink so much so that his wife had to take him to the Maison de Santé in Ghent for treatment. In the period leading to the elections of 1912 it had happened again. The alienists diagnosed him with 'dipsomania on the occasion of the electoral period' and explained in the notes how he was 'forced to drink liters of drink' in the 'electoral meetings held in cafes and estaminets'. He left after a month again but with a question mark behind the decision to let him go: 'cured? like every alcoholic'.[28]

French Melodrama in the Cinema

With drinking and drunkenness seemingly everywhere, alongside the constant need to fight against it as a threat to respectability, it should not come as a surprise that the story of the plight of the family of the middle-class drunkard continued to captivate audiences. The grandchildren of the generation of shopkeepers and clerks who used to enjoy popular melodramatic theatre were enthralled by a new form of entertainment that had become available to them beside the bar: the cinema. Socialist leader Emile Vandervelde called cinema the 'theatre of the poor man'.[29] And the type of performance, the style of writing and acting of the early films and also their success found its roots in popular melodrama.

Several existing short French films had already recounted the social problem of alcoholism. In the very early films that depicted drunkenness it was especially the representations of the outlandish hallucinations that accompanied delirium tremens that proved interesting for film makers: *Le rêve d'un buveur* (*The Dream of a Drunkard*) for example, was a very short film of less than a minute made by Pathé as early as 1898. In this film, a drunkard falls asleep on a table top in a bar and dreams about the face of his wife who pesters him about the household money, followed by a scène in which he is taken away by two policemen to an asylum afflicted by delirium tremens. Then there was the short feature from 1902 by Ferdinand Zecca *Les victimes de l'alcool* (*Victims of Alcohol*), in which a prosperous worker ruins his family when he cannot resist the temptation of drink and he finally ends up squirming in a padded cell in the madhouse. In 1902 film distribution was still very limited and if this film reached a Belgian audience, it would have been in tents at local fairs and in vaudeville theatres, and its audience would have been decidedly working class.[30]

Yet when Pathé issued a long version of *Les victimes de l'alcool* with the same title, this time directed by Gérard Bourgois in 1911, the situation had changed to be different. The appearance of the first fixed cinema theatres in cities like Brussels and Antwerp in the early years of the twentieth century, broadened the audience for cinema attracting also middle-class audiences, those people who had previously been regular visitors to performances of popular drama in theatres.[31] This shift in audience ran parallel with an important modification of the story of *Les victimes de l'alcool*. Apart from its length, the main difference between the original from 1902 and the 1911 remake was that Jean, the protagonist, had been a working-class drunkard in the earlier film and would become ten years later a petit-bourgeois drunkard.[32] Instead of wearing a workman's shirt and cap, which he did in the 1902 version, the drunkard of the updated story in 1911 sported a waxed moustache and a bowler hat. For the rest the drama had remained more or less the same, although we learn more about the drunkard's children. The son Jacques turns to crime and becomes involved with a housebreaking gang, and his little sister Marie suffers from tuberculosis and dies. Beaten in her battle against vice and misery, the drunkard's wife lights a stove and kills herself while Jean loses his reason and is carried away to the madhouse.

The temperance movement had understood the power of the cinema as a propagandist tool and endorsed screenings featuring the drunkard.[33] But it is hard to believe that the production houses – certainly more interested in profits than morals – would have taken on this particular subject matter because of a concern with public welfare. Rather, they knew that a social melodrama about the plight of the family of a drunken father was a tale that would grab audiences and that was likely to do well at the box office. Popular drama was essentially sensationalist and always in search of new narratives. Witnessing the middle-class drunkard fail to conform to expected social conduct linked back to real-life anxieties and offered sensation and scandal: the ingredients for successful melodrama. The fall from grace for the lower middle-class family was much more dramatic than for a working-class family, which was seen to be accustomed to live with drink and its excess and for whom drinking was always represented as 'normal'.

Equally, the possibility of a descent into madness offered vast opportunities for melodrama: the loss of reason symbolized the ultimate fear of many a bourgeois trying to conform. The madhouse was constructed in this representation once more as the final destination of the drunkard and a prime site for sensational drama and outlandish performance. An English reviewer of the 1911 version of this film elatedly described the last scene in the madhouse:

> Pent in a narrow straw-padded cell, we see the maniac raving and gibbering in the agony of his lunatic fury ... with foam dripping from his distended jaws the mad man hurls himself upon the ground, clawing with his bleeding fingers at his face, his clothing and everything about him.[34]

A few months later, in January 1912 in Brussels, in almost all of the more than 100 cinemas the city boasted, the 'heartrending drama' *Le poison de l'humanité* (*The Poison of Humankind*) was shown.[35] This film was distributed by the French company Éclair and directed and written by Emile Chautard and Victorin Jasset was a great success in Belgian cinema. This film brought the drama of *Les victimes de l'alcool* again a step further. In Chautard's film the drunkard had made first a journey up the social ladder – an ambition many of the petite-bourgeoisie viewers most certainly shared and his higher social position, made for a more spectacular downfall. The first part *Les fautes d'une père* (*The Mistakes of a Father*) introduces Morin, an intelligent engineer, full of energy who through hard work had become rich. Having succeeded on his own merit, he marries the daughter of his boss and becomes part of the haute bourgeoisie. But of course, all goes wrong when he takes to drink. Subsequently, in a second part of the great social drama, *L'Hérédité maudi* (*The Cursed Heredity*), the dire hereditary consequences are exposed, when Morin's excessive drinking does not only turn out to affect his own children but also future generations.[36] It affects the family until the fourth generation. The *Kintematograph and Lantern Weekly* acknowledged that this was a theme 'that was current opinion among some groups that were in contact with learned societies', hereby acknowledging the scientific roots of the ideas of degeneration.[37] While in *Les victimes d'alcool* the son's criminality and the daughter's disease can possibly be attributed purely to environment and milieu, in *Le poison de l'humanité* there can be no doubt that the alcoholism of the father has fundamentally affected his biology – and with it the 'race' more generally.

The main difference between the theatre of the mid-century and the films more than half a century later was precisely the addition of concepts of alcoholic heredity and physical degeneration in the latter. In mid-century melodramas the drunkard always completely disappears in the end, dies after having repented or kills himself unable to live with his guilt. The children are not affected by vice or disease; instead, they are healthy, work hard and survive the distress their father's downfall has caused and modestly clamber out of the social and financial pit dug by the father. These mid-century stories belong to an earlier, although not less melodramatic, moral universe where high morals and willpower were central and the drunkard was responsible for the downfall of himself and his family and where biological heredity was not implicated.

However, half a century later, this has changed: the popular films *Les victimes de l'alcool* and *Le poison de l'humanité* show that ideas that vices of the drunkard live on through future generations had become very convincing and that the focus on the hereditary aspects of drink added to the drunkard's downfall and the film's dramatic potential. There were no heroes in these dramas, only victims, and the faith of the whole of humanity was involved. This prevalence in dramatic fiction of notions that were at the same time also recorded by medical professionals in their textbooks and case notes, indicates a smooth flow of ideas between science and popular culture. In addition, the popularization of ideas pertaining to biology and medicine also points towards 'what people really thought of science and how they liked to use it'.[38] The terrible outcome of disease brought upon innocent victims and the ultimate loss of control in alcoholic madness and disastrous effects to generations to come, fuelled the melodrama. The unavoidability of the dreadful results of alcoholism, set now in biological, unequivocal terms, persuasively reinforced the tragedy and therefore added to its attraction.

Inventing Fairy Tales

Madness as a consequence of excessive drinking and some ideas of hereditary generation were to be found much earlier in Belgium, in a fairy tale titled *Eene uitvinding des duivels. Helsche geschiedenis* (*An Invention of the Devil. A History from Hell*), written by Conscience, in which he tells the story of how the devil invented gin. Conscience had started to think about the subject of drunkenness for a second time after a debate about the problems of the 'gin-plague' organized by the Société littéraire de Courtrai, a discussion society that the writer himself had set up and which convened in Café Belge over a pint.[39]

Perhaps he hoped that the fairy tale form would interest his potential readers in the countryside. The reader is introduced to the court of Queen Death, with her courtiers: Mother Plague and her daughter Cholera, Father Famine with son Typhus and Knight War. Other courtiers are named after other diseases: Yellow fever, Chickenpox, Mania, Epilepsia, and so on. They all feel bored and complain to their Queen about lack of occupation. The Queen is not well herself: 'Nerves are the worst plague to us women', she complains, 'and even queens on the throne do not escape it'.[40] But then a message arrives that her cousin, King Lucifer, has invented a death potion which would solve the joblessness of the inhabitants of hell. The devil arrives with his own following: the Sins, the Vices and the Crimes, and he explains how he invented a poison that

> by its taste and its effects would bewitch man in such way that he would gulp it down as a life-giving and comforting foodstuff … it would suffocate the moral powers of man and load him with sins and evil deeds and thus guide him into the vortex of hell.[41]

Queen Death, however, on realizing how bad the potion tastes, does not want to believe him. To prove his point, the devil presents her with a wooden box with holes to look through, in which scenes from the future can be seen demonstrating the effects his poison will have. The different moving-image panoramas that Queen Death glimpses through the devil's time machine correspond to familiar sensational narratives of the mid-nineteenth century; narratives that would be taken up again in the real cinema of the early years of the following century. First, there is the story of a poor ruined drunkard's household, with a crying mother and hungry, dying children. The peep-show reveals how a lewd 'gentleman' offers money to the drunkard's daughter and how, instead of protecting her, he laughs, 'stupid and furious as an unreasonable animal'.[42] While the drunkard's daughter turns to prostitution out of desperation, the drunkard himself goes insane. The next disastrous scenario displayed in the devil's viewing-box tells of the struggles of a wealthy family who had sent their son to university where he had become 'slave of the poison' of the devil.

He cannot finish his studies, disappoints his family and finally kills himself.[43] A scene in a lunatic asylum follows, where those who had become insane as a result of their drinking have to spend their miserable days. Then we look inside a prison, where all those who have committed crimes under the influence of alcohol are locked up, among whom a husband who in his bout of drunkenness had axed his wife's head off. A fifth scene shows a ship in a storm, which was doomed to perish. Because of the mistakes the inebriated crew made the vessel could not be kept under control.

These scenes, chronicled to illustrate the curse of alcoholism in the mid-nineteenth century are the same stereotypical stories that would be ceaselessly used and reiterated by the medical anti-alcohol campaigners in years to come. Conscience not only cited drink as a cause of poverty and misery but also established a connection between drink and both crime and lunacy. But while the story was written in 1864, the temperance movement that would retell these imaginary scenes over and again would only come into existence in Belgium and also in France a decade later. However, in Protestant countries, the United States of America and Britain and also in Germany and the Netherlands, an anti-alcohol movement was already prominent from the first half of the nineteenth century.[44]

In Britain temperance was a mass movement which claimed in the mid-nineteenth century a following of hundreds of thousands.[45] At the heart of their propaganda was such melodramatic imagery of the possible dangers of drink and parts of this cultural repertoire had crossed the Channel. George Cruikshank, the illustrator of Charles Dickens's *Oliver Twist*, famously published a serious of temperance drawings depicting the gradual ruin of a family as a result of alcohol, titled *The Bottle*. These eight plates were available in Britain for the first time in 1847 where they had caused a sensation.[46] Fifteen years later, in 1862, the series of *The Bottle* was introduced in Belgium by hygienist, early temperance campaigner and translator Paul Bouquié-Lefebvre, who published the drawings in Brussels under the title *Les dangers de l'alcoolisme*.[47] Hendrik Conscience was most certainly familiar with these drawings as he knew Bouquié-Lefebvre from translation work he had done for him.[48] The similarities between Cruikshank's influential illustrations and what Conscience described in *The Invention of the Devil* are immediately apparent.

Madness had constituted the final stage of degradation both in Cruikshank's drunkard and in Conscience's fable as insanity was a possible outcome of drinking the devil's potion. Conscience described the alcoholic inhabitants of the asylum as follows:

> [they behave] like stupid animals, with whom all feeling, all reason, all conscience had disappeared. They are death and still alive, they carry a person's name, but are no longer human beings. Among them, there are many whose head staggers, whose limbs tremble, whose features are deformed into the faces of monkeys. What makes them tremble and stumble, is a disease, which is called delirium tremens.[49]

The idea of the asylum as a desirable place to house delirious drunkards was hereby accommodated further into general acceptance and shared beliefs. Three years after Conscience published his story of delirium tremens in the asylum, the affliction would become officially established as belonging in the asylum when the minister of justice formally stated it to be a condition that allowed for legal internment in a lunatic asylum.[50] But whereas delirium tremens was a known problem that was also in other settings more often associated with the asylum, another form of drunkenness that Conscience also located in the lunatic asylum was hardly heard of. In his story some educated drunkards had become mad and placed in the asylum because they had drunk an extraordinary liquor: absinthe:

> All these miserable creatures were once powerful because of their reason, powerful by their intelligence, powerful by their science ... What are they now? A lump of numb meat, less intelligent than the most stupid animal. Ah, they mixed my poison with green herbs and gave it the name 'absinthuim helveticum', and thus strengthened its power on the soul, without diminishing the power on the body.[51]

Historians have tried to understand the extraordinary preoccupation with absinthe in France and its impact in Belgium at the fin de siècle.[52] But in 1864 when Conscience wrote about it, still very little attention was given to the drink and its supposing mind-destructive properties. The British popular temperance narrative did not mention absinthe, and even in France where moral panic related to the drink would become most widespread, its negative effects were only just being explored. It was in the same year *The Invention of the Devil* was published that absinthe specialist Valentin Magnan presented the first results of his research into the effects of absinthe on the brain.[53] Could Conscience have read those articles, published in a specialist medical periodical when researching his story? He was interested in modern medicine as he evokes it further as well, but certainly these early clinical studies would not have been general knowledge in 1864.[54] Absinthe was hardly known in Belgium and definitely not in the Flemish countryside where Conscience envisioned his reading audience. Moreover, as in France at this time only wealthy people would be able to afford the drink, which would only become more readily available in the last decades of the century.[55] And even then, absinthe was always drunk by specific groups interested in the cultural connotations of a bohemian and artistic way of life attached to the undeniably French drink.

Drinking absinthe became part of a bohemian lifestyle and became a favourite aperitif among modern decadent French artists and writers, many of whom, like Victor Hugo and Charles Baudelaire, had been prosecuted in Paris and had found refuge in Brussels. In 1864 Conscience had just moved from the provincial town of Kortrijk to Brussels where he witnessed how the drinking of absinthe at the hour of the *apéritif* was emulated by local artists and writers. One of those who developed a special fondness for the drink was Conscience's French translator Léon Wocquier, a professor at Ghent university who could be spotted working at his translations in a bar called la Carpe in the university quarter at the Kortrijksepoort, 'with a glass of absinthe'.[56] But in 1860, aged only thirty-nine, he had to be admitted in the mental institution le Strop in the same city after suffering from 'illness in his head' for many years.[57] There the doctors agreed that it was indeed abuse of alcoholic drinks, especially absinthe, but also a bad heredity, excessive use of tobacco and 'debauchery', that had led to his current mental calamity, which was recognized as 'general paralysis' and 'dementia'.[58]

And this was not the only case of madness related to drink that Conscience had been close witness to within his intimate circle. In the same year, 1860, when Wocquier was admitted, another friend the priest and classicist Domien Cracco had died in the same private asylum.[59] And ten years earlier, Conscience's good friend, the poet Theodoor van Ryswijck, had passed away aged thirty-eight, having lost his reason after an 'undisciplined and carefree life, having known misery all the way'.[60] In a letter to his editor, explaining the problems he encountered with his French editors after his translator had fallen ill, Conscience exclaimed: 'It is frightful, this Disease of Writers', referring both to Wocquier's excessive drinking and the lifestyle that accompanied it as well as to the *paraysie general* that he and the doctors believed was the result of it.[61] Léon Wocquier died in the Maison de Santé le Strop in 1864. The night after his friend's death Conscience had started to write *An Invention of the Devil*.[62] By importing and introducing new narratives of drunkenness and madness to his Flemish readers, Conscience was influenced by and at the same time influenced the way excessive drinking was understood in the mid-nineteenth century and set the scene for its interpretation in the latter half of the century.

Towards the end of the nineteenth century, the narrative linking madness with alcoholism and artistic genius was firmly established. Alcohol was believed to grant intellectual and creative energy and as such it was also deemed indispensable for painters and writers, who subsequently would often drink too much of it, anti-alcohol writers explained.[63] A particular idea of 'alcoholic art' – indicating modern avant-garde art – was introduced.[64] Symbolist and decadent artists such as Rops and writers such as Verhaeren presented themselves and were both celebrated and reviled as deviants and outcasts: as mad, drunken and pathological geniuses. Cesare Lombroso in his influential work on genius and degeneration had listed many drunken artists to illustrate his point that 'many man of genius have abused alcoholic drinks'.[65] After Vincent Van Gogh exhibited in Brussels in the salon of Les Vingt in 1890, the art critic Albert Arier famously described the artist, who had drunk absinthe in great quantities during his time in Arles and who was now staying in a mental hospital as 'a fanatic, an enemy of the bourgeois sobriety and minutiae, a sort of drunken giant'.[66] Mad and drunken delirium were always closely linked with extraordinary artistic inspiration, the opposite of pedestrian middle-class ordinariness and thus as a sign of genius. Now in a context of degeneration theory and fin-de-siècle symbolist and decadent art, alcohol becomes the fuel that powered the creative energy of the degenerated mad genius.

The artistic free spirit, embodied by absinthe, was easily understood in terms of loss of reason, in the context of the strictly ordered social system of nineteenth-century Belgium as defended by Conscience and the dominant social opinion with him. He certainly disapproved of the bohemian lifestyle that rejected his own bourgeois values. The restrained and dignified morality campaigner Conscience felt he needed to caution his readers about the risks of drunkenness and rebellion, which he feared most within in his own circle.

Fears and anxieties engendered by a social system under threat were very prominent in one last very significant scene in the story of the *Invention of the Devil*. After having seen the ravages of delirium tremens and *absinthisme*, Queen Death is still not convinced of the damaging powers of the Devil's potion. 'In an hour', she said, 'Mother Plague can kill thousand times more'. To convince her, the devil showed her one last, devastating scene proving the destructive powers of his poison. She looked through the camera in the future and was confronted with an apocalyptic panorama: a scene of what could be understood as racial degeneration. The devil comments:

> an entire race of humans passes by, the kind which one calls on earth 'working class people'. There are men, women, elderly and children. The long use of my poison has made its effects hereditary from father to son. [They are] a degenerate [*verbasterd*] race, that seems to be stooped under a general curse. All are yellow or colourless, with hesitant eyes and emaciated limbs. One is hunchbacked, the other limp, some are bent; many have red, tearful eyes; but all are without power and courage; the blood that's running through their veins is as watery as the blood of insects.[67]

Theories of alcoholic heredity were already established within the medical world in 1864 when Conscience wrote this. But, overall, it was only at the end of the century that such ideas were making a more profound impact in on wider general culture. As in the case of absinthe, Conscience's early attention here to these medical themes, certainly contributed to the spread of those ideas within wider Belgian society.

The terrifying metaphor of the group of degenerated workers as insects, infesting society, is very striking. The image Conscience depicted here, of 'a race of humans passing by ... stooped under a general curse', was repeated, in a different context almost thrity years later, when social painter Eugène Laermans depicted the then current theme of a workers' strike in the painting *Un soir de grève/Le drapeau rouge* from 1893. It shows an enormous crowd of grey clothed men, women and children, a sea of heads and workers' caps, with the factory in the background, walking silently, ominously, behind an enormous red socialist flag. In his new home in Brussels, Conscience must have noticed emaciated workers marching past on their way to the factories. Attributing their evident appalling physical condition to alcoholic heredity and not to their miserable living conditions as a result of economic exploitation was a likely reading of such a scene by a bourgeois writer wanting to dissociate himself of the responsibilities of his own class.

The sad cortège of degenerate workers, Queen Death sees, is accompanied by ghosts of disease flying around them, and the Devil explains:

> My poison has created those ghosts who you can see accompanying them ... they are the ailments and diseases that are called: Scrophula, Rachitis, Anaemia, Ascitses, Atrophia, Cachexia, Cacochymia[68]

The diseases mentioned here, which for Conscience originate in the excessive use of gin, would by others rather be associated with malnutrition and bad hygiene, or in general, with the kind of living conditions the workers and farmers had to endure. Health was always a vital concern and sickness a threatening reality among the lower classes and diseases were menacing the people like so many unattainable ghosts. It was unlikely that Conscience's working and middle-class reading public understood the medical terms quoted. But the inventory of their Latin names gave the account a terrifying ring, which suited the supernatural element of the diseases' representation as ghosts.

Conscience's fairy tale, so dreamlike and fantastic, was in fact far from it. His bizarre tale had its roots firmly embedded in the writer's experience with drunkenness in his own environment. His readers would in turn take up the elements he introduced, some of them for the first time in Belgium, adding them to their own cultural repertoire when thinking about drunkenness. Popular theatre, film and literature took on particular narratives of drunkenness, and audiences identified with them, morphed and reshaped them to become part of what it meant to be drunk. For the middle classes who saw their place in society as self-made and sometimes uncertain, drunkenness was always a condition that should belong to the other but that at the same time always threatened to invade their world.

4 DRUNKENNESS AND THE UPPER CLASSES

The Belgian haute bourgeoisie combined titles and land with new industrial and commercial wealth and was notorious for its extravagant eating and drinking habits.[1] The upper classes liked to show off with lavish banquets and their drink of choice was usually wine.[2] This had always been the preferred drink among the nobility and the haute bourgeoisie and it also became increasingly popular towards the end of the nineteenth century among the broader middle classes.[3] Ordinary people would not get to know the taste of wine until the second half of the twentieth century, apart from when taken as a medicine.[4] In 1851, in Conscience's famous story *de Loteling* a wealthy benefactor offered a strengthening medicinal sip of 'marvellous (wonderdaedigen)' Spanish wine to the wounded and sick poor Jan who said about it, 'full of surprise': 'God what is this? ... it warms so well inside'.[5] Here Conscience, always the moralizer, not only insinuates that wine was completely unfamiliar to the ordinary people but Jan's surprise also indicates his innocence and modesty towards a drink so intimately linked to wealth and luxury.

In Ghent in 1876 at the wedding of Benjamin Ingels, the medical superintendent of the public mental asylum Hospice Guislain, more than ten courses were served all combined with different matching wines: with the oysters came Souterne, with the turbot and the foie-gras champagne, while burgundy accompanied the venison filet. In between courses a sorbet was served on cherry liqueur and after that followed pheasant with St Julien, 'buisson' of lobster with Hochheimer and finally desert of orange fruit salad with Rhine wine. Of course we do not know how much of each offering was actually drunk and we can only assume from the amount of drink that was listed on the menus and the festive context that some or a lot of drunkenness followed.

Camille Lemonnier described in *La fin des bourgeois*, published in 1892, the drinking habits of the mine-exploiting family Rassenfosse. Like every wealthy family the Rassenfosses celebrated weddings, births and job-appointments with lavish banquets consisting of all kinds of exquisite foods and wines. However, Lemonnier described them as gluttonous, unable to keep their consumption in check and always exaggerating. At the wedding of his sister, for example, one of the brothers manages to drink three bottles of champagne by himself.[6] One of the sons-in-law is a very heavy drinker who daily empties three bottles of burgundy. He makes it a point of honour to make his guests drunk 'until vomiting' with a selection of great vintages from his cellars.[7] The idea that this type of decadence passed from father to son is conveyed in a scene in the book when during the celebrations after the christening of a new baby in the family, the drunken male family members christen the baby a second time with champagne among much laughter.

Alcohol was part of the lifestyle of the bourgeoisie and not only at parties and special occasions. Trying to stay away from it in bourgeois circles in the nineteenth century would prove difficult indeed. Apart from drinking wine with meals, taking aperitifs before and digestives after meals in the shape of all kinds of fashionable liquors and mixed drinks like vermouth-cassis, picon-curacao, bitter-citron, was a widespread habit.[8] Anti-alcohol campaigner Juliaan Melchior, who revealed his popularizing stance by writing in Flemish, was a rare voice commenting on the double standards or perhaps the false beliefs related to the type of drink that was drunk and the impact it had on one's health. He pointed out that 'many clerks, bourgeois and wealthy people do admit that gin is a poison, but they believe that fine liquors ... can be beneficial for one's health because they are ... expensive and unadulterated'.[9]

The decadence of lavish drinking parties and the taking of aperitifs and digestives might have been an accepted practice, but from the moment a person was known to have 'taken to drink', he or she was an embarrassment for the family, a black spot that was preferably not mentioned and rarely referred to, even by anti-alcohol campaigners. 'Drunkenness', admitted Dr van den Corput, sometimes could indeed also affect 'the unemployed man of independent means or any inactive man whose intelligence was kept unoccupied'. As a result, such people would look for distractions from boredom in the form of strong alcoholic drinks. The doctor concluded: 'even some learned man, like countryside doctors, cumbered by a rude and ungrateful job or lawyers without clients or misunderstood dreamers sometimes yield to the deceiving appeal of spirits'.[10] Other stories of such unproductive and unfulfilled wealthy alcoholics in Belgium in the nineteenth century were found back in the registers of the exclusive Maison de Santé in Ghent and also here and there in contemporary literature. Some believed drinking to excess among the rich was, like the scourge among the working classes, also something new that belonged to fast modern lifestyles. It was seen as a problem of young people who were caught in the wear and tear of modern life. A witness on the Government Commission in 1886, for example, acknowledged that most certainly bourgeois drinking existed, but he called it the prerogative of the youth of a new 'modern' generation.[11]

The patient registers give us a unique insight into the drunkenness of the rich. Here the patients in addition to their mental confusion, suffered from shattered reputations and damaged status. The idea of being considered 'mad' and being locked up in an asylum added greatly to this. For example, a wine merchant in his forties kept on running into troubles with the authorities because of his excessive drunken and 'improper' conduct. He was brought to the Maison de Santé by his family who could no longer control his behaviour. Between 1883 and 1892 he was locked up in the asylum no less than five times. But he himself claimed that he was not ill, 'neither physically or mentally'. He argued that his incarceration as a lunatic was an act of vengeance by the doctor who had provided the medical certificate in order to ruin his *réputation devant le monde*,[12] and that it was not him but his family who were crazy. He started to write to the magistrate demanding his release, but the medical superintendent contradicted his requests in his own report, which he based on the evidence of the patient's parents and the mayor and the police officer from his town. '[He] is a man who cannot behave himself appropriately in polite society any longer. He drinks, spends all his money and drives himself into ruin'.[13] When the medical superintendent saw the wine merchant arriving for the fourth time, he became much more fatalistic and was now convinced he had made the right diagnosis of 'dipsomania': 'Here he is calm, like during his previous stays, but I am of the conviction that, when released, he would give himself over again to all kinds of eccentricities.'[14]

It was exactly these 'eccentricities' of drunkards that led them to be taken to the asylum, to be locked away from society. The problem was the excessive drinking and inappropriate behaviour *in public*. The boundaries of tolerance that had to be crossed before behaviour became unacceptable were much more restricted for the upper classes.[15] As previous chapters have shown, among the lower classes drinking could still be seen as 'normal': it formed part of their culture or even 'interested' behaviour, because it helped them to forget their misery.[16] For upper-class drunkards the situation was very different. It was felt they had much more to lose: their respectability and that of their families and therefore excessive drinking outside the boundaries of sociability for them was social madness, interpreted as physical insanity. In this light the effort to transform drinking upper-class men into diseased patients in the last quarter of the nineteenth century seemed appropriate and this can explain the larger number of 'alcoholics' kept for treatment in the upper-class asylum.[17]

Wives and Families

Although it was much more addressed by moralizers when it affected the lower classes, wives of drunkards of the upper classes could also become stuck in the vicious circle of drink and violence. Wives of wealthy drunkards did have a bit more freedom than their counterparts of the poorer classes. Historian Mieke Claes explained how an elaborate judicial procedure such as divorce, requiring the husband to pay maintenance for her household and her children was unattainable for working-class women, but it could potentially become an option available to wealthy wives of violent and drunken husbands.[18] In practice in the courts, habitual drunkenness and violence that accompanied it was not generally accepted as a reason for divorce by Belgian judges, although there had been the rare case where for wealthy women the 'true scandals' that drunkenness had provoked were interpreted as a 'gross insult', which could be a justification for divorce.[19] But divorce was a very drastic measure indeed and came with its own grave loss of reputation. Before going as far, there was another option open to middle and upper-class wives: the Lunacy Law provided women with certain powers to have their drunken husbands committed in an asylum when they had become a threat to domestic peace. Letting their squandering, drinking husbands be declared insane could offer wealthy women a chance to safeguard their fortune and avoid financial and social ruin. However, when drunkards had sobered up in the asylum, there was often no reason to keep them and they were sent home again. For example, a cotton merchant from Lokeren always became violent after overindulging in wine, so much so that his wife had to flee her home with their child. In July 1881, the town council issued an order for his internment as a lunatic and he was brought to the Maison de Santé le Strop by the police sergeant. But after ten days of observation the medical superintendent had to admit that the only symptoms he could notice with this man were 'signs of nervousness and a heightened sensitivity'. 'Not in his deeds, nor in his words can I find sufficient grounds to prolong his stay in the asylum and I feel that our resident has to be liberated'.[20]

Also the looming consequences of the loss of the all-important social respectability through drunkenness and the association with madness prevented many from having their husbands or sons admitted to the asylum and it always remained a last resort.[21] Many wives, sisters and mothers opted to take care of their alcoholic family members in the privacy of the home until this was no longer an option. This is shown in the Ghent case books in the example of a wealthy building contractor from Bruges who had started drinking after financial misfortune. He had squandered what was left of the family fortune and had become increasingly violent as a result of his addiction. His wife decided that she was no longer able to deal with his behaviour and consequently made the bold decision to abandon him. Unable to be left to his own devices, the drunkard was then taken care of by his sister. But in spite of the strictest surveillance, he still managed to succumb to 'his favourite passion'. Once under the influence he always menaced and threatened his family. Finally, the sister also decided she could not handle his excesses anymore and asked for his admission in the Maison de Santé.[22]

Some alcoholics, mostly those from wealthier backgrounds, presented themselves voluntarily at the asylum as it was the only place where they could undergo a detoxification treatment. A French businessman came to Ghent in August 1897 after he had tried in vain to kick the habit there already several times beforehand. This time he gave consent to his wife to have him legally committed. A special arrangement was made in order to weaken the inevitable link with lunacy: it was agreed with the family that he would stay in the Maison de Santé to do a 'hydropathic cure' and to rest in order to 'habituate himself to abstain from alcoholic beverages' but unlike other patients he would be allowed to go in and out on his own responsibility. The doctors stated clearly in his record: '[he] is not a *malade d'esprit* in the real sense of the word: he is unbalanced [*déséquilibré*] as a result of alcoholism'. Very soon, however, the agreed arrangement fell through. By the end of September, the businessman had given in to his cravings, which had led to '*libations copieuses*' in town. His wife now intervened immediately and took her husband back home again; not because he was the much needed breadwinner as was the case with many working-class families, but because of fears of lack of discretion and loss of respectability for the family.[23]

Most bourgeois drunkards denied their problems and were unwilling and unable to change their ways. Advertisements in Belgian local papers for medicines that promised to cure drunkards were aimed at wives, mothers and daughters. The British Coza powder was sold in Belgian pharmacies, advertised as being able to provoke repugnance to alcohol in any drunkard.

> Coza powder does its work so silently and surely that wife, sister or daughter can administer it to the intemperate without his knowledge, so that he is unaware of what effected his reformation.[24]

The *British Medical Journal*, in its quest to unmask quack remedies declared Coza powder to be made up of bicarbonate of soda with a bit of cumin and cinnamon powder and so its effects were clearly doubtful.[25] Temperance organizations, with doctors at their helm, called for a boycott of such products.[26] But that patent medicines such as this were popular indicates again the initiative and the often fraught measures that were taken up by women as part of their role in the cure and care of drunkenness. Those husbands who were brought to the asylum were exceptions; they were taken away as a last resort after their drunken behaviour had led to other, unacceptable behaviour. Most drunkards would stay at home and were being cared for by their families. And mostly upper-class drunkards would also not accept that their drinking habits were out of control and they would be outraged and insulted if one was to treat their habit as a problem or a disease.[27] Doctors were advised in their professional journals to be cautious when diagnosing alcoholism among their wealthy patients if they wanted to retain their clientèle:

> One might as well not call the things with their name and tackling the enemy indirectly, you can remark that such and such stomach trouble warrants pure mineral water or milk ... Thus you will safeguard the immediate health interest of your client, who will believe you and will obey you if you talk of his disease of the kidneys, the stomach etc. but do not admit, certainly not initially, that you identified him as a man consumed by alcohol.[28]

Habitual drunkenness was too widely associated with everything lower class: poverty, immorality violence and weakened willpower.

Corrupted Morals

Among the upper classes drunken behaviour was also regularly associated with broader moral corruption, often including sexual excess and violence. It is in this narrative that we find the roots of the relationship between alcoholic excess and sexual excess and the idea that 'alcoholism leads to libertinage and sponsors prostitution'[29] that would become so prominent in the discourse on drunkenness of the last decades of the nineteenth century.

The clearest early example is to be found back in Eugène Zetternam's *Mijnheer Luchtervelde. Waarheden uit onzen tijd* (*Mister Luchtervelde. Truths from our Time*), a novel about a drunken and debauched factory owner written in the revolutionary year 1848, still a moralizing tale but with class conflict at the heart of the story. In 1885 it certainly had become understood as such when it was chosen as the first Flemish work to be serialized in *De Vooruit*, the socialist newspaper in Ghent.[30]

The Mr Luchtervelde of the title is a wealthy industrialist who is bad to the core. He mistreats animals and shows pleasure in other people's suffering. He is also known to visit 'those detestable houses one cannot name'.[31] A sexual pervert, he pursues all the female workers in his factories, fathering a long list of illegitimate children. This theme of the drunken, sexually predatory bourgeois, or alternatively his idle and corrupted son, who sinisterly tries to seduce honourable working-class and farmer's daughters, resurfaced countless times in Belgian fiction.

Zetternam took it a step further than most of his contemporaries, as he presents Luchtervelde in a drunken fit raping his own wife.[32] Although there are many examples of drunken workers who became violent to their wives, marital sexual violence remained reserved to the upper-class debauched drunkard. This fits in with a preoccupation with sexually transmitted diseases among the higher classes that provided essential drama. The middle-class angel of the house was now being cast in the role of suffering wife par excellence, the ultimate victim of the drunkard. Historians have studied the link between excessive drinking and syphilis as something that goes far beyond just a preoccupation with disease. The obsession with syphilis and drunkenness in the later decades of the nineteenth century represented deep seated anxieties about gender and class.[33] Zetternam introduced this highly fraught subject of venereal disease as early as in 1848, although in extremely obscured terms. After the rape, Clara, the wife, starts to feel strange, 'as if lechery had stung me' and like 'her blood was rotten in her veins'. When she finally dares to call a doctor, she writes in the diary: 'I suffered the punishment for lascivity and had never lived in sin! I was infected with that secret plague sent to the world only to punish humankind for its animal-like brutishness [*hunne dierlijkheid*].'[34]

This vague description of what had happened to Clara shows how Zetternam expected his readers to know from the few morally loaded indications he provided, what 'the secret plague' was. Also the descriptions of Clara's treatment, with 'murderous means' were vague but indicative enough, assuming that readers would recognize the signs of the harsh mercury treatment, perhaps from examples in their own environment.

In the last decade of the nineteenth century those of the upper classes who through their decadence and immoral behaviour, their sexual and alcoholic excess throughout subsequent generations had lost vigour and power and had accumulated weak constitutions, were felt to be degenerate, the 'animal like brutishness', as described in 1848 became in the second half of the century introduced within an evolutionary context.

Corrupted Blood

In 1905, in *Het bolleken* [*The Little Ball*] Cyriel Buysse described how the boring, numbing life in the countryside, combined with a predestined heredity, led its upper-class inhabitants to drink. Inspired by the death of a country gentleman whom Buysse knew, he created Nonkelken.[35] Nonkelken is a wealthy man of leisure, one of 'the village dignitaries', who has passed a life of pleasure in his 'little castle'. His life consists of eating and drinking, hunting, horse riding, archery and visits to the pub. Every morning Nonkelken can be found in the local village pubs behind his little glass of gin. He has never married but enjoys a passionate sexual relationship with his maid, Flavie. When Nonkelken becomes ill, he feels in his throat a little ball and it is as if that could be removed, he would become better. When after Nonkelken's death in the beginning of the story, his cousin Vital asks the doctor what has actually been wrong with his uncle, the answer is, 'brutally accenting the last syllable of the word as if it had three o's: "l'alcool"'.[36] The little ball is, according to the village doctor, simply an infection of the oesophagus, caused by the vast amounts of gin Nonkelken has drunk.[37]

Buysse's irony hinted at the ignorance of Nonkelken who rejects superior medical cures and believes instead that alcohol was invigorating, while ignoring its destructive power over time:

> especially in the early morning he felt very bad and it only became better, but very much so, after having drunk a few glasses. That was the best and even the only means, much more efficient than all the powders and pills and mixtures the doctor made him take.[38]

However, Buysse also criticized the easy diagnosis of the village doctor. Many late nineteenth-century medical specialists understood the disturbing sensation of a 'lump in the troat' as a traditional symptom of hysteria, caused by emotional disorder or anxiety known as 'globus hystericus'. And so perhaps also Nonkel's 'bolleken' indicated more than simply the somatic outcome of his alcohol habit.

Buysse inferred that Nonkelken's life was empty and lonely and he also alluded to the problem of alcohol dependence and its possible psychological causes, overlooked by the village physician. Nonkelken himself considers drink as the solution for his problems rather than its cause, implying underlying veiled trouble for which alcohol seemed to offer a consolation. Buysse thus underlined the lack of insight into a patient's mental health by a pretentious but ultimately uninformed medical practitioner, who, like the general public, too readily ascribes Nonkelken's disease and cause of his death directly to alcoholic and sexual excess.

Also the entire village know and are convinced that Nonkelken has died from 'l'alcool et Flavie'. Indeed, Flavie was his maid with whom he had a passionate sexual relationship. After Nonkelken's death his heir and nephew Vital gives up his law studies in the city and moves to the countryside to take up residence in the 'little castle'. Vital makes up his mind never to indulge like his uncle had done:

> How was it possible, he thought [that] Nonkelken had gradually killed himself with a slow working poison ... Drink, with which came the tendency for all kinds of other excesses was the enemy, the great enemy, the vengeful enemy of the happiness of wealthy people. He should never forget this; he would be always on his guard.[39]

Of course, inevitably the opposite happens and after a failed marriage proposal, even a cultured and critical city dweller like Vital cannot avoid his hereditary predisposition within the numbing environment that was life in the small village and he too turns to the bottle.

Vital knows, nevertheless, that too much drink could be harmful for his health and his friend, the brewer's assistant Taghon, explains that:

> Gentlemen, who went on regular nights out and especially brewers and distillers, who were obliged to drink much, in the long run started to suffer from their kidneys. The doctors called this 'albumerie', or discharge of albuminous matter, or 'uremie', all those strange names they invented to scare patients and to keep them under treatment as long as possible, while the situation [*het zaakje*] was very normal in the end and could be checked by the patients themselves without any problems.[40]

Doctors were represented as characters keen on meddling and interfering, tricking people into believing that only they held expertise on health. Yet with doctors' powerlessness with regards to alcohol, people would rely on patent medicines that claimed to end their craving forever. Powders and potions were sold over the counter, which could be added 'secretly' to the drunkard's favourite tipple.[41]

Taghon teaches Vital of an intriguing practice of adding a liquid bought from the apothecary to a test tube filled with urine which will keep his health in check while allowing him to continue to drink: after letting the urine settle overnight one would notice 'a grey, yellowish substance, as fine sand' at the bottom of the tube. If there is only a little bit of it, Taghon explains, there is no problem and one can happily continue to drink, but if there is a lot, one had to drink less for a few days until the level of the substance had come down again: 'it was as if your doctor was always in the drawer of your night table'. All gentlemen in the village know about this 'health barometer' and use it, but they do not mention it to their doctor because they would not agree. But Taghon reassures Vital he should: 'just let them talk and quietly continue as you were doing, because everyone understood very well why the doctors were against it'.[42] Upper-class drinkers appropriated modern laboratory science for their self-diagnosis over which they claimed as much expertise as the specialists. And indeed, like elsewhere in Europe, Belgian doctors during the whole nineteenth century continued to campaign against such practices.[43] Vital's doctor also disapproves strongly: he declares it quackery and maintains that it should be denounced by the government.

Ultimately, in Buysse's novel, self-medication proves unsuccessful and, like his uncle, Vital also eventually dies from alcoholism. By showing the futility of the drunk's own attempt to control his abuse, Buysse equally criticized the ignorance of the patient and his easy belief in that which appears to be scientific and therefore seems to be offering an infallible solution. But he also questioned the specialist's responsibility faced with alcoholic disease. When the doctor is called to the little castle to help Vital in the midst of an attack of *delirium tremens*, he leaves with an excuse, abandoning his patient. The final deathbed scene in *Het bolleken* was certainly sensationalist as true to the naturalist formula the drunkard goes mad. Buysse's description of Vital's attacks of delirim tremens including visions of rats was most certainly inspired by Coupeau's drunken madness that had horrified readers of Zola's *Assommoir* almost thirty years earlier and that was in its turn directly based on Valentin Magnan's clinical reports of his patients in the Parisian hospitals.[44] And half a century after Hendrik Conscience had introduced the drunkard's decline into madness and delirium tremens, the terrible visions and convulsions at the end of Vital's life still offered a terrific, horrific, dramatic ending, leaving readers astounded when closing the book.[45] Vital had been a degenerate drunk, it was in his blood through the connection with his uncle. And his mind-numbing country environment that seemed to entangle him had done anything but redeem him.

A preoccupation with the health of future generations of upper classes and a warning against precisely this danger of passing the drinking vice onto one's descendents was also the key message in a rare representation of bourgeois drinking among the propaganda of the temperance movement. A postcard published by Le Bien Social in 1900 was titled *Double nouvel-an* (*Double New Year*) and shows in the first scene celebrations of New Year among a small bourgeois family in a very lavish interior. The father is smoking a thick cigar and the mother is filling a glass held up by their boy of around eight years of age with champagne. This first scene carries the caption: 'the first glass'. This first glass has triggered the taste for alcohol in the little boy and consequently the right-hand illustration shows 'the last glass'. We see the same boy as a man now so many New Years' later lying on the floor in a squalid attic room, dressed in rags with the empty glass and bottle next to him.[46] The seemingly innocent first glass was in fact the trigger that had led to the moral, physical and financial demise of the little boy later in his life. A bad heredity could be triggered all too easily in an environment of unconstrained hedonistic luxury and dangerous decadence.

In the French-speaking part of the country novelist Camille Lemonnier was equally fascinated by the concept of drink and degeneration. In *La fin des bourgeois* the Rassenfosse family, which now in its third generation of opulent living, has suffered from racial decline as a result of too much luxury and debauchery and is heading to its final dissolution.[47] Although the writer experimented with a Huymans-like symbolist style in this novel, Lemonnier's universe still remains naturalistic and accordingly the characters in the novel are necessarily defined by both their heredity and their environment. The family members all represent various types of what Lemonnier saw as the degenerated haute bourgeoisie. There are hysterical daughters and decadent dandyish sons, mentally retarded brothers and pathologically obese cousins. But none of these characters are represented as degenerate alcoholics per se. Alcohol and the exuberant use of it are simply taken for granted, serving to illustrate the decadence of the family. One heavy drinker in the family is Regnier, the over-sophisticated son of mine-owner Charles Rassenfosse. Regnier Rassenfosse also drinks out of boredom, in order to give some flavour to the monotony of his aimless life. In the literature of the mid-nineteenth century, drunkenness and other vices among the upper classes had been explained as avoidable immoral choices. But now in the 1890s and 1900s in *La fin des bourgeois* and *Het bolleken*, the strong hereditary aspect that was added to the story of the debauched bourgeois seems to have made willpower and moral choice redundant. Regnier himself acknowledges that the cause of his 'behaviour' is located in his physical degeneration and he puts this forward as an excuse for not making any efforts to better his ways. But Lemonnier was never morally neutral in his naturalism: he also described how Regnier feels very ill at ease about his privileged position in society when realizing how miserable the workers in his family's mining enterprise were. Regnier's act of rebellion, his reaction against this injustice, is to squander his father's money in gambling, prostitutes and drink.

In the Ghent Maison the Santé in the 1880s similar opinions and moral judgements about upper-class decadence and decline permeated case histories of upper-class drunkards like that of Baron Gustave van R. and his son Raymond. Here also the taint 'in the blood' had eradicated their willpower. For Gustave and Raymond who were members of a rich old and noble family, like for the fictional Rassenfosses, excessive drinking belonged to an opulent sphere of overindulgence. In March 1885 Baron Gustave was brought for the first time terribly drunk to le

Strop. The baron expressed confused and grandiose ideas that could very well be linked to the delirium caused by tertiary syphilis, but nothing in the case notes referred to this, as it was not until later in the century that Dr Alfred Fournier made the direct link between this type of behaviour and the dreaded venereal disease. In the asylum, where Baron Gustave was not drinking, he 'behaved well' according to his case notes, but 'he expresses ideas that are not according to his social position'.[48] This idea of expressing ideas according to one's social position became increasingly important for the Belgian bourgeoisie in order to maintain its identity as the hegemonic class. According to the treating physician, the baron also mistakenly 'believed that he could recover his reputation by parading a luxury lifestyle'. The legal responsibility of the drunken and well-connected baron, now declared insane, was taken up by his solicitor and financial trustee, Jules de Burlet. As member of the Catholic Party, de Burlet would become the country's prime minister in 1894, at the time of a political earthquake when the introduction of universal multiple suffrage introduced the first socialist deputies to parliament. Representing a sick and alcoholic member of the Belgian upper classes, de Burlet observed the flaws in what was known as the 'racial health' of traditional ruling families. Doctors and lawyers, the professional middle classes, through their diagnosis and classification of alcoholism and degeneration, by taking on legal responsibilities of the mad and debouched upper classes and by detaining those accused of public drunkenness and unruly behaviour created order. In doing so, both doctor and lawyer forged their own professional identities when deciding over who should and who should not play a part in the country's public life. Ultimately it was their moral judgement that ruled. And so Baron Van R. was not considered fit and his doctor answered to his lawyer: 'Considering his moral situation, I cannot declare that this dispsomaniac patient can be set in liberty'. It was not his health or public responsibilities that the doctor and the lawyer assessed; instead they called it his 'moral situation'.

Nevertheless, the intervention of this very important magistrate did secure a certain amount of freedom for the baron. The medical superintendent agreed to grant him occasional breaks – 'to see if his pathological desire for alcoholic drinks has ceased'.[49] And so Baron Gustave was allowed to leave the asylum now and then. One evening, however, he was brought back by a policeman. He was drunk again and had 'caused a scandal in town': in one of the bars he had visited while drunk, a ring was stolen from his finger. Consequently he was no longer allowed to leave the Maison de Santé and he stayed until his death, aged forty-one. The alcoholic baron was represented in the patient registers as unable to take up the responsibilities of his position in society. He certainly did not behave according to the rules of propriety laid out for him in line with his social standing: his drinking habits and his behaviour in public were unacceptable. Finally, as his ring went missing, he also lost control over his possessions, the last remnant of his social supremacy.

On the Streets

The theft of the baron's ring symbolized much larger contemporary events happening on the streets of the Belgian cities. The class tensions played out on the streets in those years had a direct impact on many and the material and psychological effect is hard to gauge. As the worker's demands for general suffrage magnified in the last year of the century, a wealthy inhabitant of Ghent entered the Maison de Santé in November 1894 in the midst of an attack of *delirium tremens*. He was completely out of his mind: he shouted about socialists destroying his house and raved about them shooting in the suburbs of Antwerp.[50] In fact, in Antwerp half a year earlier, the workers had indeed come out on the streets demanding the vote. Repression of that march had led to violence with deaths and wounded as a result.[51] It is not known how and if this person got involved in the street violence or what happened to his house. He probably lost his house, as after the events this rich man moved away from Antwerp to Ghent. Had this bourgeois taken to drink to forget the horrible events of that day? Or had it been a catalyst which made him express underlying terrors? This example illustrates significant moments of role reversal, indicating the immense psychological impact that the rise of the socialist movement made on the mind of the Belgian bourgeoisie and its symbolic relationship with drunkenness. Through his excessive drinking this proprietor had also abandoned the bourgeois positivist ideal of rationality and control on which his hegemonic identity was based. In his alcoholic delirium he behaved himself unreasonably, furious and out of control, like the workers on the streets behind the red flag were usually represented.

In the previous year of 1893, another year of social and political cataclysm in the struggle for general suffrage, one of Baron Gustave's two sons was also admitted to the Maison de Santé. His mother had requested admission for her son who had not only been heavily drinking, but also smoking since the age of sixteen. He had started a career in the military, but 'extravagant acts' had made those around him doubt the state of his mental health. He expressed incoherent ideas and he believed the police persecuted him and also that he was going to die. Is it possible that this paranoia was a symptom of syphilis caught in the barracks?[52] Raymond was only twenty-three-years old when he came to stay with the Brothers in Ghent. Possibly, like fictional Regnier Rassenfosse, young and gilded Raymond R. found it hard to disregard the shocking class differences around him and the ferment that was brewing on the Belgian streets around that time. Or perhaps his delusions had another source: as an officer in the army he could have been involved in the controlling of one or more of the many workers' strikes for general suffrage in 1893 and this had possibly left a deep impact.[53] According to the doctor in le Strop, the reasons for his madness were to be found elsewhere and he believed that Raymond was 'a young man who had abused everything [*de tout*]: women, alcoholic drinks, game, tobacco'. The doctor certainly remembered Raymond's father when he added: 'combined with his hereditary predispositions, this "overwork" [*surménage*] has led to the mental derangement he presents at the moment'. Raymond stayed for thirty-six years in the asylum until his death, just like his father.[54] His madness had been a given as an irreversible result of his tainted blood; considering the laws of heredity Raymond's 'life of eccentricities' did not come as a surprise.

For the liberal and enlightened bourgeoisie the examples of drunken and debouched members of the upper classes showed how a conservative and self-indulgent upper class could no longer sustain itself within the new values a changing society demanded. Their obstinacy, isolation and bad behaviour had possibly even fuelled social instability. Their excessive drinking debased them to the same immoral level as the working classes they so abhorred and was at odds with their claims to social and moral supremacy.

This same moral judgement was illustrated on canvas in what has been called the first realist painting in Belgian art history. It heralded a new time of 'modern' art but was in fact still a morality painting. *A l'aube* (*At Dawn*) (see Figure 4.1), although provocative, pleased visitors to the Brussels Salon in 1875 and made its creator, Charles Hermans promptly famous. The theme of drunkenness in a 'realistic' setting had been previously reserved for smaller scale genre-paintings with a moral message but became now for the first time presented on a large scale, a format that until then was reserved for grand historical themes.[55] The positive reception of the large and explicitly 'modern', impressionist work sanctioned and reinforced the system of belief of a progressive fin-de-siècle bourgeoisie the painting conveyed.

It shows a group of workers with 'resigned manners of martyrs',[56] who on their way to work stumble upon bourgeois drunken revellers leaving a restaurant. Towards the end of the century there were many such places in the Belgian cities: sumptuous cafés and restaurants who had perhaps modest entrances but had interiors like real palaces, with mirrors, paintings and gilded decoration, like the luxurious Café du Phare in Liège: a magnificent building, opened with much pomp in 1886 – the year of such social and political turmoil. The interior was lavishly decorated with wall paintings and there was an enormous billiard room, which had twenty tables.[57] Many of those places frequented by upper-class men had private rooms. On the billboard outside the door of the establishment Hermans's drunken party-goers exit we can read that this was also the case here: they do not only serve dinners but additionally have 'salons' and 'cabinets' on offer: smaller rooms, strictly private.

'Always Less and Less in the Home'

At the centre of attention of *A l'aube* are not the two men in their expensive but crumpled suits, with their top hats crooked on their hats, but rather the drunken women that accompany the men. It was immediately clear to all that these women were far from respectable.

The workers in the painting watch the scene with abhorrence and one of them, the father, looks at his young son with a meaningful frown. The miners come across as unexpectedly clean, healthy and well-dressed: the father is depicted as wise and knowing, his child bright and well-nourished and so seems is the blushing mother. In contrast, the drunken prostitutes come across as the opposite of clean and healthy: their skin is pale and their eyes lie deep in dark sockets. Their magnificent dresses cannot cover up their moral ugliness, written on their faces and displayed through their drunken behaviour. The disapproving look on the father's face is the central narrative vector in this representation, expressing the important moral message of the work: placing duty opposite pleasure, poverty versus luxury and virtue against vice.[58] Public drunkenness had become the ultimate signifier to delineate respectability for women and once more was it linked with sexual promiscuity and loose morals.

The way in which public drunkenness indicated the crossing of the borders of respectability for women is also superbly shown in Buysse's in *Het bolleken*. Cousin Vital used to meet his mistress Irma in a *café-concert* in the city. One day they meet a credulous inhabitant of his village who believes the charade: he is very impressed with the 'lady' who accompanies Vital. Buysse's mocking of the gullible neighbour indicates a shared understanding with the reader of what really was going on. And what was really going on was an unsurpassable difference in class between himself and his lover, which is also recognized by Vital himself. Irma is a Flemish social climber and in order to create a more sophisticated identity for herself, she speaks French. By having her speak the language abominably, Buysse immediately clarifies the class and gender rules of the *café-chantant*. Although Irma tries very hard, it was ultimately not only her abominable French that gave her real social standing away. 'She wanted to pretend to be a sophisticated lady', explained Buysse, 'he [Vital] knew she was different; because he had witnessed her more than once, half drunk with champagne, blaring as the street girl she actually was'.[59] So while dress could perhaps cause confusion about women's actual standing in society, a weary and unhealthy countenance, ghastly French but especially public drunkenness would eliminate all doubts.

Figure 4.1: Charles Hermans, *A l'aube (At Dawn)*, 1875 © Royal Museums of Fine Arts of Belgium, Brussels.

Yet upper-class women certainly did drink alcohol. They enjoyed sweet liqueurs and the Hasselt Jenevermuseum's collection of colourful advertisement posters for sweet liquors like Anisette and Elixir d'Anvers shows that such drinks were marketed towards wealthy and stylish female consumers. Women would take alcohol very often as a medicine, since it was considered to be helpful for all kinds of female ailments and doctors prescribed it frequently.[60] We also know that some upper-class ladies drank excessively and that this was considered extremely problematic. Very occasionally there is a reference to female excessive drinking in the temperance press. Anti-alcohol campaigner Dr Auguste Jansen dryly commented: 'Often one sees ladies and even children take a liking [*prendre goût*] to those sweet drinks and make immoderate use of it'.[61] The very limited information that is available for the female patients of the Ghent asylums indicates that in the 1850s there were more women with problems related to alcoholic abuse among those of the upper class in Maison de Sainté than among the larger population of the public asylum.[62] But female higher-class drinking was something that was very rarely mentioned. Even those avant-garde painters and writers keen to shock, who had depicted drunken women from the lower classes, never represented alcoholic bourgeoises. The lack of representations of inebriated upper-class women shows how severely inappropriate and unthinkable such behaviour was. Even more than for working women, for ladies drinking too much was socially completely unacceptable and because it was considered 'the ultimate humiliation', it would always remain private.[63] It was to be kept hidden from the world as it completely undermined the sacred social role set apart for the lady as 'angel of the house'.[64]

The Belgian reticence concerning female middle and upper-class drinking was certainly in stark contrast with the British public discourse at the same period. In Britain, the theme of female middle-class drunkenness dominated the discussions of the medical profession and the reformers in the late nineteenth century.[65] But also mainstream publications like the *Spectator* and the *Gentleman's Magazine* ran articles on the trouble of 'secret drinking' and 'overstimulation in women'.[66] Although this question needs much further research, one explanation for this discrepancy can be political: active middle-class women were a much more real threat to the social status quo in Britain and their succumbing to a 'male' vice such as drunkenness indicated their presence on the public stage. Already in the 1860s was women's suffrage seriously debated in Britain, and middle-class women activists were at the forefront of public life when campaigning against social injustice.[67] In Belgium, a first feminist-organized movement only came into existence in the last decades of the nineteenth century. A preoccupation with women leaving their allotted space and entering the public sphere and with it possibly taking up habits that were previously prerogatives for men, like drinking, was a concern voiced in Western Europe more generally towards the end of the nineteenth century. Such confusion about shifting conventional gender roles caused by women taking up employment and leaving the home had worried social observers also in France. Belgian temperance doctors quoted French specialist on madness Paul Garnier who wrote: 'Especially in the large cities the woman tends more and more to copy the man in her lifestyle, she now frequents bars and is always less and less in the home'.[68]

5 DRUNKENNESS IN THE COLONY

The story of alcohol in the Congo as part of a history of Belgium begun when the country's colonial venture took off in 1885. While at home class tensions soared, the ambitious businessman–king Leopold II was recognized by the other European powers as the owner of l'État indépendant de Congo, the Congo Free State. Less than a quarter of a century later, under pressure of accusations of exploitation, the king was made to let the Belgian state take over the running of his territory.[1] The story of the Congo as part of the story of Belgium, as a 'fixed feature of the mental furniture of the Belgians', is something historians of Belgium have only recently begun to consider.[2] The experience of imperialism and colonialism became part of what it meant to be Belgian. An initial exploration into how the remarkable and intricate stories of drunkenness in the Congo were understood in Belgium illustrates how they added another cultural category of 'race' to the multitude of representations of alcohol. This small chapter can thus offer a rough outline of the possibilities for research in the story of the Congo as part of Belgian narratives and an invitation for further research and additional analysis.

Alcohol and Colonialism

Since the Portuguese had arrived with European spirits and wines the sale of alcohol had always been a cornerstone of the European African enterprise and its economy had become dependent on it. In Leopold's economic venture the Congo became a new market for Belgian produce, like spirits. Consequently he forbade the native inhabitants from brewing their own 'indigenous beer' and Belgian gin was exported in vast amounts in its stead – alcohol often of very bad quality, which had proved difficult to sell at home.[3] This low-quality alcohol became known as 'trade gin' and it was used to pay the African workforce and as currency when doing all kinds of business in Africa.

Constant De Deken, who travelled to Congo in 1892 as a missionary, told in his travelogue how his steamer stopped several times on route along the river Congo to disembark nothing but alcohol. In fact, there was not much else besides it in its hold: 'thousands of hectolitres of poison to kill the blacks, or to brutalize them'.[4] On the way back home to Belgium, of course the ship was filled with rubber and palm oil. De Deken explained how bottles were used as *monnaie d'exchange* (commodity money) and that even the missionaries bartered for fresh food and fish with alcohol.[5] Official arrangements sanctioned Belgian colonials indeed to pay for local produce with alcohol and as part of Leopold's economics of exploitation part of the wages of the railway workers were paid out in alcohol.[6] Such common practices were always explained and often justified by referring to the law of offer and demand of the free market and this way of doing trade was presented as originating from a local African demand.

Free trade had been the condition upon which the Berlin Act had conceded Leopold his Congo Free State and as 'trade follows no flag' it was those who provided the cheapest gin and rum who made the largest profit. Arthur Conan Doyle, in his polemic against Leopold's running of the Free State summed up the situation concisely: 'If a chief desires gin for his ivory, it is clear that the nation which supplies that gin will get the trade and that which refuses, will lose it'.[7]

In 1907 American journalist Richard Harding Davis wrote about his encounter on his way to Africa with a trader working for an English firm who used to trade in slaves, but had now diversified to selling gin. He told him how the firm bought substandard alcohol from the Germans, who made their gin out of potatoes, then they put a colouring in it and a label on it that said 'Jamaica' or 'Demerara' and sold it at the wharf at the harbour of Antwerp with enormous profit.[8]

Gin had been at the heart of the colonial venture in a much more fundamental manner than just as a currency for trade or as wages in exchange for African labour. When at the onset of Leopold's colonial adventure Henry Morton Stanley had travelled across Congo to sign treaties with local chiefs on behalf of the king alcohol had been the cornerstone of his negotiation practices. 'Without it (rum) friendship or trade is impossible on the Lower Congo', he wrote.[9] Friendship meant convincing local chiefs to sign treatises which would in effect hand over their lands and Leopold's agents thus managed on their 'treaty making campaigns' in less than four years to sign 400 such agreements.[10] Rum, or disguised cheap gin, had been fundamental to this endeavour.

Gradually abroad, but also at home, reports about the seriousness of Leopold's forced labour practices and scandalous mistreatment of the local population started to cause resistance. At the same time, disapproval of the use of strong liquors as an intrinsic part of the colonial effort was expressed.[11] In the very early days of the colonial enterprise doctor and temperance campaigner Alphonse Moëller had already asked: 'Is it not painful to think that we are to send the pioneers of civilization, but that they carry in their luggage barrels of "eau de vie" and gin?'[12] His question was asked in terms of morality, laying bare the double standard underlying the practice of selling gin to the natives. In a similar vein, in Ghent cafés the contradiction of what was happening in the Congo provided abundant inspiration for sarcastic song lyrics. 'In his first lesson a savage does not learn how to honour God', sung Karel Waeri about the missionary effort of Belgian Catholic colonizers, 'but about the bottle of liquor'.[13] Similarly to what had happened in relation to the 'question of labour' at home, in the case of the Congo socialists and progressive liberal politicians shared in the protests.[14] They pressurized the government to urge the king to take measures to limit the import of alcoholic drinks into the colony or, as was mentioned by a socialist delegate in a parliamentary debate, to put a halt to 'poisoning [of] the negroes'.[15]

So when King Leopold next faced bankruptcy and needed to find more funds for his colonial enterprise, he saw the potential of raising import duties for alcoholic drinks in the Congo. This could help to relieve his financial troubles and would equally appease his critics. But it also meant he had to forego the free trade agreement with the other great powers. Between 1898 and 1890, Leopold organized an international anti-slavery convention in Brussels, which would use a humanitarian argument of combatting slavery to convince the other colonial powers to relinquish the principle of free trade in the part of the Congo the Belgian king already had claimed for himself. As for the alcohol question on the African continent, Leopold actually agreed to a treaty banning the import of alcoholic liquor in Africa. The British and the Americans had always been important participants around the colonial decision-making table and as countries where the protest against Leopold's regime had been first voiced and most loudly, Leopold now more than ever needed to curry their favour. It had been the American and British anti-alcohol campaigners who had most fervently asked for measures against the sale of alcohol by the colonial powers and so apparently swayed by their arguments, the Belgian king agreed to the prohibition. In practice, the ban would only strengthen Leopold's position in central Africa, as it would prevent other countries from negotiating new land arrangements with local rulers that were not yet under contract with the Belgian king and thus cripple their colonial expansion and trading enterprises there.[16]

And so officially, in 1898, Leopold decreed that sale of all alcohol to the local people was completely forbidden in the Free State and that production of alcohol in the country itself was no longer allowed. The alcohol that continued to be sold legally, to white colonial officials and traders for their own use, would carry very heavy duties that would go to the Belgian coffers. In the first decade of the twentieth century, import duties on alcohol amounted to almost 50 per cent of its value. Special permission had to be obtained before Europeans could carry any spirituous liquor inland. State officials were only permitted to buy three litres of spirits each month. But there was no limit on the amount of beer and every white man was given one litre of red wine each day as a ration.[17] Absinthe on the other hand was completely forbidden in Congo, even for consumption by Europeans. While in Belgium its consumption was not so widely spread, it was a very popular drink among white colonials and in Léopoldville it was easily smuggled in from Brazzaville, the French side of the river.[18]

The anti-slavery measures, together with the anti-alcohol legislation that Leopold introduced were endlessly used in propaganda supporting Leopold's civilizing mission in the Congo. The law came at a moment that criticism on his colonial enterprise was growing and it was hailed by those endorsing Leopold's regime as a radical step for which the king deserved credit. Supporters of Congo would raise the argument that these were measures that would help the black populations to espouse European values of sobriety and rationality and to improve themselves towards a better state of affairs. These arguments echoed the calls for reform by anti-alcohol campaigners aimed at the purported gin-crazed lower-class populations at home.[19]

Those who were critical of the situation in the Congo Free State, however, argued that the abolition of alcohol was only undertaken under the guise of philanthropy but that it was in fact indicated purely by self-interest. Arthur Conan Doyle wrote in his virulent pamphlet *Crime of the Congo* that the king was not in the least concerned about the moral or physical condition of the black workers. He explained that for the part of the Congo where there was free trade the abolition of alcohol would remove competition, whilst in the large parts of the country where free trading principles were abolished, with no more need to compete for trade, alcohol was no longer useful to Belgian companies and their shareholders. In fact, he concluded, it would 'simply detract from the quality and value of their slave population'.[20]

Drunken Natives

Drinking alcohol was very much part of African culture, as Justin Willis has shown in detail for nineteenth-century East Africa.[21] The local people brewed their own beer from sugarcane: massanga and palm wine called malafou. According to Emile Storms, a member of a scientific expedition in Katanga in 1898, the blacks drunk enourmous quantities of it, '20 or 30 liters a day until they dropped down in a drunken stupor'.[22] Additionally, Africans used European drinks that had been introduced with colonialism. The narrative of the drunken black native in Belgium goes back a long way and it is one that has proved extremely resilient. Research based on Belgian newspapers of the 1950s shows that a stereotype of the black native as a drunkard was widespread, while the drinking habits of the colonial white population were being ignored or excused.[23] Also in nineteenth-century sources many stories featuring drunken natives can be found.

One of the most enduring manifestations of this narrative can be read in the diary of Stanley, in his description of a meeting with the chiefs of the Mgangila plateau in 1886:

> I had a visit yesterday from several chiefs of Mgangila plateau, who were tricked out in the cast-off finery of Europe. Most of the lackey coats had their large buttons stamped with unicorns. Too much gin-drinking was indulged in by the natives. I attempted to frighten them with hideous pictures of the effects of indulgence in gin; but one blear-eyed man, whose eyes were even then red with alcoholic fire, declared that he was never so happy as when glass after glass was poured down his open mouth. He acted the intemperate man remarkably well, proving that he understands by experience what a figure he exhibits when inebriated.[24]

The British explorer represented the African delegation as looking pathetic in their cast-off European uniforms. Like Herman's prostitutes, they were dressed up, or 'tricked out' says Stanley, thinking to fool us into believing that they stood for something they would never truly emanate: respectability.[25] But by mentioning the heraldic symbol on the buttons of the coats originally belonging to servants, Stanley reaffirmed their essential commitment and subjugation to Europe's ruling classes. Their drunkenness was taken for granted, as they were in fact not drunk when they met Stanley, but he sees it in their eyes and their familiarity with the experience of drunkenness was confirmed by its provoked 're-enactment'. By presenting the Africans as essentially drunk, Stanley emphasizes their savagery and their irrationality and this consequently corroborated what he and most other Europeans were already convinced of, that Africans were fundamentally incompetent to negotiate as equals with rational and sober Europeans.

The chief's red eyes radiating with fire belied a brutality and barbarity deep within him, woken up by too much drink. Like the revolutionary workers at home, chiefs who came forward with a point of view that they wanted to be heard were represented as untrustworthy and insignificant through their inert drunkenness; they were 'exhibiting a figure', not to be taken seriously. The African chiefs had decided clearly and defiantly that they preferred the irrational option of drunkenness above taking on board Stanley's elaborately illustrated advice towards temperance. As part of the white man's burden to civilize Africa, Stanley saw it as his duty to remind Africans to stop drinking. The chief's reluctance to accept the consequences of this behaviour and instead his insistence to stubbornly hang on to this drunken way of life, indicated to Stanley and his readers that the chief's petition and his version of the story could never be acceptable, even before he had even started to set out his position.

In his description of his meeting with the alcoholic chiefs, Stanley presented himself as temperance campaigner, set out like so many missionaries to teach the natives sobriety and civilization. He himself, however, like most others working with Africans, paid his own local staff out in alcohol and handed out what he called 'grog rations' every morning.[26] Also he defended his practice as inevitable as the demand came from the local people themselves. He was simply 'compelled' to hand out the alcohol rations in order for the workers to even start doing their jobs and it was the natives themselves, Stanley explained to his readers, who insisted their work was to be paid for in drink 'in lieu of a portion of their wages'.[27] Similar concerns were heard at home at this time, when liberals defended the right to produce and sell alcohol without the state intervening with attempts to combat abusive use of it. A similar argument, that drinking habits were simply too deeply entrenched in the people's habits to regulate them from above, was brought up in the African context.[28] Both natives in the colonies and the lower classes at home were represented as living traditional lifestyles in which alcohol use and abuse were very much part.

What is furthermore remarkable is that for Stanley the drunkenness that resulted from handing out alcohol so freely among his crew was never an undesirable consequence and he defended it as follows: 'I have not seen any ill-effects from this as yet; on the contrary, it has increased their sociality, and made people otherwise silent open their minds frankly'.

When drunkenness facilitated the relation between colonizers and natives to the advantage of the Europeans it was not considered inconvenient. Also, drinking as part of social rituals smoothed out cultural difference and communication difficulties, when all parties became drunk and trust between colonized and colonizer seemed finally possible. Leo Frobenius, a German collector and ethnographer, was taken along by Belgian agents on a research trip to several local villages and a lot of drink and ensuing drunkenness accompanied their visits. While talking to the natives and recording their habits Frobenius was also interested in their objects and artwork for purchase and also here, a steady flow of palm wine smoothed negotiations.[29] As he made out, the drunkenness of his hosts allowed him to take special and sacred objects he would normally not be trusted with and so also here drunkenness is presented as a helpful means to obtain what he desired. However, when excessive drinking endangered natives' ability to do work for the Europeans, as it often did in their eyes, or if it allowed them to speak their 'otherwise silent minds' too frankly, as perhaps the chiefs had done when joining forces together for the negotiations on the Mgangila plateau, then their drunkenness was described in negative terms.

African drunkenness meant many things. Initially, early on in the colonial adventure, colonizers understood native drunkenness as part of the bad habits of the native, which needed to be curbed, educated and reigned in – pacified and colonized. The natives' excessive drinking habits were the result of an ignorant acceptance of a potentially dangerous product offered to badly informed, child-like populations that should instead be taught to make an informed decision as to what was right and wrong. But as the century came to its final decade, most agreed that the urge to drink was lodged deeply within the individual native's biological makeup. It was understood that the indigenous populations, being less evolved and in possession of 'unchained passions' were by their biological constitution more susceptible to alcoholic drinks. While for Stanley in the 1880s drinking was still related to habits and customs, English traveller Marcus Dorman who was a supporter of the Leopold regime, explained it concisely twenty years later: 'The native is a curious mixture of simplicity and cunning. He is very fond of strong alcohol, but does not care much for wine'.[30]

These characteristics attributed to Africans were again very similar to those that middle-class observers and travellers to Belgium would mention when describing the character of the lower classes. Also for Belgian workers it was said that they preferred gin over wine, equally interpreted as an indication of less delicate and sophisticated tastes and preferences rather than a result of unequal purchasing power. And while at home in Belgium the farmers and workers were depicted as drunk by design, with an urge to drink that was part of their internal make-up, Africans were thought to be predestined to drunkenness in a similar way, as part of their character and their position on the evolutionary ladder. Dorman continued with a story of a black servant who tried to steal whiskey:

> The mess boy here apparently stole some whisky and instead of filling the bottle up with water added red wine to the requisite amount. Of course the colour led to instant detection and of course he knew nothing about it, but he lurched about violently as he waited at dinner and it was obvious the new European drink was acting rather forcibly. It is very troublesome to have to lock up every bottle when travelling, yet it is absolutely necessary. There is, however, I hear, a patent lock, which can be fixed over the cork and is easily fastened to the bottle. This is worth remembering.[31]

The moral of this story is that European superior intelligence and technology could keep elemental African passions and urges in check. By calling the situation 'troublesome', Dorman's language recalls the idea of the 'white man's burden'. Protecting Africans against themselves from their own incontrollable drives, in this case an urge for intoxicating liquor, became part of the colonizer's rhetoric. And surely in this case, Dorman simply did not want to share his expensive whiskey with his black servant. So the lock became a practical, rational solution for a problem of African character that ultimately at its heart could never be cured completely.

The understanding that the African was racially inferior and by his moral and biological lack of development was unable to resist alcohol when offered, made the crime of offering alcohol to Africans worse and heightened the white man's responsibility not to feed the natural urge of the natives. In this narrative the Congolese were presented as 'noble savages' who lived simple lives in which their environment provided everything they needed. Africans were in this version depicted as naturally indolent before the Europeans had arrived who had then made them dependent on alcohol, which was used to force natives to do work for Europeans. As a biologically inferior species, once introduced to drink they would necessarily give themselves over to it and what was more, they would continue to do so towards the extermination of their race. As a race destined to die out in the struggle for existence, alcohol only accelerated a natural process, many thought. Temperance doctor Emile Caudelier, a very prominent voice in this debate, wrote not without a serving of sarcasm in his brochure *Le Gin et le Congo* in 1895:

> Of all the means the civilized man of the Arian race has imagined to tame, enslave and exterminate the primitive races if needed, there is no means more direct, more infallible than to introduce among them the taste for alcohol.

The African's apparent savagery illustrated for the Europeans the idea of evolutionary regression in front of their eyes and it worried them profoundly. Ethnologist Joseph Maes was open and honest when he wrote:

> the obscene dancing scenes in the middle of the night in the villages of the primitives in our colonies might very well be interesting for studies, science and ethnography, but they fill me with a profound feeling of horror.[32]

This 'profound feeling of horror' was caused not because this type of behaviour was so unfamiliar and different from his own, but rather because it was in many ways very similar. Joseph Conrad described this same sense of unease felt by the Europeans when looking at natives' performing a ritual:

> They howled and leaped and spun and made horrid faces, but what thrilled you was just the thought of their humanity – like yours – the thought of your remote kinship with this wild and passionate uproar. Ugly. Yes, it was ugly enough, but if you were man enough you would admit to yourself that there was in you just the faintest trace of a response to the terrible frankness of that noise, a dim suspicion of there being a meaning in it which you – you so remote from the night of first ages – could comprehend.[33]

Their 'obscene dancing scenes' and 'passionate uproar', often performed in a state of inebriety, were similar to the Europeans' own behaviour when drunk, a reminder of a constant lurking of savagery under the coat of civilization, accessed when under the influence. Getting drunk was turning native. Alcohol could bring out the African in all of us, the primitive essence of what came before civilization and it would let us slide down on the evolutionary ladder.

Colonial Drinking

The scenario in which white settlers capitulated to drink was much more disconcerting than the story of the 'natural' drunkenness of the Congolese. The rational white man on his mission to civilize was meant to stay sober. But many did not, and the many warnings we read against excessive drinking in the tropics indicate that there was a real problem with excessive drinking among the white population. 'Alcoholic drink is the greatest enemy of the white in Congo', warned for example Pieter De Wit after having travelled to the colony in 1899.[34]

And drunkenness among the white population in Congo was not uncommon at all. Maarten Coutenier showed how Charles Lemaire and the members on his scientific expedition finished in no time the 120 litre of Bordeaux wine, champagne, absinthe and plum gin they had taken along. When asking for more in a letter home Lemaire explained his need for more drink by calling it a 'comfortable solace'.[35]

Alcohol softened the harsh living conditions of the explorers and settlers. The Congo was a place of rough business dealings and little camaraderie. Disillusioned colonial Henri Van Booven wrote in his autobiographical novel *Tropenwee* about the experience of his alter ego Jules: 'Friendship was here something unheard of and no one seemed to understand anything about politeness, in those parts of the world he never knew anything but an environment of cold, badly equipped men full of grimy animal-like sensuality, who know only to talk about drink and women. They were cruel'.[36]

Cyriel Buysse's novel *De zwarte kost* (*The Black Fare*) published in 1898, told a similar story. Fortuné Massijn, a bored petit-bourgeois inhabitant of a dull Flemish village, a notary-clerk, travels to the colony in search of adventure but soon finds out that the situation on the ground is very different from what he had expected it to be. Massijn writes home to his former employer, the notary: 'you have no idea how much the Europeans here drink'.[37] He further discovers that the settlers not only drink excessively but also misbehave badly, giving themselves over to orgies with local women. Although he fiercely disapproves of such practices, the influence of the colonial environment also drives Massijn to succumb to them. He takes a local girlfriend and soon after dies from 'fièvre hématurique': malaria.

The threat of drink and savagery of the Dark Continent was also conveyed in an episode told in the diary of physician Jules Amerlinck. Amerlinck was employed as doctor in what became known as the Bia-Francqui-Cornet expedition to Katanga to find precious metals. One night whilst staying in Kinshasa he heard cries for help and when he went out to explore he found an agent, Auberg, lying on the road, covered in soil and vomit. Auberg did not answer any of Amerlinck's questions, so he decided to order the servants to have him helped back to his bed. Later he was told by the other agents at the station that Auberg had drunk large quantities of of absinthe and a whole bottle of cognac, which he had stolen from the warehouse. The doctor gave him some ammonia to drink. Twenty drops of *ammoniaque* in a glass of water was indeed the treatment for *empoissement par l'alcool* as suggested in Dr Dryepondt's *Manuel du voyageur et du résident au Congo* (1910), the hand-book each prospective Congo traveller was suggested to take.[38] This made him vomit even more and then the doctor let him sleep to *cuver son vin*, to sober up. The next morning Auberg was dead. Amerlinck ended his diary entrance with a very meaningful remark. 'It was an absinthe poisoning' he wrote: 'in Europe they will say: another victim of the Congo'.[39]

Like Amerlinck, most held the tropical alien environment liable for the pollution of the colonials' vigorous moral and physical European health. Both Massijn and Auberg, like so many other whites on the continent, had succumbed to Africa. This story tapped into the widespread European paranoia that cohabitation with the natives combined with drinking, the harsh climate and terrible diseases would lead to moral and physical degeneration. Alcohol was at the same time both the catalyst and the outcome of this disintegration. At fault for why white rational colonizers would take to the bottle in the first place was Africa: the Dark Continent itself. In the words of Nigerian writer Chinua Achebe, Africa was seen as 'a place where man's vaunted intelligence and refinement are finally mocked by triumphant bestiality'.[40] Metaphorically, this was exactly the place excessive alcohol use was believed to lead people to. Hence the white man's excessive drinking was the result of this Africa-effect. His behaviour became Africanized when clear boundaries between the sober, rational European and the irrational, drunk native were blurred through drink.

The reasons that explained why rational Europeans would reach for the bottle could be always traced back to the African environment. The horrors of the Congo, we read, were such that colonials took to the bottle to forget and to be able to endure the African harshness. Apart from harsh living conditions and rough dealings amongst colonials themselves, there was a longer list of other African horrors that were believed to lead to alcohol excess. Firstly there was the stress on the boat. Without even having yet set foot on African soil already the long trip towards the continent – a voyage of three weeks on board of a crowded steamship with an on-board bar – were circumstances that could according to some lead those more susceptible individuals to become inveterate drunkards. Massijn wrote from on board to his friends in the village about taking cocktails in the bar, two concepts his friends and family at home had never heard of.[41]

Once arrived in Africa there was a whole gamut of tropical diseases waiting to assault the unprepared traveller. It was generally accepted that dysentery, sleeping sickness, malaria and so forth could all be prevented with wine. A physician had advised prospective Congo traveller missionary Constant De Deken to keep warm with a long flannel undershirt and to drink wine to stave off microbes. 'Two glasses are worth more than one' had been his motto.[42] Due to its *propriétés toniques et digestive,* wine was, according to Belgian physicians who advised prospective travellers, always healthy for the white residents in Congo when drunk with meals. To illustrate this position on wine, pioneer in tropical medicine Dr Dryepondt compared his view and that of the Belgian colonizers with that of the protestant missionaries in the Congo – English and Americans – who, he said, were generally 'leatowtlers [*sic*]'. He felt he needed to explain this very alien concept to his readers: 'they are opponents of alcohol in whatever form and they never drink wine'.[43] But, he argued, although they generally lived in more comfort than the agents of the Belgian state and its companies and while their work was not as tough, the overall mortality amongst this group of whites in the Congo was not any less. In fact, Belgians in the Congo were given one litre of red wine each day as a ration to stay healthy. Additionally, the state also allowed each white man two bottles of champagne and port wine every three months as 'medical comfort' in case of sickness.[44] So African disease and drunkenness were in more than one way connected: drink could prevent disease as well as console and soothe those who had still succumbed to illness.

Another reason put forward to explain the large proportion of colonial officials who fell prey to drunkenness was the blandness of colonial life, a boredom attributed to 'African lethargy'. Once established in position as clerk of a trading company or as a government official, the daily reality of the Belgians in the colonial stations was one of tedium; an environment that would foment heavy drinking. The heat made work hard and the indolence that was according to many typical behaviour of the black natives could rub off, they feared, on the Europeans in Africa as well. Jules Amerlinck explained the life of emptiness and idleness he witnessed among white administrators and explorers shared Amerlinck's dread for being stationed in a colonial outpost. Like Emil Torday, who spent four years in Katanga province as a colonial official before becoming a traveller, and wrote about the community of Belgian officials in Léopoldville:

> There was much drinking going on at that time and although a bottle of beer cost three francs, enormous quantities were consumed. Some of us founded a ... newspaper called 'le Petit Leopoldvillain', the subscription was a case (48bottles) of beer per annum; this was drunk by the editorial staff. I really think we were a miserable lot and even our gaiety had a bitter taste.[45]

In contrast to this behaviour, the German colonial success was ascribed to their unusual work ethic: 'they do not go ... to drink absinthe or whiskey, or to play dominoes or cricket. They work twice as long as do the other white men'.[46]

Additionally, the loneliness of the whites far from home was offered as a reason for their heavy drinking. This problem was caused, according to some, because of the lack of white wives. Indeed, it seemed a simple solution to a grave problem: inviting wholesome Belgian wives who would exert a strong moral power over their husbands to stay in line. They would keep a clean nice home so there would no longer be the need to find sociability elsewhere. This story surely sounded familiar to those who had read propaganda of anti-alcohol campaigners at home. If they would have had a Belgian wife with them in the colonies, Belgians in the Congo would 'instead of pursuing those questionable pleasures of the young men, mostly not suitable for the tropics, stay in the circle of his family, which can only be beneficial for his health and his wallet'.[47] Those 'questionable pleasures of young men' (*twijfelachtige genoegens van den jonkman*) were of course not only drink, but also, and most worryingly, sex – sex with local women. The inescapable tandem sex and drink led here in Africa to something even more dangerous and threatening: the dreaded spectre of miscegenation. Going native in the Congo meant to drink like blacks and to have intercourse with black women. This would inevitably bring damnation for those who believed in God and degeneration of the race for those who believed in Science.

One last explanation given for the excessive drinking of whites in Congo was the constant threat and fear of attacks by a savage and violent indigenous population. Their behaviour was seen as unpredictable and difficult to keep under control. Local officers would resort to drink to keep their nerves under control. Richard Harding Davies ironically describes as such the 'illuminated picture of discipline' displayed by an inebriated Belgian 'glazed-eye' official, the 'grossly fat, colourless, coatless, purple faced and perspiring' captain of the port at Leopoldville when directing his sentries to violently disperse a crowd of local women. The next morning, Davies tells us cynically, this man was 'exceedingly unwell, trying to calm his nerves with absinthe which is not particularly good for nerves'.[48]

Absinthe became particularly problematic in those last decades of the nineteenth century and first of the twentieth century. More than anything, the unsettling reality the Europeans experienced in the jungles of the 'heart of darkness', a feverish encounter with 'a black and incomprehensible frenzy'[49] mimicked the experiences of hallucinatory drunkenness provoked by the intoxicating effects of absinthe on the mind. More than other liquors this particular drink provoked feelings and carried meanings similar to those experienced and attributed to the colonial experience. Both the 'savage' indigenous drunkard to be dealt with in the colonies and the absinthe drinker, who was also considered a potential problem at home, signified dissonance: profound, clear and potentially dangerous 'otherness'. The encounter both with the absinthe drinker and with the native drunkard invoked meanings of degeneration and possible racial decline. Both were contrary to what 'civilization' stood for and threatened the known, ordered customs of society. Both bohemian fin-de-siècle artists at home, typical absinthe drinkers and drunken Congolese in Africa were situated outside known and trusted rationality and order.

The official complete abolition of absinthe in the colony in 1898 can be understood as addressing a real problem. Absinthe was the cause of much devastating drunkenness among white colonials and it was most certainly much more widely drunk in the colony than in the motherland. Moreover, it also seemed a calculated move motivated by commerce: as a French drink its sale did not benefit the Belgian economy.[50] And the outlawing of absinthe was important ideologically, driven by a need to protect the idea of civilization on which the project of colonization was built.

In the Belgian colony, drunkenness became both an ideological and political tool used both to defend and attack colonial practices. Drunkenness was compellingly present both among native populations and white settlers. However, meanings of drunkenness also here changed according to who did the drinking and to what type of behaviour the resulting drunkenness led to. The language in which both the natives' and Belgian colonists' abuse of alcohol was discussed showed many parallels with the language of class used at home to describe the decadent artists', the workers' and the farmers' drinking. Constructed as belonging to the Other, it always established difference, in the colony as it did at home.

PART II: THE POLITICS OF DRUNKENNESS

In the nineteenth century drunkenness became understood as a social problem and the drunkard a character that needed to be controlled. How this should be done was the subject of discussion among different political ideologies that shaped Belgium in the second half of the nineteenth century. Drinking and getting drunk carried ideological meanings about responsibility and self-control which the different political factions, the conservative Catholics, the liberals and later the socialists and feminists used for their political agendas. Their different interpretation of the social problem became a rhetorical tool in ideological battles. And the multitudinous ways drunkenness was constructed as a social problem in need of checking shed light on anxieties and concerns of those proposing its solution in the fast-changing society that was Belgium in the second half of the nineteenth century. Variegated narratives of drunkenness point out political tensions between the social classes, between conservative and progressive forces and between city and countryside.

6 LAISSEZ FAIRE, LAISSEZ BUVER: 1830–86

Before the mid-1880s Belgian governments were extremely reluctant to address the subject of drunkenness and unwilling to regulate both consumption and production of alcohol, especially when compared with neighbouring countries such as Britain and the Netherlands.[1]

Drunkenness, Poverty and Madness

Before the second half of the century, political and social theorists only addressed drunkenness indirectly when forced to reflect on possible reasons and solutions for the problem of poverty after the so-called 'crisis of Flanders'. In 1848 severe potato famines had led thousands of Flemish farmers to ruin and many travelled to the industrial centres to find alternative employment. But in spite of the crisis, when the 'spring of the people' set Europe on fire, docile Belgian farmers and workers and modest petit-bourgeois did not take to the barricades and the unsettling question of socialism was not yet raised. However, the combination of manifest poverty at home and revolution abroad meant that for the first time lower-class drunkenness came to be considered a social problem. Catholic social reformer Edouard Ducpétiaux contemplated the problem of poverty in 1850. His answer to the crisis combined notions of Malthusianism and Christianity.[2] The farmers and workers would, he maintained, be able to struggle their way out of destitution through education and the promotion of moral and religious feelings.[3] Sobriety was one important aspect of this exercise in self-control. Following up on his initial work on poverty, Ducpétiaux then published in 1855 the results of a survey of wages and consumption: *Budgets économiques des classes ouvrières en Belgique* (*Economic Budgets of the Working Classes in Belgium*) in which he distinguished two different sorts of workers. Some were sober, hard-working and honest, but the majority, he alleged, lived immoral and irregular lives in self-afflicted poverty. As a rule these workers would spend their wages on drink and debauchery. Increasing wages therefore could not be a solution. As a matter of fact, the existence and survival of sober workers proved that wages were sufficient.[4] Many mid-century middle- class people would have shared Duscéptiaux's opinion that drunkenness was 'one of the dominant vices of the worker, transmitted unremittingly from fathers to children', that could and should be remedied with moral solutions.[5] His views very much resounded in further culture and this narrative of the good sober versus the unruly drunken worker would become central to the understanding of drunkenness in the second half of the nineteenth century.

Ducpétiaux's views on poverty and related crime led directly to reforms in poor relief and of the penal system in Belgium. In 1866, he promoted a law that was consequently passed in parliament 'on the repression of vagrancy and beggary'. Having studied the ways in which other countries dealt with their undesirables, his new law would enable the state for the first time to arrest people in the street often under the influence of drink when they could not show evidence of any wealth or status. Vagrants that were frequently also problem-drinkers were then to be sent to special mendacity depots or 'agricultural colonies' where they were made to work.[6]

Edouard Ducpétiaux also contributed significantly to the reorganization of mental asylums in Belgium. Following his work on the reorganization of care of the insane and in collaboration with *aliéniste* Joseph Guislain, the first lunacy law was passed in Belgium in 1850. This law aimed to protect citizens against accidents caused by insane persons.[7] A ministerial circular – an administrative directive – by the minister of justice Jules Bara of 1867, explained that 'because people suffering an attack of *delirium tremens* can be a danger for society', disorderly drunkards threatening to endanger other members of society could be taken into confinement in a mental asylum under the same lunacy act.[8] Research into the admission registers of the Ghent public mental asylum shows that drunkenness was always a prominent concern and among those who were arrested and sent to the asylum, up to a third had problems related to drink.

However, the condition for committal, a state of *delirium tremens*, was an ambiguous affliction and one that was difficult to identify. Minister Bara was well aware of this. He cautioned that outlining the terms of incarceration was complicated and suggested that it would depend on the circumstances and the characteristics of the particular case. He described how some sufferers, after the attack had subsided, returned completely to their normal and calm self and how they recovered completely, so that they could no longer be kept in the mental asylum. But, he insisted, there was a second category of drinkers, those whereby after the *folie furieuse* had subsided 'the disease entered a next phase'. They would feel an overwhelming need for drinking, which 'can be considered as a real mania'. Minster Bara warned that it would be fatal for public safety, but also for the well-being of the people themselves to let drinkers of this nature go free and thus allow them to give themselves over to new bouts of drinking.[9] It was up to the medical authorities to decide which type of drinker they were dealing with.

Report of Frère-Orban 1869

Drunkenness as a problem in its own right was placed on the Belgian political agenda for the first time two years later, when liberal minister of finance Walthère Frère-Orban presented a report on the 'abuse of intoxicating drinks' before the Chamber of Representatives in 1869, which called for some form of state interference in the unlimited production and sale of alcohol in the country. Indeed, the gospel of free trade allowed for mostly unrestricted production and sale of alcoholic drinks in Belgium. Temperance societies offered up endless worrying evidence that consumption of gin was on the rise over the course of the nineteenth century.[10] At the very end of the century, after the introduction of a licence to sell and a higher tax on strong liquors in 1899 its sales dropped, after which beer would become the drink most heavily consumed.[11] Also here Belgium seemed to be in a league of its own: consumption of beer was two times higher than in Germany and drank six times more of it than the French.[12]

Frère-Orban's well-documented report revealed a notion of the over-consumption of drink as a male and working-class vice and more importantly, of its fabrication and sale as a powerful economic force that essentially needed to be maintained within a free market place. The Minister of Justice's report borrowed much of its ideas from the work of Edouard Ducpétiaux. Because there had been little attention on drinking habits in Belgium, the evidence Frère-Orban used to underpin his report came mostly from other places where there had been more concern with drink, notably from England, the United States of America and the Netherlands: countries where temperance societies were long established and that could present a long record of anti-alcohol legislation. For the minister of finance, like for most nineteenth-century policy makers, statistical evidence was most convincing, but of course accurate information on the amount of drink that was consumed in Belgium proved difficult if not impossible to find.

Frère-Orban affirmed that 'of all vices, drunkenness [*ivrognerie*] leads most directly to moral and physical degradation', but he added immediately that it was also a very difficult problem to solve. Being in favour of a minimal state, the minister believed that governmental action was certainly not necessarily the right solution for this particular problem. The situation in England illustrated this very well: although this was a nation with more legislation designed to restrict drunkenness, the country suffered more than any other from the effects of immoderate use of strong liquors, the minister told the members of parliament.[13] There was indeed much statistical evidence produced in Britain to underline the problems of excessive drinking, while there was none in Belgium, which perhaps rather indicated how an enhanced interest in Britain shed a brighter light on a problem that was simply not acknowledged in Belgium.[14]

As the brewing industry had become a vital part of the Belgians' economy, the liberal mind of Frère-Orban considered the licensing of drinking places as an infringement on the principle of free trade, and total prohibition, as some proposed, would mean a complete economic disaster and had to be prevented by any means. Frère-Orban's argument against government intervention in matters concerning drink remained forever vague and it left much space for interpretation. He held that before considering any sort of action, policymakers should 'consider very carefully the character, the habits and the institutions of the nation'. 'It was important to be extra mindful in trying to destroy drink abuse', so said the minister of economy, because 'it finds its sources in the traditional habits of the people'.[15]

In Belgium, without licensing laws, anyone could open a bar, one just needed to pay a business licence, just like any other shopkeeper. The only expenses required were the cost of a barrel of beer and a few bottles of spirits. Many workers indeed did so to supplement their income. There were different categories into which a business could fall and the criteria to decide which tariff one had to pay were based on the value and profits of the establishment.[16] When historians of drunkenness in France claimed that France had a much higher concentration of bars than any other industrial nation with one bar per eighty-two inhabitants in 1914, they overlooked Belgium with a bar per forty habitants in 1887 and one per thirty-two inhabitants by the turn of the century.[17] By way of comparison, powerful temperance movements and licensing regulations meant that British industrial cities such as Manchester or Newcastle counted only one public house per 175 inhabitants in the late nineteenth century.[18]

The many prominent drink sellers and high-ranking individuals with interests in the brewing industry were now simply too influential.[19] Too many leading persons in towns and villages owned bars or were involved in the drinks trade, and these people obstructed any legislation on the regulation of the sale of drink.[20] By the end of the century, the situation had slightly changed and in 1889 a new law stipulated that those who wanted to sell alcohol needed a licence to do so. However, so much resistance and protest was voiced that it was abolished twenty years later.[21]

As late as in 1907, banker and mine owner Paul de Smet de Naeyer, ex-prime minister and then finance minister for the Catholic Party, was still speaking out against regulating public houses:

> One cannot dream of legally restricting the number of public houses. Any legislation for such a purpose would be contrary to the spirit of professional and commercial liberty. It would be arbitrary for it could not be based upon any fair or rational foundation.[22]

Most bars were very small and not profitable but those visited by wealthier clientele, where more expensive beverages than just gin and beer were sold, could do exceedingly good business and would therefore fall into a higher tax category. Shopkeepers paying higher business rates had become eligible to vote in 1849. Richer public house owners would thus have become voters and many had opened a bar especially to be entitled to vote. By 1871, no less than 10 per cent of those taking part in the ballot were café-owners, a considerable part of the liberal bourgeoisie.[23]

Although this regulation was blamed for encouraging drinking and therefore causing drunkenness, Frère-Orban defended it. He maintained that the constitution held that direct taxes were taken into consideration for a vote and the business license was certainly a direct tax.[24] It was hardly surprising that Frère-Orban watched over the interests of the rich publicans as he owed much of his political career to them.[25] His future liberal governments would be in place partly owing to the vote of wealthy café-owners, brewers and drink-sellers. When in 1870 a Catholic government came to power, they immediately passed a law that excluded the business taxes from selling alcohol from those qualifying for franchise. This decision was taken, not out of consideration for possible excesses of drunkenness, but out of political interest as public house owners would as a rule vote liberal.

Whereas there was no central government legislation in Belgium on public drinking at the time Frère-Orban was writing his report, a few local provincial councils had some regulation in place to keep the problem in check. In 1860 the province of Antwerp prohibited the peddling of liquors and issued acts to punish public drunkenness. These rules were, however, in practice mostly ignored and several towns falling under this provincial jurisdiction completely and openly disputed the new rules. The city of Lier, for example, did not agree with the stipulations of the provincial law on public drunkenness and they defended their position with the argument that 'because of the publicity a repressive legal proceeding brings with it', this law could 'needlessly destroy the reputation of honourable men as nobody is completely to be sheltered from an incidental drunkenness [*une ivresse accidentelle*] as a result of exceptional circumstances'.[26]

This objection by the city council of Lier addressed what was in fact a crucial aspect when it came to control of excessive drinking: the issue of class. Drinking was indulged in by all classes, but surely not all of it called for repression by the law? The minister Frère-Orban used this same objection when explaining why national legislation for drunkenness would be unworkable. One simply could not ascertain at which point moderate drinking became excessive drinking, he said. Drunkenness was too indefinite a condition: 'when does a socially acceptable activity change into a socially repugnant evil?' asked the minister rhetorically. Thus, when he then raised the question of what sort of drunkenness the state should penalize, it became in essence a question about which drunkards should be punished.

Because of course, although drunkenness was generally depicted as a problem affecting the working classes, it was clear to all that it also extended to other groups in society. Yet, it was impossible to think that the respectable gentleman in an inebriated state returning from a café could be arrested in the same way that a common working-class drunkard would. Surely, members of parliament reading the report could think of an instance whereby someone of their own class, if not themselves, had been completely drunk after a chic dinner? But what would happen in such cases was that 'friends would generally show the delicate attention to wrap him up in a carriage and to drive him home, so he escapes publicity'.[27] For people belonging to lower social classes, however, drinking and drunkenness would be much more public and more problematic, and it was felt to be much more threatening to the social order.

Frère-Orban therefore differentiated between 'voluntary' and 'involuntary' drunkenness, 'accidental' or 'habitual' drunkenness, and 'public' or 'non-public'. He believed that governments were only justified to punish 'public drunkenness', as a result of the scandal it would provoke and the dangers that it could possibly imply to public order.[28] But what he called 'accidental' or 'involuntary' and 'non-public' drunkenness had to escape all penalties.

According to the minister habitual indulgence in alcoholic drink (*ivresse habituelle*) on the other hand should be punished since it was always voluntarily. It would lead to the vice of drunkenness (*ivrognerie*). The difference between *ivrognerie* and *ivresse* does not exist in English; both mean 'drunkenness', but *ivrognerie* refers to repeated heavy drinking while *ivresse* is the result of a particular drinking bout.[29] Frère-Orban never used the word *alcoolisme*, but instead talked about people who were *adonné a l'ivrognerie* ('devoted to repeated heaving drinking').

The minister concluded that the most effective way to combat the plague of drunkenness was not through state intervention or licensing but by 'moral means'. Because drinking was seen as a personal moral failure, it was the responsibility of the individual to keep it under control. Not everyone, however, had the necessary moral fortitude to make the personal decision to drink only within 'acceptable limits' and the working classes and their children were believed to be in need of guidance. The minister therefore promoted private initiatives such as temperance movements and anti-alcohol education, both to be supported with government subsidies. The 'traditional habits and customs of the people', which had seemingly served as such an important line of argument to oppose possible government intervention, were no longer a hindrance, although of course the moralizing campaigns proposed now as an alternative were equally intended to change these habits.

When drinking became at long last an issue in Belgian politics in 1868, it was mainly out of concern for the economic status quo and for the conservation of liberal freedoms of trade and import. The vague conclusion of the report on 'the abuse of intoxicating drinks' was that 'one is allowed to doubt the action of public powers to combat drinking'.[30] As an advocate of a minimal state and maximum freedom of the individual, Frère-Orban's answers to the drink question were evasive, contradictory and inconclusive. Internal incoherencies and his vain attempts to delineate between different types of drunkenness indicate that the problem of drunkenness were too widespread and its meanings too nebulous and broad for the state to control.

7 CATHOLICS, LIBERALS, SOCIALISTS: CHANGE AND DRINK: 1880–9

After six years of liberal governments under Frère-Orban, the Liberal Party was severely defeated by the conservative Catholic Party in 1884. The Catholics would now remain in control of government until 1914 and the political understanding of drunkenness would shift accordingly. As political tensions grew the people's drinking habits became weapons in political propaganda.

Socialist Challenge

In 1885, fifty-nine professional associations – cooperatives, trade unions, and so on – joined to form the Belgian Workers' Party to improve the abysmal living and working conditions of the Belgian labourers. The party promoted a very moderate and reformist version of socialism but even so, very strong religious affiliations among much of the lower classes, especially in Flanders, prevented the party from bringing together more than a small section of the working class. And as suffrage was still linked to property, there were no poor workers that could vote for their own new party.[1] So first on the socialist political agenda was the need to change the unfair voting system.

However, for the traditional parties, Catholic and liberal, there was no such need; in their eyes the working classes were not ready to vote yet, as they were seen as uneducated, drunken and lazy. Good, sober workers would eventually earn enough money by hard work, which would then qualify them to vote.[2] But the rise of the socialist movement and its impact on the workers would now lead the Catholics towards some form of social action too as they tried to lure people back to their camp. The Catholic reaction to the political transformations was one of 'change in order to preserve', an attitude reflected in their stance on drinking. They also began to understand the power of the theme of sobriety within the worker's political awakening. Catholics had always taught moral and Christian values from the pulpit and in the classroom and temperance was one of those. Now in the present political climate they became convinced the subject was in need of further attention. By 1905, there were eighteen officially recognized temperance societies in Belgium in receipt of government subsidies and all of them were Catholic, while the few socialist temperance organizations that existed did not receive government support at all. The first temperance organization established in Belgium had been officially pluralistic, it aimed to attract 'citizens from all stands, from all beliefs from all parties'.[3] In fact, its members were recruited among wealthy groups in society and temperance became overall a Catholic cause. Most of the Catholic temperance movement's government money was spent on propaganda campaigns in the form of calendars, post-cards, periodicals and exhibitions to convince workers to stay away from alcohol and to save their money through prudent living. Through such propaganda they also hoped to convey their own political message. This led socialist deputies to question whether the real motives behind the organizations were not political.[4] For example, a story printed in an anti-alcohol publication in 1899 told of how a socialist militant was inciting workers against their patrons. The agitator insisted that his fellow workers should have the right to a horse and carriage like the capitalists. Among his audience was a 'converted' drinker – religious language was omnipresent in this discourse – who 'knew that many among them who considered their wages insufficient often drank half or a third of it'. When at that very moment the landlord of the pub passed in his own carriage the teetotaller shouted: 'You want to know where your carriage is? Look, the pub-landlord is driving it'.[5] For Catholics, not redistribution of wealth but frugality by moderation was the proper and acceptable way to reach social fairness.

Especially in the smaller centres and villages deeply embedded in Catholic structures, people reacted negatively, even violently against any form of socialist campaigning. In the eyes of the traditional parties, those promoting socialism were dangerous agitators. Socialists were godless individuals who had forsaken the church, who were debauched and above all drunken:

> From the moment the road of the church is taken away from them, they briskly walk the road of political meetings, where their yearning for amusement and sensual pleasures is stimulated, after which they ... go and apply the doctrine of their seducers in the gin-bars, where they intend to satisfy their animalistic urges.[6]

The hysterical tone of this extract from a publication which offered hints and tips to free the Flemish villages of socialist 'herecy', sheds light on the seriousness of the concern that existed about the corrupt influence the growing city, with its industrial modernity, political awareness and drunkenness seemed to have on traditional ways and values of the conservative countryside. Widespread mayhem and drunkenness would be the dramatic result if naïve farmers, who had previously been deferential under Catholic guidance, were thrust into politics.

That socialists were often made out as drunkards was not unrelated to the policy on drinking the socialist party itself had initially endorsed. Unlike their political opponents in the 1880s, the early socialists had not taken a stance against alcohol abuse and had not tried to promote moderation or abstinence, insisting that a glass now and then was the right of the workers for whom it was the only form of distraction. They believed that the worker had a right to his drink, a strategy that delivered them many supporters in the earlier years of the movement.[7]

The bourgeois parties' zeal to impose moderation illustrated for the socialists their actual underlying project, which was the undermining of the worker's identity, of which sociable drunkenness formed part. Popular bar songs condemned the hypocritical attitude of the bourgeoisie against workers' drinking:

> O rich men, all your days are dedicated to wealth. And when the worker before his labour drinks a pint of beer sometimes, this you cannot accept. And you squander the riches won with sweat and blood by those who slave for you.[8]

If the workers were abusing alcohol, it was because of the miserable conditions they, and the farmers as well, had to toil under. Together with the liberals, socialists fumed against what they called the Catholic hypocrisy relating to drinking and promiscuity and in their narratives drunken and licentious priests and monks featured prominently.[9]

The Spring of 1886

In the spring of 1886 the already strained class antagonisms in Belgium exploded. The general strike that erupted in the southern industrial areas spread spontaneously.[10] As discussed earlier, most Belgian bourgeois commentators were convinced that the strikes had been stirred up by drunken agitators. The victimized bourgeois owners identified the root as the uprisings as the malicious influence of the bar.[11] In Belgium, like in many other places, political grievances were expressed and discussed in bars. More than once anti-alcohol pamphlets described the bar as 'the home of socialism'.[12] The fact that socialist meetings took place in meeting rooms behind the cabaret seemed for many a very good reason to fulminate against it. Anti-alcohol campaigner Gaussin wrote:

> Strikes are coalitions very often formed by alcohol. Who do we see at the front of the movement but evil and mentally defective [*tarés*] beings of incorrigible intemperance. Who are those who they manage to recruit first? The idlers hanging around in bars, denigrators of property and family. It is in the bars that strikes ferment, it is in dives that popular uprisings are organized, it is in clubs made up by malcontents and those worn out by alcohol that revolutions and other disorders of the same kind are hatched.[13]

Strikes were understood not as a political means of pressure used by workers to obtain change, but as an outcome of the innate laziness and drunkenness of socialist workers. The spontaneous strikes and workers' revolts of 1886 were forcefully repressed and those considered responsible for the violence were arrested and tried.[14]

In court many of those arrested for revolutionary activities invoked their drunkenness as a mitigating factor. They claimed that they had acted 'under the influence' and thus in effect had been in a state of temporary madness and so hoped that responsibility could be denied.[15] Specialists indeed had argued that sometimes when drunkenness was the result of mental disease this could be considered the case.[16] A plea of drunkenness would be a valuable defence and was often proposed, but in practice it was seldom taken into account as a mitigating factor in court cases as was the case in Britain and France.[17] In the case of the Belgian insurgents of 1886 the defence of drunkenness would not lead to a reduced sentence and they were deemed fully responsible for their acts.[18]

La Commission du Travail 1886

The intensity and violence of the revolt by the normally obedient and docile Belgian workers compelled the Catholic government into action. In April 1886 a Parliamentary Commission of Inquiry was set up 'charged to enquire into the situation of industrial work in the kingdom and to study the measures that could improve it'. The commission, which became known as the Commission du Travail was to examine the social and economic conditions of the factory workers. It consisted of thrity-seven members of 'specialists', who were mostly conservatives: lawyers, clergymen and professors in economy and engineering, but no doctors.[19] However, among the witnesses invited to give evidence were several medical professionals and for the very first time also delegates of the workers. But because many workers feared for their jobs, they mostly told the commissioners exactly what they thought they wanted to hear.[20]

An entire section of the Commission du Travail was dedicated to researching the problem of what was now called *alcoolisme*. Drunkenness was dealt with under the chapter on the 'intellectual and moral state' of the workers. This section also included issues of education and illiteracy and sexual promiscuity among workers. Drunkenness was unmistakably approached as a problem of questionable morality among the working classes from the start.

The first two questions the commissioners asked their witnesses in connection with drunkenness were: 'Does intemperance rage among all classes of society?' and 'Does it affect both sexes?' This choice of questions immediately highlights a profound preoccupation with both the class and the gender aspect of the problem. Most of the answers to these questions established that it was mostly the men and only the working classes that were giving themselves over to drink. Nearly all the witnesses found that drunkenness was one of the main reasons for the appalling social conditions of the factory workers. The beer the workers drunk was believed to be alright and healthy, but as 'the worker prefers strong alcohol by natural disposition'; gin-drinking was identified as the problem that needed tackling.[21] The workers' 'natural' devotion to strong liquor was attributed to an equally 'natural' lack of morality and self-restraint. However, there were representatives of the workers who in their testimony before the commission explained how they believed that it was the terrible conditions in which the workers had to live that drove them to the public house.

In spite of such contrary assertions by several witnesses, in the final report of the Commission du Travail the general tone of the argument was familiar. Drinking was a vicious habit of the workers who wasted their wages on it and therefore landed up in poverty. Historian Eliane Gubin has concluded that the final report of the Commission du Travail was not prompted by the actual answers to the questions, but was based on the preconceived ideas and prejudices of the committee members.[22] The distinction between the 'good' worker and the 'bad' worker, as already established by people like Edouard Ducpétiaux and through stories and novels a few decades earlier, still permeated contemporary thinking. The commissioners agreed that there were indeed workers who were hard working and loyal to their employers and who managed to feed their families and thus showed that the wages they received were sufficient. The problem was located among another 'type' of worker: those that were lazy and wasted their income on drink. Therefore they lived in misery and were easily lured into the nets of the socialists.[23]

The commission proposed several plans of action in its report to the government to diminish the problem of drink, but they were not much different from what Frère-Orban had proposed two decades earlier. The promotion of temperance movements and anti-alcohol education was recommended and a sharper control on the production of adulterated and poor quality spirits. Secondly, the abolition of the so-called 'truck system' was advocated: the practice whereby part of the wages were to be paid in 'natural', meaning alcohol or paid out in pubs, which in its turn was felt to promote drinking.[24]

The truck system was effectively abolished in 1888, a late development especially when compared with other European examples. As a comparison, in Prussia, the practice of paying out part of the wages in drink was already formally abolished in 1849 and in Great Britain even as early as 1831. In fact in Britain the truck system had not involved at all the payment of wages in goods such as alcohol, but it stipulated long pay periods and the requirement that some of the wages had to be spent in the company store. This practice had been defended with an anti-alcohol argument. Long pay periods would reduce absenteeism due to drunkenness that was seen to blight Mondays following paydays and also having to spend the wages in the company store prevented workers to spend their money on alcohol.[25] The extent of the actual role of the state to curb drunkenness was still much debated in the report of the Commission du Travail of 1886 and serious reservations about it were expressed.[26] Drunkenness, after all, was a problem that affected private individuals and was therefore no business of the state. The scientific medical argument of alcoholic heredity gave ample justification for this point of view: there was nothing to be done about it. Officially, however, in the final discussions of the commission it was agreed that the argument of biological predestination should not be used as an excuse for apathy towards the problem of alcoholism, an indication that an important shift within the debate on the role of the state was on its way. Adophe Prins, professor of criminal law at the university of Brussels and general inspector of prisons and as such invited as a specialist to give evidence before the commission, contended that alcoholism as the stigma of degeneration was the genesis of all crimes and that it should be penalized when it became public. He concluded that one should attack the evil at its source and therefore punish drunkenness when it happened in public.[27]

The Law on Public Drunkenness, 1887

And so in the wake of the commission's report, the Belgian parliament proposed a law on public drunkenness amongst other cautious changes in law that would lay the basis for further social legislation. It proposed that anyone in public 'in a state of manifest drunkenness' could be arrested.

The time had now arrived to legislate against drunkenness, explained Minister of Justice Joseph Devolder when evaluating the proposal, because by 1887 Belgium was the only European country without a national law on public drunkenness.[28] In comparison, in Britain the 1871 Licencing Act had consolidated a large body of legislation curbing drunkenness going back to a much earlier period.[29] In France, a law to punish public drunkenness was approved in 1873 and in the Netherlands in 1881.[30]

Catholic member Comte Henri de Mérode, who presented the law in the *Chambre*, explained how in Belgium drunkenness was still 'firmly rooted in the national habits' and that it was a specific Belgian attitude towards it that had been the cause for this lack of state control: being drunk was still not deemed to be something embarrassing or degrading, but instead it was found to be amusing and entertaining.[31] In other words, it was not considered necessarily as unacceptable behaviour that needed to be curtailed.

Up until now public drunkards were dealt with under the regulations on vagrancy and on lunacy, but only when they caused trouble. Devolder believed that in 1887 the attitude in Belgium towards alcohol had changed, compared to a few years previously when Frère-Orban presented his report and when the 'public opinion did not directly demand a reform'.

De Mérode embraced the general feeling of unease after 1886 with arguments of 'dangerousness'. He referred to reports written by temperance doctors explaining how alcoholism would predispose people to commit certain crimes and he quoted the last report of the situation in the insane asylums in Belgium, which confirmed an alarming rise in apprehended mad alcoholics. A fear for hereditary degeneration of the Belgian race was very clearly present in the language he used in his parliamentary speech: drunkenness led straight to the 'debasement' (*abatardissement*) of the race and its physical 'decay' (*decrepitude*). He who gave himself over to drink would not only suffer from it himself, but 'he prints the permanent physical and moral stamp of his weakness onto his offspring'. Liberal Bara who was critical of the proposal accused the House of creating 'all sorts of new crimes' under the pretext of bettering the conditions of the workers.

There was, nevertheless, another type of drunkenness added to the *rapporteur*. It concerned a special class of 'professional drinkers', difficult to define, but so much more dangerous: he referred here to the 'unlucky sufferers of chronic alcoholism' who partook quietly in civil and political life, while in actual fact were semi-irresponsible. Was he perhaps talking from his personal experience with his parliamentary colleagues? Medical opinion called this condition, he said, 'a morbid state as a result of a sometimes very slow poisoning of a regular absorption of spirits which could possibly never even have led to drunkenness [*ivresse*]'.[32] This pathology, explained De Mérode, because that was what it was, partially deprived the sufferer of his faculties, especially of his will, and it could even induce him to commit crimes.[33] But the idea of possible legislation regarding this type of drunkard, which they knew all too well, was laughed at. There were certainly 'plenty of such irresponsible individuals in politics and in the civil service all over the world'.[34] The members furthermore agreed that it was a very unlikely prospect that a Belgian citizen would voluntarily surrender his liberty to enter a treatment clinic, as was done in Britain and as some eminent doctors had proposed. 'One has to know our habits very badly to believe that an alcoholic could provoke his own imprisonment!', exclaimed De Mérode. He concluded that 'the greatest abuses were to be feared' and that as legislators they were incompetent to 'review this delicate point in more detail'.

Instead, the drunkenness that would fall under this legislation was of a different type, it was the moral vice of the badly educated working class. But how to distinguish between the two different types of drunkenness? The idea of 'manifest drunkenness' as the proposed law stipulated could indicate both types of drunkenness. Radical liberal Bara understood this when he explained that the proposal on the table dealt with an issue that in theory could affect everyone, all classes in society. There was not even 'ecclesiastical immunity', he said in an acerbic sneer to the Catholics, which provoked again much laughter in the house.[35] The solution here for Bara was to leave the state out of it altogether: 'let us not make laws for all the vices of human nature, we do not have a mission to reform society and to let virtue rule everywhere'.[36]

However, such need to protect personal liberties and the disregard for meddling in moral issues when legislating for public drunkenness was annulled when dealing with prostitutes. Since the time of Napoleon they had been the subject of rigid government control in Belgium and when a prostitute breached the regulation of her trade with 'scandalous behaviour' or with drunkenness or fraud, she was sent to prison straightaway.[37] By the 1880s illegal prostitution thrived in neighbourhoods where official prostitution was forbidden, often in bars. Some members of parliament wanted to see the confusion over the regulations of the sale of drink in brothels cleared up within the bill on public drunkenness and much discussion time in the chamber was devoted to it.[38] Much attention in the chamber was devoted to this particular aspect of the law on drunkenness because a debate on drink and brothels really addressed the problem of syphilis, and that was very much on the mind of those involved in the debates.[39] Syphilis, like alcoholism, was a problem that affected all social classes and especially to those of the bourgeoisie who took full advantages of the services on offer in brothels.

In 1887 when the final law on public drunkenness was passed through parliament, with many amendments, it had become a law to punish drunk and disorderly behaviour. The formulation of 'manifest drunkenness', which had been such an obstacle, was amended to 'a state of drunkenness causing disorder, scandal, or danger to oneself or others'.

The new law stipulated higher fines if it involved someone having a profession demanding 'greater caution', like civil servants. The time devoted to deciding which 'type' of drunkenness to include and this addition of higher fines for professionals affected by the bill, indicated how much concern there was about drunkenness amongst the better off. But it was ultimately left to the integrity of the individual judge, a fellow and therefore perhaps sympathetic bourgeois, to come to a verdict and to decide what exactly entailed disorder and scandal in a particular case. So ultimately the law would always target the working classes whose drinking was much more public and more easily interpreted as disorderly.

Pub landlords would be liable to punishment when serving drink to already drunk customers or to children younger than sixteen unaccompanied by an adult when consuming on the premises, though children were still allowed to buy drink to take home with them. There was further a clause to prevent the accumulation of debts in the public house, a measure that was as much to the economic benefit of pub landlords as to drunkards. While the final law of public drunkenness included a check on the sale of alcohol in brothels, nowhere in it was a regulation or licensing of any kind for ordinary bars mentioned.

Ultimately, it was required that the text of this law against public drunkenness should be advertised in all public houses in the two languages of the country. This obligation was often ridiculed: one landlord had hung it up in the toilet, joking that it was the most important place in his bar.[40]

Local governments were in charge of the enforcement of the new regulation, but local councillors were often also local brewers and bar owners who chose to ignore the regulation.[41] In general the law was never taken very seriously and it was often mocked. In a song especially dedicated to it, cabaret singer Karel Waeri in Ghent presented it as a perfect opportunity to play a practical joke on a pub landlord, referring to the article that the publican could be punished for serving drink to drunken patrons. When arrested in the street a drunkard could denounce the pub landlord whose services had brought him to his present state. And soon, sang Waeri, there would be no one left to implement the law, as the entire police-corps would be locked up in prison. As drinking on the job was not considered problematic in nineteenth-century Belgium, local policemen were used to drinking with the people in neighbourhood bars. Policemen were, however, forbidden by law to run a 'cabaret'.[42]

Because *garde-villes en garde-champêtres* seldom arrested people for public drunkenness and mayors were often afraid of unpopularity, in practice the *Loi d'ivresse publique* of 1887 was not commonly enforced. Apart from the practical difficulties of enforcing it, the law was also criticized for it was felt to be inefficient and unhelpful to remedy the problem of drunkenness. The last stanza of Waeri's song *De drankenwet* illustrated its futility. It relates a story of a notorious woman from Brussels who had been arrested for drunkenness time and again and after having spent once again another short sentence in prison, she simply said: 'bye gentlemen, see you later, I will be back soon'.[43] For Waeri and many other critics the law on public drunkenness dealt with the symptoms of the problem but not the causes. Not the influential brewer or distiller, but the small pub landlord and his or her costumers were duped. The socialist paper *La peuple* wrote that this law punished the poor drinker who did not have money to rent a cab to have them brought home such as the rich did when they would get drunk. The paper called upon the government to enact social reforms instead.[44]

Before the end of the century both the liberal and subsequent Catholic governments remained reluctant to take legislative action about the sale and consumption of alcohol, for the same political and economic reasons.[45] But after the political turbulence that provoked the discussions in the Commission du Travail and the passing of a first law on drunkenness, the issue of drunkenness became increasingly considered more important. Although they occasionally acknowledged the issue of drunkenness among women and middle-class men as well, lawmakers always connected excessive drinking to disorder and the way of life of the working classes and their physical and moral state.

8 REMEDYING DANGEROUSNESS: 1889–1914

A medicalized discourse on the relation between drink and the 'dangerousness' of the working classes became officially endorsed in the last decades of the nineteenth century. Unacceptable behaviour such as drunkenness became not only criminalized, but increasingly understood as pathological. That alcohol was one of the main culprits of the degeneration of a strong Belgian race was the central story of the anti-alcohol societies that were being consolidated in this period, whose names like Ligue Patriotique, set up to save 'the family and the nation against the destruction by alcohol', belied their nationalistic inclination.[1] They would call their supporters to arms with propaganda aimed at engaging their patriotic sensitivities: 'Don't drink and you'll understand your mission: to enrich and defend the country'.[2]

Reformist Socialism

When in the second half of the 1880s Emile Vandervelde came to power within the Belgian Socialist Party, the condoning of the consumption of alcohol as a 'worker's right' was written out of the official party line and instead the socialists declared open war on drink. Vandervelde stressed the importance of counteracting the poor public image of the socialist movement as associated with revolution, drunkenness and irrationality. During his entire political career, rather than supporting drink as a prerogative for the workers, Vandervelde insisted on an organized fight against alcoholism as an essential contribution to the war against capital. He wanted to persuade workers that heavy drinking endorsed a capitalist system whereby bourgeois brewers and distillers exploited the drinking working class. Also, workers' self-respect, so much needed for their political awakening, was completely annihilated by extreme drinking habits.

Vandervelde depicted the bourgeois as hypocritical drunkards themselves and he compared their attitude towards alcoholism to their outlook on prostitution.[3] Although they scorn the prostitute, bourgeois men still believed that the institution was indispensable for the existence of the bourgeois marriage. In the same way, said Vandervelde, they hate the drunkard, but his drinking is necessary for the continuance of capitalism itself: by drinking the worker numbs himself from his real misery and is incapable of revolt.[4] In 1898, Vandervelde founded within the worker's party a Ligue Socialiste contre l'Alcoolisme.[5] Inspired by the viewpoints of the teetotal leaders of British trade unions he pleaded for complete abstinence, unlike the medical bourgeois anti-alcohol leagues who championed moderation.[6]

Vandervelde was eager to use contemporary scientific and medical arguments to add strength to his case, like the claim that alcoholism contributed to 'hereditary degeneration of the race'. But, as Brice De Ruyver pointed out, as elsewhere, also here degeneration was a vague concept and what Vandervelde meant when he used the term 'degeneration' remained unclear.[7] He hinted at it being a condition affected by the debased semi-criminal environment in which children of drunken parents grew up.[8] *Milieu* necessarily had to be more important than biology within a degenerationist concept that was compatible with anticipated social change, so fundamental to the ideas of socialism.

Belgian socialist heroes were often described or indeed depicted themselves as being brought up in miserable circumstances, suffering under the hand of a drunken father. They themselves in turn, having found redemption in socialism, would have forsaken all alcoholic drink. The figure of the drunkard drowning his sorrow in drink, terrorizing his family and squandering all his money belonged to an older time, before the coming of socialism.[9] According to the new gospel of pragmatic reform socialism, honest workers had to emancipate themselves and through self-respect and solidarity overcome their miserable conditions. He wanted for example to stimulate a reading culture among the workers, stating that 'in Belgium one drinks too much and reads too little'.[10]

Although Vandervelde agreed with most other socialists that the best way to attack alcoholism was to alleviate the suffering of the workers, unlike other influential socialist leaders, such as Domela Nieuwenhuis in the Netherlands, who did not believe fairer distribution of wealth alone would make alcoholism disappear. He supported this point by referring to the excessive drinking that took place among the rich bourgeoisie.[11]

The change in tactic of the socialist campaigners towards drinking and the working class matched the model of moderate reform socialism, of social democracy that party leaders like Vandervelde embodied.[12] Moderation was the key for these socialist elites, emanating from a bourgeois liberal background.[13] A middle-of-the-road reformist strategy had led the party ultimately to political success. Mass socialist pressure ensured the introduction of a diluted version of general franchise for men in 1893. The general 'plural' franchise meant that every man over twenty-one could cast a vote, while those with money and qualifications could claim two or three votes. In spite of these restrictions one and three quarters of a million new voters were added to the electorate and Vandervelde became one of the twenty-eight socialist deputies who would occupy a seat in Europe's most bourgeois parliament for the first time.[14]

Feminism

Political success was the aim of another emancipatory movement that also took on the fight against alcohol as central to its campaign. Like the socialists who had moulded anti-alcoholism into an essential aspect of their programme, the fight against drunkenness equally contributed towards the formation of an identity for the early feminist movement, organized in Belgium in the last decade of the nineteenth century.[15] The fight against alcohol was one of the very few causes bourgeois women could publically engage in.[16]

The early feminists were liberal bourgeoisies and their movement was moderate as it fought for control over the domestic sphere, insisting that women's natural principal role as mother and wife needed protection in order to maintain the health of the Belgian race, for which one should read: the bourgeois family.[17] In the campaign against alcoholism, feminists stressed women's importance as protectors of the family and the race. They argued that women needed support to fulfil their important 'natural' role for the nation. Anti-alcoholism was central to their political message. First, women were to produce strong and healthy offspring, and secondly, they were to assert their moral influence on their husband and children as housewives and educators. Furthermore, women were considered experts in dealing with drunkards, because drunkards were to be treated as 'children and lunatics, with gentleness and firmness'.[18] In 1899 Belgian feminists founded their own temperance society: the Union des Femmes Belges contre l'Alcoolisme, with as its aim to the protection of women of the people from the negative effects of the social plague that was alcoholism.[19]

In anti-alcoholic feminist discourse it was always the drinking of men of the lower classes that needed to be countered. In a widely distributed and immediately translated propaganda brochure aimed at working-class women, Marie Parent urged them not to marry a man with a soft spot for drink. Women would not only have to put up with the violence perpetrated by drunken husbands, but would also suffer for her children, 'because vices are hereditary and the father's bad example will be a great danger to them'.[20] In order to keep husbands from taking to drink Parent offered tips on how to excel in housekeeping, so that husbands would stay home rather than go to the bar.

At the end of the 1890s the issue of votes for women was only addressed occasionally and cautiously; there was not even suffrage for all men. In the first decades of the twentieth century, anti-alcohol campaigning lodged itself at the heart of a growing campaign for suffrage for women – albeit in local elections. Within a paradigm of race and milieu, while the liberal and socially-minded feminists gathered force, arguments to grant votes to women emerged within debates on alcoholism.

For femimists such as the liberal Louis Frank and also for Catholic feminists, like Louise van den Plas, the anti-alcohol campaign was a vehicle on the route towards political change, used in campaigns and to lobby for women's political rights. To combat drunkenness the environment needed to change; a reform to be effected by the workers themselves was required, supported by the moral persuasion of their wives, who hereby could emancipate themselves as well.[21]

Catholicism

In the last years of the nineteenth century, Catholics in their temperance groups moulded the old moral Catholic anti-alcohol discourse into new shapes in order to enable it to compete with the arguments of its political enemies.[22] As part of their battle with the liberals for the rights on providing education, Catholic governments would pass legislation on temperance teaching in primary schools, and so Belgium became one of the first European countries to include specific anti-alcohol classes in the national curriculum. This also fitted in well with ideas on combatting the negative effects of degeneration through education. The 'prophylactic education of children' was according to many European specialists one of the ways out of the national and racial debacle of alcoholism and degeneration.[23]

In a circular of 3 April 1892 to the chief inspectors, Minister Jules de Burlet explained his views on the role of temperance in primary education. According to de Burlet, the anti-alcohol project in schools should include teaching children about the dangers of alcohol and he also encouraged schools to set up temperance societies for children in which they were to promise moderation for the future. It remains unclear, however, how widespread his recommendations were followed up in primary schools around the country.[24]

Catholic social campaigners modernized the old emphasis on the individual moral conscience of the workers to involve wider social responsibility by appealing to prevailing ideas of heredity and racial degeneration. Catholics were keen to adopt biological models of heredity into their anti-alcohol narratives, connecting notions of heredity to Christian notions of virtue and vice. Jos Lemmens, a progressive priest active in Catholic workers' organizations, organized an anti-alcohol movement in Liège called Bien-Etre Social in 1895. He published a collection of sermons to help clerics with anti-alcohol education of the masses. It suggested that priests preach to their congregation:

> Do not ignore that mysterious law that is called the law of heredity, in virtue of that law … the child inherits from his parents the germs of good or the taints of evil, of passion and of vice. Modern science has shown that this law finds its application particularly within the family of the alcoholic. The children of the drunkard are born with unfortunate predispositions, both in regard to their bodies and their souls. Tuberculosis, anaemia, idiocy, scrofula, falling sickness spy upon its little body, while

> at the same time a predisposition to crime, propulsion towards immorality, lack of character and violence of the passions spy on its soul![25]

Most of the Catholic anti-alcohol message used the moral educational tool which positions the drinker opposite the abstinent and so showed the dramatically opposed results of their actions.[26] The iconography of the temperance movements mirrored ideas of good versus evil, or sober versus drunk to images of health, sickness and weakness in offspring (see Figure 8.1). In one widely published picture, here on a postcard, we see the sober worker who fathered a healthy looking child, his family is happy and the tools of his carpenter trade beside him reveal a Christian connection with the Holy Family. In the picture next to it, there is the idle drunkard without tools but with bare walls and empty cupboards instead, who has produced an emaciated, misshapen baby, frightening to look at.[27]

Ideas of heredity and degeneration fitted very well within a Catholic ideological framework. Medicine and science were powerful and convincing new social influences that added additional authority to what always had been inescapable dogmatic 'truths'. The concept of the vice of the individual harping back to the original sin, which the church needed to emphasize, could through ideas of heredity, become a 'social' issue.[28]

By the end of the nineteenth century always-louder socialist pressure had left the traditional political parties with no choice but to listen to the voice of the working classes and to accept universal suffrage. The panic caused by the first anarchic socialist uprisings had subsided somewhat and with it the emphasis on alcohol and drunkenness as a cause of the workers' insubordination weakened as well. General strikes and demonstrations in the campaign for general franchise were now better organized by the united and ideologically reformist socialist party, and they were felt to be much more subdued than the drunken *jacquérie* of 1886. The minor social unrest that did arise was, according to Dr Bienfait, due to the true impossibility to 'contain Walloon exuberance or Flemish stubbornness, with some of them [being] of feeble intellectual development, with mental defects [tares], with little moral education'.[29]

Social Defence

Because many were convinced that the excessive public drinking that had made the workers so different and dangerous in 1886 had actually only seemingly disappeared. According to some, it now had become lodged within the biology of the 'race' of the workers and had through heredity and degeneration turned into a silent but unavoidable threat to the social and physical health of the nation. This idea of the 'internalization' of drunkenness through heredity drove discussions leading in the last decades of the nineteenth century towards social legislation in the name of what became known as the doctrine of 'social defence', a principle which fitted in well with the ideology of the ruling Catholic government.

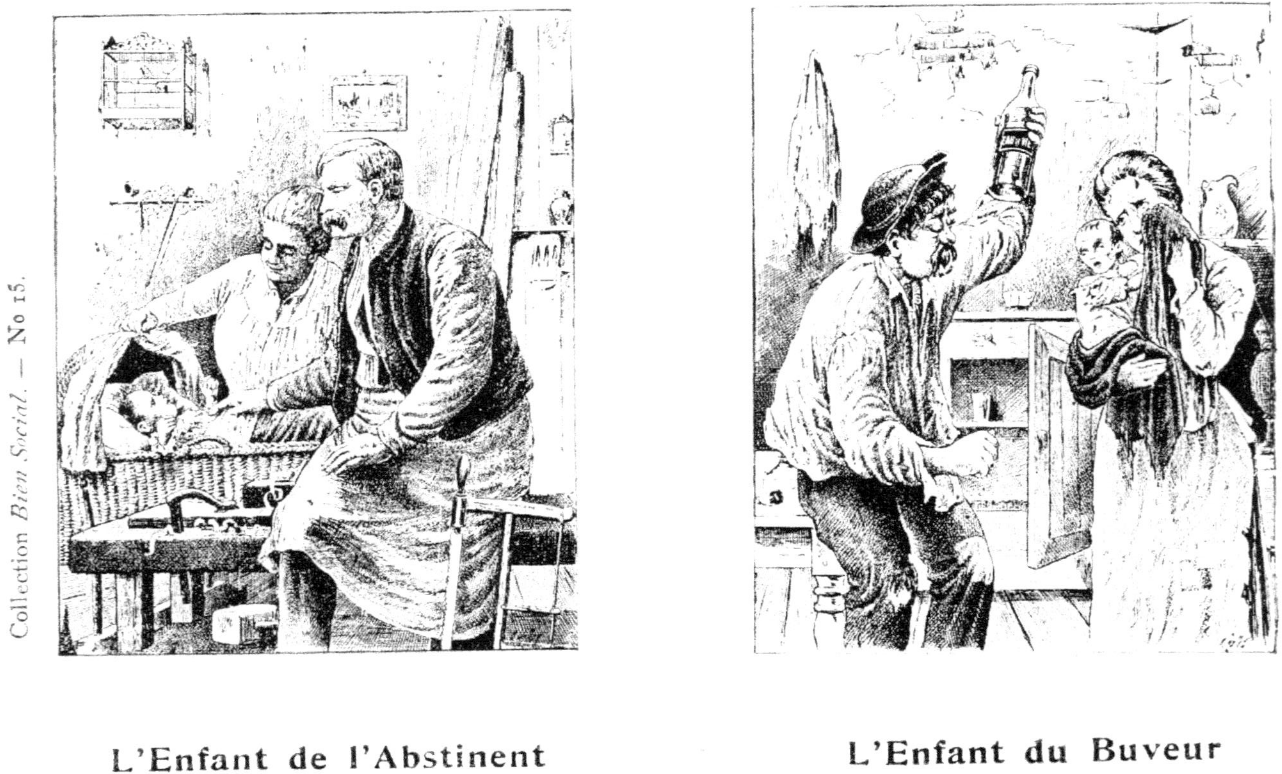

Figure 8.1: *L'Enfant de l'abstinent. L'Enfant du buveur (The Child of the Abstainer, the Child of the Drinker),* Temperance Postcard. Collection Le Bien Social. Journal illustré mensuel contre l'alcoolisme, 15 (1902) © Collectie Nationaal Jenevermuseum, Hasselt.

Most of these changes were introduced by Catholic Minister of Justice Jules Lejeune between 1887 and 1894 and were inspired by the thinking of his close advisor, Adolphe Prins, who never held a direct political post himself but who became a key player in late nineteenth-century Belgian social politics.[30] Prins had already taken the political stage as a specialist in the Commission du Travail in 1886, arguing for the penalizing of public drunkenness as the 'genesis of all crimes'. Combining ideas of criminal law and psychiatry, Prins introduced the idea of 'social defence', which asserted that the social body needed to be protected from degeneration through the malign influence of dangerous individuals. Drunkenness and the solutions to combat it that Prins proposed illustrate very well where the new idea of social defence differed from traditional criminal law, for which responsibility was at the heart of what made an act criminal or not.[31] Alcohol was for Prins, the 'destructeur de responsabilité', and if this were used as a criterion for punishment many violent acts would have to be necessarily acquitted.

> We find in the labouring classes lazy and brutal drunkards who refuse to work, who mistreat their wives, who wear themselves out to gain the daily bread and his children by whom the father instills fear and disgust. It is known that those repugnant scenes even sometimes turn to horrible scenes of killing and rape[32]

Therefore dangerous alcoholics should be eliminated from society before their pernicious habit, or indeed inborn defect, could manifest itself. [33] Such measures of 'moral hygiene' were espoused to prevent the nightmarish scenario Prins had painted. With this in mind, Jules Lejeune started effecting penal reform. He firstly revisited and reformed Ducpétiaux's law on vagrancy in 1892, which was badly implemented. He built new reform institutions separately for those who were vagrants and clearly not willing to work: 'owing to idleness, drunkenness or immorality', while those unfortunates who could not work due to illness or forced unemployment were to be housed in different Welfare Colonies with a more lenient regime.[34] It would be interesting to research how the justices of the peace made this distinction in practice, in individual cases.

However, the experiment was not successful: by the turn of the century, three quarters of the 6,000 detained in the reform institution of Merxplas were there already for at least the fourth time.[35] Many of those arrested as vagrants and incarcerated were people with long -standing drink problems and this contributed to their recidivism. Most foreign observers of the penitentiary colony project who had been initially interested in the experiment, were no longer convinced of its efficacy after visiting.[36] Seebohm Rowntree called the inhabitants of the agricultural colonies 'human wreckage' and instead of offering rehabilitation he saw the institutions as 'permanent asylums for those ruined by drink, for the indolent, the incapable and the old'.[37] Official consumption statistics continued to show a steep rise in the sale of alcohol, which showed clearly that the locking away of unwanted destitute alcoholics was inefficient.[38]

And so the problem of drunkenness and dangerousness continued to haunt bourgeois political minds and in 1895 Lejeune, who had now become senator, chaired a Government Study Commission in relation to the Question of Alcoholism. Fifteen commissioners met forty-one times between April 1895 and June 1897 and over this time they analysed endless statistics, graphs and facts showing the irrefutable relationship between drunkenness and all kinds of social evils. Among the commissioners were seven medical experts, this time most of them active in the temperance movement.

The commission unanimously adopted the position that 'alcoholism of the parents transmits to the children and hits [*frappe*] the offspring with a hereditary taint [*une tare héréditaire*]'.[39] Their final report listed how alcohol, through heredity had contributed to an increase of madness, dementia, simple-mindedness, epilepsy and many other diseases of the body, but mostly to a rise in afflictions of the mind. It also revealed, once again, the enormous influence alcohol abuse was alleged to have on poverty, criminality, immorality and suicide.

A second section of the report presented possible solutions for the problem. At first sight not much had changed since the time of the laissez-faire approach of Waltère Frère-Orban. The commission suggested a programme of alcohol-education in schools and government support for private initiatives in the shape of temperance societies.

State intervention into the production and sale of alcohol was still not mentioned as an option, although the report did recommend a significant rise of taxes and the licensing of bars. But new and most remarkable was that the commission of 1895–7 also proposed the incarceration 'for a period considered necessary for their recovery of accused drunkards when judged dangerous'.[40] After the committee had presented its findings, its president Lejeune followed up on this recommendation and, this time in the senate, presented an act for the 'incarceration of dangerous lunatics'. It recommended the establishment of special asylums for criminal lunatics and drunkards. In fact, he had already proposed this act in 1890, but then it had failed to reach a second reading and it had also not included the category of drunkards. The act had been strongly supported from its initial stages by eminent psychiatrists. The minister would say later that 'the measures presented in my bill were almost dictated by the *Acacémie Royale de Médicine*'.[41] Now, in 1897, with the findings of the Study Commission behind him, Lejeune had added a category of individuals to the list of persons suitable for forced incarceration in special institutions that had not been there seven years earlier: alcoholics (*des alcoolisés*). The *alcoholisés* that were to be sent to special asylums were those who had been acquitted of a crime because of 'legal irresponsibility' due to chronic alcoholism. It would also concern individuals who had been found guilty of serious crimes whilst in a state of drunkenness. Moreover, the category would include those who had incurred four sentences for public drunkenness within a period of four years.[42] However, not unexpectedly, the proposal was severely criticized as infringing on personal freedoms and was rejected again.

In comparison, in Britain an Inebriate Act was passed in 1898 which enabled local authorities to set up special reformatories to treat habitual drunkards. Until the First World War, when the experiment came to a halt, fourteen such reformatories dealing with 4,590 inmates were established.[43] The major difference was that these reformatories that had become reality in Britain catered mainly for women, while the special asylums proposed in Belgium envisioned only men as their potential clientele. Female drinking was not under consideration in this context in Belgium, a discrepancy that deserves further enquiry.

Alcoolisés were still a target-group when the proposal for special asylums for criminal lunatics was, once again fruitlessly, put before the house a third time in 1909, proposed by a group of six members of parliament, among whom included the socialist Emile Vandervelde. The law was finally passed only in 1930, but by that time the specific category *alcoolisés* had disappeared again and the 'law on social defence' – as it became known – would only include 'abnormals, habitual delinquents and criminal adolescents'. While 'social defence' justified the need to organize direct forms of social control, especially through changes in criminal justice, with its emphasis both on willpower and on hereditary degeneration, it laid bare essential contradictions within late nineteenth-century ideas on drunkenness. Alcohol once more had proved a subject too ambiguous to deal with as an indiscriminate 'condition' in a law that would be applicable to the entire population, rich and poor, male and female.

Absinthe

Liesbet Nys has told the story of how, after the experiment in the colony to forbid the sale of absinthe in 1898, a ban on the professed hazardous anise liquor in Belgium followed in 1906.[44] In sharp contrast to the lengthy discussions over legislation regarding other aspects of alcohol sale and use, the ban of absinthe both in the colony and at home was passed at once, unanimously, without much serious debate. The legislation to ban absinthe served to demonstrate interest and goodwill on the part of the Belgian government to tackle issues at the forefront of the medical and wider public debate: the preoccupation with the growth of alcoholism and madness and the perceived decline of the race. The government could now pride itself on listening and acting upon those concerns of 'social defence' related to drunkenness. And as it was a French drink its ban did not affect in any way those important 'habits and mores of the people'. As it was hardly produced in Belgium, it could not cause offence to anyone with a political or economic interest in its sale and production. And as it was hardly drunk in Belgium, apart by some bohemian anti-social groups, nothing would really change. Contemporaries quickly made these observations too and the regulation was ridiculed. One publication wrote that Belgium should receive as much congratulations for the passing of this law 'as a eunuch because he stays chaste'.[45]

Epilogue

WWI and the Vandervelde Law

The First World War was a breaking point not only for the general history of Belgium but also specifically for the history of alcohol, as it was in France, Britain and the United States of America.[46] As in most countries at war, in Belgium drastic action was taken as a result of the shortage of raw materials. The government strictly controlled the production of alcohol and its consumption became outright forbidden in non-occupied territory. Psychiatrist Auguste Ley observed that as a result, during the war the number of people suffering from alcoholic madness had seriously decreased. After the war, Ley remained at the forefront of a campaign that canvassed for this emergency legislation to become permanent once the war was over.[47]

And so prohibition became a reality in Belgium, a development that deserves much further and detailed historical exploration. From 29 August 1919 onwards, socialist Minister of Justice Emile Vandervelde forbade the sale of small amounts of alcoholic beverages. This meant in practice those that were served in pubs. This was certainly a drastic shift, surely compared with the unwillingness to regulate the sale of alcohol in previous years.[48] To prevent alcohol abuse moving from public places to private homes, the new law quadrupled the excise duty on strong liquor. Shopkeepers could only sell alcohol in minimum quantities of two litres – so that the purchase of it would be too expensive for the weekly workers' budget.

Ten years later in 1929 alienist Auguste Ley again concluded that the incidences of madness related to drunkenness had once more decreased dramatically after the war.[49] Vandervelde himself noted in a report on the success of his law in 1923 that the number of vagrants locked up in the colonies and convictions for public drunkenness in Belgian prisons had declined: noticeably, while there had still been 625 drunkards detained in Vorst in 1912, none were counted in 1919 and a year later only 9.[50]

The First World War and the Vandervelde Law can be seen as marking the end of an era where alcohol represented madness and degeneration, and embodied the social threat of an irrational working class. It symbolizes how liberal ideologies had shifted and reconstruction and social democracy were now on the agenda.[51] The period of prohibition in Belgium after the first war and the cultural and social context of the Vandervelde Law belongs to a new chapter in Belgian history. It can be seen as the final chapter of the story of the making of modernity and social change in the nineteenth century. I believe, nonetheless, that the Vandervelde Law of 1919, together with the extension of suffrage in the same year – one vote for one man – is the first chapter in a new, post-war history of social democracy in Belgium and as such its needs more detailed historical investigation.

In the period of the long nineteenth century in Belgium until the outbreak of the First World War, politicians were interested in drunkenness when it became problematic for the smooth running of society, specifically when an individual's problem became a 'social problem'. This meant in practice mostly lower-class public drunkenness. While initially drunkenness was linked to poverty and personal failure, the concept of degeneration had direct influence on how drunkenness was understood as a social problem in the last quarter of the nineteenth century.

The political and ideological narratives of drunkenness show how excessive consumption and its condemnation provided a framework within which to construct 'the other': the drunk, and thus to construct their own political identity and to promote its claims. So while drunkards always proved a very difficult category to legislate for, largely because they were to be found within all echelons of society, it was precisely because excessive drinking was constructed as a vice of 'the other' that it became a convenient topic for straightforward political propaganda, which took on aspects of both morality and biology according to the agenda that was followed.

PART III: DRUNKENNESS AND ITS SPECIALISTS

In Catholic Belgium, excessive drinking and habitual drunkenness were condemned as a vice. Once one yielded to the temptation, faith and willpower were the solutions religion offered to combat the immoral urge to drink. As in the rest of Europe, in nineteenth-century Belgium the problem of drunkenness became ever more an area of expertise of science and medicine. This medicalization of morality in general and drunkenness in particular has been interpreted as a social and cultural shift in the second half of the century: excessive drinking was removed from the realm of religious morality where it had lingered for centuries and instead was claimed by the positivistic world of scientific medicine. Historians have seen this as part of a wider process of the professionalization of doctors, who forged themselves through expansion of their expertise as a hegemonic group in society.[1] By calling the increasingly powerful body of medical professionals, 'the new confessors', Karel Velle, following Michel Foucault, has argued that doctors in Belgium generally assumed social roles performed in earlier times by the clergy. Sociologists have further argued that the construction of drunkenness as a disease coincided with the consolidating of medical professional identities.[2]

This chapter will illustrate how this process was both scattered and uneven. Different emerging specialties claimed expertise on the subject of alcoholism. In the mid-nineteenth century those who were interested in the problem of drunkenness were mostly men involved in matters of public health, so-called 'hygienists'. Towards the end of the century, doctors studying alcoholism defined themselves mostly as specialists of mental illness: psychiatrists, who claimed expertise by constructing both madness and drunkenness as a disease. At the same time, ideas of heredity and degeneration found their way into the understanding of alcoholism and drunkenness.[3] Up to the First World War, with contributions of criminal anthropologists, ideas of inborn criminal traits were added on to psychiatric approaches and its ideas of normal and most importantly abnormal behaviour.

Medical discourse would transform the drunkard from a morally reprehensible person into a sick person. Peter Scholliers has explained that by changing *ivrognerie* into *alcoolisme* and focussing on the scientific aspect of alcohol and on its clinical consequences, doctors introduced medical thinking about alcohol into common sense language.[4] Liesbet Nys has suggested that this process was not straightforward when she wrote that the history of medicalization should not be understood simply as a 'nefarious collaboration of experts and state authority imposed from above'.[5] By looking closely at the language used by specialists to talk about drunkenness and placing this within the context of broader societal change, this part of the book will show that the medicalization of drunkenness was as a complex cultural event.[6] As a social phenomenon with many outcomes, drunkenness offered complicated and multifarious possibilities for scientific and medical interpretation. In their turn the continuities and transformations in the medical understanding of drunkenness were inspired by how drunkenness was understood in broader society.

In the second half of the nineteenth century, medical practitioners published ever-increasing numbers of texts on the 'scourge of drunkenness'. The term 'alcoholism', coined by the Swedish doctor Magnus Huss in 1849 to refer to excessive drinking as a disease, was already being used by Belgian doctors in the 1850s.[7] According to Alfred Bienfait, *chef-de-clinique* of the main hospital in Liège and one of the founders of the temperance movement in Belgium, the difference between *ivrognerie* and *alcoolisme* was that the first has always existed, but the second condition was new and a result of the industrial production of cheap spirits typical for the age.[8] Alcoholism was, according to the specialists, a sign of the times – a problem of modern living. And it was in establishing that slippery difference between trouble-free drunkenness and problematic alcoholism, between vice and disease, that specialists felt their duty lay.

Doctors produced so-called *manuels populaires*, handbooks written deliberately in 'simple language', aimed at the working classes. Based on what they explained were unambiguous scientific truths, those manuals provided information to educate the lower classes about the dangers of excessive drinking with the aim of changing their behaviour. It is questionable, however, whether or not the intended audience ever read these 'hygiene' manuals, given the fact that many Belgian workers were illiterate or not interested in reading. Furthermore, as some contemporaries noted themselves, they would be wary of following advice proffered by members of a social class so far removed from their daily reality. Medical specialists were perceived as an elite group in society, as being out of touch with workers' actual lives, or even worse, as representatives of the class that subjugated them.[9]

Impact aside, what we can infer from reading and analysing medical advice manuals is what type of drinking behaviour and whose drinking the middle-class writers found unacceptable. Which narratives of drunkenness did the specialists use and circulate to convey their message and what does this tell us about their own preoccupations and anxieties? Answers to these questions can be found in another type of medical publication that informs the following chapters: medical works on alcoholism aimed at colleagues. It is in these specialist publications that self-professed specialists on drunkenness often most clearly communicated their doubts often about what exactly constituted drunkenness and how it should be defined.

The third type of source pertaining to the specialists included here are the case notes from the two mental institutions in Ghent. We learn how medical theory was applied in practice, where the reality of drunkenness was given meaning by the specialists who defined it differently according to whom the drunkard was and which behaviour he exhibited. Written between the lines are 'common sense' denominators of social class and of gender and indications of the forging of identities and of shifting power relationships. The case notes related to an essentially unstable concept such as drunkenness expose the mutability of cultural categories and social boundaries. Translated in equally fluid medical language, those categories and boundaries were accepted and contested, interpreted and constructed.

9 HYGIENISTS

In the mid-nineteenth century Belgian doctors by no means formed a closely-knit body and a Belgian Académie Royale de Médicine was only established in 1842 as a professional exclusive organization.[1] Many of the medical practitioners in nineteenth-century Belgium who wrote down their opinion on drunkenness were elite figures, whose view on many important matters was held in high esteem. Within this medical elite, the *hygiénistes* formed a specialized group of doctors interested in the physical and moral conditions of the working classes or *l'hygiène public*. They gathered and published statistical evidence on the unsanitary living conditions of the new urban workers and also on what they called their 'moral state', which included drinking habits.[2] Precursors in Belgium had been doctors Daniel Joseph Mareska and Julian Heymans who examined in the 1840s for the first time the living situation of the people employed in the Ghent cotton mills.[3] They condemned the workers' abuse of gin, which they described as a 'typical' moral failing of the working-class population that could eventually also affect their physical health.[4] Mareska and Heyman, like most hygienists of their time, did endorse a moderate use of gin, as it was commonly accepted that alcohol was a stimulant that would warm the body in cold weather and provide strength and energy needed for heavy physical and mental efforts. For most of the nineteenth century beer and wine were considered 'hygienic drinks' which, given that they were prepared in an honest way, were thought to be beneficial. As in Britain and France, it was only towards the end of the nineteenth century when physiological research proved the opposite was true that such deeply seated beliefs were gradually discarded by most medical professionals, however not among the people.[5] In many rural communities there was no running water and the water from the pump on the farmyard was not pumped deep enough to be of any good quality. As late as 1906, Dr Jean Demoor of the University of Brussels believed it was the task of the hygienist to teach the workers a fear for water and he wrote 'If you drink, drink beer, but never take water'.[6]

Belgian doctors insisted on maintaining a strict difference between 'hygienic drinks', which were fermented drinks (wine and beer) and distilled drinks (spirits, above all gin). The drink of the rich – wine – and the Belgian national drink

– beer – were represented as healthy. They would favour appetite, help digestion and activate intellectual activity.[7] Beer was praised from a nationalistic perspective. Such ideas were inspired by a romantic vision of beer drinking, by memories of a long lost time before industrialization when there was no widespread use of gin and also no proletariat. Doctor Boëns was convinced that because drinking beer was characteristic of the Belgian way of life, it should be considered a necessary item in the countrymen's diet. As beneficial and nourishing as Belgian beer traditionally brewed from natural ingredients was believed to be, one had to be on one's guard for the adulterated German, Bavarian variant, which became increasingly popular in the second half of the nineteenth century.[8] Throughout the century, medical specialists expressed a constant anxiety about the quality of the national drink and its pureness, while at the same time they speculated about the quality of the Belgian race being 'tainted' by contagious diseases and alcoholism. The concern with the pureness of the beer always represented deeper anxieties. According to the hygienists, the effects of beer on the body were completely opposite to those of distilled alcohol. While beer was wholesome, gin was thought to make its drinker aggressive and violent.[9] While beer embodied tradition, gin represented modernity.

Doctors continued to prescribe alcohol as therapy for all kinds of ailments. The problem that medical temperance doctors pinpointed was that unlike with other medical 'fashions' like bloodletting, in this instance the people themselves had access to alcohol and would make uncontrolled use of it 'with great pleasure'.[10] Ordinary people used alcohol as a prophylactic against all types of disease. During the cholera outbreak of 1866, people had entrusted their lives in the sanitary effects of alcohol. Meanwhile they disregarded the other, official medical advice of basic sanitation that would prevent the disease spreading.[11]

The treatment offered to alcoholics in asylums and private Maisons de Santés was equally not one of abstinence. In the Maison de Santé le Strop in Ghent the large daily lunch was always accompanied with half a bottle of wine and a tumbler of beer.[12] Gin and wine were also offered as treatment in the Ghent asylums for sufferers of chronic alcoholism, because it was considered dangerous to abstain at once. An exception was the sanatorium of Fort Jaco in Uccle ran by Dr Auguste Ley, where alcohol was absolutely forbidden.[13] Ley was a fervent campaigner for complete abstinence, not only for the patients but also for the staff of asylums. When his own staff, unhappy with these rules, had all resigned, Ley had to find new personnel in more temperate Holland.[14] Whereas in other countries complete abstinence had been for years preferred practice in asylums, in Belgium a similar scheme was viewed as too radical.[15] By the last decade of the century, however, the patient registers indicate that total abstinence became the treatment of choice for alcoholism. When for example in 1904 a desperate but very well connected dipsomaniac entered the Maison de Santé in Ghent he was put on a regime of one bottle of wine and two litres of beer a day, while a special delivery of alcohol free beer from London was arranged.[16]

Doctors increasingly questioned the beneficial effects of alcohol and sometimes even started to express reservations about beer and its reputation as *boisson hygiènique*. One of the most prolific temperance campaigners in Belgium, Hippolyte Barella wrote in 1900: 'For the development of *alcoolisme*, one does not necessarily need to resort to distilled drinks. So-called hygienic drinks, fermented drinks like wine, cider and beer can equally engender it'.[17] But twenty years earlier, Barella had still asserted that 'abuse of Belgian beer does not produce a pathological state that one could call alcoholism' and like most hygienists he combined a conviction of the healing character of alcohol with a strong condemnation of its abuse.[18] *Usi, sed non abusi* ('Use but do not abuse') was the motto of the temperance movement Barella had set up a year earlier.

The medically organized anti-alcohol movement in Belgium owed much to the efforts of a few ardent medical supporters and was very much influenced by what was happening in the French medical world and on the wider European stage.[19] Barella had become physician in service of the Societé Anonyme des Charbonnages de Bascoup et de Mariemont since 1868 in Chapelle-lez-Herlaimont, the town where he would became mayor. In 1895 he became president of the Royal Academie of Medicine. During his life he campaigned in all fields of 'public hygiene'. He successfully lobbied for the legal obligation to declare the presence of contagious diseases, for isolation pavilions in hospitals and for organized disinfection services; he also lobbied for stricter regulation of prostitution.[20]

In 1879, together with his colleagues Louis Martin and Theodore Belval, he set up the Association Belge contre l'Abus des Boissons, was the first national organization of its kind in Belgium born within hygienist circles. As in France, the anti-alcohol movement in Belgium was organized and dominated by medical professionals. The organization, which would later change its name to Ligue Patriotique contre l'Alcoolisme, had 174 initial members of whom seventy-nine were likeminded medical professionals. From the late 1870s onwards articles on alcoholism furthermore started to appear more frequently in the *Bulletin de l'académie de médicine de Belgique*.[21] Like many other aspects pertaining to 'hygiene', drunkenness was considered a personal responsibility of the working-class individual even though it affected the entire social body. The task of the hygienist temperance campaigner was to investigate the possible bad influence of dirt, immorality and excessive drinking on the workers' health and to edify people about these threats.[22] They advocated the merits of moderation and clarified the dangers of intemperance for both mind and body. For the doctors of the Ligue drinking was always a problem of the working-class male, while the Belgian temperance movement remained a relatively small-scale, bourgeois group. Its direct influence on policy making remained limited, certainly when compared with the popular mass following temperance and abstinence movements attracted in Britain, or even in Holland where it had had significant political influence. For the hygienists of La Ligue Patriotique drunkenness was a major problem of the working classes, while temperance remained a relatively small-scale, mostly middle class cause. Even when with the Ligue's support in the last decades of the nineteenth century many small local temperance movements were organised to popularize the hygienic anti-alcoholic canon, temperance remained a relatively small-scale movement in Belgium, certainly when compared with the enormous popular following temperance and abstinence movements attracted in Britain, or even in neighboring Holland.[23] By the end of the nineteenth century, the Ligue patriotique had no more than 3,700 members and all of them were bourgeois.[24]

As elsewhere in Europe, the influence of the *hygiènistes* grew in the last part of the nineteenth century as Pasteur's bacteriological revolution and changing perceptions about the importance of the social versus the individual resulted in new discourses on 'contagion'.[25] In 1884, Barella, among others, launched a specialist publication on hygiene in all its aspects: *Le Mouvement hygiénique*. Drunkenness was located at the centre of discourses on contagion, closely intertwined with other diseases like cholera and tuberculosis that were equally thought to be conceived amidst the poverty and squalor of the slums of the city proletariat and in their public houses and that seemed to infect the whole of society.[26] Contemplating the devastating cholera epidemic of 1866, Dr De Mayer remembered twenty years later that in his town of Boom, near Antwerp, the epidemic had made most of his casualties among the poorer classes who were as a rule inveterate drinkers. The disease had only killed two bourgeois and one of them, he recalled, had been a drunkard and the other one had just returned from a local fair, where he had drunk a few glasses too many.[27] For Dr De Mayer the epidemic was caused by the drinking of too much alcohol, which weakens the body and makes it more susceptible for disease, not by unsanitary living conditions.

In 1898, Hippolyte Barella with Alfred Bienfait set up a new temperance movement aimed specifically at medical professionals: the Societé Médicale Belge de Tempérance, whose quarterly bulletin appeared as a supplement with *Le Mouvement hygiénique*. The Sociëté, a small professional organization with only 170 effective members by 1902, aimed with its bulletin to inform doctors of the dangers of alcohol-excesses and chronic alcoholism, and it published, for example, informative drawings of vital organs in temperate bodies, compared with the insides of and alcoholic patients.[28] It also tried to dissuade doctors from making too generous use of alcohol in their prescriptions.[29] Their main message was that drunkenness, like other illnesses formed in the lowest regions of society, could rapidly spread, multiply and cause horrible chaos, which eventually would threat the entire social body.[30]

The idea of contagion, at the core of the hygienic canon, was undeniably confirmed with the discovery of germ theory. But this theory of contagion became problematic in the case of alcoholism: no 'alcoholic germ' had been identified under the microscope. This was equally the case with syphilis. While science was making discoveries about the origins of many diseases, the causes of syphilis remained a mystery for the medical profession until the first decades of the twentieth century. Without a germ to explain its spread, their genesis and the root of both problems continued to be explained in terms of inappropriate behaviour.

Both syphilis and alcoholism clearly also affected the upper classes, and so it was untenable to approach syphilis and drunkenness uniquely as a public health problem due to bad environment and lack of education, when there were sober workers and bourgeois drinkers. And so the medical specialists' attention shifted from the environment of the drinker to his mind and body, while ideas of moral responsibility remained central to the debate.

Degeneration and Social Hygiene

In the latter half of the nineteenth century the idea of hygiene would become that of social hygiene as theories of degeneration explained the rise of alcoholism in society. According to Jules Morel, degenerates were people who had deviated from the 'normal type'. Ideas of heredity had always formed part of the thinking about drunkenness and this new medical discourse took on and transformed older narratives. The concept of 'degeneration' was already in 1850 used by a Belgian doctor P. J. A. Vandeven, to explain 'the propagation of the morbid causes ... of misery', and it combined aspects of social environment, morality and heredity. Vandeven grouped drunkenness among wide-ranging elements, such as debauchery, child labour, laziness and even nakedness, which would work together to 'drain the life-sources of rich and poor alike'.[31]

The central question in a Lamarckan model of degeneration was whether drinking led to bad heredity or whether a bad constitution caused drinking?[32] With French specialist Paul-Maurice Legrain, Belgian doctors acknowledged how drunkards and their children would thus find themselves in 'a terrible vicious circle' being degenerates themselves because of their drinking, but also creating degenerate children.[33]

The idea of degeneration was fuelled by Christian notions of ideas of good and bad behaviour, instantly recognizable in the discourse of Catholic medical practitioners on drink and its dangers. Honorary physician in the Brussels hospitals and Catholic senator Dr Édouard van den Corput was one of the most influential amongst them. As president of the Commission Médicale de Brabant, he was much involved with public health issues and he campaigned for radical causes such as cremation and alcohol legislation and in 1897 he proposed – without success – a licensing law in the senate.[34] Van den Corput was convinced that the abuse of alcohol had fatal repercussions for the survival of the species. This was because of a law in physiology which he called 'the law of heredity or of atavism'. He explained that this law had only recently been given attention but had in fact always existed. The central belief in Christianity, the idea of original sin, was in fact this same law of nature, he explained. This meant that the arguments that were for centuries used by religion to 'enforce its moral education' could now be efficiently substituted by a positivist explanation.[35]

Original sin became the primal hereditary defect: *la tare originelle* and Darwinism became dogma. It came with its own Final Judgement. As alcoholics were a 'stigmatized' race that was fatally destined to extinction, the problem of alcoholism contained within its own solution: alcoholic drink was 'the selective agent that makes useless beings disappear'.[36]

Historians have identified degeneration as a politicized medical theory with wide repercussions in culture, with its roots in a fear for revolution and a preoccupation with decline of civilization of the hegemonic middle classes who introduced and utilized the concept.[37] Surely, increasingly and most significantly after 1886, ever more concerns were heard about lower-class alcoholics contributing to the degeneration of the Belgian race.[38] After the troubles with the workers, the Commission du Travail that was set up to discuss the condition of the workers also called upon medical witnesses. And some of these witnesses referred to the hereditary aspects of drink. Dr De Mayer for example, a physician in the ceramics industry of Boom near Antwerp, warned the commission about the effects of alcoholism in the offspring. In this regard, he believed, alcoholism was indeed a serious curse for society. Taking the intemperance of the Belgian workers in account, it was no wonder he said, that there were numerous people suffering from physical and intellectual illnesses such as epilepsy and hydrophaly and so many who were unsuitable for any education.[39]

Also army doctors in the last decades of the nineteenth century were worried about the health of the nation as the fitness among Belgian soldiers seemed to have remarkably weakened because of the effects of alcohol among the lower classes. [40]

By the end of the century new emerging theories of hereditary transmission spurred supporters of the Lamarckian theory to defend themselves and to explain how the passing of acquired characteristics in effect worked.[41] The theory of germ cells they proposed fitted the discourse of the hygienists very well. Finally, the alcoholic germ that would account for the contagious aspect of the plague of alcoholism was identified. It was to be found within the individual and could be 'turned on' by the environment. As with the tuberculosis germ, there was no cure, but prophylactic measures could be put in place to combat its spread. For Hippolyte Barella, a good education for example could possibly avoid the 'hatching of the hereditary germs'. He suggested resourceful 'measures of social hygiene':

> to educate the abandoned and remove them from the atmosphere of vice; to take care of the unfortunate children of criminals, drunkards, thieves, vagabonds and prostitutes; to move workers away from their horrible shacks ... etc.[42]

In 1881, the Belgian Royal Academy of Medicine organized an essay-writing contest to answer the following question: 'What are the effects of alcoholism on material and physical matters of the individual, as well as on his offspring?'[43]

The winner of the competition was the alienist Francois Lentz who subsequently published a bulky volume on the topic in which he concluded that madness was one of the main results of alcohol abuse. After many elaborate chapters, he concluded that 'a certain vagueness [*obscurité*] still reigned over the nature and the manifestations of this transmission of which it is not always easy to isolate the different factors'.[44] Ideas of alcoholic heredity and degeneration were as flexible and broad as drunkenness itself. What was clear was that through degeneration the drunkard had become a deviant who could infect the whole of society and who needed to be cared for by specialists.

10 ALIENISTS

Deviance was the area of expertise in the new discipline of psychiatry. Madness and drinking had always been linked in several ways: a state of drunkenness could be considered a temporary state of insanity; a brief loss of reason. Classically trained doctors would be familiar with Seneca's dictum that 'drunkenness is nothing but a state of self-induced insanity'.[1] Specialists and lay people agreed that heavy drinking was undeniably a cause of mental instability.[2] Dr Eduard Van Coillie estimated that 30 to 40 per cent of the patients who had passed through the *asile-dépot* of the St-Jean hospital where he worked in Brussels before 1897 had been alcoholics turned insane through drinking.[3] Mad-doctors could not explain the precise connection between alcoholism and mental disease, or how the two functioned together. They reasoned that as drunkenness annihilated reason, prolonged drinking would affect the nerves and the brain in a permanent and irreversible way, so excessive drinking could cause madness. But excessive drinking was equally constructed as the result of madness: the unexplainable obsessive craving for the substance seemed akin to mania. And finally, drunkenness was, like madness, a very difficult disease to cure and institutionalization often seemed the only solution.[4] All specialists agreed that there were various types of drunkards suffering from different forms of drunkenness and some of them, but not all, were to be fitted into the new nosologies of mental disease that were being compiled in the mid-nineteenth century.

In his classification of mental disease of 1852 alienist Jospeh Guislain identified different forms of drunkenness as a form of mania. Guislain is often referred to as the 'Pinel of the North', for humanizing and professionalizing the care of the insane and he was the founder of Belgium's first public asylum in Ghent. Elaborating on the influential theories of French alienist Jean Etienne Esquirol who had categorized alcoholics as 'monomanics', for Guillain 'an unremitting need to swallow fermented liquors or spirits' became *manie ébrieuse*. By making alcoholism a disease, Jan Goldstein argued, Esquirol had – controversially– eradicated the drinker's moral responsibility.[5] Therefore, it was important to carefully separate out different possible forms of alcoholic madness: *manie crapuleuse* was clearly different from 'dipsomania', and even more different from 'oinmania': an unexplainable urge to drink wine. Also, comparable symptoms were not always to be interpreted similarly. *Delirium tremems* for example, could, in Guislain's opinion, be considered no more than an acute syndrome, but on the other hand 'in many circumstances it was to be treated as a mental disease [*il appartient aux phrénopathies*]'. Guislain did not offer objective markers on which to base his separation of the different categories, but ideas of what was considered appropriate behaviour for a particular person in a given social context were central to his classification. In 1852, however, Guislain remained unworried about the actual situation in Belgium, where compared to other countries few sufferers of mental disease as victims of alcoholism were to be found, 'in spite of the extreme cheapness of gin'. He himself did not have much experience with the problem of madness caused by drunkenness. In 1849 he had only seen eight patients that needed treatment for madness as a result of immoderate alcohol drinking and in the years before that there had not been many at all.[6]

Things changed in the latter quarter of the nineteenth century, when it was felt everywhere in Europe that mental illness was dramatically increasing.[7] The ostensibly incontrollable growth of the asylum population was generally blamed on the rise of alcoholism and syphilis.[8] The official registration of statistics in Belgium, the *Annuare statistique du royaume* of 1898 stated that there had been an escalation in alcohol consumption since 1850 and a parallel increase in madness, whereby the latter was immediately identified as the 'deplorable result' of the former.[9] Significantly, the doctors who would specialize in the treatment of mental patients had organized themselves for the first time in 1869 in the Société Phréniatique, an organization that would change its name to Société de Médecine Mentale de Belgique in 1873. This name-change reflected the specialization's ambition to take up a central role in the field of medicine.[10] In 1893, a disquieting report of the committee of assistant inspectors of *asiles* stated that the number of people in Belgian asylums had doubled over the last ten years and that 6 per cent of the total admissions were for 'alcoholic madness' (*folie alcoolique*).[11] Many other dramatic statistics that indicated increases on both fronts were presented in the last quarter of the century. Numbers never really added up, but they do give evidence of the moral panic felt by those compiling them. The most dramatic records came from those offering the most drastic solutions. For example, penal justice expert Adolphe Prins, who argued for an overhaul of the justice system by rethinking the concept of responsibility through the concept of *défense sociale*, claimed that Belgian asylum population grew in the period between 1881 and 1901 by 88 per cent and that the number of those interned because of alcoholism had increased by 227 per cent.[12] By the end of the century prominent psychiatrists enlisted their expertise in the campaign against alcohol abuse. Renowned Professor Xavier Francotte from the University of Liège for example or August Mahaim, the eminent student of Auguste Forel, both wrote propaganda brochures to spread the message that alcoholism was linked to madness in dangerous and dramatic ways.[13]

The Asylums in Ghent

Research in the patient registers covering the entire period 1851–1914 of two asylums for men in Ghent, the public Hospice Guislain and the private Maison de Santé le Strop, shows at once that drunkenness was in both institutions always a prominent concern.[14] The registers also confirm an increase in the incarceration of the mad in general and those suffering from problems related to alcohol specifically over the course of the nineteenth century.[15] The presence of drinkers in the nineteenth-century psychiatric hospital has been studied for France.[16] Canadian historian Patricia Prestwich thoroughly researched the population of different Parisian institutions based on the records of the admission office. She concluded that the relationship between psychiatry and alcoholism was at all times ambivalent. In work she did specifically on the female alcoholic population of the Parisian hospitals she reflected upon the gendering of drunkenness and the complex links between the medical specialists, the patients and their families.[17]

The Hospice Guislain in Ghent was inspired by the enlightened ideas of its founder and although the day to day care was always taken up by the members of the religious order of the Brothers of Charity, both asylums remained after Guislain's death in 1860 under the auspices of prominent Belgian alienists. Guislain was succeeded by his deputy and student Benjamin Ingels, co-founder of the Société de Médicine Mentale de Belgique.[18] His successor as medical director in the hospital in 1886 was Jules Morel, an equally important figure in Belgian psychiatry: together with Auguste Vermeulen, superintendent in the Maison de Santé le Strop in Ghent and François Lentz he was charged with inspecting the Belgian mental institutions for the minister of justice. Like so many others working in this field in the 1880s and 1890s in Belgium, Morel was interested in the relationship between degeneration, crime and alcoholism, as demonstrated by his attendance of the 'Congress of Criminal Anthropology' in Brussels in 1892 and his publications of works on recidivist criminals and specifically on alcoholism.[19] Morel stayed on in the Hospice Guislain as director until 1896 when he left to take up an appointment as medical superintendent of the public asylum in Mons. He was succeeded by Dr De Moor, about whom very little is known.[20]

In 1843 the Maison de Santé le Strop was opened in the green outskirts of the city. It was a luxury institution for twenty-five patients from the upper classes of society.[21] Le Strop was considered the most modern private hospital in Belgium and it received patients from all over the country. It was run by Guislain's student Auguste Vermeulen together with the Brothers. Vermeulen became the president of the Société de Médicine Mentale de Belgique and he combined his position in the Maison de Santé in Ghent with the job of medical superintendent in the asylum for alienated women in Ghent run by the 'Sisters of Charity'. He was, as mentioned above, with Lentz and Morel, in charge of inspection of Belgian's three public asylums. Vermeulen stayed on as superintendent of le Strop his entire life and it was only in 1896 that he was followed up by Dr. T. Maere.[22]

These medical superintendents were responsible for the admission of patients based on an assessment of their symptoms during an initial consultation. The admissions where alcohol played a part in the assessment of the patient's problem can be divided up into two groups. Firstly there were those where excessive drinking was seen as the cause or a contributory factor in a mental disorder. While it was thought to be a cause of madness in only 8 per cent of the entries in the private hospital, alcohol was referred to as a contributing factor in 18 per cent of the registrations in the public asylum Hospice Guislain. Among patients of the public Guislain asylum excessive drinking was generally identified as a contributing factor for other mental health problems, while they were also more frequently sent away as not belonging in the asylum. Poverty was often seen as the crux in the relation between drunkenness and madness. Dr Peeters, the director of the *colonie des aliénés* in Gheel where the insane were boarded among the farmers, declared that all those sent to him from the nearby beggars' colonies were victims of strong liquor.[23]

The patients from the poorer echelons of society in the asylum Hospice Guislain were often recorded as leading 'irregular lives'. Time after time the answer to the question 'do you indulge in excessive drinking?' had to be a straightforward 'yes', as numerous working-class individuals had regular encounters with drunkenness, especially at the weekend. In many cases where drinking was recorded as important in the aetiology of their disease, the patients were old and suffered from mental problems related to their age. They had become unmanageable but had nowhere to go. Often their complaints would be associated with histories of heavy drinking, as in the case of a seventy-three-year-old factory labourer who suffered from 'senile dementia' and whereby 'not a single Sunday had passed over the last few years without alcoholic excess'.[24]

But it is the other, smaller group of patients that are of most interest for the cultural and social understanding of drunkenness and psychiatry: those patients who were admitted to the hospitals specifically because of their excessive drinking habits.

About 15 per cent of patients in the Ghent asylums were diagnosed with some form of alcoholism.[25] Excessive drinking by itself was much more frequently considered a form of madness and a reason for a prolonged stay in the asylum among patients from the upper classes than it was among the poor patients. But also, of course, upper-class patients were generally given much more attention from doctors and a much more elaborate diagnosis.[26]

Madness, Drink and Degeneration

Joseph Guislain had already in 1852 illustrated that alcoholism could be a hereditary cause for madness with an example of a whole generation of lunatics, all brothers and sisters and children of a mother who consumed strong liquors 'in quantities so considerable that during a whole series of years she was to be found in a state of complete drunkenness'. This woman had never been mentally ill, however, and neither was her husband nor any other member of the family. Therefore her entire *descendance* of *aliénés* had to be necessarily the result of her drinking.[27]

In the Maison de Santé le Strop only about twenty patients talked about the medical background of their family. In contrast to what can be read in the registers of the Hospice Guislain, in only four cases was it revealed that the father was abusing alcohol and there was only one mention of maternal negative influence: a mother who used to be 'nervous'. In general, instead of exactly defining who suffered what, as in the lower-class asylum notes, the observations of the richer patients were much more broad and vague. Patients would not easily give away specific cases of alcoholism or madness in their immediate family because of fears of damaging the family's reputation. Doctors in their turn would also be more inclined to protect the 'privacy' of the family history in the registers, which were after all official judicial documents.

The Belgian alienists widely engaged with the ideas of *alcoolo-dégénérescence* of their French colleagues Benedict Morel and Valentin Magnan, and they eagerly participated in the various discussions these ideas provoked.[28] The Brussels' medical periodical the *Santé* wrote triumphantly in 1857, the year of publication of Morel's influential work on degeneration: 'it is beyond doubt now that the children coming forth from drunken parents can be born violent, as murderers, debauched etc. just like they can be born idiots, predisposed to madness and suicide'.[29]

With an increased concern over the future of the entire Belgian race came an emphasis on 'abnormality' in children and how this was related to drinking habits of the parents. After 1900 several specialists published alarming results of their research into this topic. Auguste Ley, for example, researched the background of pupils in a recently organized special school for blind, deaf, dumb and mentally retarded children in 1912 and found what he was looking for: many alcoholic fathers, mothers and grandfathers.[30] And it was not physical suffering only that the hereditary burden of alcoholism inflicted on these children: young children of drunkards were often cruel, unkind, enjoyed the suffering of others and liked to torture animals, the specialists explained. When these children grew up they would be lazy and lack discipline, they would easily devote themselves in their turn to drink and debauchery and land up in beggars' colonies, prisons and lunatic asylums.[31] In this last possible outcome of parental drinking, an example of *dégénérescence morale*, alcoholism was not directly passed on to the next generation, instead what was passed on was a lack of willpower and a failing character, which in its turn would again lead to unbridled drinking.

The theory of inheritance of acquired characteristics vindicated the prevalence of moral overtones in a biological theory on habitual drunkenness as it implied that individual action had consequences for future generations. Hippolyte Barella illustrated this generational process of degeneration into 'abnormality' among alcoholic workers with photographic evidence, in a lecture given to the Académie Royale de Médicine on the role of alcohol as a predisposing cause of both mental retardation and moral failure.

He showed his audience portraits of the third and the fourth generations of alcoholic degenerates whom he had encountered in his practice among the miners in the Borinage. (see Figure 10.1) Inspired by theories of criminal anthropology, he linked their physiognomy to their inborn defects: he analysed the external characteristics of their faces and concluded that their 'elongated, asymmetric faces', 'deep eyebrow-folds' or 'prolonged chins' indicated a condition of abnormality. Their drunken degeneracy had become part of their biology and was etched undeniably on their faces.

Although this series of photographs was presented to illustrate scientifically a particular diseased physiognomy it did of course much more: the pictures shocked and elicited pity. It was especially the last picture of the small child alone that solicited strong emotions from viewers. A vulnerable child, almost seven years old in a sailor's suit looks cheekily in the camera. But he is not an innocent child; the capture tells us we are looking at a creature that is in fact 'rotten' both biologically, indicated by his dental caries we learn about and morally – even worse, sexually – in his constant obsession with masturbation. He is also mentally retarded and suffers from tics and epileptic attacks. He could be Julken from Buysse's *De biezenstekker*. His picture is isolated from the other pictures of the men of his family that are all called 'third generation'. The child, its portrait set aside in a separate frame, belongs to the fourth and last generation of this lineage: he was the final outcome of his parents' diseases and vices and he represented the end of the line where his race died out.

In Ghent, although heredity appeared very important in the diagnosis-based questions in the register, the patients themselves mentioned social problems as the beginning of their struggle with drink. Poverty was frequently mentioned, love problems and financial problems were other difficulties mentioned that would have led people to find consolation in drink.[32] These were sometimes understood in terms of 'moral heredity', especially when they could be explained in terms of moral failure. Psychiatrists called 'moral heredity' the condition whereby a 'deprived taste has developed under the influence of bad examples'.[33] In other words, environmental causes were accounted for in biological language.

Figure 10.1: Series of photographs of family of degenerated drunks, *Bulletin de l'académie royale de médicine*, 2 (1897), p. 964 © Royal Library of Belgium, Brussels.

And so it was for example under the heading 'heredity' that the doctor mentioned that an alcoholic patient was the son of *une prostituée clandestine*.[34]

Degeneration seemed to be everywhere in Belgium in those last decades of the century, in literature and broader culture and in almost all medical writings. The pre-printed registers in Ghent changed layout a few times over the period to include ever more questions about hereditary *tares*, *signes*, *marques* or *stigmates* of degeneration and about predisposing factors. But in spite of this, in daily practice, alcoholic degeneration on the whole rarely formed part of a diagnosis. Dr De Moor's enthusiastic first diagnosis of degeneration, of a weaver admitted to the Hospice Guislain for epilepsy, was only in 1895. In his case notes he wrote excitedly, as if he had discovered a new species: 'Alcoholic excess, son of a drunken father. It is very probable that we find ourselves before a congenital degenerate'.[35] And after this first degenerate, only nine other patients in the public asylum were pinpointed as degenerates. Prestwich came to the same conclusion for the Paris asylum. 'Although alcoholism was considered to be both a symptom and a cause of hereditary degeneracy', she wrote, 'in only 43 cases of over 1200 in this study were alcoholic patients labelled as "degenerate"'.[36]

As was the case with drunkenness and mental disease more generally, it was often not clear why in practice one patient was diagnosed as degenerate and another not. It has been argued that *dégénérescence* was a working-class condition or was generally linked to poverty and assigned to the working masses.[37] But in Ghent the doctors identified cases of degeneration in both asylums and unexpectedly there were relatively many more patients diagnosed as degenerate among the wealthy in le Strop than among the much larger, poor population of the public Guislain asylum.[38]

In Ghent 'degeneration' was reverted to when there was a need for a strong moral judgement in the clinical diagnosis. Degeneration was added to cases where the drinking was combined with other unacceptable social and moral behaviours. The clearest example here is the case of one of two Irish priests, who at arrival was diagnosed simply with *dipsomanie*. When it emerged, however, that he had been involved in sexual acts with young boys, his diagnosis was changed and the priest became a *dégénéré moral* suffering from *alcoolisme*. Initially the register stated that there was 'no information' about his family, but later it was added that he had a brother who had stayed in an asylum, another one who had drowned and an epileptic sister.[39] Information about family heredity was included now to emphasize and reinforce the diagnosis. The morally neutral term dipsomania was replaced by the morally loaded notion of degeneration.[40]

Delirium Tremens

Of all alcoholic mental afflictions, it were mostly the dramatic convulsions and outlandish visions that accompanied what was called 'acute alcoholism' that took hold of people's minds. The notion of alcoholic madness found its way into the public imagination and the medical temperance rhetoric used dramatic representations of alcoholic mania to deter people from drink. Theatrical illustrations in the *Almanach de la tempérence*, edited by the Ligue Patriotique contre l'Alcoolisme, showed for example how the shocked patrons of a pub gathered around the dramatically seizing body of a drunkard who 'after emptying his twentieth glass crashed into a fit of epilepsy',[41] or how a delirious women was tied on a cart on her way to the asylum.[42] As discussed in previous chapters, literature and film used the character of the mad alcoholic to great accomplishment.

Alcoolisme aigu, or 'acute alcoholism', was a very common diagnosis in the public asylum. This diagnose indicated a passing form of drunkenness; extreme drunkenness, but a fit that would be over rapidly after which health would be restored. This diagnosis, simply 'acute alcoholism', was one reserved exclusively for those who were brought into public asylum, for the lower classes. In the upper-class Maison de Santé, however, not one case of 'acute alcoholism' was recorded – mostly because people would have not been brought to the asylum when in such state, although there were more than a few upper-class drunkards brought in by the police after misbehaving in public.

More than one in ten of the alcoholic patients in the Hospice Guislain were diagnosed with drunkenness related to 'delirium', as in, for example, *delire alcoolique*. Mostly the symptoms were described in the patient notes simply as 'délire'. They often involved violent behaviour, as this was for many patients the main reason why they were incarcerated in the first place. Patients shouted and fought back when being forcefully detained. There were a lot of incoherent ideas expressed and the doctors recorded much 'overexitement' (*surexitation*)and much trembling.[43] Many suffering from alcoholic mania were delusional: they believed they were very rich or important for example, but there is no evidence to be found in the casebooks of such colourful hallucinations so powerfully described in both the contemporary medical temperance writings and in literature and film. There were no visionary hallucinations of rats or monkeys or crawling vermin like those referred to in both the medical text and in the broader cultural understanding of the phenomenon.[44] Valentin Magnan in France had also linked this type of hallucination to the excessive use of absinthe, but none of the patients in the asylums in Ghent was mentioned as suffering from 'absinthisme', nor was absinthe mentioned as a tipple of choice by either the lower or the upper-class lodgers. Or perhaps this behaviour was so common that the alienists did not feel the need to make a note of it when describing patients' symptoms?

French and English doctors had described delirium tremens already in the beginning of the nineteenth century and Joseph Guislain had prominently elaborated on it in a Belgian context in 1850.[45] And Magnan's interpretation of alcoholic mania as delirium tremens in the 1870s was prominent in the Belgian understanding of the phenomenon. When discussed in this context, delirium tremens became a specific medical condition, a separate and identifiable mental affliction, brought on by the poison alcohol.[46] There was no suggestion in the contemporary medical text or in the case notes of a link between withdrawal and delirium, although interestingly patients were sometimes offered alcoholic drinks to prevent further attacks. What is striking when exploring the different forms of alcoholic madness in the asylum notes, is that in the lower-class asylum only two patients were diagnosed with the 'official', psychiatric term for drunken delirium: *delirium tremens*. But while this condition was rare in the public Hospice Guislain, it became the diagnosis of choice for almost one in five patients who entered the private Maison de Santé le Strop with an alcohol-related problem.

With the concept of 'delirium tremens', upper-class heavy drinking was represented as a disease, different from lower-class 'acute alcoholism'. Imbedded in one's particular biological constitution it became a condition that implied that the sufferer was no longer responsible. Unlike the drunkard who had brought his symptoms upon himself, for the sufferer of *delirium tremens* it was something that had gotten out of hand, beyond his control. As previously noted, Guislain himself had explained how delirium tremens could be considered no more than an acute syndrome, but that 'in many circumstances it was to be treated as a mental disease'.[47] Thus, when upper-class drunkards were brought to the asylum in this acute state of alcoholic madness, they were not simply labelled with 'alcoholism aigu' or 'delire alcoolique' as they would have been in the public asylum. Among the bourgeoisie, the problem was given its scientific Latin name – it became a disease. So while the workers were still responsible for their state – through their excess – the upper-class diagnosis no longer even referred to alcohol or drunkenness. Instead, delirium tremens, with a suitable clinical – scientifically sounding and discreet abbreviation: *d.t.*, became a disease that overcame the sufferer. Vice and moral responsibility were much less involved when the problem was labelled as such.

Dipsomania

The most evident class-related diagnosis, whereby drunkenness became classified as a disease, was that of *dipsomanie*. Guislain had already mentioned 'dipsomania' as an uncontrollable urge for alcoholic drink.[48] In the early versions of the patient registers of the Maison des Hommes Aliénés he diagnosed four patients from as early as 1850 with the affliction. The concept of dipsomania was taken on by Valentin Magnan in France who connected it with heredity and from his

1884 *Leçons cliniques sur la dipsomanie,* immediately published in *Le scalpel,* the Belgian asylum doctors learned that the *dipsomane* was different from the ordinary drunkard in that the former had been already a lunatic before taking to drinking while the latter only had become insane because of drinking.[49] Dipsomania was not even a form of *alcoolisme* but a distinct disease, an actual mental disorder in its own right.[50] For specialists in degeneration it was heredity that distinguished normal from abnormal drunkenness and established the difference between *ivrognerie* and *dipsomanie.* Whereas with the ordinary drunkard the need to drink was a result of his habit and of 'his internal struggles at the mercy of the occasion', the dipsomaniac reached for the bottle as a result of his predisposition. He was, in other words, born with it.[51] When it was accompanied by a craving for other substances such as such as for example chloral, dipsomania was always the diagnosis of choice. Dipsomania delineated forms of drunkenness that were not only incontrollable but also 'abnormal', suffered by people that would normally not ostensibly drink extensively, like women, among which it would be typically found according to Magnan

As with other labels of drunkenness, the term 'dipsomania' was never consistently used; but when it was resorted to, it was always to clearly distinguish the mentally ill 'dipsomaniac' from the 'normal drinker'. Specialists cautioned their colleagues to be particularly meticulous in this diagnosis, because it would be extremely dangerous to confuse 'periodical drinking bouts as a result of social circumstances with "dipsomania"'.[52] The main difference was ultimately based on the accountability for one's actions and the moral responsibility this entailed: 'the dipsomaniac was irresponsible because he is insane, the ordinary drunkard is irresponsible because he is nothing else but wicked [*vicieux*]'.[53] The emphasis both on disease instead of vice and on heredity instead of environment took away the dipsomaniac's responsibility for his or her actions. For criminal anthropologist Raymond de Ryckere, dipsomania was an important form of manic pathological drunkenness, a degenerative mental disease that was specific to women. It consisted of a compulsive need to drink, which would reveal itself mainly during menstruation or pregnancy. Young girls would develop this form of madness, often in puberty and the manifestations of the disease very often disappeared again with the menopause.[54] But de Ryckère urged for watchfulness: very often, he knew, drinking women of higher social classes were wrongly diagnosed as *dipsomanes* by their doctors 'out of politeness [*par politesse*]'.[55] They would not necessary suffer from dipsomania; they would rather be affected by ordinary 'abnormal drunkenness'. Suffering from a disease such as dipsomania would take away responsibility for one's actions, explained legal mind de Ryckere and this was only permissible in certain scenarios. He acknowledged that it remained unclear precisely what would turn abnormal drunkenness into 'dipsomania', but argued that what was clear was the complexity of the diagnosis, and that the expertise of specialists was vital and must be relied upon.

Once more medical professionals appointed themselves as the final arbitrator but all disagreed or failed to explain on which grounds precisely the demarcation between vicious drinking and dipsomania was to be made. Hippolyte Barella admitted that it was indeed difficult to define rigorously limits between drinking prompted by an immoral character and drinking driven by a mental disease. But he was convinced, he wrote cynically, that the workers he saw drinking every Monday certainly did not do so because they suffered from a disease, but rather just because they liked to indulge in drink.[56]

Patricia Prestwich noted how French psychiatrists did not frequently find 'dipsomaniacs' among those admitted for excessive drinking in the Paris public asylums, and that most of them were women.[57] Edward Brown also noted the lack of this particular diagnosis in asylums in the United States of America.[58] Also in the Ghent public asylum it was a rare diagnosis: after Guislain's death in 1860, until 1914 only two further patients in the Hospice Guislain were called 'dipsomaniacs'. However, in the Maison de Santé le Strop, where rich patients were taken care of, 'dipsomania' was the most common diagnosis among alcohol-related problems. 40 per cent of those who were in the Maison de Santé because of trouble with alcohol were diagnosed as such. Therefore in practice the specific diagnosis of dipsomania in the asylums in Ghent was clearly reserved for patients for whom habits of alcohol abuse were much more socially unaccepted: drunkards from the upper classes.

The interpretation that dipsomania was a diagnosis applied to those for whom excessive drinking was extremely inappropriate behaviour can also explain why in Prestwich's research in the public asylum the majority of the cases with *dipsomanie* were women. Among the Ghent male asylum population, 'dipsomania' referred to those whose habitual drunkenness was out of control and not reconcilable with the ideas of decency and propriety that to their social class demanded. When drunkenness manifested itself among the bourgeoisie, it was mostly represented as a disease: rich drunkards belonged to the category of '*névrosiques*, lacking notions of order, among those who were "unbalanced" [*déséquilibré*]'.[59]

Dipsomanie was a convenient medical term to use instead of the harsh diagnoses that were *alcoolisme* and *ivrognerie*, immediately associated with the inferior working classes.

A good example of an upper-class dipsomaniac is the case of Jean D, a violent man from a very well established family, who was brought to the Ghent Maison de Santé in 1905. He was not only diagnosed as a dipsomaniac but also as degenerate. His drinking was so out of control that on arrival he immediately stole and drunk a bottle of *eau de mélisse de Carmen*, a herbal alcoholic preparation which the Brothers used as a medicine and he also downed seven bottles of beer and one and a half bottles of wine. His illustrious family included a long list of mentally affected and alcoholic members.[60] Moral judgement, however, still clearly coloured this diagnosis and the adding of 'degenerate' to the neutral term of dipsomania confirmed this.

In spite of a growing use of medical terminology to indicate problematic drinking and an increasing acceptance of hereditary causes for madness, medical language most certainly did not exclude moral judgement. Moreover, the treatment proposed to dipsomaniacs called upon the patient's sense of wrong and right. Morality was built into the medical theory of dipsomania: a distinctive feature of a dipsomaniac was that after having given in to the uncontrollable impulses he or she usually felt guilty.[61] In Ghent as late as 1887, drunkards were still treated in the asylums with *moralizations*, a variation of the moral therapy Guislain originally had introduced.[62] Sentiments of guilt and regret were continuously promoted and those of modesty and subservience endorsed.

The social implications contained within a medical theory became ever more evident when considering how the asylum doctors in Ghent interpreted the theory and daily applied it in practice. Confronted with drunkards from specific social backgrounds it was felt to be more 'acceptable' and 'normal' for a farmer or worker to show an inclination for drinking, while it was socially much more problematic – deviant, and thus 'pathological' – for, for example, a proprietor, a pensioned priest or a medical student.[63] Its medical, Latinized language, using terms like *dipsomanie* and *delirium tremens* instead of drunkenness and alcoholic madness, carves out specific meanings for the problem of drunkenness. This was in fact a constant and familiar process in the particular language politics of bilingual Belgium. When deciding on the exact nature of the drinking habits of Flemish lower-class patients, bourgeois doctors were speaking and writing in French. Here as always in Belgian history, language, class and power were closely connected, resulting in complex negotiated exchanges. An uneven relationship was played out in the encounter between patient and doctor who always mediated, translated and transformed the patient's experiences through the case notes.

General Paralysis

Not only mania, but also dementia was identified as a mental disorder that could be caused by drunkenness. In the late nineteenth century doctors were especially worried about the large number of people in asylums suffering from 'general paralysis of the insane'. General paralysis was a mysterious affliction until it became after 1913 definitively identified as the tertiary stage of syphilis.[64] Guislain himself in 1852 referred to *dementia paralytica* as caused by alcoholism.[65] And in 1861, German psychiatrist Griesinger wrote: 'drunkenness especially appears to possess much in common with general paralysis'.[66] Later in the decade also Valentin Magnan at St Anne confirmed that general paralysis was caused by alcoholism.[67] Indeed several neurological indicators of general paralysis, like trembling of the tongue, shaking of the hands and difficulties in talking were also to be found in chronic alcoholics.[68] Behaviours that were described in the Ghent asylum records as indicators of long-term drinking could very well have been linked to syphilis: hallucinations, ideas of persecution, ideas of grandeur.

As Liesbet Nys has shown, in Belgium the topic of syphilis was always directly related to the problem of drunkenness, especially in the later years of the nineteenth century.[69] The precise link between general paralysis, syphilis and thus sex would not be established until the first years of the twentieth century and it would take longer for it to become fully understood. Until then alcoholism was mostly offered as its cause and it remained considered for much longer as a main contributory factor. The softening of brains observed in post-mortem rooms was interpreted as being caused by the organ being steeped in alcohol for too long.[70] Dr Bernard Lefebvre from the University of Louvain and honorary physician of the *asiles des aliénés* of that city called general paralysis the 'fatal mindless state [*abrutisemment*] in which all alcoholic diseases converge'.[71] The patient registers of Ghent reflect this general consensus in the ongoing discussion about the causes of general paralysis. Of all the hospital notes analysed here, almost one in five of the cases of mental disease whereby alcohol was identified to be responsible for its occurrence were cases of *démence paralytique*, *folie paralytique* or *paralysie alcoolique*. When there was no information on the drinking habits of the paralytic patients, as for example in the case of a day labourer suffering from paralytic dementia in the Hospice Guislain, the superintendent filled in 'probably', where the register asked if the patient abused alcoholic drinks, thus in effect creating a presumed cause derived from the nature of the disease.[72]

The ambiguity between biology and morality, disease and free will in dealing with drunkenness in the asylum was never clearer than in cases of those suffering from *paralysie générale*. As the cause of paralysis drunkenness was accompanied by other excesses, particularly sexual. 'Alcohol and women' were then the 'substances' that were overindulged in, leading to disease. In one case the disease itself was called 'passion in Baccho et in Venere'.[73] Also the idea of *surmenage* (overwork) was brought up as a cause of general paralysis, which had been understood as physical or mental exhaustion due to stress.[74] Perhaps it can also euphemistically indicate another type of over-indulgence. It certainly indicates an overall failing not only of physical strength but also moral strength and willpower. The neurological terminology used when making that most objective and scientific of all observations, when the disease was after death finally confirmed in organic brain lesions, was 'softening of the brain' (*ramollissement cérebrale*).

This equally indicates softening and weakening of willpower and morality which were thought to have their seat in in this all-important organ.

When ascribing venereal excess and intemperance as causes for terrible diseases such as general paralysis, the disease was explained in moral terms: the symptoms and the suffering were interpreted as a punishment of sin, of undesirable social behaviour. Sexual promiscuity was more than once implicated in a diagnoses of degeneration in the registers, showing how the 'alcoholic taint has left its traces'.[75]

The confusion that led to heated debates in the medical community towards the end of the century about the causes of dementia paralytica or general paralysis – the question if excess in general and more specifically chronic alcoholism was enough to account for the condition – was reflected in the registers. As the syphilitic origins of the disease were slowly becoming evident in Europe's research labs, the diagnoses of general paralysis resulting from alcoholism became occasionally accompanied with a tentative 'S' in the registers, sometimes alongside a question mark. Syphilis also became identified as a cause for *paralysie genérale* and in the pre-printed registers it acquired together with alcoholism a place under 'harmful influences'.

Symbolically, sexual excess and abuse of alcohol were most certainly linked to the disease of general paralysis or *démence paralytique*, with or without a correctly identified causal micro-organism. Its association with excess and depravity, with drink, sex and physical and mental fatigue and laziness, made it another medical diagnosis that was set within the realm of morality, of misbehaviour that was internalized and that through disease now faced its inescapable punishment. An inability to reign in one's comportment and a lack of self-control would lead to dramatic final destruction, to annihilation of that which makes one human: our mental capabilities.

The study of the representation of *paralysie générale* and its perceived and consequently contested connection with excessive drinking deserves much more elaborate study. Here, within the analysis of the social construction of medical representations of alcoholism, it provides a good example of the prevalence of preconceived ideas on decency and appropriate behaviour within the medical diagnoses of drunkenness.

11 CRIMINAL ANTHROPOLOGISTS

Contemporary themes of morality and responsibility were linked to heredity and degeneration in the explanation of drunkenness by a new group of specialists who called themselves criminal anthropologists. The Italian psychiatrist Cesare Lombroso had introduced in the 1870s this new science but it was the doctrine as exposed by Alexandre Lacassagne's French school that was enthusiastically adopted among the progressive liberal circles of the Free University of Brussels in the final two decades of the nineteenth century and the beginning of the twentieth century.[1]

Criminal anthropology combined forces of both legal and medical specialisms and drew on biological models and ideas of evolution to scientifically research the genesis of and possible solutions for deviations of normal behaviour, like excessive drinking.

In 1891 Minister of Justice Jules Lejeune introduced research units on mental medicine in Belgian prisons as part of his thorough reorganization of the prison system, inspired by his preoccupation with 'social defence'. Ernest Masoin, professor at the medical faculty of the University of Louvain, led a team examining the mental constitution of violent criminals in the central prison of the same city. In 1896, the same year in which Jules Dallemagne classified a passion for drink among the 'biological and sociological stigmata of criminality',[2] Masoin published the results of his research: a set of statistics in which he compared prisoners who were in a state of drunkenness or who were 'habitual drunkards', with the level of the violence of their crime. There was a clear link between the two. For the worst criminals, 'the proportion was enormous': 41 per cent had been drunk when committing the crime and no less than 60 per cent were habitual drunkards.[3] Masoin could do no else than conclude that 'above all alcohol was to blame for the genesis of the gravest offences'.[4] The statistics were overpowering and would convince the remaining sceptics in the Belgian medical and judicial establishment that:

> In every alcoholic hides a possible or even a probable murderer, he is a dangerous being heading towards crime. His progeny is not less dangerous [*redoubtable*]; or his taints lead him to crime as well, or else he will be incapable to make a living and will hence become a burden on society.[5]

Since 1850 drunkards that were a danger to others could already be forcefully detained in an asylum.[6] The principle for admission for both asylums in Ghent was the same for all: a demand for confinement accompanied by a medical certificate was enough to have a patient legally committed. The drunkard could be brought in by the police or by a concerned family member as long as a medical certificate was attached to the demand for detainment. Some worried that individuals could be wrongfully convicted at the request of someone wanting to get rid of a troublesome relative. In Britain such fears had led to fierce debates and as a result the law there prevented the incarceration of drunkards against their will.[7] In the Belgian asylums the superintendent had the final responsibility for the correctness of the claim and he had to make sure no innocent men or women would be locked up in his asylum by wicked or profit-seeking family members.[8]

To justify their decision to have a patient formally incarcerated the physicians in Ghent referred in their notes repeatedly to the *Circulaire Ministrielle*, the ministerial document that gave them such powers.[9] Many alcoholic patients of lunatic asylums did protest against their incarceration and there was the possibility to file a complaint with the magistrate against their confinement, but as many among them, especially in public asylums, were illiterate and badly informed, this protection of liberty seemed to exist for most cases only on paper. Nevertheless there were a few examples of men who were arrested for public drunkenness and transferred to the asylum by the police that were declared *non-aliéné* after having written a letter of complaint to the magistrate. Some patients in the upper-class asylum fought long epistolary battles to be released. Their campaigns were sometimes successful, but mostly fruitless. But the lunacy law only allowed for the institutionalization of drunkards who were considered dangerous; as soon as the drunken was fit, or the madness had subsided, they were to be freed. Many argued that drunkards needed their own specialized institutions.[10] In the name of 'social hygiene', the affected individual was to be cut off from the rest of society, so he could do no harm.[11] In neighbouring countries, special 'inebriate asylums' had been created in the second part of the nineteenth century. In Britain, the Habitual Drunkards Act of 1870 had provided government licences for specialist asylum care. Dedicated private institutions in America and all over Europe received wealthy alcoholics voluntarily in order to kick the habit, and some European governments had also introduced public reformatories where criminal drunkards could be forcefully locked up.[12] In Britain in 1898 a new Inebriates Acts had become law, which granted the state powers to provide asylums in which habitual drunkards could be forcibly detained.[13]

In 1892 Dr Alfred de Vaucleroy, the secretary of the Ligue Patriotique contre l'Alcoolisme, complained that in Belgium 'not one establishment so far exists: the alcoholic, who wants to heal himself, can only choose between the hospital and the lunatic asylum'.[14] This was certainly so for poor alcoholics, but wealthier drinkers who wanted to dry out had a few more options available. Alcoholic members of respectable families were sometimes 'pensioned off' or went on their own initiative to health resorts such as the hydropatic Kneipp-sanatorium in Bonsecours, whose proprietor Dr Gustave Delaunois presented himself as a specialist on drunkenness.[15] The waters from the pilgrimage town of Bonsecours were believed to have both medicinal and religious powers. Therapeutics and religion were equally linked when wealthy drunkards were admitted into convents of religious orders, for a 'retreat' to get better. For instance, the Carthusian monks in Ghent would receive alcoholics in their monastery, where they were believed to be completely sheltered from worldly temptations.[16] Well-off alcoholics would also be admitted, forcibly or voluntarily, into private lunatic asylums.

However, in these private institutions, in the asylums and the *maisons de santés*, no patient who behaved adequately could be forcibly detained. The law allowed the doctors to retain people only as long as they would pose a danger so society or him or herself. But the 'sobering up' of alcoholic lunatics did not mean that they were healed.[17] In Ghent, dipsomaniacs and other drunkards were not often declared 'cured' on leaving and their prognostic was presented in legal language: 'doubtful with regards to recidivism'.[18] But even so they had to be sent home if they wanted to and many of them were to revisit the asylum over and again. The same problem of reoffending that was worrying lawmakers and criminologists in relation to crime in general worried those discussing the topic of drunkenness. As all drunkards could be potential criminals, criminologists, hygienists and alienists argued that they were to be controlled and constrained in prison-like provisions.

The topic of special inebriate asylums was much debated after 1890 when Jules Lejeune had included alcoholics among the category of dangerous lunatics in his social legislation in the name of 'défense social'.[19] It was prominently raised at an international anti-alcoholic congress held in Belgium in 1897, where the Swiss Professor Auguste Forel spoke positively from his experience at his drinkers' health clinic (*Trinkerheilstätte*) in Ellikon-an-der-Thur, which he had set up in 1888 together with Eugene Bleuler, and where drunkards were treated by means of complete abstinence. In the discussion that followed the contributors, among whom Hyppolyte Barella argued for the introduction of 'preventative penalties' in the Belgian legislation.[20] Some brought up issues of personal liberty while others questioned whether enough drinkers would be cured to justify the public costs of special asylums.[21] Forel argued that it 'was better to prevent than to cure' and that it was completely in the public interest that 'those harmful and incurable beings' should be incarcerated.[22] According to the ideas of hereditary degeneration, the race of alcoholics would of course eventually die out, so their incarceration in special homes would not only protect society from their criminal nature, but prevent them from procreating and thus spreading their degenerate 'taints'. The Belgian specialists eagerly took on Forel's liberal and eugenic opinions on the connection between alcohol and mental illness.[23] In this utilitarian eugenic argument, the general good for society would justify, in theory, the locking up of degenerated alcoholics.[24]

However, in practice, dealing with so many different types of drunkenness, one of the major problems in the discussion about incarceration was how one was to determine who precisely had to be locked up, why and for how long. This question was not new: psychiatrists dealing with alcoholic lunatics in the asylums had to think about this issue daily. Joseph Guislain had already in the mid-nineteenth century asked his students in relationship with delirium tremens: 'Can we lock up any man who is affected by maniacal over-excitement as a result of immoderate use of drink?'[25] His own answer was that it depended on the ways in which the patient presented himself and the opinion the psychiatrists could form about the individual's mental and physical state. If experience had proven that it was impossible to 'correct the vicious habits' of the patient, nothing would be more beneficial than to confide him into 'strange hands' and to submit him to the regime of a 'sanitary establishment'.[26] The alienist was in charge of deciding who was fit for the asylum and who should not be admitted based on an assessment of individual behaviour.

Half a century later the physician together with the magistrage had become the approved authority on deciding which drunkards were to be incarcerated. For Francois Lentz it was only the drunkards who were affected with a real somatic disease of the brain that ought to be locked up in institutions. He did not clarify how he would determine this group, but he was interested in the possibilities alcoholic asylums would offer doctors to study the specific pathology of the disease.[27] Lacking so far a biological marker to separate diseased from immoral drunkards, Barella found it self-evident that the entire responsibility to decide lay with the medical profession, who were 'generally men of a proven honesty'. He continued: 'one cannot have an absolute rule, it depends from case to case, but it is important that the *médécin aliéniste* should not be forced to act against science and against his own conscience'. With science he meant criminal anthropology and the laws of degeneration of the race. Based on the extent of the 'dangerousness' of the patient, the doctor should make his assessment and thereby be 'left completely free to decide and not restrained by the letter of rules and regulations'.[28] The doctor had become judge and his personal high moral standards had to guarantee the correct medical and moral treatment of drunkards as potential patients, lunatics or criminals.

Female Drunkenness

One form of drunkenness that was always to be considered unacceptable and therefore pathological was excess committed by bourgeois women. Dr Auguste Janssen wrote: 'Nothing is more revolting than a drunk women. If one can still feel a slight respect for a man who drinks, a woman loses in such circumstances every right of respect and sympathy'.[29] However, female drinking was seldom mentioned in contemporary writings, not even in the medical temperance press and when it was, it almost always concerned working-class women. Experts on the subject were convinced that 'alcoholism was less frequent among women than it is among men and among women, only those belonging to the inferior classes have an inclination towards drinking'.[30]

But initial research into the very scant evidence that remains for both female asylums in Ghent shows that in the 1850s there were inebriate ladies finding refuge behind the walls of the asylum. In fact, habitual drunkenness was a greater problem for the 'pensionnaires' who paid for their stay than for those who were cared for by public expenditure, where it was more prominently recorded as a contributing factor for madness.[31]

In 1899, in *L'Alcoholisme féminin*, Raymond De Ryckère shockingly argued that alcoholism among middle and upper-class women was on the rise. The subject was considered such a scandalous condition, a taboo subject, that it was thought fit for a monograph in the series *Bibliothèque de Criminologie* edited by the leader of the French school of criminal anthropology, Alexandre Lacassagne. *L'Alcoolisme féminin* was the twentieth book in the series, which further included titles on for example, 'deviant' sexuality, delinquent children and sadistic sex-crimes. De Ryckère was particularly interested in pathological crime among women.[32] He had started his career as public prosecutor in Antwerp and then had made a splendid legal career in the tribunals of Brussels. Initially specializing in maritime law, he grew to be gripped by legal medicine and criminal anthropology and became a freelance collaborator to Lacassagne's periodical, the *Archives d'anthropologie criminelle, de criminologie et de psychologie normale et pathologique*, to which he contributed news from the Belgian criminal anthropological front.[33] Raymond De Ryckère had read and quoted French and British essays on the subject of female drinking and was the only Belgian author who pondered more extensively about drinking bourgeoises. Modern middle-class ladies had lost that unconscious sensation, De Ryckère observed, which working-class women had never possessed in the first place: that in poisoning themselves they poisoned at the same time the children that had to be born from them.[34] They used to refrain from drinking out of a knowledge of their role in society as safeguards of morals and educators of children, but also as guardians of the race.[35] De Ryckère was convinced that female drinking led to the degeneration of the race, which had up until this point always been 'guarded by the feminine sex'.[36]

Inspired by the general theories on drunkenness and madness as for example exposed by Dr Francois Lentz, De Ryckère identified two forms of female drunkenness.[37] First there was 'abnormal drunkenness [*ivresse abnormale*]' – female intemperance could never be 'normal' – and secondly, he described 'pathological drunkenness [*ivresse pathologique*]'. With 'abnormal drunkenness', problem drinking among women came about as a direct result of their excessive alcohol consumption. The reason given as to why women would reach this state was 'to change their conditions': out of boredom. Alcoholism among upper-class ladies was described by De Ryckère as a predicament that often came about as a result of the blandness of their lives. Mostly drinking women would carry with them an enormous sadness and almost all of them, he wrote, 'have lived their tragic and painful novel of their life, that often make real novels fade away'.[38] De Ryckère's description of the drinking lady found its origins and echo in fictional narratives. The way he represented the upper-class alcoholic and her novel-like life bore great resemblance with stories of 'tragic' passionate heroines of the literature of the period. Probably De Ryckère had read *Anna Karenina*, published in 1877, as he quotes Tolstoy further on. Rather than with examples from real life, his portrait of the middle-class inebriate seemed to be associated with the figure of the divorced, morally collapsed and opium addicted Anna, irreversibly heading towards dramatic self-destruction.[39] The need to revert to fiction is significant: only on the pages of a novel could the female addict solicit compassion as a suffering heroine and curiosity as a fallen woman. In a novel's pages she remained just that, a titillating possibility, while in real-life drawing rooms the female addict would ruin names and reputations. Female bourgeois drinking was so unacceptable that it was always necessarily criminal behaviour, but also always diseased and therefore belonged in the realm of legal medicine, an ultimate case for specialists.

Drunkenness became a problem for specialists as soon as they wrote about it, discussed it and organized it. When doing so they never employed one general term to refer to the problem of excessive drinking but instead they used an increasingly particular terminology. A wide vocabulary was devised in order to construct different models of drunkenness, ranging from 'drunkenness' (*ivresse* and *ivrognerie*), 'alcoholism' (*alcoolisme aigu* and *chronique*) to 'delirium tremens' and 'dipsomania'. The meaning of these concepts themselves was never consistent, they differed from case to case and were often contradictory, as the social terms in which drunkenness was debated always shifted. Clearly, diagnoses were dependent on more than the amount of alcohol the patient had consumed and patients with a different social background were diagnosed with different problems, even though they presented the same physical symptoms. For Mariana Valverde the instability of the discursive network shows a failure of the medical profession to consolidate their power.[40] Drunkenness was indeed an ambiguous state, with aspects of free will and disease always intersecting, a state that was at all times difficult to explain and contain in language. Nonetheless, the continuous attempts at classification by specialists could also indicate exactly the opposite: it can be seen as an essential mechanism and a necessary step towards the establishing of that power. Classifying drunkenness is controlling it, as deviant behaviour, belonging to the other. Hence the medicalization of drunkenness can no longer be understood as a transparent progressive shift whereby ideas of vice in the judgement of drunkenness were shed and taken over by assessment guided by scientific and biological knowledge. Instead it becomes a process in which the borders between acceptable and non-acceptable conduct, normal and abnormal behaviour were discussed. In this process, the language of vice and morality was contradicted, but equally taken on, transformed and proliferated into new medical terminology. Drunkenness was interpreted in the discourse of the specialists within different models of disease and its spread: contagion, madness and degeneration. The ambiguous language of drunkenness, written by medical and legal professionals with the pen of a dominant liberal bourgeois ideology, carried with it wider social meanings. It thereby constructed and was at the same time influenced by essential cultural dichotomies not only between morality and biology, or free will and determinism, but also between, for example, the group and the individual, men and women, and the upper and lower classes.

CONCLUSION

As drunkenness was experienced within a social, historical space, it was understood in different ways for distinct individuals in particular moments, ways that expressed historically specific values and fears. I have looked in different places where he, or she, became a subject of concern. At certain times various interpretations existed of how much of a certain beverage was considered 'too much' and for whom what type of behaviour as a result of intemperance was felt to be problematic. Generally, drunkenness represented a moment of chaos in which seemingly permanent cultural boundaries became blurred. Defining drunkenness therefore entailed asserting, negotiating and constructing social identities. Starting from this premise that representations of excessive drinking were fundamental signifiers for culture, 'the drunk' became a guide into important historical changes in Belgian society in the second half of the nineteenth and the first decade of the twentieth.

Various narratives of drunkenness, shaped by and also forming experience, were produced at the intersection of so many social, political and medical ideas. They were certainly ambiguous, even contradictory and always shifting, but continued to recur over the period in different shapes and forms. They addressed mostly the fantasies and fears of the middle classes for whom drunkenness had become a serious issue of concern in the mid-nineteenth century and were endorsed by bourgeois social commentators, progressive lawmakers, asylum doctors and modern authors and artists. Only very rarely do we hear the voice of the drinker him or herself or his affected family, but if we do, it becomes clear how he or she actively participated in the negotiation of his or her place in society.

With the established social order endangered and working classes and women demanding participation in society, the dominant culture needed to assert itself and reassess its value system. Moderation became a fundamental idea within the formation of a 'modern' bourgeoisie. The nineteenth-century narratives of drunkenness reflected middle-class ideas about morality, about free will and social organization, but also negotiated opinion and so these narratives participated in the construction of a historically specific, powerful hegemonic middle-class voice. Against a backdrop of an all-embracing process of modernization and change, undesirable drunkenness was considered as belonging to the immoral and sick other, which in its turn defined the moral, healthy self.

The vague but seemingly universal nature of habitual drunkenness, seemingly unexplainable outside morality and only curable by the drinker him or herself, offered complications and contradictions to doctors and lawmakers concerned about exact definitions and comprehensive demarcations to label 'deviance'.

Various narratives of drunkenness emerged in the last half of the nineteenth century towards the First World War from people's experiences with drunkenness, taken on and negotiated in various settings. First, central to the bourgeois understanding of drunkenness in the mid-nineteenth century, was the narrative of the drunken unruly farmer and drunken revolutionary worker. The ceremony of drinking was always political and ideological: it made men and it sealed belonging, but when undertaken by an impoverished besieged working class, it was considered as potentially dangerous. As working-class groups demanded their share in the running of society and traditional rural areas had to face social transformations, the figure of the male working-class drunkard became a metaphor for loss of control and property and preoccupations about inevitable changes prevalent in the fast changing late nineteenth-century society. When the country was put on the map by European diplomats in the 1830s it was ruled by a small elite circle, while at the end of the century, first lower middle class then workers' demands had led to a dramatic increase in those who participated in politics. By the end of the century social action had obtained for each man at least one vote. In the countryside, where drunkenness was so much part of the way of life on special days, the habitual drunkard, who continued to pervert the right order of things also on normal days, represented turmoil and insubordination. In the mid-nineteenth century drunkenness was seen as a moral failure of a particular group in society, as undesirable type of behaviour not in line with the demands of modern civilization, but possibly also something that could be righted by education.

Towards the end of the nineteenth century, like all over Europe, fears were expressed about the degeneration of the race and drunkenness was essential to this dramatic decline. The growing and broadening idea of degeneration went alongside a 'subjectivation' of the idea of drunkenness. An emphasis of the problem of drunkenness as a social problem in the mid-nineteenth century gave way to a judgement of the individual drunkard. And so especially after the shocking revolutionary events of 1886, in addition to a fundamental moral failure, drunkenness became part of the biological make-up of undesirable individuals. It became judged on much harsher terms as a congenital defect, belonging to a certain type of class or person. The drunkard came to represent the essence of what was believed to be the racially specific uncivilized nature of the Flemish, from a Walloon perspective, of the Walloons from a French perspective and from the African from everyone's perspective. The positivist paradigm of degeneration contained a set of ideas as flexible as drunkenness itself. Middle-class professionals, doctors and lawyers would become its self-professed specialists. The medical theories linking drunkenness with degeneration allowed for two explanations with different outcomes. Drunkenness could be seen as part of the milieu that would kindle inborn defects. Socialism and feminism took this on to argue for social change. However, drunkenness was also understood as lodged within biology itself, part of the racial make-up of particular groups. For this interpretation, change was always futile and it fitted in with a conservative ideology.

Ideas of a 'dangerous' alcoholic, whose civil rights were to be subordinated for the greater good of society, permeated the medical and legal discussions on alcoholism in the later part of the century. In the context of 'social defence', further legislative measures were proposed, widely discussed and partially taken on to constrain and contain disorderly lower-class drunks. 'Social defence' was profoundly influenced by medical discourse, which towards the end of the century placed ever more emphasis on the 'criminal drunk'. In the discipline of 'criminal anthropology' notions of degeneration were used to plead for the forced incarceration of drunkards as potential criminals. In the representation of male working-class alcoholics, drinking and violence were always combined and the argument of 'dangerousness' became the signifier for the diagnosis of lower-class alcoholics. The ostensibly unbiased medical language preferred by doctors and the legal categories invented by law makers, involved highly prejudiced opinions as to what constituted unacceptable drinking habits. Aspects of heredity were often put forward to account for environmental factors contributing to the onslaught of drunkenness and to explain moral dissipation. In the narratives on drunkenness, the language of 'degeneration' went hand in hand with that of melodrama. Degeneration, whether moral or biological, represented a spectacular downfall and told of a social order being dramatically disturbed.

Fictional representations of drunkenness embodied widely shared social meanings and were informed and consequently adapted and reshaped by readers' and authors' experiences. Contemporary writers and artists mostly endorsed the belief system of reformist liberalism and condemned drunkenness for corrupting the essence of its hegemony: rationality and moderation. Towards the end of the century, writers and artists articulate a more critical standpoint and their representation of the drunk spelled out contradictions and tensions prevalent in the social world they experienced.

The antagonist of the figure of the revolutionary drunkard/farmer was that of the good, sober worker. While the former was depicted as wasting his wages on drink and therefore living in self-afflicted poverty, the latter's quiet existence would confirm that the limited wages he received were in fact sufficient. The revolutionary working-class drunkard was described as poor and frustrated, easily lured into political movements for change like revolutionary socialism. The image of the good, sober worker and farmer on the other hand, who was happy and contented, was brought into play to show that social change was not the answer, but rather frugality and temperance were instead. The liberal reformist cause fundamentally relied on this contradictory character, who, paradoxically managed to curb the typical or even inborn passions of his social class. This contradiction between an inborn tendency to drink that medical specialists had identified on one hand, together with the idea of self-betterment through moderation and education that the same specialists and 'liberal' bourgeois would preach on the other, was predominant in the narratives of drunkenness.

The home was another middle-class fundament that was always represented as threatened by too much drink: drunkards would not want to return to its protective walls, would instead drink in public rather than at home, were often represented as losing it altogether by squandering their income, would be able to save up to buy one when saving from drink, and so on. Property was at the heart of a bourgeois organization of society. The stereotypical wife of the drunkard, as suffering victim, represented the moral values and family model of the hegemonic middle classes, under attack by drink. With her moral superiority she was to convince the worker to stay away from the pub and to urge him to remain at home, within the framework of tradition. The narrative of the suffering wife represented a bourgeois appreciation of the domestic sphere in a society where working-class women were decidedly active in public life, albeit with very limited civil rights.

The figure of the victim wife, reproduced tirelessly in melodramatic songs, paintings and drama, also became a means to place and give meaning to existing realities. The prescriptive ideology of femininity in the nineteenth century endowed women with an important moralizing role in the fight against alcohol and a responsibility for maintaining the respectability of their families. The option of forced incarceration of drunken husbands in a lunatic asylum, for example, gave wives an opportunity to protect their families from domestic violence, although their dependence on their husband's income often prevented this for women of the lower classes. For women in the higher classes, confinement of squandering husbands and debauched sons was a means to safeguard their respectability and fortunes.

Respectability and its loss became the key concern when dealing with drunkards of all classes, but it was mostly depicted as fundamentally a middle-class concern. To the middle classes, owing to their often precarious economic situation, drunkenness could easily cause a terrifying throwback into the lower classes. The concept of degeneration, as an unavoidable moral and biological downfall added to this idea. The medical temperance movement and popular melodrama took up this threatening prospect of a 'fall from grace' steeped in a possible reality.

In the colony drunkenness was a concern among the administrators of the overeas possession. Those who were meant to civilize instead had become savages themselves. Here it was the impact of the environment of Africa itself that was mostly blamed for the moral and physical downfall.

Within a changing society, the self-indulgent lifestyle of the wealthy bourgeoisie, including their excessive drinking became increasingly criticized. While previously the lavish consumption of wine and liquors had always been a way to parade one's wealth and position in society, it became in the later decades of the century ever more questioned as fitting behaviour for a self-conscious ruling class.

The good, sober worker returned in a second double-act; in opposition to another incongruous character, that of the drunken decadent bourgeois. A strong moral condemnation was reserved for those among the higher classes who had become slave to the bottle and thus such excessive drinking would be mostly hushed up or denied. The discussions surrounding the loss of willpower as a moral and medical affliction testify to the importance of this faculty for the liberal, free enterprise on which the Belgian organization of society was based. In the asylum those rich patients whose actions were considered morally unacceptable were sometimes called 'degenerates'. The decadent bourgeois drunkard was also represented as sexually deviant. Especially in the later years of the century when anxieties about syphilis were at their height, upper-class men's sexual exploits with prostitutes were often linked to and even blamed on their excessive drinking habits.

The hegemonic voice on drunkenness of the progressive bourgeoisie connected heavy drinking with obsolete values of a type of self-indulgent bourgeois proprietor, who, by his ruthlessness was felt to have contributed to the social conflict society was facing in the second half of the nineteenth century. The representation of the decadent drunken bourgeois helped to endorse the esteem for the opposite position of an enlightened bourgeoisie, presenting itself as an example of moderation and self-control. The theme of personal responsibility was important here, as it was another important characteristic that excessive drinking seemed to annihilate.

However, constructing drunkenness as belonging to the immoral other became increasingly problematic and ambiguous when dealing with drunken members of the bourgeois class. Drinking remained a fundamentally important aspect of a bourgeois lifestyle, just as it played a significant part in working-class culture. Therefore, the moral judgement of excessive drinking as formulated by the liberal section of the bourgeoisie had to be carefully negotiated. Doctors realized that drunken, anti-social behaviour was not a unique signifier for problem-drinking, when otherwise respectable middle and upper-class men inadvertently ruined their family's fortunes and all-important respectability when becoming gradually and silently dependent on alcohol. The ruling classes hesitated to take legislative action to curb drunkenness, not only because their own financial interests were directly caught up with the production and sale of drink, but also because of the widespread habit of excessive drinking among their own bourgeois class. The bourgeois drunkard, if condemned by law, would necessarily have to receive similar treatment as drunken lower-class individuals – a consequence that was unimaginable.

It had to become possible therefore, in particular cases, to identify drunkenness as another form of deviant behaviour, different from that caused by deprived morality. When it was explained as a disease it no longer called for reform and punishment, but for medical care and was therefore not any more directly related to immorality. Doctors could decide to diagnose the middle-class drunkard with a form of 'abnormal drunkenness'. The disease of 'dipsomania', for example, came to explain an uncontrollable craving for alcoholic substances specific to women, and, as the evidence from the Ghent private asylum showed, to bourgeois drinkers. But although the language had changed, moral judgement still prevailed. While classifying drunkenness, hygienists, alienists and criminologists, forged their own professional identities and negotiated the meaning of what it was to be drunk both through their writings as in their consultation rooms and on the ward of the asylum.

Drunkenness was not only called 'abnormal' when it affected members of the bourgeoisie, but always when it concerned women. As middle-class women demanded their rightful space not only in but also outside the house, in literature and art, the innocent suffering wife, and especially passive wife, the defender of the hearth and guardian of male sobriety, became supplanted by a possibly threatening active, sexually perverted fallen woman, who would drink excessively herself. Subversive naturalist art and literature depicted drunken working women as unnatural, degenerated and neglectful mothers.

But even in the most 'dissident' corners, there continued to be a reticence about what remained ultimately the 'unthinkable': bourgeois female drinking. For women, excessive drinking behaviour was always compromising what it meant to be a woman: femininity itself. By becoming drunk in public, women overstepped unwritten social rules, which made their position towards men unclear and alarming. The drunken bourgeoisie was a character that only rarely received attention, a matter that because of its horrendousness had to be hushed up. However, towards the end of the century, with women increasingly participating in the public sphere, some writers apprehensive of changes occurring in society, dared sometimes to address this taboo subject. For women drinking too much was considered without exception deviant behaviour and for ladies the act was unspeakable. Female drinking, more than anything else, undermined the moral pillars of society and the health of the nation. Firmly imbedded in culture, narratives on drunkenness were always ambiguous. Drunkenness was disquieting because it crossed seemingly stable cultural borders. The irrationality and unruly behaviour of the drunk became symbolic for a challenge to assumptions about power and control. Consequently, it was to receive a different meaning according to each scenario in which it was set. Hence

I hope to have demonstrated through the narratives of drunkenness explored here that changing ideas on drunkenness reflected and at the same time also constructed the ways in which society was organized in Belgium from 1850 to 1914.

NOTES

Introduction

1. G. Deneckere, E. Gubin, J. P. Nandrin, and E. Witte, *Nouvelle histoire de Belgique, Vol. I 1830–1905* (Tielt: Lannoo, 2005), p. 14.
2. P. Van Den Eeckhout, 'Eten en gegeten worden. Historici en Consumptiegeschiedenis in België (19e–20e eeuw)', *Tijdschrift voor sociale geschiedenis*, 28 (2002), pp. 373–90, on p. 371.
3. M. Douglas, *Constructive Drinking: Perspectives on Drink from Anthropology* (Cambridge: Cambridge University Press, 1987), p. 8.
4. P. Cohen, *The Symbolic Construction of Community* (London: Routledge, 1993), pp. 12, 53, 115.
5. For drunkenness in Belgium see the work of Pieter Scholliers and Liesbet Nys. For Britain: A. A. Pruitt, 'Approaches to Alcoholism in Mid Victorian England', *Clio Medica*, 9:2 (1974), pp. 93–102, and G. Johnstone, 'From Vice to Disease? The Concepts of Dipsomania and Inebriety, 1860–1908', *Social and Legal Studies*, 5 (1996), pp. 37–56. For France: J. C. Sournia, *Histoire de l'alcoolisme* (Paris: Flammarion, 1986) and D. Nourrisson, *Le buveur du XIXe siècle* (Paris : Albin Michel, 1990). For the United States of America: H. G. Levine, 'The Discovery of Addiction: Changing Conceptions of Habitual Drunkenness in America', *Journal of Studies of Alcoholism*, 23 (1978), pp. 143–74, and P. Conrad, and J. W. Schneider, *Deviance and Medicalization, from Badness to Sickness* (St Louis: Mosby, 1980). pp. 73–109.
6. P. Scholliers, 'The Medical Discourse and the Drunkard's Stereotyping in Belgium, 1840–1919', in A. Fenton (ed.), *Order and Disorder. The Health Implications of Eating and Drinking in the Nineteenth and Twentieth Centuries* (East Linton: Tuckwell Press, 2000), pp. 227–39.
7. L. Nys, '"De grote school van de natie", Legerartsen over drankmisbruik en geslachtsziekten in het Belgische leger (ca. 1850–1950)', *Bijdragen en Mededelingen tot the Geschiedenis der Nederlanden*, 65:2 (2000), pp. 392–425.
8. L. Nys, '"De ruiters van de Apocalyps": alcoholisme, tuberculose, syphilis en degeneratie in medisch België. 1870–1940', in J. Tollebeek, J. Van Paemel and K. Wils (eds), *Degeneratie in België 1860– 1940: een geschiedenis van ideeën en praktijken* (Louvain: Louvain University Press 2003), pp. 11–42, and L. Nys, '"Nationale plagen": hygiënisten over het maatschappelijk lichaam', in L. Nys, De Smaele, J. Tollebeek and K. Wils (eds), *De zieke natie: over de medicalisering van de samenleving, 1860–1914* (Groningen: Historische Uitgeverij, 2002), pp. 220–41.

9. J. Tollebeek, J. Van Paemel and K. Wils (eds), *Degeneratie in België 1860–1940: een geschiedenis van ideeën en praktijken* (Louvain: University Press, 2003), and M. Dupont-Bouchat, *La Belgique criminelle, droit, justice, société* (XIVeXXe siècles) (Louvain la Neuve: UCL et Academia-Bruyland, 2006).
10. L. Nys, '"Groene toverdrank of gebottelde epilepsie?": absint in België omstreeks 1900', in Tollebeek et al. (eds), *Degeneratie in België 1860–1940*, pp. 155–82.
11. R. Cooter, 'Medicine and Modernity', in M. Jackson (ed.), *The Oxford Handbook of the History of Medicine* (Oxford: Oxford University Press, 2011), pp. 100–16, on p. 103.
12. L. Jordanova, *Languages of Nature: Critical Essays on Science and Literature* (Brunswick, NJ: New Rutgers University Press, 1986), p. 34.
13. M. Poovey, *Uneven Developments: The Ideological Work of Gender in Mid-Victorian England* (Chicago, IL: University Of Chicago Press, 1988), p. 2; and L. Jordanova, *The Look of the Past. Visual and Material Evidence in Historical Practice* (Cambridge: Cambridge University Press, 2012), pp. 3–6.
14. R. Williams, *The Long Revolution* (London: Hogarth Press, 1961), p. 47.
15. L. S. Jacyna, *Lost Words: Narratives of Language and the Brain, 1825–1926* (Princeton: Princeton University Press, 2000), pp. 4–5.
16. P. J. Corfield, *Language, History and Class* (Oxford: Basil Blackwell, 1991) p. 27.
17. J. R. Walkowitz, *City of Dreadful Delight: Narratives of Sexual Danger in Late-Victorian London* (Chicago, IL: University of Chicago Press, 1992), p. 9.
18. M. Foucault, *L'archéologie du savoir* (Paris: Gallimard, 1969), p. 67.
19. M. Foucault, *Abnormal: Lectures at the Collège de France 1974–75* (London: Verso, 2003), p. 313.
20. C. Hall, *White, Male and Middle-Class: Explorations in Feminism and History* (Cambridge: Polity, 1992), p. 24.
21. '*Vormen* van het leven en van de gedachte zijn het, wier beschrijving hier beproefd is. Den wezelijken *inhoud* te benaderen, die in die vormen heeft gerust, – zal het ooit het werk zijn van geschiedkundig onderzoek?', J. Huizinga, 'Herfsttij der Middeleeuwen', in J. Huizinga, *Verzamelde werken. Deel 3*, ed. L. Brummel (Haarlem: H. D. Tjeenk Willink & Zoon, 1949), p. 3.
22. For example, P. Van Den Eeckhout and P. Scholliers, 'De hoofdelijke voedselconsumptie in België, 1831–1939', *Tijdschrift voor sociale geschiedenis*, 9 (1983), pp. 274–301.
23. T. Brennan, 'Towards the Cultural History of Alcohol in France', *Journal of Social History*, 21:1 (1989), pp. 71–92.
24. G. Eley and K. Nield, *The Future of Class in History: What's Left of the Social?* (Ann Arbor, MI: University of Michigan Press, 2007).
25. M. Bloch, *The Historian's Craft* (Manchester: Manchester University Press, 1954), p. 61, and J. Tosh, *The Pursuit of History* (New York: Longman, 1999), p. 183.
26. From an address delivered by Baron R. du Sart de Bouland, governor of the Provincial Council of Hainaut, at the opening of the session, 7 July 1903 as quoted in B. S. Rowntree, *Land and Labour: Lessons from Belgium* (London: Macmillan, 1911), p. 412.
27. Ibid., p. 528.
28. B. Anderson, *Imagined Communities: Reflections on the Origin and Spread of Nationalism* (Verso: London. 1983), p. 4; C. Strikwerda, 'If All of Europe were Belgium: Lessons in Politics and Globalization from one Country', *Belgisch tijdschrift voor de nieuwste geschiedenis – Revue belge d'histoire contemporaine*, 35:4 (2005), pp. 503–22.
29. P. Penn-Hilden, *Women, Work, and Politics: Belgium, 1830–1914* (Oxford: Clarendon Press, Oxford. 1993), p. 14.

30. J. C. H. Blom and E. Lamberts, *History of the Low Countries.* (New York: Berghahn Books, 1998), p. 264.
31. For a survey on Belgian's archives see P. Van den Eeckhout and G. Vanthemsche (eds), *Bronnen voor de studie van het hedendaagse België, 19e–20e eeuw* (Brussels: Koninklijke Commissie voor Geschiedenis, 2009).
32. Hilden, *Women, Work, and Politics*, p. 14.
33. On pillarized archives and documentation centres see P. Pasture, 'Views from Abroad: Foreign Historians on a Small State by the North Sea. With Reflections on Historical Writing in Belgium and Elsewhere', *Belgisch tijdschrift voor de nieuwste geschiedenis – Revue belge d'histoire contemporaine*, 35:4 (2005), pp. 413–33.
34. P. Van den Eeckhout, 'The Quest for Social History in Belgium (1848–1998)', *Archif für Sozialgeschichte*, 40 (2000), pp. 321–36, on p. 330.
35. What remains of the records of two female asylums ran by the Sisters of Charity in Ghent is very limited covering only a few years. See V. Vanoverschelde, 'Tot herstel der krankheid van mijn zwakke geest is nodig. De psychiatrische praktijk in het Sint-Jozefshuis en het *maison de santé* te Ghent door de Zusters van Liefde en Jozef Guislain 1808–1806)' (Student Dissertation, University of Ghent, 2008).
36. C. Geertz, 'Thick Description. Toward an Interpretation Theory of Culture', in *The Interpretation of Cultures. Selected Essays* (New York: Basix, 1973), pp. 3–30.
37. On food and drink and the making of identities, see P. Scholliers, 'Meals, Food Narratives and Sentiments of Belonging in Past and Present', in P. Scholliers (ed.), *Food, Drink and Identity. Cooking Eating and Drinking in Europe since the Middle Ages* (London: Berg Publishers, 2001), pp. 3–20.
38. E. P. Thompson, *The Making of the English Working Class* (Harmondsworth: Penguin, 1986), pp. 8–13.
39. For example, in G. Crossick, 'Metaphors of the Middle: The Discovery of the Petite Bourgeoisie (1880–1914)', *Royal Historical Society Transactions*, 4 (1994), pp. 251–79. See also P. Van Den Eeckhout in P. Scholliers, 'Social History in Belgium: Old Habits and New Perspectives', *Tijdschrift voor sociale geschiedenis*, 23:2 (1997), pp. 147–81, on p. 165.
40. J. W. Scott, 'Gender: A Useful Category of Historical Analysis', *American Historical Review*, 81 (1986), pp. 1053–75.
41. S. Eriksen, 'Alcohol as Gender Symbol', *Scandinavian Journal of History*, 24:1 (1999), pp. 45–73.
42. M. Poovey, *Making a Social Body: British Cultural Formation 1830–1864* (Chicago, IL: University of Chicago Press, 1995), p. 153.
43. C. Lemonnier, *Salon de Paris, 1870* (Paris: Morel, 1870), p. 232.
44. E. d' Oliveira, *'De jongere generatie' (Vervolg op 'de mannen van '80'): Gesprekken met vertegenwoordigers van de nieuwere richting in onze literatuur; tevens een enquête naar enkele beginselen in ons nationaal geestelijk leven* (Amsterdam: Maatschappij voor goede en goedkoope lectuur, 1914), p. 65.
45. J. S. Allen, 'History and the Novel: Mentalité in Modern Popular Fiction' *History and Theory*, 22 (1983), pp. 233–52.
46. M. Poovey, 'Reading History in Literature: Speculation and Virtue in Our Mutual Friend', in J. Smarr (ed.), *Historical Criticism and the Challenge of Theory* (Urbana, IL : University of Illinois Press, 1993), pp. 42–80.
47. S. Maza, 'Stories in History: Cultural Narratives in Recent Works in European History', *American Historical Review*, 51:5 (December 1996), pp. 1493–515, and A. Kane,

'Reconstructing Culture in Historical Explanation: Narratives as Cultural Structure and Practice', *History and Theory*, 39 (October 2000), pp. 311–30, on p. 314.

48. Poovey, 'Reading History in Literature', p. 47.
49. J. Kocka, 'The Middle Classes in Europe', *Journal of Modern History*, 67 (December 1995), pp. 783–806, on p. 783.
50. J. Nicholls, *The Politics of Alcohol: A History of the Drink Question in England* (Manchester: Manchester University Press, 2008), pp. 2–3.
51. H. Small, '"In the Guise of Science": Literature and the Rhetoric of 19th Century English Psychiatry', *History of the Human Sciences*, 7 (February 1994), pp. 27–55, on p. 47.

Part I: Drunkenness and the People

1. H. Pirenne, *Histoire de Belgique, Vol. VII. De la révolution de 1830 á la guerre de 1914* (Brussels: H. Lamertin, 1932), p. 262; and E. W. Herbert, *The Artist and Social Reform. France and Belgium 1885–1898* (New Haven, CT: Yale University Press, 1961), p. 67.

1 Drunken Farmers

1. K. Van Isacker, *Mijn land in de kering: 1830–1980* (Antwerp: De Nederlandsche Boekhandel, 1978), p. 225.
2. C. Baudelaire, *Arm België* (1864) (trans. edn: Amsterdam: Joyce & Co., Arbeiderspers, 1975), p. 122.
3. Ibid., p. 32.
4. Blom and Lamberts, *History of the Low Countries*, pp. 232–3.
5. A. De Winne, *Door arm Vlaanderen (1903)* (Louvain: Van Halewyck, 2001), p. 125.
6. On drunkenness in the sixteenth centurym see S. Van Bouchaute, 'Grenzeloos drinken? De enscenering van de herberg en het drinken in de beeldende kunst en literatuur tijdens de lange zestiende eeuw', in D. J. Baetens and D. Jacobs, *De kunst van het drinkien. Herberg – en drinkscenes in de Belgische schilderkunst* (Hasselt: Van Der Wiele, 2011), pp. 11–31.
7. C. Buysse, 'Guustje en Zieneken' (1887), in C. Buysse, *Verzameld werk [van] Cyriel Buysse. Deel IV*, ed. E. Van Elslander and A. M. Musschoot (Brussels: Manteau, 1974), pp. 40–83, on p. 47.
8. P. Burke, 'Bakhtin for Historians', *Social History*, 3:1 (1988), pp. 85–90, on p. 85.
9. E. Pirson, *L'alcoolisme à la campagne* (Louvain: Polleunis, 1903), p. 11; and *Bulletin de la Société médical belge de tempérance* (April 1902), p. 365, and (September 1905), p. 395.
10. H. Charriaut, *La Belgique moderne. Une terre d'expériences* (Paris: Flammarion, 1910), p. 17.
11. E. Verhaeren, *Les campagnes hallucinées. Les villes tentaculaires* (Paris: Gallimard, 1982), p. 59.
12. G. Eekhoud, *Kermesses. Contes* (Brussels : Kistemaeckers, 1884), and G. Eekhoud, *Nouvelles kermesses. Mœurs Flamandes* (Brussels: Veuve Monnom, 1887).
13. De Winne, *Door arm Vlaanderen*, p. 54.
14. H. De Smaele, *Rechts Vlaanderen. Religie en stemgedrag in 19e eeuws België* (Louvain: Louvain University Press, 2009), p. 314.
15. C. Lemonnier, 'Les Concubins', in *Ceux de la glèbe* (Paris: Albert Savine, 1889), pp. 69–114, on p. 107.
16. *Bulletin de la Société médical belge de tempérance* (November 1908), p. 424.

17. C. Buysse, 'Het recht van de sterkste' (1893), in Buysse, *Verzameld werk [van] Cyriel Buysse. Deel I.*, ed. Van Elslander and Musschoot, p. 49.
18. S. Streuvels, *The Long Road*, trans. E. Crankshaw (Boston, MA: Twayne, 1976), p. 83–4, and C. Buysse, 'Het leven van Rozeke van Dalen' (1906), in Buysse, *Verzameld werk [van] Cyriel Buysse. Deel II*, ed. Van Elslander and Musschoot, pp. 1–302, on p. 67, and Buysse, 'Het recht van de sterkste', p. 55.
19. C. Buysse, 'Op het kleine gehucht' (1901), in Buysse, *Verzameld werk [van] Cyriel Buysse. Deel II*, ed. Van Elslander and Musschoot, pp. 864–909, on p. 891, and Buysse, 'Het recht van de sterkste', pp. 143–5.
20. C. Lemonnier, *La vie belge* (Paris: Bibliotheque Charpentier, 1905), p. 105.
21. Rowntree, *Land and Labour*, p. 412.
22. Van Isacker, *Mijn land in de kering*, p. 53.
23. De Smaele, *Rechts Vlaanderen*, pp. 314–15.
24. Van Isacker, *Mijn land in de kering*, p. 52.
25. H. Boëns, *La bière au point de vue médical, hygiénique et social* (Brussels: Manceaux, 1878), p. 145.
26. S. Van De Perre, 'Noble Drinking, Wine Consumption in Belgium, 1830–1914', in P. Janssens and S. Zeischka, *The Dining Nobility: From the Burgundian Dukes to the Belgian Royalty* (Brussels: Vrije Universiteit Brussel Press, 2008), pp. 60–80, on p. 63. P. Scholliers, *Food Culture in Belgium* (Westport, CT: Greenwood Press, 2009), on p. 54. Van Den Eeckhout and Scholliers, 'De hoofdelijke voedselconsumptie in België, 831–1939'.
27. De Winne, *Door arm Vlaanderen*, p. 109.
28. F. Gaussin, *Le fléau moderne: traité complet médico-moral de l'alcoolisme; causes, effets, remèdes* (Namur: Wesmael-Charlier, 1901), p. 225, and Buysse, 'Het leven van Rozeke van Dalen', pp. 17–19.
29. D. Boulger, *Belgian Life in Town and Country* (London: G. Newnes, 1904), p. 96–7.
30. C. Buysse, 'Het bolleken' (1905), in Buysse, *Verzameld werk [van] Cyriel Buysse. Deel II*, ed. Van Elslander and Musschoot, pp. 305–458, on p. 424.
31. M. Van Den Berg, *De volkssage in de provincie Antwerpen in de 19de en 20ste Eeuw* (Ghent: Koninklijke academie voor Nederlandse taal- en letterkunde, 1993), p. 1231.
32. P. Burke, *Popular Culture in Early Modern Europe* (London: Temple Smith, 1978), pp. 149–77. R. Bauman, *Story, Performance and Event: Contextual Studies of Oral Narrative* (Cambridge: Cambridge University Press, 1986.) p. 2. L. Dégh, *Narratives in Society: A Performer-Centered Study of Narration* (Bloomington, IN: Indiana University Press, 1995), p. 41. R. Darnton, 'Peasants Tell Tales. The Meaning of Mother Goose' in R. Darnton, *The Great Cat Massacre* (New York: Vintage Books, 1985), pp. 9–72.
33. The Germanic languages department of the Catholic University in Louvain have collected folk-stories online at http://www.volksverhalenbank.be/.
34. K. Brandes, 'Inleiding', in E. Zetternam, *Mijnheer Luchtervelde* (Ghent, 1943), p. 2.
35. H. Conscience, *The Curse of the Village; and the Happiness of Being Rich. Two Tales* (trans. edn: London: Lambert & Co., 1855), p. 140.
36. Ibid., pp. 46–50.
37. Ibid., p. 54.
38. M. Boone and H. Gaus, *Dagelijks leven: sociaal-culturele omstandigheden vroeger en nu* (Deurne: Baart, 1982), p. 149.
39. H. G. Dumont, *La vie quotidienne en Belgique sous le règne de Léopold II (1865–1909)* (Brussels: Le Cri, 1996), pp. 82–3, and D. P. Blok, *Algemene geschiedenis der Nederlanden. Deel XII* (Haarlem: Fibula-Van Dishoeck, 1981), pp. 100–1 ; and C. Buysse,

'Het gezin van Paemel' (1902), in Buysse, *Verzameld werk [van] Cyriel Buysse. Deel VI*, ed. Van Elslander and Musschoot, p. 767–822, on p.789.
40. E. Vandervelde, *Le parti ouvrier et l'alcool* (Brussels: Brismée, 1898), p. 5.
41. E. Vanhaute, *Heiboeren. Bevolking, arbeid en inkomen in de 19de-eeuwse Kempen* (Brussels: Vrije Universiteit Brussel Press, 1992), p. 211.
42. Conscience, *The Curse of the Village*, pp. 115–6.
43. 'Huwelijkstwist (duo)', and ' De dronkaard en zijne vrouw (duo)', in P. Waeri, *Verzameling der volledige kluchtige en politieke liederen van Karel Waeri den Gentschen Beranger* (1899; Ghent: Historische Heruitgeverij, 2001), pp. 235, 442–3.
44. V. Turner, 'Social Drama's and Stories about Them', *Critical Inquiry*, 7:1 (Autumn 1982), pp. 141–68, on p. 156.
45. M. Parent, *Le rôle de la femme dans la lutte contre l'alcoolisme* (Brussels: Ligue Patriotique contre l'Alcoolisme, 1890).
46. Conscience, *The Curse of the Village*, p. 108.
47. http://www.volksverhalenbank.be/ FBECK0291–0291; RCELI0226–0226; TDANI0300–0300; COOMS0181–0181; APRIN0187–0187, 0188, 0189; APRIN0203–0203; DTRUY0132–0132.
48. Conscience, *The Curse of the Village*, p. 130.
49. Ibid., p. 133.
50. Ibid., p. 104.
51. Postcard: la Ligue Patriotique contre l'Alcoolisme (Brussels, 1910), Jenevermuseum, Hasselt. See Chapter 10, p. 155.
52. M. Oris, 'Hygiène publique et médicalization dans une cité industrielle. Seraing au XIXe siècle et au début du XXe siècle', *Revue Belge de Philologie et Histoire*, 73 (1995), pp. 983–1009, on p. 984 ; and H. Kuborn and H. A. O. Devaux, *Aperçu historique sur l'hygiène publique en Belgique depuis 1830* (Brussels: H. Lamartin, 1904), p. 31.
53. M. A. Van Andel, *Volksgeneeskunst in Nederland* (Utrecht: Boekhoven, 1909), p. 170.
54. Conscience, *The Curse of the Village*, p. 34.
55. Ibid., p. 72.
56. *'[ze] hadden het in hunne bovenkamer en lieten zich meer voorstaan dan aan boerenmenschen wel past'*. H. Conscience, *De plaeg der dorpen* (Antwerpen: J. P. Van Dieren, 1855), p. 15.
57. The English translation was published as *The Long Road*, in Boston in 1976, translated by E. Crankshaw.
58. B. Vanheste, 'Een tweede eeuw voor Streuvels? Gedachten over een literatuursociologisch programma', in T. Piet (ed.), *Een tweede eeuw? Jaarboek I van het Stijn Streuvelsgenootschap* (Tielt: Lannoo, 1995), pp. 13–30, on p. 13.
59. C. Scudamore, *Belgium and the Belgians* (Edinburgh: William Blackwood & Sons, 1901), p. 17.
60. Ibid.
61. Charriaut, *La Belgique moderne*, p. 17.
62. Streuvels, *The Long Road*, p. 55.
63. Ibid., p. 83.
64. Ibid., p. 105.
65. Ibid., p. 108
66. See Chapter 9, pp. 143–4.
67. S. Streuvels, 'Veld en dorp', in M. Rooses (ed.), *Vlaanderen door de eeuwen heen, Eerste deel* (Amsterdam: Elsevier, 1912), pp. 1–61, on pp. 40, 44–5.

68. Laermans depicted the poor always as outcasts; see H. Todts, D. Cardijn-Oomen, and N. Monteneye, *Het volk ten voete uit. Naturalisme in België en Europa* (Ghent: Ludion, 1996), pp. 157–61. P. Baudson, 'Du constat à l'interprétation. L'art social de Jospeh Stevens à Eugène Laermans', in P. A. Roberts-Jones, *Eugène Laermans, 1864–1940* (Brussels: Crédit Communal, 1995), pp. 51–65. This theme of the drunkard being violently cast out of rural society is also the subject of a painting of monumental size painted ten years earlier by Denmark's foremost naturalist painter L. A. Ring.
69. J. Tollebeek, 'Degeneratie, moderniteit en culturele verandering. Een Belgisch perspectief', in Tollebeek et al. (eds), *Degeneratie in België 1860–1940*, pp. 299–320, on p. 304.
70. Streuvels, *The Long Road*, p. 114.
71. B. Woestenborghs, 'Les travailleurs saisonniers flamands en France de 1870 à 1970', in A. Morelli (ed.), *Les émigrants Belges. Réfugiés de guerre, émigrés économiques, réfugiés politiques ayant quitté nos régions du XVième siècle à nos jours* (Brussels: Éditions Vie Ouvrière, 1998), pp. 205–12.
72. S. Vanden Borre, 'Union et fraternité. Verenigingen van Belgische migranten in Roubaix in de tweede helft van de negentiende eeuw', *Belgisch tijdschrift voor de nieuwste geschiedenis – Revue belge d'histoire contemporaine*, 39:3–4 (2009), pp. 369–404, on p. 371.
73. De Winne, *Door arm Vlaanderen*, p. 118. P. J. Derainne, 'L'hostilité aux ouvriers Belges en France au XIXe Siècle', in Morelli (ed.), *Les émigrants Belges*, pp. 101–14.
74. E. Vandervelde, *Essais socialistes: l'alcoolisme, la religion, l'art* (Paris: Alcan, 1906), p. 79.
75. *Bulletin de la Société médical belge de tempérance* (April 1902), p. 363.
76. De Winne, *Door arm Vlaanderen*, p. 48. C. Buysse, 'De Biezenstekker' (1900), in Buysse, *Verzameld werk [van] Cyriel Buysse. Deel IV*, ed. Van Elslander and Musschoot, pp. 639–63, on p. 658, and Buysse, 'Het recht van de sterkste, p. 64. E. Hélin, 'Reconstituer l'histoire des 'bricteux' saisonniers', in A. Morelli (ed.), *Histoire des étrangers et de l'immigration en Belgique de la préhistoire à nos jours* (Brussels: Éditions Vie Ouvrière, 1992), pp. 213–28.
77. Commission du travail instituée par arrêté royal du 15 avril 1886, *Volume II. Procès verbaux des séances d'enquêtes concernant le travail industriel* (Brussels: A. Lesigne, 1887), pp. 45, 713.
78. Commission du travail instituée par arrêté royal du 15 avril 1886, *Volume I. Réponses au questionnaire concernant le travail industriel* (Brussels: A. Lesigne, 1887), p. 1102.
79. J. Van Parijs, *Het leven, niets dan het leven: Cyriel Buysse en zijn tijd* (Antwerp: Houtekiet, 2007), p. 123.
80. E. J. Brill, *Handelingen en levensberichten van de maatschappij der Nederlandsche; letterkunde te Leiden, 1942–1943* (Leiden 1944), pp. 26–7. Digitale Bibliotheek voor de Nederlandse Letteren: http://www.dbnl.org/.
81. C. Buysse, 'Driekoningenavond' (1899), in Buysse, *Verzameld werk [van] Cyriel Buysse. Deel II*, ed. Van Elslander and Musschoot, pp. 823–65, and A. M. Musschoot, *Cyriel Buysse* (Antwerp: Manteau, 1996), p. 323.
82. Streuvels, *The Long Road*, p. 54.
83. E. Calemeyn, *De onthouding* (Bruges: Brugsche Onthoudersbond, 1894), p. 15.
84. Buyssche, 'De biezenstekker', p. 646.
85. J. Melchior, *De jeneverplaag, of het alcoolisme in België* (Hasselt: Ceysens, 1896), p. 60; and C. Steverlynck, *Kleine martelaars: een historisch document over misbruikte kinderen, kindermishandeling, incest en prostitutie* (Antwerp: Icarus, 1997), p. 239.
86. Buyssche, 'De biezenstekker', p. 653.
87. Ibid., p. 654.

88. Tollebeek, 'Degeneratie, moderniteit en culturele verandering. Een Belgisch perspectief', p. 308.
89. I want to thank Bernadette Bonnier at the Musée Félicien Rops for her help when I tried to find out more about this etching.
90. Nys, '"Groene toverdrank of gebottelde epilepsie?", p. 162. B. Noël, *La rebuveuse d'Absinthe – Autour de l'oeuvre de Félicien Rops* (Sainte Marguerite des Loges: Éditions BVR, 2005).
91. R. Stijns, *Hard labeur* (Rotterdam: M. Boogaerdt Jr) and (Brussel: De Vlaamsche boekhandel, Leo. J. Krijn, 1904), p. 56.
92. B. Bonnier, L. Leblanc, D. Prioul and H. Védrine, *Rops suis, aultre ne veulx estre* (Brussels: Complexes, 1998), p. 96.
93. H. Pirenne, *Histoire de Belgique. Vol.VII. De la révolution de 1830 à la guerre de 1914* (Brussels: H. Lamertin, 1932), p. 262. as quoted in E. W. Herbert, *The Artist and Social Reform. France and Belgium, 1885–1898* (New Haven, CT : Yale University Press, 1961), p. 67.

2 Drunkenness and the Working Classes

1. J. P. Rioux, *La révolution industrielle, 1780–1880* (Paris: Editions Du Seuil: 1971), p. 101.
2. N. Kerr, 'Alcohol and Drug Habits', in T. L. Stedman (ed.), *Twentieth Century Practice: An International Encyclopedia of Modern Medical Science by Leading Authorities of Europe and America. v. 3. Occupation Diseases, Drug-habits and Poisons* (London: Sampson, Low, Marston, 1895), p. 126.
3. E. J. Hobsbawm, *The Age of Empire, 1875–1914* (London: Abacus, 1994), p. 99.
4. M. Reynebeau, *Een geschiedenis van België* (Tielt, 2003), p. 149.
5. *Bulletin de la Société médical belge de tempérance* (September 1898), p. 352, planche V.
6. P. Scholliers, 'Een vijand die men kennen moet. Jenever in België in de 19de en Vroege 20e Eeuw', in E. Van Schoonenberghe (ed.), *Jenever in de Lage Landen* (Antwerp: Stichtig Kunstboek, 2004), pp. 138–77, on p. 152; Deneckere et al., *Nouvelle histoire de Belgique, Vol. I 1830–1905*, pp. 120–1.
7. Boulger, *Belgian Life in Town and Country*, pp. 75–6.
8. A. Forel, *The Sexual Question: A Scientific, Psychological, Hygienic and Sociological Study for the Cultured Classes* English adaptation by C. F. Marshall, *Die Sexuelle Frage* (1905; London: Rebman, 1908), p. 329.
9. Commission du travail, instituée par arrêté royal du 15 Avril 1886. Volume II. *Procès verbaux des séances d'enquêtes concernant le travail industriel* (Brussels), section D. 7, p. 72.
10. Commission du travail, instituée par arrêté royal du 15 Avril 1886. Volume I. *Réponses au questionnaire concernant le travail industriel* (Brussels), pp. 1105, 5418.
11. De Winne, *Door arm Vlaanderen*, p. 43.
12. Scholliers, 'Een vijand die men kennen moet', p. 155.
13. V. Robert, 'De arbeidersbeweging in Belgie', in J. A. Van Houtte (ed.), *Algemene geschiedenis der Nederlanden Deel XI. Van liberaal naar sociaal getij, 1885–1914* (Zeist: W. De Haan, 1961), pp. 24–59. F. Laurent, *Les sociétiés ouvrières de Gand* (Ghent: Clemm & Hoste, 1877), p. 2.
14. N. Hirano, 'Le retour des immigrés belges à la suite des événements de Lens à Liévin à août-septembre', in *Belgisch tijdschrift voor de nieuwste geschiedenis – Revue belge d'histoire contemporaine*, 37:3–4 (2007), pp. 307–23.
15. Heusy, *Un coin de la vie de misères*, p. 34.
16. Ibid., p. 35.

17. 'Het glas', in Waeri, *Verzameling der volledige kluchtige en politieke Liederen van Karel Waeri den Gentschen 'Beranger'*, p. 357.
18. Dumont, *La vie quotidienne en Belgique*, p. 107.
19. For more on this, see Chapter 7, p. 120.
20. E. Zetternam, *Mijnheer Luchtervelde. Waarheden uit onzen tijd* (Antwerp: J. E. Buschmann, 1848), p. 197.
21. B. Brouwers, *Literatuur en revolutie* (Boom: Meppel, 1971), pp. 192–243.
22. H. Nyssen, 'Introduction', in C. Lemonnier, *Happe-chair* (1886; Brussels: Editions Labor, 1994), pp. 8–9.
23. Lemonnier, *Happe-chair*, p. 191.
24. P. Aron, 'Dans l'ombre de Germinal. Happe Chair de Camille Lemonnier', *Bulletin de la Société d'etudes des lettres françaises de Belgique*, I (1982), pp. 1–11, on p. 8.
25. P. Aron, 'Les arts et les lettres de 1886: Lorsque la race Wallon-Flamand se révaillait au contact des infernales cuisines industrielles', in Bruwier et al. (eds), *1886, La Wallonie née de la grève?*, p. 153.
26. J. Puissant, 'Le bon ouvrier, mythe ou réalité du XIXe siècle. De l'utilité d'une biographie. J. F. J. Dauby (1824–1899)', *Revue belge de philologie et d'histoire*, 56:4 (1978), pp. 878–929.
27. P. De Witte, *Alles is omgekeerd: hoe de werklieden vroeger leefden (1848–1918)* (Louvain: Kritak, 1986), p. 115.
28. H. Boëns, *Traité pratique des maladies, des accidents et des difformités des houilleurs* (Brussels: Tircher, 1862), p. 24.
29. *Bulletin de la Société médical belge de tempérance* (August 1901) p. 378. V. Desguin, *De l'abus des boissons alcooliques* (Paris: E. Donnaud, 1876), p. 2. Gaussin, *Le fléau moderne*, p. 225
30. J. S. Roberts, 'Drink and Industrial Work Discipline in 19th Century Germany', *Journal Of Social History*, 15:1 (Autumn 1981), pp. 25–38, on p. 26.
31. Y. Crispeels, 'De strijd tegen het drankmisbruik in Belgie, eind 19e begin 20e eeuw' (Student Dissertation, Katholieke Universiteit Leuven, 1982), p. 193.
32. P. Heusy, *Un coin de la vie de misères* (Paris: Oriol, 1883), p. 33.
33. Charriaut, *La Belgique moderne*, p. 343.
34. T. Gautier, *Un tour en Belgique et en Hollande* (Paris: l'Ecole des Loisirs, 1997), p. 48.
35. Van Isacker, *Mijn land in de kering*, p. 223. W. S. Haine, *The World of the Paris Cafe: Sociability among the French Working Class, 1789–1914* (Baltimore, MD: Johns Hopkins University Press, 1999), p. 57.
36. *Annales Chambre.* Séance du 19 July 1887, p. 1660. Boulger, *Belgian Life in Town and Country*, pp. 96–7.
37. *Annales Parlementaires*, Chambre, Séance du 19 July 1887, p. 1660.
38. Scudamore, *Belgium and the Belgians*, p. 17.
39. R. Leboutte, 'A propos de la condition ouvrière en Wallonie, fin 18e–19e siècle', in M. Bruwier, N. Caulier-Mathy (eds), *1886, La Wallonie née de la grève? Colloque organisé a l'université de Liège les 29 Octobre, 14 et 29 Novembre 1986* (Brussels, 1990), p. 22.
40. *Bulletin de la Société médical belge de tempérance* (November 1908), p. 421.
41. Blom and Lamberts, *History of the Low Countries*, pp. 252–307. For France, see P. E. Prestwich, *Drink and the Politics of Social Reform: Antialcoholism in France since 1870* (Palo Alto: Society for the Promotion of Science and Scholarship, 1988). Nourrisson, *Le buveur du XIXe siècle*. For Britain: J. M. Golby, and A. W. Purdue, *The Civilization of the Crowd. Popular Culture in Britain 1750–1900* (London, Sutton, 1999), p. 119.

Nicholls, *The Politics of Alcohol.* For Germany: I. Vogt, 'Alkoholkonsum, Industrialisierung und Klassenkonflikt', in G. Vögler, and K. von Welck (eds), *Rausch und Realität: Drogen im Kulturvergleich, Vol. 1* (Reinbek: Rowohlt Verlag, 1982), pp. 202–11.

42. P. Waeri, 'Het Dubbel Bier', in *Verzameling der volledige kluchtige en politieke liederen van Karel Waeri den Gentschen beranger*, p. 291.
43. Douglas, *Constructive Drinking*, p. 8.
44. Haine, *The World of the Paris Café*, pp. 22–32.
45. H. Wouters, *Documenten betreffende de geschiedenis der arbeidersbeweging ten tijde van de internationale (1866–1880)* (Louvain: Editions Nauvelaerts, 1970), p. 1639.
46. J. Van De Merwe, *Gij zijt kanalje, heeft men ons verweten! Het proletariërslied in Nederland en Vlaanderen* (Antwerp, Utrecht: A. W. Bruna & Zoon, 1974). H. Vandecaveye, 'Het proletariërslied, een sociaal-kulturele verschijningsvorm van de socialistische arbeidersvereniging', *Belgisch tijdschrift voor de nieuwste geschiedenis – Revue belge d'histoire contemporaine*, 6:2 (1980), pp. 171–202.
47. On violence and especially political violence in Belgian history, see X. Rousseaux, 'C'est arrive près de chez vous/Het geweld van België. La violence est-elle un objet d'histoire des Belges?', in G. Kurgan-Van Henterijk (ed.), *Un pays si tranquille: la violence en Belgique au XIXe siècle* (Brussels: Editions de l'Université de Bruxelles, 1999), pp. 9–40.
48. E. Caudelier, *L'alcoolisme en Belgique* (Brussels: Ligue Patriotique contre l'Alcoolisme, 1889), p. 42.
49. *Bulletin de l'Académie royale de médecine de Belgique*, 11 (1897), p. 854.
50. G. Deneckere, *Sire, het volk mort. Sociaal protest in België (1831–1918)* (Antwerp-Baarn-Ghent: Hadewijch/AMSAB, 1997), p. 236.
51. R. Harris, *Murders and Madness: Medicine, Law And Society in the Fin De Siècle* (Oxford, 1989), pp. 245–6. S. Barrows, 'After the Commune. Alcoholism, Temperance and Literature in the Early Third Republic', in J. M. Merriman (ed.), *Consciousness and Class Experience in Nineteenth-Century Europe* (New York: Holmes & Meier Publishers, 1979), pp. 205–18.
52. Dupont-Bouchat, *La Belgique criminelle, droit, justice, société*, p. 271.
53. Prestwich noted a similar scenario for the Parisian public asylums. P. E. Prestwich, 'Family Strategies and Medical Power: "Voluntary" Committal in a Parisian Asylum, 1876–1914', *Journal of Social History*, 27 (1993), pp. 798–819.
54. L. P. Boon, *Pieter Daens, of hoe in de hegentiende eeuw de arbeiders van Aalst vochten tegen armoede en onrecht* (1971; Amsterdam: Arbeiderspers, 1986), p. 39.
55. 'Kom t' huis' in Waeri, *Verzameling der volledige kluchtige en politieke liederen van Karel Waeri den Gentschen beranger*, p. 61.
56. P. Aron, *La Belgique artistique et littéraire: une anthologie de langue française (1848–1914)* (Brussels: Complexe, 1997), p. 129 ; and H. Todts, D. Cardijn-Oomen and N. Monteneye, *Het volk ten voete uit. Naturalisme in België en Europa* (Ghent: Ludion, 1996), pp. 17–18.
57. D. E. Stark, 'Charles De Groux et le réalisme social dans la peinture Belge', in J. Dewilde, J. M. Duvosquel and A. M. Meessen-Doneux (eds), *Charles Degroux, 1825–1870 et le réalisme en Belgique* (Ghent: Snoeck-Ducaju & Zoon, 1995), pp. 41–56.
58. H. Kuborn, *Topographie médicale du royaume, elaborée en vertu de l'arrêté royal du 20 Juillet 1889 par la Société royale de médecine publique et de topographie médicale. Zone VII: Bassins houillers* (Liége: H. Vaillant-Carmanne, 1909), p. 9.
59. Parent, *Le rôle de la femme dans la lutte contre l'Alcoolisme.*
60. *Bulletin de l'Académie royale de médecine de Belgique* (1900), pp. 87–8, and 96–7.

61. E. Gubin, 'Home Sweet Home'. L'image de la femme au foyer en Belgique et au Canada avant 1914', in *Belgisch tijdschrift voor de nieuwste geschiedenis – Revue belge d'histoire contemporaine*, 22:3–4 (1991), pp. 521–68, on p. 534. P. Penn-Hilden, 'The Rhetoric and Iconography of Reform: Women Coal Miners in Belgium, 1840–1914', *Historical Journal*, 34:2 (1991), pp. 411–36.
62. Commission du travail instituée par arreté royal du 15 avril 1886, *Volume IV. Comte rendus des séances plénières. & mémoires, rapports, lettres etc. envisageant la question ouvrière dans son ensemble* (Brussels: A. Lesigne, 1887), p. 107.
63. Rowntree, *Land and Labour*, p. 413.
64. *Happe-chair* (1886; Brussels: Editions Labor, 1994), p. 125.
65. *Bulletin de la Société médical belge de tempérance* (November 1908), p. 422.
66. 'De mosselkaai', in Waeri, *Verzameling der volledige kluchtige en politieke liederen van Karel Waeri den Gentschen beranger*, pp. 333–6.
67. D. Keymolen, *Ongewenst seksueel gedrag op de werkplek in het 19de eeuwse België* (Louvain: Hoger instituut voor de arbeid, 1990), p. 45.
68. *Bulletin de la Société médicale de tempérance* (November 1908), pp. 867–8.
69. S. Herman, 'De grenzen van seksueel geweld. Schuld en schande in Vlaanderen tijdens de 19e eeuw', in *Tijdschrift voor sociale geschiedenis*, 23:1 (2002), p. 63.
70. In *Het bolleken* Eleken was clear about Vital's advances: 'This was as far he was allowed to go, not further'. Buysse, *Verzameld werk [van] Cyriel Buysse. Deel II*, ed. Van Elslander and Musschoot, p. 391. Sidonie in *Het volle leven* told her suitor Odon clearly: 'It cannot last like this any longer, it's one thing or the other', in C. Buysse, 'Het volle leven' (1908), in *Verzameld werk [van] Cyriel Buysse. Deel IV*, ed. Van Elslander and Musschoot, pp. 461–614, on p. 542.
71. Lemonnier, *Happe-chair*, p. 336.
72. M. Biron, *La modernité Belge: littérature et société* (Brussels: Editions Labor, 1994), p. 99.
73. P. Prestwich, 'Female Alcoholism in Paris, 1870–1920. The Response of Psychiatrists and Families', *History of Psychiatry*, 14:3 (2003), pp. 321–36.
74. Charriaut, *La Belgique moderne*, p. 219.
75. Commission du travail instituée par arreté royal du 15 avril 1886, *Volume II. Procès verbaux des séances d'enquêtes concernant le travail industriel* (Brussels: A. Lesigne, 1887), Section D. 7. on p. 72.
76. Commission du travail instituée par arreté royal du 15 avril 1886. *Volume I. Réponses au questionnaire concernant le travail industriel*, pp. 836, 314.
77. Lemonnier, *Happe-chair*, p. 117.
78. 'Gentsche kafépraat (Duo)', in Waeri, *Verzameling der volledige kluchtige en politieke Llederen van Karel Waeri den Gentschen beranger*, pp. 333–36.
79. Lemonnier, *Happe-chair*, p. 123.
80. B. Dijkstra, *Idols of Perversity: Fantasies of Feminine Evil in Fin-de-Siède Culture* (Oxford: Oxford University Press, 1986). M. Biron, *La modernité Belge: littérature et société*, p. 105.
81. It is not known if this statue still exists and if so, where. I need to thank Dorine Cardyn-Oomen at the Koninklijk Museum Voor Schone Kunsten Antwerpen, Francesca Vandepitte at the Musées Royaux des Beaux Arts de Belgique and Bruno Fornari of the Museum voor Schone Kunsten, Gent for their information relating to Lambeaux and this work.
82. V. Pica, 'Artisti contemporanei: Jef Lambeaux', *Eporium*, 20:117 (September 1904), p. 172.

83. A. Eylenbosch, *Jef Lambeaux 1852–1908, ou les passions d'un faune* (Saint-Gilles Les Rencontres Saint-Gilloises, 1990), p. 5.
84. C. Conrardy, 'Le statuaire Jef Lambeaux', *Savoir et Beauté*, 13 (June 1933), p. 298.
85. L. Ery, 'Notes d'art. Jef Lambeaux', in *Le Thyrse. Revue de littérature d'art et de critique*, 2:3 (June 1900), p. 26.
86. Dumont, *La vie quotidienne en Belgique*, p. 216.
87. Lemonnier, *Happe-chair*, p. 344.
88. A. Forel, *Die sexuelle frage* (1905), trans. C. F. Marshall, *The Sexual Question: A Scientific, Psychological, Hygienic and Sociological Study for the Cultured Classes* (London, 1908), p. 329.
89. P. Aron, 'Dans L'ombre de Germinal. Happe-Chair de Camille Lemonnier', *Bulletin de la Société d'études des lettres françaises de Belgique*, 1 (1982), p. 8.
90. Lemonnier, *Happe-chair*, p. 63.
91. Forel, *The Sexual Question*, trans. Marshall, p. 329.
92. Lemonnier, *Happe-chair*, p. 337.
93. Ibid., p. 351.
94. Ibid., p. 353.
95. As quoted in C. Havelange, 'De uitvinding van de wanorde. Het negentiende-eeuwse verbond tussen collectiviteit en gezondheid', in Nys, et al. (eds), *De zieke natie*, p. 84.

3 Drunkenness and the Middle Classes

1. H. Todts, *James Ensor. Schilderijen en tekeningen uit de verzameling van het Koninklijk museum voor schone kunsten Antwerpen* (Schoten: BAI, 2008), p. 80.
2. A. Corbin, *Le miasme et la jonquille: l'odorat et l'imaginaire social XVIIIe-XIXe siècles* (Paris: Aubier Montaigne, 1982).
3. A. Labrie, *Zuiverheid en decadentie. Over de grenzen van de burgerlijke cultuur in West-Europa 1870–1914* (Amsterdam: Bakker, 2001), p. 89.
4. Dumont, *La vie quotidienne en Belgique*, p. 74.
5. Crossick, 'Metaphors of the Middle', pp. 251-79.
6. S. Lilar, *Une enfance gantoise* (Paris: Bernard Grasset, 1976), p. 15. G. Kurgan-Van Hentenryk, 'Une classe oubliée: la petite bourgeoisie de 1850 à 1914', in S. Jaumain, and G. Kurgan-Van Hentenryk (eds), *Aux frontieres des classes moyennes: la petite bourgeoisie belge avant 1914* (Brussels: Éditions De l'Université de Bruxelles, 1992), pp. 15–24.
7. S. Jaumain, 'Les petits commerçants et la frontière entre petite bourgeoisie et classe ouvrière (1880–1914)', in Jaumain and Kurgan-Van Hentenryk (eds), *Aux frontieres des classes moyennes*, pp. 101–9, on pp. 106–107.
8. G. Crossick and H. G. Haupt, *The Petite Bourgeoisie in Europe 1780–1914* (London: Routledge, 1997), p. 190.
9. Jaumain, 'Les petits commerçants', p. 107.
10. Lemonnier, *La vie belge*, p. 107.
11. D. Lesko, *James Ensor, The Creative Years* (Princeton: Princeton University Press, 1985), p.18.
12. A. Swinbourne, *James Ensor* (New York: Museum of Modern Art, 2009), p. 84.
13. Lilar, *Une enfance gantoise*, p. 38.
14. L. Nead, *Myths of Sexuality: Representations of Women in Victorian Britain* (Oxford: Basil Blackwell, 1988), p. 180.

15. R. Ankaert, 'Les cabaretiers-cafétiers à la fin du XIXe siècle', in Jaumain, and Kurgan-Van Hentenryk (eds), *Aux frontieres des classes moyennes*, pp. 29–57, on p. 31.
16. Walkowitz, *City of Dreadful Delight*, pp. 50–2.
17. G. J van Bork, and P. J. Verkruijsse (eds), *De Nederlandse en Vlaamse auteurs van middeleeuwen tot heden met inbegrip van de Friese auteurs* (De Haan, Weesp, 1985), p. 314.
18. Brouwers, *Literatuur en revolutie*, pp. 182–3.
19. P. F. Van Kerckhoven, *De dronkaerd. Drama in dry bedryven* (Antwerp, 1854), p. 4.
20. *Le Mouvement hygienique* (October and November 1886), p. 372 ; and 'L'art alcoolique', in *Bulletin de la Société médical belge de tempérance* (October 1901), pp. 513–6.
21. Van Kerckhoven, *De dronkaerd* p. 21.
22. Ibid., p. 5.
23. As quoted in Dumont, *La vie quotidienne en Belgique*, p. 79.
24. J. Lalouette, 'L'alcoolisme et classe ouvrière en France aux alentours de 1900', *Cahiers d'histoire*, 13:1 (1997), pp. 89–107.
25. E. Witte, 'Electorale agenten aan de vooravond van de partijformaties', *Belgisch tijdschrift voor nieuwste geschiedenis – Revue belge d'histoire contemporaine*, 1: 2 (1969), pp. 216–53. on p 251.
26. G. Deneckere, *Geuzengeweld, anticklerikaal straatrumeour in de politieke geschiedenis van Belgie, 1831–1914* (Brussel: VUB press, 1998), p. 95.
27. C. Buysse, *'n Leeuw van Vlaanderen* (1900 ; Brussels: De Lage Landen, 1943), on p. 134.
28. Maison de Santé le Strop. Régistre médical, [G] 1223, 14 juin 1912.
29. S. Hayward, *French National Cinema* (London, Routledge, 1993), p. 50. A. L. Williams, *Republic of Images: A History of French Filmmaking* (Cambridge, MA: Harvard University Press, 1992).
30. G. Sadoul, *Histoire générale du cinéma* (Paris: Denoel, 1973), p. 74. J. J. Vincent, *Naslagwerk over de Vlaamse film* (Brussel: C.I.A.M. 2000), p. 31. J. Kermabon, *Pathé: Premier empire du cinéma* (Paris: Centre Georges Pompidou. 1994), p. 61.
31. G. S. Jowett, 'The First Motion Picture Audiences', in J. L. Fell (ed.), *Film before Griffith* (Cambridge: University of California Press, 1983), p. 200. D. Biltereyst, and P. Meersuit, *De verlichte stad. Een geschiedenis van bioscopen, filmvertoningen en filmcultuur in Vlaanderen* (Louvain: LannooCampus, 2007), pp. 239–40.
32. *'Pathé i film' XXIV Mostra internazionale del nuovo cinema. Pesaro, 11–19 juinio 1988* (2004), p. 20.
33. T. Lefebvre, 'Les victimes de l'alcoolisme (Pathé 1902)', *Archives. Institut Jean Vigo – Cinémathèque de Toulouse*, 50 (mai, 1992), pp. 8–9.
34. 'In the Grip of Alcohol, a Wonderful Drama', in *The Bioscope* (July 20, 1911), pp. 109–12.
35. *Het Volksgeluk* (1 January 1912), p. 2; and G. Du Champs, M. Convens and A. Visscher, *beelden uit de Belle Epoque* (Brussels: Reader's Digest, 1988), p. 153.
36. M. Starks, *Cocaine fiends and Reefer Madness: an Illustrated History of Drugs in the Movies* (New York and London: Cornwall Books, 1982), p. 30.
37. *Kinematograph and Lantern* (October 1911), as quoted in D. Robinson, 'Influence du cinema Français sur le marché londonien', in J. A. Gill and M. Langy (eds), *Les vingt premières années du cinema Francais, actes du colloque international de la Sorbonne nouvelle 4, 5 et 6 Novembre 1993* (Paris: Presses de la Sorbonne nouvelle, 1995), pp. 337–50, on p. 350.
38. R. Cooter, *The Cultural Meaning of Popular Science: Phrenology and the Organization of Consent in Nineteenth-Century Britain* (Cambridge: Cambirdge University Press, 1984), p. 2.

39. E. Willekens and G. Degroote, *Hendrik Conscience en zijn tijd* (Antwerp: Stichting Mercator-Plantijn, 1983), pp. 133, 153.
40. H. Conscience, *Eene uitvinding des duivels. Helsche geschiedenis* (Antwerp: J. P. Van Dieren, 1865), p. 17.
41. Ibid., p. 50.
42. Ibid., p. 52.
43. Ibid., p. 53.
44. B. Harrison, *Drink and the Victorians: The Temperance Question in England, 1815–1872* (Pittsburgh: University of Pittsburgh Press, 1971); J. S. Roberts, *Drink, Temperance and the Working Class in Nineteenth Century Germany* (Boston, MA: Allen & Unwin, 1984). J. C. van der Stel, *Drinken, drank en dronkenschap: vijf eeuwen drankbestrijding en alcoholhulpverlening in Nederland* (Hilversum: Verloren, 1995).
45. J. M. Golby, and A. Purdue, W. *The Civilization of the Crowd. Popular Culture in Britain 1750–1900* (London: Sutton, 1999), p. 123.
46. R. Upstone and C. Holden, *George Cruikshank's The Worship of Bacchus in Focus* (London: Tate Publishing, 2001), pp. 16–18.
47. P. Bouquié-Lefebvre wrote *Des causes et des résultats de l'intempérance, ainsi que des moyens de la prévenir & de la combattre* in 1857, but had already published 10 years earlier an article on the abolition of strong liquors, translated from Flemish, in the Brussel's *Gazette médicale Belge*.
48. Willekens, *Hendrik Conscience en zijn tijd*, pp. 99, 104.
49. Conscience, *Eene uitvinding des duivels*, p. 54.
50. See further Chapter 7: The Alienists, pp. 155-6.
51. Conscience, *Eene uitvinding des duivels*, pp. 54–5.
52. P. E. Prestwich, 'Temperance in France: The Curious Case of Absinthe', *Historical Reflections/Réflections Historiques*, 6:2 (1979), pp. 301–20. Nys, '"Groene toverdrank of gebottelde epilepsie?"', pp. 155-82.
53. V. Magnan, 'Accidents determinés par l'abus de la liqueur d'absinthe', *L'Union Médicale*, Nos. 92 and 94 (1864), pp. 227–32 (92), and pp. 257–62 (94).
54. B. Conrad, *Absinthe: History in a Bottle* (San Francisco, CA: Chronicle Books, 1988), p. 20.
55. Prestwich, 'Temperance in France: The Curious Case of Absinthe', p. 302.
56. E. M. H. Seyn, *Dictionnaire des écrivains Belges. Bio-bibliographie. Tome II* (Bruges: Editions Excelsior, 1930), pp. 2095–6.
57. G. L. Degroote, J. L. H. De Schuyter, and J. P. Van Dieren, *Hendrik Conscience en zijn uitgevers. Brieven met inleiding en toelichting door Dr. Gilbert Degroote en Jan De Schuyter* (Brussel: Elsevier, 1953), p. 104.
58. Maison de Santé le Strop. Registre Médical, 9:10 (10 Mary 1860).
59. Degroote, *Hendrik Conscience en zijn uitgevers,* p. 104. Maison de Santé le Strop. Livre de Clinique, 5 (8155), p. 18.
60. E. M. H. Seyn, *Dictionnaire des écrivains belges bio-bibliographie*, p. 2095.
61. Degroote, *Hendrik Conscience en zijn Uitgevers,* p. 104.
62. M. A. Conscience, 'Conscience als mensch', *Ons volk ontwaekt* (10 Augustus 1912).
63. *Le Mouvement hygienique* (October and November 1886), p. 372.
64. 'L'art alcoolique' in *Bulletin de la Société médical belge de tempérance* (October 1901), pp. 513–6.
65. C. Lombroso, *The Man of Genius* (London: Scott, 1891), p. 54.

66. G. Pollock, 'Artists Mythologies and Media Genius: Madness and Art History', in *Screen*, 21 (1980), pp. 57–96, on p. 66.
67. Conscience, *Eene Uitvinding des Duivels*, pp. 57–8.
68. Ibid., p. 58.

4 Drunkenness and the Upper Classes

1. L. Vandervelde, *Monarchs and Millionaires* (London: Thornton Butterworth, 1925), p. 21.
2. S. Vloeberg, *Tot we barsten. Een impressie van het banket in de 19e reuw in drie Belgische steden: Leuven, Mechelen en Diest* (Student Dissertation, Katholieke Universiteit Leuven, 1991).
3. Van De Perre, 'Noble Drinking, Wine Consumption in Belgium, 1930–1914', p. 62.
4. A. J. Bijsterveld, E. Niesten, Y. Segers and I. Steen (eds), *Suikerbonen en beschuit met muisjes. Eetgewoonten bij sleutelmomenten in het leven* (Louvain: Nederlands centrum voor volkscultuur, 2005), p. 134.
5. H. Conscience, *De loteling* (Antwerp: J. Buschmann, 1851), p. 138.
6. C. Lemonnier, *La fin des bourgeois* (1892) (1892; Brussels: Editions Labor, 1986), p. 64.
7. Ibid., p. 97.
8. *Le Globe illustré: Journal de la famille*, 30 (27 April 1890).
9. Melchior, *De jeneverplaag, of het alcoolisme in België*, p. 85; and *Het Volksgeluk* (9 September 1911), p. 69.
10. É van den Corput, *L'Alcoolisme, l'hérédité et la question sociale* (Brussels: H. Lamertin, 1895), p. 24.
11. Commission du travail instituée par arrêté royal du 15 avril 1886. *Volume I. Réponses au Questionnaire concernant le travail industriel* (Brussels: A. Lesigne, 1887), p. 1105. p. 5352.
12. Maison de Santé le Strop. Registre médical, G 120, 1 August 1883.
13. Maison de Santé le Strop. Registre médical, D 26, 11 July 1885.
14. Maison de Santé le Strop. Registre médical, D 55, 10 March 1888.
15. Prestwich, 'Female Alcoholism in Paris, 1870–1920'.
16. M. Foucault, A. Baudot and J. Couchman, 'About the Concept of the "Dangerous Individual" in 19th-Century Legal Psychiatry', *International Journal of Law and Psychiatry*, 1 (1 February 1978), pp. 1–18, on p. 5.
17. see part 3: Drunkenness and the Doctors
18. M. Claes, *'Il est Impossible d'etre féministe sans être antialcoolique': Marie Parent (1853–1935) een voorvechtster in de strijd tegen alcoholisme* (Licenciaatsverhandeling, Katholieke Universiteit Leuven. 2000), p. 45.
19. *Het Volksgeluk* (February 1911), p. 13; and J. Hoegaerts, 'Legal or Just? Law, Ethics and the Double Standard in the Nineteenth Century Divorce', *Law and History Review*, 26:2 (Summer 2008), pp. 259–84, on p. 279.
20. Maison de Santé le Strop, Registre médical, G 91, 2 July 1881; and Registres matricules, [B] 91.
21. C. Mackenzie, *Psychiatry for the Rich: A History of Ticehurst Private Asylum, 1792–1917* (London: Routledge, 1992), p. 102.
22. Maison de Santé le Strop. Registre médical, G. 88, 3 May 1881.
23. Maison de Santé le Strop. Registre médical. D. 183, 23 August 1897.
24. This is the wording of the advertisement as it appeared in English local papers e.g. *Harrowgay Advertiser*, 27 March 1907. The Belgian papers carried a translated text, for

example, *Het land van Aalst* (7 June 1908) that also gave the address of local pharmacies where the product could be purchased.

25. 'The Composition of Certain Secret Remedies. XXIII. Inebriety Cures', *British Medical Journal* (10 April 1909), p. 909.
26. *Le messager belge*, 13:11 (November 1908), p. 170 as quoted in J. De Brauwere, *Het beeld van alcohol. Een historische discoursanalyse van de antialcoholcampagnes tussen 1879 en 1919* (Student Dissertation, Vrije Universiteit Brussel, 2007), p. 65.
27. H. Barella, *Rapport de la commission à laquelle a eté renvoyé le mémoire de M. le docteur Mora, à Brunehamel, relatif à l'alcoolisme* (Brussels: Manceaux, 1881), p. 5.
28. *Bulletin de la Société médical belge de tempérance* (August 1901), p. 370–71.
29. *Bulletin de la Société ,édical belge de tempérance*, 65 (December 1911).
30. H. S. Vreckem Paul, *De invloed van het Franse naturalisme in het werk van Cyriel Buysse* (Brussels: Tijdschrift van de Vrije Universiteit Brussel, 1968), p. 17; and B. De Nil, 'Zetternam en Zola. De Vlaamse sociaal demokraten en hun literaire mythen vóór 1914', *Brood en Rozen*, 3:1 (1998), pp. 7–24.
31. E. Zetternam, *Mijnheer Luchtervelde. Waarheden uit onzen tijd* (Antwerp: J. E. Buschmann, 1848), p. 145.
32. Ibid, p. 163.
33. See Nys, '"De ruiters van de apocalyps"', pp. 11–42.
34. E. Zetternam, *Mijnheer Luchtervelde. Waarheden uit onzen tijd*, p. 165.
35. J. Van Parijs, J. *Het leven, niets dan het leven: Cyriel Buysse en zijn tijd* (Antwerp: Houtekiet, 2007), p. 351.
36. Buysse, 'Het bolleken', p. 308.
37. W. Marcet, *On Chronic Alcoholic Intoxication: or Alcoholic Stimulants in Connexion with the Nervous System; with a Synoptical Table of Cases* (London: J. Churchill, 1860).
38. Buysse, 'Het bolleken', p. 307.
39. Ibid., p. 316.
40. Ibid., p. 446.
41. F. Pirlot, 'l'Alcoolisme en Belgique de 1830 à 1950. Mythe et réalité' (Student Dissertation, Université de Liège, 1993), p. 144; and *Het Volksgeluk* (April 1912), p. 29.
42. Ibid.
43. K. Velle, *De nieuwe biechtvaders: de sociale geschiedenis van de arts in België* (Louvain: Kritak, 1991), pp. 170–4; and C. Havelange, 'Quelques aspects du discours médical pendant la 2nd moitié du XIXe Siècle', *Belgisch tijdschrift voor de nieuwste geschiedenis – Revue belge d'histoire contemporaine*, 16 (1985), pp. 175–99.
44. J. P. Rousseaux, 'l'Alcoolisme et co-alcoolisme dans l'Assommoir d'Emile Zola', in J. P. Roussaux, B. Faoro-Kreit and D. Hers (eds), *L'alcoolique en famille: dimensions familiales des alcoolismes et implications thérapeutiques* (Brussels: De Boeck & Larcier, 2000), pp. 143–8.
45. Buysse, 'Het bolleken', pp. 455–6.
46. J. De Brauwere and D. Jacobs, '"Le premier verre – le dernier verre", Het antialcoholdiscours op een postkaart', in E. Dekens, J. Debrauwere and D. Jacobs (eds), *Pierre le buveur et Jean l'abstinent* (Hasselt: National Jenevermuseum, 2009), pp. 47–65, on p. 58
47. C. Hanlet, *Les écrivains Belges contemporains de langue Française: 1800–1946* (Liège: H. Dessain, 1946) p. 117.
48. Maison de Santé le Strop. Registre médical, D 22 (11 March 1885) ; and Hospice Guislain. Registres matricules, p. 22.

49. Maison de Santé le Strop. Registre médical, D 34 (18 February 1886); and Hospice Guislain. Registres matricules, p. 34.
50. Maison de Santé le Strop. Registre médical, D (10 November 1894).
51. Deneckere, *Sire het volk mort*, p. 295.
52. For the Belgian discourse on alcoholism and syphilis in the army, see Nys, '"De Grote School van de Natie"', pp. 392-425. and further esp. Chapter 9: Hygienists on pp. 142-3 and Chapter 10: Alienists on pp. 159-61.
53. On the actions of 1891 and 1893 see Deneckere, *Sire, het Volk Mort*, pp. 278–305.
54. Maison de Santé le Strop. Registre médical, D 119 (14 September 1893); and Maison de Santé le Strop. Registre médical, D 119. On the idea of surménage see also further Chapter 10: Alienists, pp. 160.
55. D. Marechal (ed.), *Musée d'Art Moderne. Oeuvres choisies* (Brussels: MRBAB, 2001), pp. 54–5, as quoted in http://www.opac-fabritius.be. P. Baudson, 'Du Constat à l'Interprétation. L'Art Social de Jospeh Stevens à Eugène Laermans', in P. A. Roberts-Jones, *Eugène Laermans, 1864–1940* (Brussels: Crédit Communal, 1995), pp. 51–65.
56. T. Denoël and P. Legrain, *Le nouveau dictionnaire des Belges* (Brussels: Le Cri, 1992), p. 369. C. Lemonnier, *L'École belge de peinture, 1830–1905* (1906; Brussels: Labor, 1991), p. 144.
57. Ankaert, 'Les cabaretiers-cafétiers à la fin du XIXe siècle', p. 31 ; and *Le Globe illustré: Journal de la famille*, 50 (11 September 1887).
58. C. Jewitt and R. Oyama, 'Visual Meaning: A Social Semiotic Approach', in T. Van Leeuwen, and C. Jewitt (eds), *Handbook of Visual Analysis* (London: Sage, 2003), pp. 134–56.
59. Buysse, 'Het bolleken', p. 350.
60. Boëns, *La bière au point de vue médical, hygiénique et social*, p. 100. *Le Scalpel*, 16 (23 October 1881). *Bulletin de la Société médical belge de tempérance*. (June 1900), p. 294.
61. A. Jansen, *De l'usage et de l'abus des boissons et des liqueurs alcooliques. Manuel d'instruction populaire* (Namur: Wesmael-Charlier, 1880), p. 4.
62. Vanoverschelde, 'Tot herstel der krankheid van mijn zwakke geest is nodig', p. 112.
63. *De Sint Jansbode. Maandschrift tegen alcoholism*, 28 (28 January 1894), p. 114.
64. L. Duffin, 'The Conspicuous Consumptive. Woman as an Invalid', in L. Duffin and S. Delamont (eds), *The 19th Century Woman, her Culture and her Physical World* (New York: Croom Helm, 1978), p. 29.
65. See A. Vleugels, 'Class, Gender, Alcohol and Anti-Social Behaviour in the Making of the Habitual Drunkards Act, 1870–1879', in S. Pichard (ed.), *Antisocial Behaviour in Britain since the 18th Century: Sociological and Political Perspectives*, forthcoming.
66. For example: 'Women and Alcohol', *Spectator* (18 February 1871), p. 1870; or 'Over-stimulation in Women', *Gentleman's Magazine*, 244 (1879), p. 111.
67. Walkowitz, J. *Prostitution and Victorian Society: Women, Class and the State* (Cambridge: Cambridge University Press, 1982).
68. V. De Vaucleroy, *L'hérédité alcoolique. Conférence faite à l'assemblée générale de la Ligue patriotique contre l'alcoolisme, le 6 novembre 1892, à Mons* (Brussels: Secrétariat Permanent De La Ligue, 1893), p. 7; and Gaussin, *Le fléau moderne* both quoted the French doctor P. Garnier, *La folie à Paris: Etude statistique, clinique et médico-légale* (Paris: J. B. Baillière 1890).

5 Drunkenness in the Colony

1. D. Van Reybrouck, *Congo, een geschiedenis* (Amsterdam: De Bezige Bij, 2010), p. 21.
2. B. Ceuppens, D. Van Reybrouck and V. Viaene, *Congo in Belgie, koloniale cultuur in de metropool* (Louvain: Louvain University Press, 2009), p. 17.
3. E. Caudelier, *Le gin et le Congo* (Brussels: A. Lefèvre, 1895), p. 5. O. Louwers, and I. Grenade, *Codes et lois du Congo Belge Textes annotés d'après les rapports du conseil colonial, les instructions officielles et la jurisprudence des tribunaux* (Brussels: Weissenbruch, 1923), p. 519. G. Trolli, *Exposé de la législation sanitaire du Congo belge etdu Ruanda-Urundi* (Brussels: Ferd. Larcier, 1938), p. 603.
4. C. De Deken, *Deux ans au Congo* (Antwerp: Clément Thibaut, 1900), p. 36.
5. De Deken, *Deux ans dans le Congo*, p. 71.
6. Caudelier, *Le gin et le Congo*, pp.12–13.
7. A. Conan Doyle, *The Crime of the Congo* (New York: Doubleday, Page & Company, 1909), p. 121.
8. R. Harding Davis, *The Congo and Coasts of Africa* (New York: C. Scribner's Son, 1907), p. 65.
9. H.M. Stanley, *The Congo and the Founding of Its Free State: A Story of Work and Exploration* (1885) *Vol. 1.* (Cambridge: Cambridge University Press, 2011), p. 158.
10. Van Reybrouck, *Congo*, p. 63.
11. e.g. Anon. *Quelques vérités sur le Congo.* [s.l.] s.d. (1895?) Anon. *Catéchisme du Congo, par un ami de l'ouvrier* (Brussels: Van Campenhout, 189?), L. Van Parijs, *Les hontes de la civilisation au Congo belge dévoilée* (La Louvière, 1899).
12. As quoted in Nys, '"De ruiters van de Apocalyps"', p. 14.
13. 'De beschaving der wilden', in Waeri, *Verzameling der volledige kluchtige en politieke liederen van Karel Waeri den Gentschen Beranger*, p.149
14. J. L, Polasky, *The Democratic Socialism of Emile Vandervelde: Between Reform and Revolution* (Oxford: Berg, 1995), pp. 53–82.
15. *Annales parlementaires – Chambre des représentants*, Séance du 10 March (Brussels 1896), p. 127.
16. Caudelier, *Le gin et le Congo*, p.10. *Le Mouvement hygiénique. (M.H.)* (Brussels), 23:2 (février, 1907).
17. Trolli, *Exposé de la législation sanitaire*, p. 603. M. Dorman, *A Journal of a Tour in the Congo Free State* (Brussels, J. Lebègue and Co., 1905), p. 18.
18. Davis, *The Congo*, p. 19.
19. On how women and working classes at home were compared to native people in colonial discourse see A. McClintock, *Imperial Leather: Race, Gender, and Sexuality in the Colonial Contest* (Routledge: London, 1995).
20. A. Conan Doyle, *The Crime of the Congo* (New York: Doubleday, 1909). p. 121
21. J. Willis, *Potent Brews, A Social History of Alcohol in East Africa, 1850–1999* (Nairobi: British Institute of East Africa, 2002).
22. As quoted in Coutenier, M. *Congo tentoongesteld: een geschiedenis van de Belgische antropologie en het museum van Tervuren (1882–1925)* (Louvain: Acco, 2005), p. 85.
23. J. De Mey, '"Gelijk trossen bananen'. Beeldvorming over Congolezen in de Belgische dagbladpers ten tijde van de onafhankelijkheid (1955–1965*)* Een studie van stereotypen, clichés en vooroordelen' (Student Dissertation, Katholieke Universiteit Leuven, 2004).
24. Stanley, *The Congo and the Founding of Its Free State, Vol. I*, p. 202.
25. See above chapter 4: Drunkenness and the Upper Classes, pp.83-6.

26. Stanley, *The Congo and the Founding of Its Free State, Vol. I,* p. 193.
27. Ibid. pp. 194, 202.
28. See further chapter 6: Laissez Faire, Laissez Buvez 1830-1886, pp.108-10.
29. J. Fabian, *Out of our Minds: Reason and Madness in the Exploration of Central Africa* (Berkeley, CA: University of California Press, 2000), pp. 23–30.
30. Dorman, *A Journal of a Tour in the Congo Free State,* p. 79.
31. idem.
32. As quoted in Coutenier, *Congo tentoongesteld,* p. 291.
33. J. Conrad, *Heart of Darkness* (London: Penguin, 2007), p. 44.
34. P. De Mey, *Van Antwerpen naar Stanley-Pool, Reisindrukken etc.*, (Turnhout: Joseph Splichal, 1899), p. 255.
35. Coutenier, *Congo tentoongesteld,* p. 189.
36. H. Van Booven, *Tropenwee* (Amsterdam: Van Holkema and Warendorf, 1905), p. 70.
37. C. Buysse, 'De zwarte kost' (1898), in Buysse, *Verzameld werk [van] Cyriel Buysse. Deel IV,* ed. Van Elslander and Musschoot, pp. 405–55, on p. 442.
38. G. Dryenpondt, and E .Van Campenhout, *Manuel du voyageur et du résident au Congo II. Guide practique d'hygiène, de médecine et chirurgie* (Brussel: Hayez, 1910), p. 114.
39. J. Amerlinck, *Carnets de route, Expédition au Katanga avec M.M. Bia et Francqui (mai 1891–avril 1893),* Samedi 5 Septembre 1891 (Brussels, ed. Le R. Marinel, 1991).
40. C. Achebe, 'An Image of Africa: Racism in Conrad's 'Heart of Darkness'', *Massachusetts Review,* 18 (1977). Reprinted in J. Conrad, *Heart of Darkness, an Authoritative Text, Background and Sources Criticism,* ed. R. Kimbrough (1961; London: W. W Norton and Co., 1988), pp. 251–61.
41. Buysse, 'De zwarte kost', p. 439.
42. De Deken, *Deux ans au Congo,* p. 33.
43. Dryenpondt and Van Campenhout *Manuel du voyageur et du résident au Congo,* pp. 38–9.
44. Dorman, *A Journal of a Tour in the Congo Free State,* p.18.
45. E. Torday, *Camp and Tramp in African Wildes, A Record of Adventures, Impressions* (London: Seeley, 1913), p. 21.
46. Davis, *The Congo,* p. 56.
47. De Mey, *Van Antwerpen naar Stanley-Pool,* p. 255.
48. Davis, *The Congo,* p. 31.
49. Conrad, *Heart of Darkness,* p. 40.
50. Nys, '"Groene toverdrank of gebottelde epilepsie?"', pp. 175–6.

6 Laissez Faire, Laissez Buver: 1830–86

1. For a comparison of policy agendas of different European countries see. J. R. Greenaway, *Drink and British Politics since 1830: A Study in Policy Making* (Basingstoke: Palgrave Macmillan, 2003), p. 196.
2. E. Ducpétiaux, *Mémoire sur le paupérisme dans les Flandres* (Brussels: M. Hayez, 1850).
3. Penn-Hilden, *Women, Work, and Politics,* p. 53.
4. Scholliers, 'Een vijand die men kennen moet', p. 142.
5. E. Ducpétiaux, *De l'intempérance et de l'ivrognerie dans la classe ouvrière* (Brussels: Wauters, 1843), p. 4, as quoted in Declerck, 'Genèse du discours anti-alcoolique en Belgique' . 37.

6. E. Ducpétiaux, *Colonies agricoles, écoles rurales et écoles de réforme pour les indigents, les mendiants et les vagabonds et spécialement pour les enfants en Suisse, en Allemagne, en France, en Angleterre, dans les Pays-Bas et en Belgique. Rapport adressé à M. Tesch, Ministre de la Justice, par Ed. Ducpétiaux* (Brussels: Lesigne, 1851).
7. E. Ducpétiaux, *De l'etat des aliénés en Belgique, et ees moyens d'améliorer leur sort: extrait d'un rapport adressé au ministre de l'intérieur, suivi d'un projet de loi relatif au traitement et a la séquestration des aliénés* (Brussels: Laurent Frères, 1832). W. Van Waesberghe, 'Het Belgische krankzinnigenbeleid in de XIXe eeuw', *Annales de la Société Belge d'Histoire des Hôpitaux et de la Santé Publique*, 22 (1984), pp 69–96.
8. See further Chapter 11: Criminal Antropologists, p. 164.
9. 'Circulaire ministérielle du 12 août 1867', in *Recueil des circulaires, instructions et autres actes emanés du ministère de la justice, ou relatifs à ce département années 1866–67* (Brussels: M. Weissenbruch, 1868.), p. 169.
10. For example : *Bulletin de la Société Médical Belge de Tempérance* (September 1898) p. 352. Planche V.
11. Scholliers, 'Een vijand die men kennen moet', p. 152.
12. Deneckere et al., *Nouvelle histoire de Belgique, Vol. I 1830–1905*, p. 121.
13. H. J. W. Frère-Orban, *De l'abus des boissons enivrantes. Renseignements déposés à la chambre des représentants* (Brussels: M. Hayez, 1868), p. 24.
14. Nicholls, *The Politics of Alcohol*, p. 3.
15. Frère-Orban, *De l'abus des boissons enivrantes*, p. 4.
16. R. Ankaert, 'Les cabaretiers-cafétiers à la fin du XIXe siècle', in. Jaumain and Kurgan-Van Hentenryk (eds), *Aux frontieres des classes moyennes*, pp. 29–57, on p. 35.
17. P. E. Prestwich, *Drink and the Politics of Social Reform: Antialcoholism in France since 1870* (Palo Alto: Society for the Promotion of Science and Scholarship, 1988), p. 16; and M. R. Marrus, 'Social Drinking in the Belle Epoque', *Journal of Social History*, 7:2 (Winter 1974), pp. 120–28, on p. 115. *Annales parlementaires – Chambre des représentants.* Séance du 19 July 1887 (1659) ; Statistique Générale de la Belgique, *Exposé de la situation du royaume de 1876 à 1900* (Brussels: Becquart-Arien, 1909). pp. 313–14 ; and *Annales Chambre.* Séance du 15 July 1887, p. 1660.
18. Hansart *Parliamentary Papers. Reports from the Commissioners*, 1878–9, X, 'Proceedings of the Select Committee on Intemperance House of Lords', p. 16 and p. 173.
19. *Annales parlementaires. Sénat.* Séance du 4 August, 1887, p. 516.
20. *Annales Sénat.* Séance du 15 July, 1887, p. 1645–49.
21. Ankaert, 'Les cabaretiers-cafétiers à la fin du XIXe siècle', p. 43.
22. As quoted in Rowntree, *Land and Labour*, p. 413.
23. H. Verboven, 'Jenever en fiscaliteit', in E. Van Schoonenberghe (ed.), *Jenever in de Lage Landen* (Antwerp: Stichtig Kunstboek, 2004), pp. 179–89, on p.183.
24. Frère-Orban, *De l'abus des boissons enivrantes*, p. 138.
25. E. Witte, J. Craeybeckx and A. Meynen, *Politieke Geschiedenis van Belgie: van 1830 tot Heden* (Antwerp: Standaard, 1990), p. 57.
26. Frère-Orban, *De l'abus des boissons enivrantes*, p.117.
27. A. Faidherbe, *Leçons sur l'Alcoolisme* (Brussels: Société contre l'alcoolisme, 1904). as quoted in Pirlot, 'L'Alcoolisme en Belgique de 1830 à 1950. Mythe et réalité', p. 59.
28. Frère-Orban, *De l'abus des boissons enivrantes*, p. 112
29. Brian Harrison discusses in this context the difference between French and English drinking habits, which has become known as the French paradox: the French seem to

drink more over a long period of time, while English drunkenness is characterized by sporadic excessive drinking bouts. Harrison, *Drink and the Victorians*, p. 25.

30. Frère-Orban, *De l'abus des boissons enivrantes*, p. 153.

7 Catholics, Liberals, Socialists: Change and Drink: 1880–9

1. V. Lorwin, 'Belgium, Religion, Class and Language in National Politics', in R. A. Dahl (ed.), *Political Opposition in Western Democracies* (New Haven, CT: Yale University Press, 1960), pp. 147–87, on p. 156.
2. G. Deneckere, *België op het breukvlak van twee eeuwen* (1900; Tielt: Lannoo, 2006), p. 67.
3. De Vaucleroy, *Premier congrès national Belge contre l'alcoolisme. Liège, 1905. Compte rendu* (Brussels: Sécrétariat Général du Congrès, 1906), p. 52.
4. B. Heyselbergs, 'Onstaansgeschiedenis van de wet Vandervelde en het impact op het alcoholgebruik' (Student Dissertation, Katholieke Universiteit Leuven, 1960), pp. 90–1.
5. Vaderlandschen Bond tegen Alcoolism, *Almanak der matigheid* (Brussels, 1899), p. 68.
6. F. Sterck, *Onze dorpen en de sociale kwestie* (Ninove: Anneessens, 1891). as quoted in B. De Nil, 'Het dublieme verschil. Tussen naturalisme en 'geslachtsdeelrealisme'. De Vlaamse sociaal-democratie en seksualiteit in de toman vòòr 1914', in D. De Weerdt (ed.), *Begeerte heeft ons aangeraakt: socialisten, sekse en seksualiteit* (Ghent: Provinciebestuur van Oost-Vlaanderen, 1999). p. 427.
7. Crispeels, 'De strijd tegen het drankmisbruik in België', p. 60.
8. P. Waeri, 'Geene scholen meer!', in Waeri, *Verzameling der volledige kluchtige en politieke liederen van Karel Waeri den Gentschen beranger*, p. 53.
9. 'Klachten van pastoor en koster over het Gents Gemeentekerkhof'; 'De drij paters'; 'Er moet vanalles zijn'; ''t nieuw Woeste ministerie'; 'Geene scholen meer!', in Waeri, *Verzameling der volledige kluchtige en politieke liederen van Karel Waeri den Gentschen beranger*, pp. 239, 359, 448, 471 and 453.
10. Witte, Craeybeckx and Meynen, *Politieke geschiedenis van België*, p 73.
11. Gaussin, *Le fléau moderne*, p. 223. E. Caudelier, *L'alcoolisme en Belgique* (Brussels: Ligue Patriotique contre l'Alcoolisme, 1889), p. 26. E. Van Coillie, *Alcoolisme et habitations ouvrières* (Brussels: Soc. Belge De Librairie, 1892), pp. 30, 205–18.
12. 'Le cabaretisme', in *Journal de la Ligue patriotique contre l'alcoolisme*, Brussels (January–February, 1891), p. 386.
13. Gaussin, *Le fléau moderne*, p. 223.
14. Penn-Hilden, *Women, Work, and Politics*, p. 162.
15. Van Coillie, *Alcoolisme et habitations ouvrières*, p. 30.
16. F. Lentz, *De l'alcoolisme et de ses diverses manifestations, considérées au point de vue physiologique, pathologique, clinique et médicolégal* (Brussels: Manceaux, 1884), p. 564.
17. Harris, *Murders and Madness*, p. 254; and R. Smith, *Trial by Medicine: Insanity and Responsibility in Victorian Trials* (Edinburgh: Edinburgh University Press, 1981).
18. J. Biesmans, 'Negentiende passionele misdrijven. Beelden en werkelijkheid' (Student Dissertation, University of Ghent, 2001).
19. Scholliers, 'The Medical Discourse and the Drunkard's Stereotyping in Belgium', p. 321.
20. Dumont, *La vie quotidienne en Belgique*, p. 123.
21. Commission du travail instituée par arrêté royal du 15 avril 1886, *Volume V. Procès-verbaux des séances de l'enquête agricole* (Brussels: A. Lesigne, 1890), section D. 40, p. 657.

22. E. Gubin, 'Les enquêtes sur le travail en Belgique et au Canada a la fin du 19e Siècle', in G. Kurgan-Van Hentenryk (eds), *La question sociale en Belgique et au Canada: XIXe–XXe siècles* (Brussels: Editions De L'université De Bruxelles (Brussels. 1988), pp. 93–122.
23. J. Puissant, 'Le bon ouvrier, mythe ou réalité du XIXe siècle. De l'utilité d'une biographie. J. F. J. Dauby (1824–1899)', *Revue belge de philologie et d'histoire*, 56:4 (1978), pp. 878–929, on p. 899.
24. Deneckere, *België op het breukvlak van twee eeuwen*, p. 214. S. Vanfraechem, *Een sfeer om haring the braden: arbeidsverhoudingen in de haven van Antwerpen* (Ghent: Academia Press, 2005), p. 5.
25. Roberts, 'Drink and Industrial Work Discipline In 19th Century Germany'. G. W. Hilton, 'The British Truck System in the Nineteenth Century', *Journal of Political Economy*, 65: 3 (June 1957), pp. 237–56.
26. Commission du travail instituée par arrêté royal du 15 avril 1886. *Volume III. Rapports. Proposition des Sections et conclusions* (Brussels: A. Lesigne, 1887), pp. 191–206.
27. Commission du travail instituée par arrêté royal du 15 avril 1886. *Volume IV. Comte rendus des séances plénières. & mémoires, rapports, lettres etc. envisageant la question ouvrière dans son ensemble* (Brussels: A. Lesigne, 1887), p. 105.
28. *Documents parlementaires – Sénat.* Séance du 5 aout, 1887, p. 523.
29. Nicholls, *The Politics of Alcohol*, p. 123.
30. Nourrisson, *Le buveur du XIXe siècle*, pp. 271–2 and van der Stel, *Drinken, drank en dronkenschap*, pp. 153–6.
31. *Documents Parlementaires – Chambre des Représentants.* Séance du 24 mai, 1887, p. 162.
32. C. Petithan, *Répression de L'Alcoolisme. Interdiction, Collocation* (Liège, Grandmont-Donders, 1881) as quoted in *Documents Chambre.* Séance du 24 mai, 1887, p. 164.
33. *Documents Chambre.* Séance du 24 May 1887, p. 164.
34. *Annales Chambre.* Séance du 15 July 1887, p. 1645 and Sholliers, 'The Medical Discourse and the Drunkard's Stereotyping in Belgium, 1840–1919', p. 232.
35. *Annales Chambre.* Séance du 19 July 1887, 1650.
36. *Annales Chambre.* Séance du 19 July 1887, 1667.
37. S. De Schaepdrijver, 'Reglementering van prostitutie 1844–1877. De opkomst en ondergang van een experiment', *Belgisch tijdschrift voor de nieuwste geschiedenis – Revue belge d'histoire contemporaine*, 17: 3–4 (1985), pp. 473–506.
38. *Annales Chambre.* Séance du 19 July 1887, p. 1654.
39. Nys, '"De Ruiters van de Apocalyps"', pp. 20–1.
40. *Het Volksgeluk*, March 1912, on p. 21.
41. Melchior, *De jeneverplaag, of het alcoolisme in België*, p. 72
42. L. Van Outrive, Y. Cartuyvels and P. Posniers, *Les polices en Belgique: histoire socio-politique du système policier de 1794 à nos jours* (Brussels: Editions Vie Ouvrière, 1991), p. 66. *Le Mouvement hygiénique* (8 August 1895), p. 374. *Annales Sénat.* Séance du 4 August 1887, p. 519.
43. 'De Drankenwet', in Waeri, *Verzameling der volledige kluchtige en politieke liederen van Karel Waeri den Gentschen beranger*, p. 23.
44. *Le Peuple*, 19 April 1887, p. 1, as cited in N. Willems, 'La Loi Vandervelde et ses antécédents' (Student Dissertation, Université Libre Bruxelles, 1971), p. 71.
45. S. Declerck, 'Genèse du discours anti-alcoolique en Belgique', p. 90, n.

8 Remedying Dangerousness

1. Deneckere et al., *Nouvelle Histoire de Belgique, Vol. I 1830–1905*, p. 120.
2. H. Merzbach, in *Almanach de la Tempérance pour 1898*, p. 20 as quoted in J. De Brauwere, *Het beeld van alcohol. Een historische discoursanalyse van de antialcoholcampagnes tussen 1879 en 1919* (Student Dissertation, Vrije Universiteit Brussel, 2007), p. 54.
3. Vandervelde, *Le parti ouvrier et l'alcool*, p. 4 ; E. Vandervelde, *La lutte sociale contre l'alcoolisme* (Brussels: Presse Socialiste, 1899), p. 3.
4. Vandervelde, *Essais socialistes: l'alcoolisme, la religion, l'art*, p. 89.
5. Vandervelde, *La lutte sociale contre l'alcoolisme*, p. 1.
6. B. De Ruyver, 'De alcoholwet Vandervelde in historische en ideologisch perspectief', *Tijdschrift voor sociale wetenschappen*, 27 (1982), pp. 342–69.
7. For the medical concept of degeneration see Part III, pp. 143–74.
8. De Ruyver, 'De alcoholwet Vandervelde', p. 345.
9. For example, the biography of Karel Waeri and Pol de Witte. Waeri, *Verzameling der volledige kluchtige en politieke liederen van Karel Waeri den Gentschen beranger*, p. 4; and P. De Witte, *Alles is omgekeerd: hoe de werklieden vroeger leefden (1848–1918)* (Louvain: Kritak, 1986), p.60.
10. Vandervelde, *La Lutte Sociale contre L'Alcoolisme*, p. 1.
11. F. Domela-Nieuwenhuis, *De l'alcoolisme* (Paris, 1889), p. 225; and *La Lutte sociale contre l'alcoolisme* (Brussels: Presse Socialiste, 1899), p. 57.
12. J. L. Polasky, *The Democratic Socialism of Emile Vandervelde: Between Reform and Revolution* (Oxford: Berg, 1995), p. 33.
13. M. Liebman, *Les Socialistes Belges 1885–1914: La révolte et l'organisation* (Brussels: Editions Vie Ouvriere, 1979), pp. 50–4.
14. E. Vandervelde, *Souvenirs d'un militant socialiste* (Paris: Editions Denoel, 1939), p. 46. E. Gerard, and L. Vos, *Hedendaagse geschiedenis* (Louvain: Acco, 1995), p. 123.
15. L. Weesmaals, *De relatie tussen het antialcoholistisch vrouwelijk activisme en het feminisme in het fin de siècle in België* (Student Dissertation, University of Ghent, 2008).
16. Deneckere, *België op het breukvlak vantTwee eeuwen*, p. 67.
17. D. De Weerdt, *En de vrouwen? Vrouw, vrouwenbeweging en feminisme in België (1830–1960)* (Ghent: Masereelfonds, 1980), p. 75.
18. Parent, *Le rôle de la femme dans la lutte contre l'alcoolisme*, p. 37.
19. S. Matkava, 'L'Union des Femmes Belges contre l'Alcoolisme. 1899–1951: de la lutte antialcoolique aux militantisme féministe et pacifiste' (Student Dissertation, Université Libre Bruxelles, 1998).
20. Parent, *Le rôle de la femme dans la lutte contre l'alcoolisme*, p. 8.
21. van den Plas in *Het Volksgeluk* (November 1911), p. 1; and L. Frank, *La femme contre l'alcool. Etude de sociologie et de législation* (Brussels: H. Lamertin, 1897).
22. J. Lemmens, *L'alcoolisme et la réorganisation ouvrière* (Liège: Imprimerie Moderne, 1907).
23. B. Harris, *The Health of the Schoolchild: A History of the School Medical Service in England and Wales* (Buckingham and Philadelphia, PA: Open University Press, 1995).
24. M. De Vroede, 'Primary Education and the Fight against Alcoholism in Belgium at the Turn of the Century', *History of Education Quarterly*, 30:4 (1985), pp. 483–97. *Bulletin de la Société médical belge de tempérance* (September 1902), p. 405.
25. *Sermons de tempérance et documents pouvant être utiles aux prédicateurs de la tempérance* (Liège: Dessain, 1906), p. 36.

26. E. Dekens, Dubbel Zien, 'Het antialcoholoffensief in beeld', in E. Dekens et al. (eds), *Pierre le buveur et Jean l'abstinent* (Hasselt:National Jenevermuseum, 2009), pp. 21–6, on p. 23.
27. Postcard. Collection *Le bien social*, no. 15. 1902.
28. R. Nye, 'Degeneration and the Medical Model of Cultural Crisis in the French Belle Époque', in S. Drescher, D. Sabean and A. Sharlin (eds), *Political Symbolism in Modern Europe: Essays in Honor of George L. Mosse* (New Brunswick, NJ: Transaction Books, 1982), pp. 19–41.
29. *Bulletin de la Société médical belge de tempérance* (June 1913), p. 181.
30. S. Christiaensen, *Tussen klassieke en moderne criminele politiek: leven en beleid van Jules Lejeune* (Louvain: Louvain University Press, 2004).
31. Dupont-Bouchat, *La Belgique criminelle, droit, justice, société*, p. 271.
32. A. Prins, *La défense sociale et les transformations du droit pénal* (Brussels: Misch et Tron, 1910), pp. 18–9.
33. M. Van De Kerckhove, 'Discours juridique et discours psychiatrique. Aux sources de la loi de la défense sociale', *Droit et Société*, 3 (1986), pp. 279–302.
34. E. Deiss, *Études sociales et industrielles sur la Belgique. Notes de voyage* (Paris: Guillemin, 1900), p. 181.
35. Van Isacker, *Mijn land in de kering*, p. 92.
36. J. C. Pringle, 'The Belgian Detention Colony at Merxplas', *Economic Review*, 19 (1909), pp. 261–81.
37. Rowntree, *Land and Labour*, p. 489.
38. Scholliers, 'The Medical Discourse and the Drunkard's Stereotyping in Belgium', p. 233.
39. Ministère de l'Agriculture, *Commission d'etudes relatives à la question de l'alcoolisme. 1895–1897. Rapports généraux* (Brussels: A. Lesigne, 1897), p. 20.
40. Ministère de l'Agriculture, *Commission d'etudes relatives à la question de l'alcoolisme. 1895–1897. Rapports généraux* (Brussels: A. Lesigne, 1897), p. 102.
41. *Bulletin de L'Académie Royale de Médicine de Belgique*, 12 (1889), p. 554; and *Bulletin de la Société de médicine mentale de Belgique*, 92 (June 1899), pp. 209–21 ; and *Annales Sénat.* Séance du 23 February (1899), p. 115. M. Van De Kerckhove, 'L'organisation d'asiles spéciaux pour aliénés dangereux', in F. Tulkens (ed.), *Généalogie de la défense sociale en Belgique (1880–1914)* (Brussels: E. Story-Scientia, 1988), p. 125.
42. Van De Kerckhove, 'L'organisation d'asiles spéciaux pour aliénés dangereux', pp. 121–2.
43. G. Hunt, J. Mellor and J. Turner, 'Wretched, Hatless and Miserably Clad: Women and the Inebriate Reformatories from 1900–1913', *British Journal of Sociology*, 11 (1989), pp. 244–70.
44. Nys, '"Groene toverdrank of gebottelde epilepsie?" Absint in België omstreeks 1900', pp. 155-82.
45. Nys, '"Groene toverdrank of gebottelde epilepsie?" 175.
46. Nourrisson, *Le buveur du XIXe siècle*, pp. 287–306. Greenaway, *Drink and British Politics Since 1830*, pp. 91–113; and G. W. Gutzke, 'Gender, Class, and Public Drinking in Britain during the First World War', in J. S. Blocker and C. L. Warsh (eds), *The Changing Face of Drink: Substance, Imagery, and Behaviour* (Ottawa: Les Publications Histoire Sociale – Social History Inc, 1997), pp. 291–319.
47. A. Ley, *L'aliénation mentale et l'alcoolisme à Bruxelles pendant la Guerre* (Brussels: Impr. des Travaux Publics, 1919).
48. De Ruyver, 'De alcoholwet vandervelde', p. 342.
49. A. Ley, *La loi Belge de 1919 contre l'alcoolisme et ses résultats* (Paris: Doin, 1929).
50. De Ruyver, 'De alcoholwet vandervelde', p. 365.
51. Gerard and Vos, *Hedendaagse geschiedenis*, p. 154.

Part III: Drunkenness and its Specialists

1. On the use of the idea of medicalization by historians see: R. Nye, 'The Evolution of the Concept of Medicalisation in the Late 20th Century', *Journal of the History of Behavioral Sciences*, 29:2 (2003), pp. 115–29. For an introduction to the Belgian situation: K. Velle, 'Medikalisering in Belgie in Historisch Perspektief, een inleiding', *Belgisch tijdschrift voor de nieuwste geschiedenis – Revue belge d'histoire contemporaine*, 64:2 (1986), pp. 266–85.
2. Velle, *De nieuwe biechtvaders*, pp. 25–32 and M. Foucault, *The History of Sexuality. Volume 1: An Introduction* (New York: Vintage Books, 1978), pp. 56–9. D. Sevenois, *De anti-alcoholproblematiek van het einde van de 19de eeuw tot het begin van de 20ste eeuw en de rol van de medische professie hierin.* (Student Dissertation, Vrije Universiteit Brussel, 2006).
3. R. Nye, 'Degeneration and the Medical Model of Cultural Crisis in the French Belle Époque', in S. Drescher, D. Sabean and A. Sharlin (eds), *Political Symbolism in Modern Europe: Essays in Honor of George L. Mosse* (New Brunswick: Transaction Books, 1982) pp. 19–41, on p. 21.
4. See for Belgium: P. Scholliers, 'The Medical Discourse and the Drunkard's Stereotyping in Belgium, 1840–1919', in A. Fenton (ed.), *Order and Disorder. The Health Implications of Eating and Drinking in the Nineteenth and Twentieth Centuries* (East Linton: Tuckwell Press, 2000), pp. 227–39. For England: G. Johnstone, 'From Vice to Disease? The Concepts of Dipsomania and Inebriety, 1860–1908', *Social and Legal Studies*, 5 (1996), pp. 37–56. For France: Sournia, *Histoire de l'alcoolisme* and Nourrisson, *Le buveur du XIXe siècle*.
5. Nye, 'The Evolution of the Concept of Medicalisation', p. 117.
6. J. S. Madden, 'Substance Use Disorders. Clinical Section', in G. E. Berrios and R. Porter (eds), *A History Of Clinical Psychiatry: The Origin And History Of Psychiatric Disorders* (London: Athlone Press, 1995), pp. 656–67, and H. G. Levine, 'The Vocabulary Of Drunkenness', *Journal of Studies on Alcohol*, 42:3 (1981), pp. 1038–51.
7. S. Declerck, 'Genèse du discours anti-alcoolique en Belgique 1830–1970' (Student Dissertation, Université Libre Bruxelles. 1994), p. 60.
8. *Le Mouvement hygiénique* (August 1877), p. 287.
9. *Bulletin de la Société médical belge de tempérance*, 39 (March 1905), p. 140.

9 The Hygienists

1. Velle, 'Medikalisering in België', p. 266.
2. On the hygienists R. Schepers, 'Een wereld van belangen. Artsen en de ontwikkelingen van de openbare gezondheidszorg', and L. Nys, '"Nationale plagen: Hygiënisten over het maatschappelijk lichaam"', in Nys et al. (eds), *De zieke natie*, pp. 200–18 and pp. 220–41.
3. On Dr. Mareska, see A. Quetelet, *Sciences mathématiques et physiques chez les Belges, au commencement du XIXe siècle* (Brussels: Thiry-Van Buggenhoudt, 1866), p. 304.
4. G. J. Mareska and J. Heyman, *Enquête sur le travail et la condition physique et morale des ouvriers employés dans les manufactures de coton, à Gand* (Ghent: Gyselynck, 1845).
5. J. H. Warner, 'Psychological Theory and Therapeutic Explanation in the 1860's: the British Debate on the Medical Use of Alcohol', *Bulletin of the History of Medicine*, 54 (1980), pp. 235–57, on p. 253 and H. W. Paul, *Bacchic Medicine: Wine and Alcohol Therapies from Napoleon to the French Paradox* (Amsterdam: Rodopi, 2001).
6. Vandervelde, *Essais socialistes: l'alcoolisme, la religion, l'art*, p. 60.
7. Jansen, *De l'usage et de l'abus des boissons et des liqueurs alcooliques*, p. 69.

8. Boëns, *La bière au point de vue médical, hygiénique et social*, p. 151.
9. Pirlot, 'L'alcoolisme en Belgique de 1830 à 1950. Mythe et réalité, p. 50.
10. *Bulletin de la Société médical belge de tempérance* (March 1908), p. 102.
11. L . Nys, 'Moderation as a Medical Moral. The Invention of the Hygienic body in Belgium ca. 1840–1914'. Unpublished Paper. Anglo-Dutch-German Workshop: Patients' Body Perceptions, Warwick, 11–13 July 2003.
12. P. Meyers, *Het N.P.C. Sint-Alfons door de tijden heen 1843–1993* (Ghent, 1993).
13. Boulanger, 'L'alcool dans des asiles des aliénés', *Bulletin de la Société de médicine mentale de Belgique*, 146:7 (August–October 1909), pp. 359–66.
14. B. De Ruyver and J. Goethals, 'Auguste Ley 1873–1956', in C. Fijnaut (ed.), *Gestalten uit het verleden. 32 voorgangers in de rechtswetenschap, de strafrechtpleging en de criminologie* (Deurne: Kluwer, 1993) and A. Ley, *Rapport sur le service médicale du santarium du Fort Jaco, à Uccle en 1908* (Brussels, 1908), p. 13.
15. See for example, W. Tuke on beer in Asylums in Britain in *Journal of Mental Science*, 30:535 (1884–85) and *Le Scalpel* (22 April 1900).
16. Maison de Santé le Strop. Registre médical [E] 1045, 28 July 1904.
17. H. Barella, 'Note sur l'internement et la libération des irresponsables dangereux', *Bulletin de l'Académie royale de médecine de Belgique*, 14 (1900), p. 355.
18. H. Barella, *Les alcools et l'alcoolisme* (Brussels: Manceaux, 1879), p. 9.
19. E. Dekens, 'Dubbel zien, Het antialcoholoffensief in beeld', in Dekens et al. (eds), *Pierre le buveur et Jean l'abstinent*, pp. 21–6.
20. G. Leboucq, 'Barella (Hippolyte)', in *Biographie nationale*, 29:1 (Brussels: Emile Bruylant, 1967), pp. 202–4.
21. Scholliers, 'The Medical Discourse and the Drunkard's Stereotyping in Belgium', p. 230.
22. Nys, '"Nationale plagen"', p. 230 and Velle, *De nieuwe biechtvaders*, pp. 317–18.
23. On the temperance movement in Britain, see Harrison, *Drink and the Victorians*; and in Holland, see van der Stel, *Drinken, drank en dronkenschap*.
24. Crispeels, 'De strijd tegen het drankmisbruik in België', p. 57.
25. A. R. Aisenberg, *Contagion: Disease, Government, and the 'Social Question' in Nineteenth-Century France* (Stanford, CA: Stanford University Press, 1999), p. 71; and D. S. Barnes, *The Making of a Social Disease: Tuberculosis in Nineteenth-Century France* (Berkeley, CA: University of California Press, 1995), pp. 138–73.
26. Nys, '"De ruiters van d'apocalypse"', pp. 15–17.
27. Commission du travail Instituée par arrêté royal du 15 avril 1886. *Volume I. Réponses au questionnaire concernant le travail industriel* (Brussels: A. Lesigne, 1887), q. 1111, p. 5443.
28. *Bulletin de la Société médical belge de tempérance* (September 1898), p. 1; (September 1902), p. 403.
29. *Bulletin de la Société médical belge de tempérance* (March 1908), p. 102.
30. C. Havelange, 'De uitvinding van de wanorde. Het negentiende-eeuwse verbond tussen collectiviteit en gezondheid', in Nys, et al. (eds), *De zieke natie*, pp. 74–85, on p. 82.
31. P. J. Vandeven, *Considérations sur les causes de la dégénérescence de l'espèce humaine, et sur les moyens d'y remédier* (Louvain: Van Linthout, 1850), p. 7; E. van den Corput, *L'alcoolisme, ses causes mésologiques, son extinction physiologique* (Paris: Masson et Cie., 1897), p. 13.
32. *Bulletin de l'Académie royale de médecine de Belgique*, 9 (1897), p. 881. I. Dowbiggin, *Inheriting Madness: Professionalization and Psychiatric Knowledge in Nineteenth-Century France* (Berkeley, CA: University of California Press, 1991), p. 118.

33. P. M. Legrain, *Hygiène et prophylaxie: dégénérescence sociale et alcoolisme* (Paris: Carré, 1895), p. 25 and R. Huertas, 'Madness and Degeneration, II. Alcoholism and Degeneration', *History of Psychiatry*, 4 (1993), pp. 1–21, on p. 1.
34. Van den Corput, *Le poison alcool* and E. Masoin, *Discours prononcé aux funérailles de M. Ed. Van den Corput* (Brussels: Hayez, 1908).
35. Van den Corput, *L'Alcoolisme, l'hérédité et la question sociale*, p. 6; and J. Tollebeek, 'Degeneratie, moderniteit en culturele verandering. Een Belgisch perspectief', pp. 302.
36. Van den Corput, *L'Alcoolisme, ses causes mésologiques*, p. 13.
37. On alcoholism and degeneration see: W. F. Bynum, 'Alcoholism and Degeneration in 19th Century European Medicine and Psychiatry', *British Journal of Addiction*, 79 (1984), pp. 59–70; and Huertas, 'Madness and Degeneration', pp. 1–21. J. Borel, *Du concept de dégénérescence a la notion d'alcoolisme dans la médecine contemporaine. Les campagnes anti-alcooliques de 1865 à 1965* (Montpellier: Causse, 1968).
38. Nys, '"De Ruiters van de Apocalyps"', p. 28.
39. Commission du travail instituée par arrêté royal du 15 avril 1886. *Volume I. Réponses au questionnaire concernant le travail industriel* (Brussels: A. Lesigne, 1887), q. 1111, p .5443.
40. C. Petithan, *La dégénérescence de la race belge, ses causes et ses remèdes* (Brussels: H. Lamertin, 1889), p. 76 and Nys, '"De grote school van de natie"', p. 402. On Charles Petithan and his ideas of degeneration of the Belgian race see also: C. Havelange, 'La Belgique médico-sociale, l'individu, la société, la race', in G. Kurgan-Van Hentenryk (ed.), *Laboratoires et réseaux de diffusion des idées en Belgique: XIXe–XXe siècles* (Brussels: Editions de l'Université de Bruxelles, 1994), p. 25–6.
41. Bynum, 'Alcoholism and Degeneration', p. 67–8 and J. D. Woiak, 'Drunkenness, Degeneration and Eugenics in Britain, 1900–1914' (PhD Dissertation, University of Toronto, 1998), pp. 189–90.
42. *Bulletin de l'Académie royale de médecine de Belgique*, 14 (1900), p. 341.
43. *Le Mouvement hygiénique* (August 1887), p. 288.
44. Lentz, *De l'alcoolisme et de ses diverses manifestations*, p. 540.

10 The Alienists

1. Seneca, *Letters from a Stoic: Epistulae Morales Ad Lucilium*, ed. R. Campbell (London: Penguin, 1969), p. 143.
2. On madness and drunkenness: For France see: C. Quétel, and J. Y. Simon, 'L'aliénation Alcoolique en France (XIXe et 1ère moitié du XXe Siècle)', *Histoire, Economie, Société*, 7:4 (1988), pp. 507–33. For Britain see: P. Mccandless, '"Curses of Civilisation': Insanity and Drunkenness in Victorian Britain', *British Journal of Addiction*, 79 (1984), pp. 49–58.
3. *Bulletin de la Société de médicine mentale de Belgique*, 146:7 (August– October 1909), p. 360.
4. M. Valverde, *Diseases of the Will: Alcohol and the Dilemmas of Freedom* (Cambridge: Cambridge University Press, 1998), p. 43–67.
5. J. Goldstein, *Console and Classify: the French Psychiatric Profession in the Nineteenth Century* (Cambridge: Cambridge University Press, 1987), p. 178.
6. J. Guislain, and B. C. Ingels, *Leçons orales sur les phrénopathies : ou traité théorique et pratique des maladies mentales. Cours donné à la clinique des établissements d'aliénés à Gand* (Paris: J. B. Bailliere, 1880). t. 2. p. 92.

7. B. Lefebvre, *De l'augmentation du nombre des aliénés à notre epoque et des causes de cette augmentation* (Brussels: Devaux, 1866).
8. E. Shorter, *A History of Psychiatry: From the Era of the Asylum to the Age of Prozac* (New York: Wiley, 1997).
9. *Bulletin de la Société médical belge de tempérance* (September 1898), p. 352.
10. J. Godderis, 'De geesteszieken: Nieuwe inzichten en instellingszorg', in L. Dhaene, G. Hertecant, K. Velle and J. De Maeyer (eds), *Er is leven voor de dood: tweehonderd jaar gezondheidszorg in Vlaanderen* (Kapellen: Pelckmans, 1998), p. 68.
11. *Treizième rapport sur la situation des asiles d'aliénés du royaume; années 1883 à 1892* (Brussels: Goemaere, 1895).
12. Prins, *La défense sociale et les transformations du droit pénal*, pp. 15–16. On *défense sociale* see above pp. 129-131.
13. A. Mahaim, *L'alcool et les maladies mentales* (Liège: Aug. Bénard, 1901), X. Francotte, *Alcool et folie* (Liège : G. Faust-Truyen, Liège. 1899).
14. Very little material remains for the two institutions in Ghent catering for female patients. See: Vanoverschelde, 'Tot herstel der krankheid van mijn zwakke geest is nodig'.
15. If the period is divided up, an increase in the awareness of alcohol abuse in general can be clearly detected in the admission records: In the period 1851–1883 in *le Strop* 14.6 per cent of the admissions were related to alcoholism, in the period 1883–1914, it had become 18.5 per cent. In the lower class asylum, the rise was ever more dramatic: from 21.8 per cent of registrations in the *Hospice Guislain* where alcohol was implicated for the period 1851–85, it became 30.4 per cent, for the period 1885–1909.
16. Initial work has been done in this context for France by Jacqueline Lalouette who studied the population of two local, rural institutions where, according to her research, 3.2 to 6.8 per cent of the men and 0.8 to 1.3 per cent of women suffered from alcoholism. The conclusions of her study remain vague mainly outlining that many alcoholics in the hospital were employed in the local wine industries. J. Lalouette, 'Alcoolisme et classe ouvrière en France aux alentours de 1900', *Cahiers d'Histoire,* 42:1 (1997), pp. 89–107.
17. P. Prestwich, 'Drinkers, Drunkards, and Degenerates: The Alcoholic Population of a Parisian Asylum', *Social History/Histoire Sociale*, 27:53–4 (1994), pp. 321–35'.
18. R. Stockman, 'Life Within the Walls of the Guislain Mental Institution (1850–1950)', in L. De Goei and J. Vijselaar (eds), *Proceedings of the First European Congress on the History of Psychiatry and Mental Health Care* (Rotterdam: Erasmus Publishing, 1993), p. 194–203 and L. Elaut, 'Benjamin Ingels, psychiater, de vinnige', *Annalen van het Noorden* (1957), pp. 2–3.
19. *Actes du troisième congrès international d'anthropologie criminelle. Tenu à Bruxelles en août 1892* (Brussels: Hayez, 1893) and J. Morel, et Congrès national belge contre l'alcoolisme, *Rapport sur les désastres produits par l'alcoolisme (criminalité, aliénation mentale, dégénérescence)* (Brussels: Secrétariat Générale du Congres, 1907).
20. Stockman, 'Life within the Walls of the Guislain Mental Institution (1850–1950)', p. 194.
21. A. Liégois, 'Triest, Guislain en de Broeders en Zusters van Liefde', in P. Vandermeersch (ed.), *Psychiatrie, godsdienst en gezag: de onstaansgeschiedenis van de psychiatrie in België als paradigma* (Louvain: Acco, 1984), pp. 171–203, on pp. 191–2.
22. Meyers, *Het N.P.C. Sint-Alfons door de tijden heen 1843–1993.* Initial work on patient profiles in both asylums in V. Van Den Abeele, 'Het sociaal-geografisch profiel van de opgenomen krankzinnigen en het dagelijks leven in twee Gentse mannengestichten, 1857–1900' (Student dissertation, University of Ghent, 1999).
23. Melchior, *De jeneverplaag, of het alcoolisme in België*, p. 51.

24. Hospice Guislain. Registre médical, 16, 5294, 13 June 1888.
25. Prestwich has calculated that for the French public asylums diagnoses of alcoholism made up 23.8 per cent of the male admissions and that in 7.3 per cent of the cases alcohol was listed as a contributing factor. In the Ghent public asylum these numbers were respectively 8 per cent and 18 per cent, so there was clearly a much higher number of alcoholics diagnosed in Paris than in Ghent's public asylum. Prestwich, 'Drinkers, Drunkards and Degenerates', p. 325.
26. For an important discussion on the use of hospital case notes for historical analysis, see J. Andrews, 'Documents and Sources. Case Notes, Case Histories and the Patient's Experience of Insanity at Gartnavel Royal Asylum, Glasgow, in the Nineteenth Century', *Social History of Medicine,* 11:2 (1998), pp. 255–81; and G. B. Risse, and J. H. Warner, 'Reconstructing Clinical Activities: Patient Records in Medical History', *Social History of Medicine,* 5 (2004), p. 183–205; and J. Radkau, 'The Neurasthenic Experience in Imperial Germany: Expeditions into Patient Records and Side-looks upon General History', M. Gijswijt-Hofstra, and R. Porter (eds), *Cultures of Neurasthenia from Beard to the First World War* (Amsterdam ; New York: Rodopi, 2001), pp. 199–217. On questions of class and asylum care see J. Andrews and A. Digby, 'Introduction: Gender and Class in the Historiography of British and Irish Psychiatry', in J. Andrews, and A. Digby (eds), *Sex and Seclusion, Class and Custody: Perspectives on Gender and Class in the History of British and Irish Psychiatry* (Amsterdam: Rodopi, 2004), pp. 7–44.
27. *Revue des questions scientifiques* (9 January 1881), p. 497 ; and (10 October 1881), p. 551 ; and Guislain and Ingles, *Leçons orales sur les phrénopathies*, vol. 2, p. 92.
28. I. Dowbiggin, *Inheriting Madness,* pp. 118-121. and I. Dowbiggin, 'Back to the Future: Valentin Magnan, French Psychiatry and the Classification of Mental Diseases 1885–1925', *Social History of Medicine*, 9:3 (December 1996), pp. 383–408 on p. 390.
29. 'Dégénérescence et l'espèce humaine', *La Santé* (10 May 1857), p. 244 as quoted in S. Declerck, 'Genèse du discours anti-alcoolique en Belgique, p. 95.
30. *Het Volksgeluk* (December 1912), p. 81.
31. Lentz, *De l'alcoolisme et de ses diverses manifestations*, p. 556.
32. Maison de Santé le Strop. Registre médical. [E] 983. 24 January 1902; and Hospice Guislain. Registre médical 16, 5305, 7 July 1888.
33. *Revue des questions scientifique*, 10 October 1881, p. 553.
34. Hospice Guislain. Registre médical 27, 7226, 16 November 1880.
35. Hospice Guislain. Registre médical, 18, 5863, 18 March 1895.
36. Prestwich, 'Drinkers, Drunkards and Degenerates', p. 127.
37. For example, Nye, *Degeneration and the Medical Model of Cultural Crisis in the French Belle Époque*, pp. 19–41; and D. Pick, *Faces of Degeneration: A European Disorder, c. 1848–c. 1918* (Cambridge: Cambridge University Press, 1989); and Harris, *Murders and Madness*, p. 255; and in England D. Porter, '"Enemies of the Race": Biologism, Environmentalism, and Public Health in Edwardian England', *Victorian Studies*, 34:2 (Winter 1991), pp. 159–78; and R. Soloway, 'Counting the Degenerates: The Statistics of Race Deterioration in Edwardian England', *Journal of Contemporary History*, 17:1 (1982), pp. 137–64.
38. In Maison de Santé le Strop, thurteen patients were diagnosed with one or another form of *dégénérescence* (1.15 per cent), all by Dr Maere between 1899 and 1911, while, in the Hospice Guislain, as mentioned, there were only ten degenerates among the alcoholic patients in the sample (0.5 per cent).
39. Maison de Santé le Strop. Régistre médical. [E] 1020, 23 October 1903.

40. Valverde, *Diseases of the Will*, p. 57.
41. Postcard: La Ligue Patriotique contre l'Alcoolisme (Brussels, 1913), Jenevermuseum, Hasselt.
42. Postcard: La Ligue Patriotique contre l'Alcoolisme (Brussels, 1910), Jenevermuseum, Hasselt.
43. Maison de Santé le Strop. Registre médical, A 1865–1873, 1 March 1872.
44. For example: Lentz, *De l'alcoolisme et de ses diverses manifestations*, p. 471.
45. R. Porter, 'The Drinking Man's Disease: The "Pre-history" of Alcoholism in Georgian Britain', *British Journal of Addiction*, 80 (1985), pp. 385–96.
46. V. Magnan, *De l'alcoolisme, des diverses formes du délire alcoolique et de leur traitement* (Paris: Adrien Delahaye, 1874). Magnan devoted almost two thirds of this influential work on alcoholism to 'delirium tremens'.
47. Guislain et al., *Leçons orales sur les phrénopathies*, t. 2, p. 92.
48. Ibid., p. 141.
49. *Le Scalpel. Organe des garanties médicale du peuple et des intérêts sociaux et scientifique de la médicine, de la pharmacie et de l'art vétérinaire. 1850–1914* (2 March 1884) p. 230; (16 March 1884) p. 246; (20 April 1884) ; and (24 April 1884) p. 284.
50. V. Magnan, *Leçons cliniques sur la dipsomanie faites à l'asile Sainte-Anne* (Paris: A. Delahaye et E. Lecrosnier, 1884) ; and J. Dallemagne, *Dégénérés et déséquilibrés* (Brussels: Lamertin, 1894), p. 554.
51. Dallemagne, *Dégénérés et déséquilibrés*, p. 555.
52. Lentz, *De l'alcoolisme et de ses diverses manifestations*, p. 562.
53. Barella, *Rapport de la commission à laquelle a été renvoyé le mémoire de M. le docteur Mora*, p. 16.
54. R. De Ryckère, *L'Alcoolisme féminin* (Lyon: Storck, 1899), p. 29.
55. Ibid., p. 113.
56. *Bulletin de l'Académie royale de médecine de Belgique*, 15 (1881) p. 13.
57. Prestwich, 'Drinkers, Drunkards and Degenerates', p. 127. Although Magnan himself was superintendent here, at St Anne in a sample of over 1,200 cases she only counted twenty-two cases diagnosed with *dipsomanie* and most of them where women.
58. E. M. Brown, '"What Shall we do with the Inebriete?" Asylum Treatment and the Disease Concept of Alcoholism in the late Nineteenth Century', *Journal of the Behavioral Sciences*, 21 (1985), pp. 48–59.
59. E. Van den Corput, *Le poison alcool. Nouvelles considérations à propos de l'alcoolisme* (Brussels: Weissenbruch, 1895), p. 15.
60. Maison de Santé le Strop. Registre médical, [E] 1045, 28 July 1904.
61. *Le Scalpel* (23 March 1884), p. 250.
62. Maison de Santé le Strop. Registre médical, D 51, 7 September 1887.
63. Maison de Santé le Strop. Registre médical, D 10, 7 July 1884; E 983, 24 November 1902 ; and D 148, 27 September 1885.
64. C. Quétel, *History of Syphilis* (Cambridge: Polity Press, 1990), p. 164.
65. Guislain and Ingels, *Leçons orales sur les phrénopathies*, pp. 54–5, 92.
66. W. Griesinger, *Mental Pathology and Therapeutics* (1861), as quoted in E. H. Hare, 'The Origin and Spread of Dementia Paralytica', *British Journal of Psychiatry*, 105 (1950), pp. 594–626, on p. 600.
67. V. Magnan and P. Sérieux, *La paralysie générale* (Paris : G. Masson, 1894).

68. As pointed out in contemporary manuals found in the library of the hospice Guislain. For example: B. Ball, *Leçons sur les maladies mentales* (Paris: P. Asselin, 1883), p. 652; and W. Weygandt, *Atlas-manuel de psychiatrie* (Paris: J.-B. Baillière et fils, 1904), p. 585.
69. Nys, 'De ruiters van de apocalyps', pp. 26–46.
70. Lentz, *De l'alcoolisme et de ses diverses manifestations*, p. 510
71. *Bulletin de l'Académie royale de médecine de Belgique*, 9 (1875), pp. 11, 111 (1897), p. 864.
72. Hospice Guislain. Registre médical, 15, 4815 June 1881.
73. Hospice Guislain. Registre médical, 18, 5682, 3 December 1892.
74. Nys, 'De ruiters van de apocalyps', p. 28.
75. Maison de Santé le Strop. Registre médical, [E] 903, 1 September 1899, and 913, 31 December 1899 and Hospice Guislain. Registre médical. 27, 7133, 20 December 1907, and 27, 7254, 13 February 1909.

11 The Criminal Anthropolgists

1. S. Durviaux, 'Le cercle universitaire pour les études criminologieques', P. Mary and P. Van Der Vorst (eds), *Cent ans de criminologie à l'ULB* (Brussels: Bruylant, 1990), pp. 21–44 and Velle, K., 'De misdaad als kwaal. Het succes van de criminele antropologie', in Nys et al. (eds), *De zieke natie*, pp. 332–54 and R. De Bont, 'Meten en verzoenen. Louis Vervaeck en de criminele antropologie, 1900–1940', in Tollebeek et al. (eds), *Degeneratie in België 1860–1940*, pp. 185–225.
2. J. Dallemagne, *Les biologiques et sociologiques de la criminalité* (Paris: G. Masson, 1896), p. 79.
3. *Bulletin de l'Académie royale de médecine de Belgique*, 10 (1896), p. 415.
4. *Bulletin de la Société de médicine mentale de Belgique* (September 1896), p. 325
5. *Bulletin de la Société médical belge de tempérance* (October 1906), p. 420.
6. 'Circulaire ministérielle du 12 août 1867', *in Recueil des circulaires*, p. 169.
7. Brown, '"What Shall We Do with the Inebriete?"', p. 54.
8. In Britain in the nineteenth century a public debate raged about the topic of wrongful confinement of lunatics in private asylums in general. See, for example, F. L. Winslow, *On Uncontrollable Drunkenness Considered as a Form of Mental Disorder, with the Only Possible Means of Legally Dealing with Such Cases* (London: Henderson & Spalding, 1892). In Belgium there were no such qualms expressed by the public. Interestingly Lady Audley in M. E. Braddon's sensation novel of 1862 was shipped off to a Belgian Maison de Santé. M. E. Braddon, *Lady Audley's Secret* (1860–1) (London: Penguin, 1998), p. 373.
9. See Part II. On the 1850 Lunacy Law and the ministerial circular of 1867 see also above Chapter 6 Laissez faire, laissez buver, p. 106.
10. *Le Mouvement hygiénique* (April 1887), p. 158 and (August 1887), p. 287.
11. Foucault, *Abnormal*, p. 34.
12. J. Baumohl and R. Room, 'Inebriety, Doctors, and the State: Alcoholism Treatment Institutions before 1940', in M. Galanter (ed.), *Recent Developments in Alcoholism Vol. 5.* (New York: Plenum Publishing, 1987), pp. 135–74; and *Le Mouvement hygiénique* (January 1894) p. 45.
13. Nicholls, *The Politics of Alcohol*, p. 165.
14. V. De Vaucleroy, *L'Hérédité alcoolique. Conférence faite à l'assemblée générale de la Ligue patriotique contre l'alcoolisme, le 6 novembre 1892, à Mons* (Brussels: Secrétariat Permanent De La Ligue, 1893), p. 17.

15. *Het Volksgeluk* (August 1894), p. 64 and G. Delaunois, *Entretiens sur l'intempérance. misère, maladie, crime* (Brussels: Hayez, 1889) and G. Delaunois, *Les maux du buveur* (Brussels: Société Belge de librairie, 1895).
16. Hospice Guislain. Registre médical, 16, 5173, 31 August 1886.
17. *Bulletin de l'Académie royale de médecine de Belgique*, 14 (1900), p. 363.
18. Maison de Santé le Strop. Registre médical. G 120, 1 August 1883.
19. A similar debate was taking place in France in the same years. See R. Nye, *Crime, Madness and Politics in Modern France: the Medical Concept of National Decline* (Princeton, NJ: Princeton University Press, 1984), pp. 234–5.
20. *Bulletin de l'Académie royale de médecine de Belgique*, 14 (1900), p. 337.
21. *Bulletin de la Société de médicine mentale de Belgique*, 93 (1899), p. 220.
22. *Bulletin de l'Académie royale de médecine de Belgique*, 14 (1900), p. 338.
23. F. Preiswerk, 'Auguste Forel (1848–1931): Un projet de régénération sociale, morale et raciale', *Annuelles – Revue d'histoire contemporaine*, 2 (1991), pp. 25–50. Forel gave a lecture in 1907 on the *XIe International Congress on Alcoholism* on 'L'alcool et les questions sexuelles' in which he explained his theories as sexologist arguing that the use of alcohol was also the chief cause of 'sexual aberration'. On the same conference Emile Vandevelde spoke about 'alcoholism and the social question'. *Bulletin de la Société médical belge de tempérance* (June 1907).
24. Harris, *Murders and Madness*, p. 102.
25. Guislain and Ingels, *Leçons orales sur les phrénopathies*, p. 142.
26. Ibid.
27. *Bulletin de la Société de médicine mentale de Belgique*, 93 (1899), pp. 209–21 and 92 (1899), pp. 42–54.
28. *Bulletin de l'Académie royale de médecine de Belgique*, 14 (1900), p. 360.
29. '"Groene toverdrank of gebottelde epilepsie?" Absint in België omstreeks 1900', in Tollebeek et al. (eds), *Degeneratie in België 1860–1940*, pp. 155–82, on p. 165.
30. *Bulletin de la Société médical belge de tempérance* (September 1911), p. 351.
31. Vanoverschelde, 'Tot herstel der krankheid van mijn zwakke geest is nodig', p. 112.
32. R. De Ryckère, *La femme en prison et devant la mort* (Lyon: Storck, 1898) and R. De Ryckère, *La servante criminelle. Etude de criminologie professionnelle* (Paris: A. Maloine, 1908).
33. K. Velle, 'Het beeld van de magistratuur van de Belle Epoque tot na de Eerste Wereldoorlog. Casus: Raymond de Ryckere (1862–1918)', in F. Daelemans, M. Lebert, E. Bodart, L. Honnoré and J. Houssiau (eds), *Image et imagination. Recueil d'articles offert à André Vanrie à l'occasion de son septantième anniversaire. Archives et bibliothèques de Belgique*, 91, special issue (Brussels: Bibliothèque Royale de Belgique, 2010), pp. 483–518, on p.499–500.
34. De Ryckère, *L'Alcoolisme féminin*, p. 27.
35. Harris, *Murders and Madness*, p. 243.
36. De Ryckère, *L'Alcoolisme féminin*, p. 28.
37. *Bulletin de l'Académie royale de médecine de Belgique*, 12 (1898) and *Bulletin de la Société de médicine mentale de Belgique*, 90 (1898) p. 268–282 and 91 (1898) pp. 390–400.
38. De Ryckère, *L'Alcoolisme féminin*, p. 27.
39. Ibid., p. 114. C. Lemonnier, *La faute de Mme Charvet* (Paris: E. Deniu, 1895) and L. Couperus, *Eline Vere. Een Haagsche roman* (1889) (Amsterdam/Antwerp: Veen, 1991).
40. M. Valverde, 'Slavery from Within: The Intervention of Alcoholism and the Question of Free Will', *Social History*, 12:3 (1997), pp. 251–68, on p. 255.

WORKS CITED

Primary Sources

Archives museum dr Guislain, Ghent

Fonds Guislain

Maison des hommes aliénés. Livre de clinique, 2, 1851, 1511–1578.

7, 1856, 1853–1936.

9, 1859, 2151–2273.

Hospice Guislain. Registre médical, 15, August 1879–February 1885: 4674–557.

16 February 1885– August 1890: 5075–5474.

18 October 1892–June 1895: 5675–5884.

21 August 1899–July 1901: 6282–6479.

24 July 1904–May 1905: 6787–6885.

27 July 1907–May 1909: 7085–7285.

Hospice Guislain. Registres matricules: 1850–1914.

Fonds St. Alfons – Maison de santé le Strop

Maison de Santé le Strop. Livre de clinique, 1851–58.

Maison de Santé le Strop. Registre médical, B1 1861 a 1865, 1–99.

A 1865–1873, 1–146.

G 30 January 1875–17 November 1883: 1–123.

D November 1883–April 1898: 1–197.

[E] 1 April 1898–14 December 1905: 868–1084.

[F] January 1906–July 1914: 1085–1282.

Maison de Santé le Strop. Registres matricules, 1850–1914

Government Publications

Annales parlementaires – Chambre des Représentants.

Annales parlementaires – Sénat.

Documents parlementaires – Chambre des Représentants.

Documents parlementaires – Sénat.

'Circulaire ministérielle du 12 août 1867', in *Recueil des circulaires, instructions et autres actes emanés du ministère de la justice, ou relatifs à ce département années 1866–67* (Brussels: M. Weissenbruch, 1868.)

Commission du travail instituée par arrêté royal du 15 avril 1886. *Volume I. Réponses au questionnaire concernant le travail industriel* (Brussels: A. Lesigne, 1887).

—, *Volume II. Procès verbaux des séances d'enquêtes concernant le travail industriel* (Brussels: A. Lesigne, 1887).

—, *Volume III. Rapports. Proposition des sections et conclusions,* (Brussels: A. Lesigne, 1887).

—, *Volume IV. Comte rendus des séances plénières & mémoires, rapports, lettres etc. envisageant la question ouvrière dans son ensemble* (Brussels: A. Lesigne, 1887).

—, *Volume V. Procès-verbaux des séances de l'enquête agricole,* (Brussels: A. Lesigne, 1890)

—, *Volume VI. Enquête agricole. Réponses au questionnaire arrêté par la commission* (Brussels: A. Lesigne, 1890)

Treizième rapport sur la situation des asiles d'aliénés du Royaume; années 1883 à 1892 (Brussels: J. Goemaere, 1895).

Ministère de l'agriculture, *commission d'études relatives à la question de l'alcoolisme. 1895–1897. Rapports généraux (*Brussels: A. Lesigne, 1897).

Pasoinomie, 4th series, 22 (1887), pp. 336–60.

Pasoinomie, 5th series, 10:1 (1919), pp. 394–422.

Periodicals

Ligue patriotique contre l'alcoolisme, *Almanach de la tempérance* (Brussels, 1897–1900; 1902; 1904; 1912).

Vaderlandschen bond tegen alcoolism, *Almanak der matigheid* (Brussels, 1899; 1908; 1910–13).

Archives d' anthropologie criminelle et des sciences penales (Lyon-Paris: Storck [1886–92]).

Archives d' anthropologie criminelle, de criminologie et de psychologie normale et pathologique (Lyon-Paris: Storck [1893–1907]).

Le Bien social: Journal illustré contre l'alcoolisme - Het Volksgeluk. Geïllustreerd maandblad tegen alcoolism [People's Happiness: Illustrated Monthy Journal Against Alcoholim (Brussels, [1889–1914 incomplete]).

Bioscope (London), 20 July 1911.

British Medical Journal (London [1891–5]).

Bulletin de la Société de médicine mentale de Belgique (Brussels [1873–1914].

Bulletin de la Société médical belge de tempérance (Brussels [1898–1913]).

Bulletin de l'Académie royale de médecine de Belgique (Brussels [1850–1914]).

Le Globe illustré: Journal de la famille (Brussels [1885–95]).

Journal de la Ligue patriotique contre l'alcoolism (Brussels, [1890–1914 incomplete]).

La ligue. Organe belge des droits des femmes [The Alliance. Belgian Organ of Women's Rights] (Brussels, [1898–1914]).

Le Mouvement hygiénique (Brussels: Librairie médicale et scientifique, [1884–1913]).

Revue des questions scientifiques (Brussels, [1877–1914]).

Le Scalpel. Organe des garanties médicale du peuple et des intérêts sociaux et scientifique de la médicine, de la pharmacie et de l'art vétérinaire [The Lancet. Organ of People's Medical Guaranties and of Social and Scientific Interest of Medicine, Pharmacology and Veterenary Art] (Liège [1850–1914]).

De Sint Jansbode. Maandschrift tegen alcoholism [St John's Messenger. Monthly Bulletin against Alcoholims] (St Truiden [1892–94]).

Printed Works

Anon., *Catéchisme du Congo, par un ami de l'ouvrier* [Catechims of Congo, by a Friend of the Worker] (Brussels :Van Campenhout, 189?).

Anon., *Quelques vérités sur le Congo* [Some Truths about Congo] ([s.l.] s.d., 1895?).

Actes du troisième congrès international d'anthropologie criminelle. Tenu à Brussels en août 1892 (Brussels: Hayez, 1893).

Addison, H. R., *Belgium as She Is* (Brussels: C. Muquardt, 1843).

Amerlinck, J., *Carnets de route. Expédition au Katanga avec M.M. Bia et Francqui (mai 1891-avril 1893)* [Travel Journals. Expedition in Katanga with Mrs Bia and Francqui] (Brussels: Le Marinel, R. 1991).

Ball, B., *Leçons sur les maladies mentales* (Paris: P. Asselin, 1883).

Barella, H., *De l'abus des spiritueux, maladies des buveurs* (Brussels: H. Manceaux 1878).

—, *Les alcools et l'alcoolisme* (Brussels: Manceaux, 1879).

—, *Rapport de la commission à laquelle a eté renvoyé le mémoire de m. le docteur Mora, à Brunehamel, relatif à l'alcoolisme* (Brussels: Manceaux, 1881).

—, *Un mot sur l'ivresse au point de vue médico-légal* [A Word about Drunkenness from a Medical and Legal Standpoint] (Brussels: H. Lamertin, 1896).

—, *De l'alcoolisme* (Brussels, Société Belge de Librairie, 1898).

—, *Note sur l'internement et la libération des irresponsables dangereux. Prophylaxie des crimes évitables: asiles pour alcoolisés* (Brussels: Hayez, 1900).

Baudelaire, C., *Arm België* (*Pauvre Belgique*, 1864) (trans. Joyce & Co., Amsterdam: Arbeiderspers, 1975).

Boëns, H., *Traité pratique des maladies, des accidents et des difformités des houilleurs* [Practical Treatise on Diseases, Accidents and Deformities of Miners] (Brussels: Tircher, 1862).

—, *La bière au point de vue médical, hygiénique et social* (Brussels: Manceaux, 1878).

—, *L'Art de vivre. Traité complet d'hygiène et de médecine: a l'usage des gens du monde* [The Art of Living. Complete Treatise on Hygiene and Medicine: For Use by Polite Society] (Brussels: Hayez. 1878).

—, *Manuel populaire contre l'alcoolisme* (Brussels: G. Bastiné, 1897).

Boulger, D., *Belgian Life in Town and Country* (London: G. Newnes, 1904).

Bouquié-Lefebre, P. F. M., *Des causes et des résultats de l'intempérance ainsi que des moyens de la prévenir et de la combattre* (Brussels: Vanbuggenhoudt, 1857).

Braddon, M. E. *Lady Audley's Secret* (1860–1; London: Penguin, 1998).

Buysse, C., 'Het recht van de sterkste' (1893), in C. Buysse, *Verzameld werk [van] Cyriel Buysse. Deel I.*, ed. E. Van Elslander and A. M. Musschoot (Brussels: Manteau, 1974), pp. 3–149.

—, *'n Leeuw van Vlaanderen* (1900; Brussels: De Lage Landen, Brussel, 1943).

—, 'Op het kleine gehucht' (1901), in Buysse, *Verzameld werk [van] Cyriel Buysse. Deel I*, ed. Van Elslander and Musschoot, pp. 864–909.

—, 'Het leven van Rozeke van Dalen' (1906), in Buysse, *Verzameld werk [van] Cyriel Buysse. Deel II*, ed. Van Elsander and Musschoot (Brussels: Manteau, 1974), pp. 1–302.

—, 'Het bolleken' (1905), in Buysse, *Verzameld werk [van] Cyriel Buysse. Deel II*, ed. Van Elslander and Musschoot, pp. 305–458.

—, 'Guustje en Zieneken' (1887), in Buysse, *Verzameld werk [van] Cyriel Buysse. Deel IV*, ed. Van Elslander and Musschoot, pp. 40–83.

—, 'De Zwarte Kost' (1898), in Buysse, *Verzameld werk [van] Cyriel Buysse. Deel IV*, ed. Van Elslander and Musschoot, pp. 405–55.

—, 'De Biezenstekker' (1900), in Buysse, *Verzameld werk [van] Cyriel Buysse. Deel IV*, ed. Van Elslander and Musschoot, pp. 639–63.

—, 'Het Volle Leven' (1908), in Buysse, *Verzameld werk [van] Cyriel Buysse. Deel IV*, ed. Van Elslander and Musschoot, pp. 461–614.

—, 'Driekoningenavond' (1899), in Buysse, *Verzameld werk [van] Cyriel Buysse. Deel VI*, ed. Van Elslander and Musschoot, pp. 823–65.

—, 'Het gezin van Paemel' (1902), in Buysse, *Verzameld werk [van] Cyriel Buysse. Deel VI*, ed. Van Elslander and Musschoot, pp. 767–822.

Caudelier, E. *L'Alcoolisme en Belgique* (Brussels: Ligue patriotique contre l'alcoolisme, 1889).

—, *Le gin et le Congo* (Brussels: A. Lefèvre, 1895).

—, *Question de l'alcoolisme: note sur les travaux de la commission d'enquête* (Brussels: Weissenbruch, 1897).

Calemeyn, E., *De onthouding* [Abstinence] (Bruges: Brugsche onthoudersbond, 1894).

Charriaut, H., *La Belgique moderne. Une terre d'expériences* [Modern Belgium. A Land of Experiences] (Paris: Flammarion, 1910).

Conan Doyle, A., *The Crime of the Congo* (New York: Doubleday, 1909).

Conrad, J., *Heart of Darkness* (London: Penguin, 2007).

Conscience, H., *De Loteling* (Antwerp: J. Buschmann, 1850).

—, *The Curse of the Village; and The Happiness of Being Rich. Two Tales* (trans. edn: London: Lambert & Co., 1855).

—, *De plaeg der dorpen* (Antwerpen: J. P. Van Dieren, 1855).

—, *Eene uitvinding des duivels: Helsche geschiedenis* [An Invention of the Devil: A History from Hell] (Antwerp: J. P. Van Dieren, 1865).

Conscience, M. A., 'Conscience als mensch', *Ons volk ontwaekt* (10 August 1912).

Couperus, L., *Eline Vere. Een Haagsche roman* (1889) (Amsterdan/Antwerpen: Veen, 1991).

Dallemagne, J., *Dégénérés et déséquilibrés* (Brussels: H. Lamertin, 1894).

—, *Les biologiques et sociologiques de la criminalité*, (Paris: G. Masson, 1896).

De Boeck J., *L'alcoolisme au point de vue médical. Rapport présenté* (Brussels: Vve Ferd. Larcier, 1894).

—, *Patronage des aliénés et alcoolisme* (Brussels: E. Bruylant, 1897).

—, *Les frontières de la folie* [The Borders of Insanity] (Brussels: J. H. Moreau, 1902).

De Deken, C., *Deux ans au Congo*, (Antwerp: Clément Thibaut, 1900).

De Mey, P., *Van Antwerpen naar Stanley-Pool, Reisindrukken etc.* (Turnhout: Joseph Splichal, 1899).

De Ryckère, R., *La femme en prison et devant la mort* [Woman in Prison and Before Death] (Lyon: Storck, 1898).

—, *LAlcoolisme féminin* (Lyon: Storck, 1899).

—, *La servante criminelle. Etude de criminologie professionnelle* (Paris: A. Maloine, 1908).

D' Vaucleroy, V., *l'Hérédité alcoolique. Conférence faite à l'assemblée générale de la Ligue patriotique contre l'alcoolisme, le 6 novembre 1892, à Mons* (Brussels: Secrétariat Permanent De La Ligue, 1893).

—, *Premier congrès national Belge contre l' alcoolisme. Liège, 1905. Compte rendu* (Brussels: Sécrétariat général du congrès, 1906).

De Winne, A., *Door arm Vlaanderen* (1903) [Across Poor Flanders] (Louvain: Van Halewyck, 2001).

De Witte, P., *Alles is omgekeerd: hoe de werklieden vroeger leefden (1848–1918)* [Everything is Different: How the Workers Used to Live] (Louvain: Kritak, 1986).

Deiss, E., *Études sociales et industrielles sur la Belgique. Notes de voyage* (Paris: Guillemin, 1900).

Delaunois, G., *Entretiens sur l'intempérance. Misère, maladie, crime* (Brussels: Hayez, 1889).

—, *Les maux du buveur* [Diseases of the Drinker] (Brussels: Société Belge de librairie, 1895).

Desguin, V., *De l'abus des boissons alcooliques* (Paris: E. Donnaud, 1876).

d' Oliveira, E., *'De jongere generatie' (Vervolg op 'de mannen van '80'): Gesprekken met vertegenwoordigers van de nieuwere richting in onze literatuur; tevens een enquête naar enkele beginselen in ons nationaal geestelijk leven* ['The Younger Generation' (Continuation of 'the Men of '80') Conversations with Representatives of the Newer Direction in our Literature; Equally an Inquiry into Some of the Principles of Our National Intellectual Life] (Amsterdam: Maatschappij voor goede en goedkoope lectuur, 1914).

Domela-Nieuwenhuis, F., *De l'alcoolisme* (Paris: Société nouvelle de librairie, 1889).

Dryenpondt, G., and E. Van Campenhout, *Manuel du voyageur et du résident au congo.II. Guide pratique d'hygiène, de médecine et the chirurgie* (Brussel: Hayez, 1910).

Dorman, M., *A Journal of a Tour in the Congo Free State* (Brussels: J. Lebègue & Co., 1905).

Ducpétiaux, E., *De l'état des aliénés en Belgique, et les moyens d'améliorer leur sort: extrait d'un rapport adressé au ministre de l'intérieur, suivi d'un projet de loi relatif au traitement et a la séquestration des aliénés* [On the State of Insane Persons in Belgium and the Means to Ameliorate their Condition: Extract from a Report addressed to the Interior Minister, Following a Legislative Proposal with Regards to the Treatment and Confinement of Insane Persons] (Brussels: Laurent Frères, 1832).

—, *De l'intempérance et de l'ivrognerie dans la classe ouvrière* [On Intemperanc and Drunkenness among the Working Class] (Brussels: Wauters, 1843).

—, *Mémoire sur le paupérisme dans les Flandres* (Brussels: M. Hayez, Brussels, 1850).

—, *Colonies agricoles, écoles rurales et écoles de réforme pour les indigents, les mendiants et les vagabonds et spécialement pour les enfants en Suisse, en Allemagne, en France, en Angleterre, dans les Pays-Bas et en Belgique. Rapport adressé à M. Tesch, ministre de la justice, par Ed. Ducpetiaux* [Agricultural Colonies, Rural Schools and Reform Schools for Indigents, Beggers, and Vagabonds and Especially for Children] (Brussels: Lesigne, 1851).

Eekhoud, G., *Kermesses. Contes* (Brussels: Kistemaeckers, 1884).

—, *Nouvelles kermesses. Moeurs Flamandes* [New Kermises. Flemish Mores] (Brussels: Veuve Monnom, 1887).

Ery, L., 'Notes d'art. Jef Lambeaux', in *Le Thyrse. Revue de littérature d'art et de critique* 2:3 (June, 1900), pp. 25–7.

Faidherbe, A., *Leçons sur l'alcoolisme* (Brussels: Secrétariat de la Société belge de Tempérance, 1904).

Auguste F., *Die Sexuelle Frage* (1905), trans. C. F. Marshall, *The Sexual Question: A Scientific, Psychological, Hygienic and Sociological Study for the Cultured Classes* (London: Rebman, 1908).

Francotte, X., *Alcool et folie* [Alcohol and Madness] (Liège, G. Faust-Truyen, Liège. 1899).

Frank, L., *La Femme contre l'alcool. Etude de sociologie et de législation* [Woman against Alcohol. Sociological and Legal Study] (Brussels: H. Lamertin, Brussels. 1897).

Frère-Orban, H. J. W., *De l'abus des boissons enivrantes. Renseignements déposés à la Chambre des Représentants* [On the Abuse of Intoxicating Drinks. Advise offered to the Chamber of Representatives] (Brussels: M. Hayez, 1868).

Gaussin, F., *Le fléau moderne: traité complet médico-moral de l'alcoolisme: causes, effets, remèdes* [The Modern Blight: Complete Medical and Moral Treatise on Alcoholism: Causes, Effects, Cures] (Namur: Wesmael-Charlier, 1901).

Gautier, T., *Un tour en Belgique et en Hollande* (Paris: L'école des loisirs, 1997).

Guislain, J., *Traité sur les phrénopathies, ou, doctrine nouvelle des maladies mentales* (Brussels: Etablissement Encyclographique, 1833).

—, *Exposé sur l'état actuel des aliénés en Belgique, et notamment dans la province de la Flandre-Orientale* (Ghent: F. et E. Gyselynck, 1838).

Guislain, J., and B. C. Ingels, *Leçons orales sur les phrénopathies: ou traité théorique et pratique des maladies mentales. Cours donné à la clinique des établissements d'aliénés à Gand* (Paris: J. B. Bailliere, 1880).

Harding Davis, R., *The Congo and Coasts of Africa* (New York: C. Scribner's Son, 1907).

Heusy, P., *Un Coin de la vie de misères* (Paris: Oriol, 1883).

Jansen, A., *De l'usage et de l'abus des boissons et des liqueurs alcooliques. manuel d'instruction populaire* [On the Use and Abuse of Drink and Alcoholic Beverages. Manual of Popular Instruction] (Namur: Wesmael-Charlier, 1880).

—, *De l'usage et de l'abus alcooliques la classe aisée* [On the Use and the Abuse of Alcohol among the Wealthy Class] (Anvers: Buschman, 1878).

Kerr, N. 'Alcohol and Drug Habits', in T. L. Stedman (ed.), *Twentieth Century Practice: an International Encyclopedia of Modern Medical Science by Leading Authorities of Europe and America.* vol. 3: Occupation Diseases, Drug-habits and Poisons (London: Sampson, Low, Marston, 1895).

Kuborn, H., *Aperçu historique sur l'hygiène publique en Belgique depuis 1830* [Historical Approach on Public Hygiene in Belgium since 1830] (Brussels: H. Lamartin, 1904).

—, *Topographie médicale du royaume, elaborée en vertu de l'arrêté royal du 20 juillet 1889 par la Société royale de médecine publique et de topographie médicale, Zone VII: Bassins Houillers* [Medical Topography of the Kingdome, Developed by Virtue of Royal Ruling...Zone VII Coalfields] (Liège: H. Vaillant-Carmanne, 1909).

Laurent, F., *Les sociétiés ouvrières de Gand* (Ghent: Clemm & Hoste, 1877).

Lebon, L., *De l'alcoolisme en Belgique. Mémoire présenté à la conférence internationale de tempérance, Tenue à Londres, Le 6 septembre 1882, Sous le patronage de la National Temperance League* (Brussels: H. Manceaux, 1883).

Lefebvre, B., *De l'augmentation du nombre des aliénés à notre époque et des causes de cette augmentation* [On the Augmentation of the Number of Insane Persons in our Time and the Causes of this Augmentation] (Brussels: Devaux, 1866).

Lombroso, C., *The Man of Genius* (London: Scott, 1891).

Legrain, P. M., *Hygiène et prophylaxie: dégénérescence sociale et alcoolisme* (Paris: Carré, 1895).

Lemmens, J., *On 'alcoolise sans le savoir, sans le vouloir* [One Intoxicates Oneself Without Knowing It, Without Wanting It] (Brecht: Braeckmans, 1903).

—, *Sermons de tempérance et documents pouvant être utiles aux prédicateurs de la tempérance* [Temperance Sermons and Documents That Can be Useful to Preachers of Temperance] (Liège: Dessain, 1906).

—, *L'Alcoolisme et la réorganisation ouvrière* [Alcoholism and Worker's Reorganization] (Liège: Imprimerie Moderne, 1907).

Lemonnier, C., *Salon de Paris, 1870* (Paris: Morel, 1870).

—, *Happe-chair* (1886; Brussels: Editions Labor, 1994).

—, 'Les concubins', in *Ceux de la glèbe* (Paris: Albert Savine, 1889), pp. 69–114.

—, *La fin des bourgeois* (1892; Brussels: Editions Labor, 1986).

—, *La faute de Mme Charvet* (Paris: E. Deniu, 1895).

—, *La vie Belge* (Paris: Bibliotheque Charpentier, 1905).

—, *L'école Belge de peinture, 1830–1905* (1906; Brussels: Labor, 1991)

—, *Une vie d'écrivain* (1911; Brussels: Académie Royale de Langue et de Littérature Française, 1994).

Lentz, F., *De l'alcoolisme et de ses diverses manifestations, considérées au point de vue physiologique, pathologique, clinique et médicolégal* (Brussels: Manceaux, 1884).

Ley, A., *Rapport sur le service médicale du santarium du Fort Jaco, à Uccle en 1908* (Brussels, 1908).

—, *l'Aliénation mentale et l'alcoolisme à Brussels pendant la guerre* [Insanity and Alcoholism in Brussels During the War] (Brussels: Impr. des Travaux Publics, 1919).

—, *La loi Belge de 1919 contre l'alcoolisme et ses résultats* (Paris: Doin, 1929).

Ley, A., and R. Charpentier, *Alcoolisme et criminalité* (Brussels: L. Severeyns, 1910).

Lilar, S., *Une enfance Gantoise* [A Ghent Childhood] (Paris: Bernard Grasset, 1976).

Magnan V., 'Accidents determinés par l'abus de la liqueur d'absinthe' *l'Union Médicale* 1864; 92:227–32, 94:257–62.

—, *De l'alcoolisme, des diverses formes du délire alcoolique et de leur traitement* (Paris: Adrien Delahaye, 1874)

—, *Leçons cliniques sur la dipsomanie faites à l'asile Sainte-Anne* (Paris: A. Delahaye et E. Lecrosnier, 1884).

Magnan, V., and M. Legrain, *Hérédité et alcoolisme. Étude psychologique et clinique sur les dégénérés buveurs et les familles d'ivrognes* (Paris: Tours, 1889).

Magnan, V., and P. Sérieux, *La paralysie générale* (Paris, G. Masson, 1894).

Mahaim, A., *l'Alcool et les maladies mentales* (Liège: Aug. Bénard, 1901).

Malou, J., *Les cabarets* (Brussels: Devaux, 1867).

Marcet, W., *On Chronic Alcoholic Intoxication: or Alcoholic Stimulants in Connexion with the Nervous System; with a Synoptical Table of Cases* (London: J. Churchill, 1860).

Mareska, G. J., and J. Heyman, *Enquête sur le travail et la condition physique et morale des ouvriers employés dans les manufactures de coton, à Gand* [Inquiry into the Work and the Physical and Moral Condition of the Workers Employed in the Cotton Manufacture in Ghent] (Ghent: Gyselynck, 1845).

Masoin, E. *Alcoolisme et criminalité* (Brussels: L. Wintraecken et Cie, 1898).

—, *l'aAlcool et le crime* (Louvain: Polleunis et Ceuterick, 1901).

—, *Discours prononcé aux funérailles de M. le professeur Lefebvre* (Brussels: Hayez, 1902).

—, *Discours prononcé aux funérailles de M. Ed. Van den Corput* (Brussels: Hayez, 1908).

Melchior, J., *De jeneverplaag, of het alcoolisme in België* (Hasselt: Ceysens, 1896).

—, *Handboek over het alcoolisme voor lager en middelbaar onderwijs* (Hasselt: M. Ceysens, 1898).

Morel, J., and Congrès national belge contre l'alcoolisme, *Rapport sur les désastres produits par l'alcoolisme (criminalité, aliénation mentale, dégénérescence)* (Brussels: Secrétariat générale du congres, 1907).

Parent, M., *Le rôle de la femme dans la lutte contre l'alcoolisme* (Brussels: Ligue patriotique contre l'alcoolisme, 1890).

Peeters, J. A., *L'Alcool. Physiologie, pathologie, médecine légale* (Brussels: A. Manceaux, 1885).

Petithan, C., *Répression de l'alcoolisme. Interdiction, collocation* (Liège, Grandmont-Donders, 1881).

—, *La dégénérescence de la race Belge, ses causes et ses remèdes* (Brussels, H. Lamertin, 1889).

Pica, V., 'Artisti contemporanei: Jef Lambeaux', *Eporium,* 20:117 (September 1904).

Pirson, E., *l' Alcoolisme à la Campagne* [Alcoholism in the Countryside] (Louvain: Polleunis, 1903).

Pringle, J. C., 'The Belgian Detention Colony at Merxplas', *Economic Review*, 19 (1909), pp. 261–81.

Prins, A., *Criminalité et répression. Essai de science pénale* (Brussels: C. Muquardt, 1886).

—, *La défense sociale et les transformations du droit pénal,* (Brussels: Misch et Tron, 1910).

Quetelet, A., *Sciences mathématiques et physiques chez les Belges, au commencement du XIXe siècle* (Brussels: Thiry-Van Buggenhoudt, 1866).

Rowntree, B. S., *Land and Labour: Lessons from Belgium* (London: Macmillan, 1911).

Scudamore, C., *Belgium and the Belgians* (Edinburgh: William Blackwood & Sons, 1901).

Seneca, *Letters from a Stoic: Epistulae Morales Ad Lucilium*, ed. R. Campbell (London: Penguin, 1969).

Sluys, A., *Le rôle de l'instituteur dans la lutte antialcoolique. Rapport au VIe congrès international contre l'abus des boissons alcooliques* [The Role of the Teacher in the Battle against Alcoholism] (Brussels: Wintraecken, 1899).

Stanley, H. S., *The Congo and the Founding of Its Free State: A Story of Work and Exploration (1885) Vol. 1* (Cambridge: Cambridge University Press, 2011).

Statistique Générale de la Belgique, *Exposé de la situation du Royaume de 1876 à 1900* (Brussels: Becquart-Arien, 1909).

Sterck, F., *Onze dorpen en de sociale kwestie* [Our Villages and the Social Question] (Ghent: A. Siffer, 1891).

Stijns, R., *Hard labeur* (Rotterdam: M. Boogaerdt Jr., Brussels: De Vlaamsche Boekhandel, Leo. J. Krijn, 1904).

Streuvels, S., *The Long Road*, trans. E. Crankshaw (Boston, MA: Twayne, 1976).

—, 'Veld en dorp', in M. Rooses (ed.), *Vlaanderen door de eeuwen heen, Eerste deel.* (Amsterdam: Elsevier, 1912), pp. 1–61.

—, Van Andel, M. A., *Volksgeneeskunst in Nederland* (Utrecht: Boekhoven, 1909).

Van Booven, H., *Tropenwee* (Amsterdam: Van Holkema &Warendorf, 1905).

Van Coillie, E., *Alcoolisme et habitations ouvrières* (Brussels: Soc. Belge De Librairie, 1892).

Van den Corput, A., *L'Alcoolisme, l'hérédité et la question sociale* (Brussels: H. Lamertin, 1895).

—, *L'Alcoolisme public et son traitement* (Brussels: Weissenbruch, 1895).

—, *Le poison alcool. Nouvelles Considérations à propos de l'alcoolisme'* (Brussels: Weissenbruch, 1895).

—, *L'Alcoolisme, ses causes mésologiques, son extinction physiologique* (Paris: Masson et Cie, 1897).

Vandervelde, E., *Le parti ouvrier et l'alcool* (Brussels: Brismée, 1898).

—, *La lutte sociale contre l'alcoolisme* (Brussels: Presse Socialiste, 1899).

—, *Essais socialistes: l'alcoolisme, la religion, l'art* (Paris: Alcan, 1906).

—, *Souvenirs d'un militant socialiste* (Paris: Editions Denoel, 1939)

Vandervelde, L., *Monarchs and millionaires* (London: Thornton Butterworth, 1925).

Vandeven, P. J., *Considérations sur les causes de la dégénérescence de l'espèce humaine, et sur les moyens d'y remédier* (Louvain: Van Linthout, 1850).

Van der Cruyssen, A. C., *De zoon des dronkaerds* (Ghent: Vanderhaeghen, 1865).

Van Kerckhoven, P. F., *De dronkaerd. Drama in dry bedryven* (Antwerp, 1854).

Van Parijs, L., *Les hontes de la civilisation au Congo Belge dévoilée* [The Embarrassments of the Civilization of Belgian Congo Unmasked] (La Louvière, 1899).

Verhaeren, E., *Les campagnes hallucinées. Les villes tentaculaires* (Paris: Gallimard, 1982).

Waeri, P., *Verzameling der volledige kluchtige en politieke liederen van Karel Waeri den Gentschen beranger (1899)* [Collection of Comlete Satirical and Political Songs of Karel Waeri, the Beranger of Ghent] (Ghent: Historische Heruitgeverij, 2001).

Weygandt, W., *Atlas-manuel de psychiatrie* (Paris: J. B. Baillière et fils, 1904).

Winslow, F. L., *On Uncontrollable Drunkenness Considered as a Form of Mental Disorder, with the Only Possible Means of Legally Dealing with Such Cases* (London: Henderson & Spalding, London, 1892).

Zetternam, E., *Mijnheer Luchtervelde. Waarheden uit onzen tijd* (Antwerp: J.E. Buschmann, 1848).

Zetternam, E., *Mijnheer Luchtervelde* (Ghent: Het Licht, 1943).

Secondary sources

Websites

Museum Dr. Guislain:

http://www.fracarita.org/nl/europa/belgie/museum/museumonshuis.html

Vlaamse Volksverhalenbank, [Flemish Folk Story Depository] Catholic University Louvain: http://www.volksverhalenbank.be/index_nieuw.htm

Digitale bibliotheek voor de Nederlandse letteren [Digital Library for Dutch and Flemish Literature]: http://www.dbnl.org/

FABRITIUS: Fine Arts Brussels Internet and Intranet Users Multiligual Collection Database: http://www.opac-fabritius.be/.

Printed Works

Académie Royale des Sciences des Lettres et des Beaux-Arts de Belgique, *Biographie nationale,* H. Thiry-van Buggenhoudt (Brussels, 1956).

Achebe, C., 'An Image of Africa: Racism in Conrad's 'Heart of Darkness'', *Massachusetts Review,* 18 (1977). Reprinted in J. Conrad, *Heart of Darkness, An Authoritative Text,*

Background and Sources Criticism (1961), ed. R. Kimbrough (London: W. W Norton & Co., 1988), pp. 251–61.

Aisenberg, A. R., *Contagion: Disease, Government, and the 'Social Question' in Nineteenth-Century France* (Stanford, CA: Stanford University Press, 1999).

Ankaert, R., 'Les cabaretiers-cafétiers à la fin du XIXe siècle', [Inkeepers and Café Proprietors at the End of the Nineteenth Century], in S. Jaumain and G. Kurgan – Van Hentenryk (eds), *Aux frontieres des classes moyennes: la petite bourgeoisie Belge avant 1914* [At the Boundaries of the Middle Classes' The Belgian Petty Bourgeoisie before 1914] (Brussels: Éditions de l'Université de Brussels, 1992), pp. 29–57.

Ancel, M., *Social Defence, A Modern Approach to Criminal Problems* (London: Routledge, 1998).

Alfano, C. L., 'Under the Influence: Drink, Discourse and Narrative in Victorian Britain', (PhD Dissertation, Stanford University, 1995).

Allen, J. S., 'History and the Novel: Mentalité in Modern Popular Fiction', *History and Theory*, 22, (1983), pp. 233–52.

Andrews, J., and A. Digby, 'Introduction: Gender and Class in the Historiography of British and Irish Psychiatry', in J. Andrews and A. Digby (eds), *Sex and Seclusion, Class and Custody: Perspectives on Gender and Class in the History of British and Irish Psychiatry* (Amsterdam: Rodopi, 2004), pp. 7–44.

Andrews, J., 'Documents and Sources: Case Notes, Case Histories and the Patient's Experience of Insanity at Gartnavel Royal Asylum, Glasgow, in the Nineteenth Century', *Social History of Medicine*, 11:2 (1998), pp. 255–81.

Aron, P., 'Dans l'ombre de Germinal. Happe Chair de Camille Lemonnier', *Bulletin de la société d'études des lettres françaises de Belgique*, 1 (1982), pp. 1–11.

Aron, P., *La Belgique artistique et littéraire: une anthologie de langue Française (1848–1914)* (Brussels: Complexe, 1997).

Aron, P., 'Les arts et les lettres de 1886: 'Lorsque la race Wallon-Flamand se révaillait au contact des infernales cuisines industrielles', in Bruwier, M., Caulier-Mathy, N. a.o. (eds.) *1886, la Wallonie née de la grève?: Colloque organisé a l'Université de Liège les 29 octobre, 14 et 29 novembre 1986* (Brussels: Editions Labor, 1990), pp. 151–166.

Barnes, D. S., *The Making of a Social Disease: Tuberculosis in Nineteenth-Century France* (Berkeley, CA: University of California Press, 1995).

Barrows, S., 'After the Commune. Alcoholism, Temperance and Literature in the Early Third Republic', in J. M. Merriman (ed.),Ed. *Consciousness and Class Experience in Nineteenth-Century Europe* (New York: Holmes & Meier Publishers, 1979), pp. 205–18.

Baudson, P., 'Du constat à l'interprétation. l'art social de Jospeh Stevens à Eugène Laermans', in P. A. Roberts-Jones, *Eugène Laermans, 1864–1940* (Brussels: Crédit Communal, 1995), pp. 51–65.

Bauman, R., *Story, Performance and Event: Contextual Studies of Oral Narrative* (Cambridge: Cambridge University Press, 1986).

Baumohl, J., and R. Room, 'Inebriety, Doctors, and the State: Alcoholism Treatment Institutions Before 1940', in M. Galanter (ed.), *Recent Developments in Alcoholism Vol. 5* (New York: Plenum Publishing, 1987), pp. 135–74.

Biesmans, J. *Negentiende-eeuwse passionele misdrijven. Beelden en werkelijkheid* [19th century Crimes of Passion. Representations and Reality] (Student Dissertation, University Ghent, 2001).

A. J Bijsterveld, E. Niesten, Y. Segers and I. Steen (eds), *Suikerbonen en beschuit met muisjes. Eetgewoonten bij sleutelmomenten in het leven,* [Eating Habits at Key Live Events] (Louvain: Nederlands Centrum voor Volkscultuur, 2005), p. 134.

Biltereyst, D., and P. Meersuit, *De verlichte stad. Een geschiedenis van bioscopen, filmvertoningen en filmcultuur in Vlaanderen,* [A History of Cinema's Film Performances and Film Culture in Flanders] (Louvain: Lannoo Campus, 2007),

Biron, M., *La modernité Belge: littérature et société* (Brussels: Editions Labor, 1994).

Bloch, M., *The Historian's Craft* (Manchester:Manchester University Press, 1954).

Blom, J. C. H., and E. Lamberts, *History of the Low Countries* (New York: Berghahn Books, 1998).

Bonnier, B., L. Leblanc, D. Prioul and H. Védrine, *Rops suis, aultre ne veulx estre* (Brussels: Complexes, 1998),

Boon, L. P., *Pieter Daens, of hoe in de negentiende eeuw de arbeiders van Aalst vochten tegen armoede en onrecht* [Pieter Daens, or How in the 19th Century the Workers of Aalst Fought against Poverty and Injustice] (1971; Amsterdam: Arbeiderspers, 1986).

Boone, M., and H. Gaus, *Dagelijks leven: sociaal-culturele omstandigheden vroeger en nu* [Daily Life: Socio-cultural Conditions Past and Present] (Deurne: Baart, 1982),

Borel, J., *Du concept de dégénérescence a la notion d'alcoolisme dans la médecine contemporaine. Les campagnes anti-alcooliques de 1865 à 1965* (Montpellier: Causse, 1968).

Brennan, T., 'Towards the Cultural History of Alcohol in France', *Journal of Social History,* 21:1 (1989), pp. 71–92.

Brouwers, B., *Literatuur en revolutie* (Boom: Meppel, 1971).

Brown, E. M., '"What Shall We Do with the Inebriete?" Asylum Treatment and the Disease Concept of Alcoholism in the late Nineteenth Century', *Journal of the Behavioral Sciences,* 21 (1985), pp. 48–59.

Burke, P., *Popular Culture in Early Modern Europe* (London: Temple Smith, 1978).

—, 'Bakhtin for Historians', *Social History,* 3:1 (1988), pp. 85–90.

Bynum, W. F., 'Alcoholism and Degeneration in 19th Century European Medicine and Psychiatry', *British Journal of Addiction,* 79 (1984), pp. 59–70.

Ceuppens, B, D. Van Reybrouck and V. Viaene, *Congo in België. Koloniale cultuur in de metropool* (Louvain: Louvain University Press, 2009).

Claes, M., *'Il est impossible d'être féministe sans être antialcoolique': Marie Parent (1853–1935) een voorvechtster in de strijd tegen alcoholisme,* ['It is Impossible to Be Feminist Without Being Temperate: Marie Parent, a Champion of the Struggle against Alcoholism] (Louvain: Licenciaatsverhandeling, Katholieke Universiteit, 2000).

Cohen, P., *The Symbolic Construction of Community* (London: Routledge, 1993).

Conrad, B., *Absinthe: History in a Bottle* (San Francisco, CA: Chronicle Books, 1988).

Conrad, P., and J. W. Schneider, *Deviance and Medicalization, from Badness to Sickness* (St Louis: Mosby, 1980).

Conrardy, C., 'Le statuaire Jef Lambeaux', *Savoir et Beauté*, 13 (June. 1933), pp. 293–303.

Cooter, R., *The Cultural Meaning of Popular Science: Phrenology and the Organization of Consent in Nineteenth-Century Britain* (Cambridge: Cambridge University Press, 1984).

—, 'Medicine and Modernity', in M. Jackson (ed.), *The Oxford Handbook of the History of Medicine* (Oxford: Oxford University Press, 2011), pp. 100–16.

Corbin, A. *Le miasme et la jonquille: l'odorat et l'imaginaire social XVIIIe-XIXe siècles* [The Miasma and the Daffodil: Smell and Social Imagination in the Eighteenth– and Nineteenth Centuries] (Paris: Aubier Montaigne, 1982)

Corfield, P. J., *Language, History and Class* (Oxford: Basil Blackwell, 1991).

Coutenier, M., *Congo tentoongesteld: een geschiedenis van de Belgische antropologie en het Museum van Tervuren (1882–1925)* [Congo Exhibited; A History of Belgian Anthropology and the Museum of Tervuren] (Louvain: Acco, 2005).

Crispeels, Y. 'De strijd tegen het drankmisbruik in België, eind 19e begin 20e eeuw', [The Struggle Against Alcohol Abuse in Belgium, from the End of the Nineteenth Century to the Beginning of the Twentieth Century] (Student Dissertation, Catholic University Louvain 1982).

Christiaensen, S., *Tussen klassieke en moderne criminele politiek: leven en beleid van Jules Lejeune* [Between Traditional and Modern Criminal Politics: Life and Policies of Jules Lejeune] (Louvain: Louvain University Press, 2004).

Crossick, G., 'Metaphors of the Middle: The Discovery of the Petite Bourgeoisie (1880–1914)', *Royal Historical Society Transactions*, 4 (1994), pp. 251–79.

Crossick G., and H. G. Haupt, *The Petite Bourgeoisie in Europe 1780–1914* (London: Routledge, 1997).

Darnton, R., 'Peasants Tell Tales. The Meaning of Mother Goose', in R. Darnton, *The Great Cat Massacre* (New York: Vintage Books, 1985), pp. 9–72.

De Belder, J. 'Adel en burgerij, 1840–1914 ', in D. P. Blok, *Algemene geschiedenis der Nederlanden. Deel XII (*Haarlem: Fibula-Van Dishoeck, 1977), pp. 78–98.

De Beukeleer, K. *Traditionele volkse feestcultuur en modernisering. Het platteland rond Gent ca.1860–ca.1940* [Traditional Popular Culture of Celebration and Modernisation] (Student Dissertation, University Ghent, 2001).

De Bont, R., 'Meten en verzoenen. Louis Vervaeck en de criminele antropologie, 1900–1940', in J. Tollebeek, J. Van Paemel and K. Wils (eds), *Degeneratie in België 1860–1940: een Geschiedenis van Ideeën en Praktijken* (Louvain:University Press , 2003), pp. 185–225.

De Brauwere, J. *Het beeld van alcohol. Een historische discoursanalyse van de antialcoholcampagnes tussen 1879 en 1919*, [The Representation of Alcohol. A Historical Discourse Analysis of the Temperance Campaigns between 1879-1919 (Student Dissertation, Free University Brussels, 2007).

De Brauwere, J., and D. Jacobs, 'Le premier verre – le dernier verre'. Het antialcoholdiscours op een postkaart,' [The First Glass – The Last Glass, The Anti-alcohol Discourse on a Postcardin E, Dekens, J. Debrauwere and D. Jacobs (eds), *Pierre le buveur et Jean l'abstinent* (Hasselt: National Jenevermuseum, 2009), pp. 21–6.

Declerck, S., 'Genèse du discours anti-alcoolique en Belgique 1830–1970' [Origins of the Anti-Alcohol Discourse in Belgium] (Student Dissertation, Free University Brussels, 1994).

Dégh, L., *Narratives in Society: A Performer-Centered Study of Narration* (Bloomington, IN: Indiana University Press, 1995).

Degroote, G. L., J. L. H. De Schuyterand J. P. Van Dieren, *Hendrik Conscience en zijn uitgevers. Brieven met inleiding en toelichting door Dr. Gilbert Degroote en Jan De Schuyter* [H. Conscience and his Editors. Letters] (Brussels: Elsevier, 1953).

Dekens, E. 'Anti-alcoholoffensief in woord en beeld. Laat negentiende-eeuwse en vroeg twintigste-eeuwse drankbestrijding in België' [Anti-Alcohol Offensive in Word and Pictures. The Late Nineteenth Century and Early Twentieth Century Temperance Movment in Belgium] (Student Dissertation, University of Maastricht, 2006).

—, Dubbel zien, Het antialcoholoffensief in Beeld', [The Anti-Alcohol Offensive in Pictures] in E, Dekens, J. Debrauwere and D. Jacobs (eds), *Pierre le buveur et Jean l'abstinent* (Hasselt: National Jenevermuseum, 2009), pp. 21–6.

De Mey, J., '"Gelijk trossen bananen". Beeldvorming over Congolezen in de Belgische dagbladpers ten tijde van de onafhankelijkheid (1955–1965*)*. Een studie van stereotypen, clichés en vooroordelen' [Images of Congolese in the Belgian Newspaper Press at the Time of Independence] (Student Dissertation, Catholic Universtiy Louvain, 2004).

Deneckere, G., *Sire, het volk mort. Sociaal protest in België (1831–1918)* (Antwerp Baarn-Ghent: Hadewijch/AMSAB, 1997).

—, *België op het breukvlak van twee eeuwen* (1900; Tielt: Lannoo, 2006).

—, *Geuzengeweld, Anticklerikaal straatrumeour in de politieke geschiedenis van België, 1831–1914* [Anticlerical Street Noise in the Political History of Belgium] (Brussel: VUB Press, 1998).

Deneckere, G., E. Gubin, J. P. Nandrin and E. Witte, *Nouvelle histoire de Belgique, Vol. I: 1830–1905* (Tielt: Lannoo, 2005).

De Nil, B., 'Zetternam en Zola. De Vlaamse sociaal demokraten en hun literaire mythen vóór 1914', *Brood en Rozen* 3: 1 (1998), pp. 7–24.

De Nil, B., 'Het sublieme verschil. Tussen naturalisme en 'geslachtsdeelrealisme'. De Vlaamse sociaal-democratie en seksualiteit in de roman vòòr 1914', in D. De Weerdt (ed.), *Begeerte heeft ons aangeraakt: socialisten, sekse en seksualiteit* (Ghent: Provinciebestuur van Oost-Vlaanderen, 1999).

Denoël, T., and Legrain, P., *Le nouveau dictionnaire des Belges,* (Brussels: Le Cri, 1992).

Derainne, P. J., 'L'hostilité aux ouvriers Belges en France au XIXe siècle' [Hostility towards Belgian Workers in France in the Nineteenth Century], in A. Morelli (ed.) *Les émigrants Belges. Réfugiés de guerre, émigrés économiques, réfugiés politiques ayant quitté nos régions du XVeième siècle à nos jours* [Belgian Emigrants. War Refugies, Economic Migrants, Political Refugies who have Left our Regions from the FifteenthCentury to Today] (Brussels: Éditions Vie Ouvrière, 1998), pp. 101–14.

De Ruyver, B., 'De alcoholwet Vandervelde in historische en ideologisch perspectief'. *Tijdschrift voor sociale wetenschappen*, 27 (1982), pp. 342–69.

De Ruyver, B., and Goethals, J., 'Auguste Ley 1873–1956', in C. Fijnaut(ed.), *Gestalten uit het verleden. 32: Voorgangers in de rechtswetenschap, de strafrechtpleging en de criminologie* [Characters of the Past: Leaders in Legal Science, Criminal Justice and Criminal Science] (Deurne: Kluwer, 1993).

De Schaepdrijver, S., 'Reglementering van prostitutie 1844–1877: De opkomst en ondergang van een experiment'. [Regulation of Prostitution: The Rise and Fall of an Experiment] *Belgisch tijdschrift voor de nieuwste geschiedenis – Revue belge d'histoire contemporaine*, 17: 3–4 (1985), pp. 473–506.

De Smaele, H., *Rechts Vlaanderen, Religie en stemgedrag in 19e eeuws België* [Right Wing Flanders. Religion and Voting Behaviour in Nineteenth Century Belgium] (Louvain: Louvain University Press, 2009).

De Vroede, M., 'Primary Education and the Fight against Alcoholism in Belgium at the Turn of the Century', *History of Education Quarterly*, 30: 4 (1985), pp. 483–97.

De Weerdt, D., *En de vrouwen? Vrouw, vrouwenbeweging en feminisme in België. (1830–1960)* [And the Women? Woman, Woman's Movement and Feminsim in Belgium] (Ghent: Masereelfonds, 1980).

Dhaene, C., *Sint-Jozef Kortenberg: van 'Maison de Santé' tot Universitair Centrum. 145 jaar zorg voor geesteszieken, 1850–1995* (Louvain: Kadoc, 1995).

Dijkstra, B., *Idols of Perversity: Fantasies of Feminine Evil in Fin-De-Siède Culture* (Oxford: Oxford University Press, 1986).

Douglas, M., *Constructive Drinking: Perspectives on Drink from Anthropology* (Cambridge: Cambridge University Press, 1987).

Dowbiggin, I., 'Back to the Future: Valentin Magnan, French psychiatry and the Classification of Mental Diseases 1885–1925', *Social History of Medicine*, 9:3 (December 1996), pp. 383–408.

—, *Inheriting Madness: Professionalization and Psychiatric Knowledge in Nineteenth-Century France* (Berkeley, CA: University of California Press, 1991).

Du Champs, G., M. Convens and A. Visscher, *Beelden uit de Belle Epoque* (Brussels: Reader's Digest, 1988).

Duffin, L., 'The Conspicuous Consumptive. Woman as an Invalid', in L. Duffin and S. Delamont (eds), *The 19th Century Woman, her Culture and her Physical World* (New York: Croom Helm, 1978).

Dumont, H. G., *La vie quotidienne en Belgique sous le règne de Léopold II (1865–1909)* [Daily Life in Belgium Under the Reign of Léopold II] (Brussels: Le Cri, 1996).

Dupont-Bouchat, M., *La Belgique criminelle. Droit, justice, société* (XIVeXXe siècles) (Louvain-la-Neuve: UCL et Academia-Bruyland, 2006).

Durviaux, S., 'Le cercle universitaire pour les études criminologie', in P. Mary and P. Van Der Vorst(eds), *Cent ans de criminologie à l'ULB* (Brussels: Bruylant, 1990), pp. 21–44.

Eley, G., and K. Nield, *The Future of Class in History: What's Left of the Social?* (Ann Arbor, MI: University of Michigan Press, 2007).

Elaut, L., 'Benjamin Ingels, psychiater, de vinnige', *Annalen van het Noorden* (1957), pp. 2–3.

Eriksen, S., 'Alcohol as Gender Symbol', *Scandinavian Journal of History*, 24:1 (1999), pp. 45–73.

Exelmans, F., 'De lagere school en de strijd tegen het alcoholisme 1880–1914' [Primary School and the Fight against Alcoholism] (Licenciaatsverhandeling, Katholieke Universiteit Louvain, 1980).

Eylenbosch, A., *Jef Lambeaux 1852–1908, ou les Passions d'un faune* (Saint-Gilles: Les Rencontres Saint-Gilloises, 1990).

Fabian, J., *Out of our Minds: Reason and Madness in the Exploration of Central Africa* (Berkeley, CA: University of California Press, 2000), pp. 23–30.

Foucault, M., *L'Archéologie du savoir* (Paris: Gallimard, 1969).

—, *The History of Sexuality. Volume 1: An Introduction* (New York: Vintage Books, 1978).

—, *Madness and Civilization: a History of Insanity in the Age of Reason* (London: Tavistock Routledge, 1989).

—, *Abnormal: Lectures at the Collège de France 1974–1975* (London: Verso, 2003).

Foucault, M., A. Baudot and J. Couchman, 'About the Concept of the "Dangerous Individual" in 19th-Century Legal Psychiatry', *International Journal of Law and Psychiatry*, 1 (1 February 1978), pp. 1–18.

Geertz, C., 'Thick Description. Toward an Interpretation Theory of Culture', in *The Interpretation of Cultures. Selected Essays* (New York: Basix, 1973), pp. 3–30.

Gerard, E., and L. Vos, *Hedendaagse geschiedenis* [Contemporary History] (Louvain: Acco, 1995).

Godderis, J., 'De geesteszieken: nieuwe inzichten en instellingszorg' [The Mentally Ill: New Insights and Institutional Care] in L. Dhaene, G. Hertecant, K. Velle and J. De Maeyer (eds), *Er is leven voor de dood: tweehonderd jaar gezondheidszorg in Vlaanderen* [There is Life Before Death: Two Hundred Years Health Care in Flanders] (Kapellen: Pelckmans, 1998).

Goffman, E., *The Presentation of Self in Everyday Life* (Woodstock, NY: Overlook Press, 1973).

Golby, J. M., and Purdue, A. W. *The Civilisation of the Crowd. Popular Culture in Britain 1750–1900* (London: Sutton, 1999).

Goldstein, J., *Console and Classify: The French Psychiatric Profession in the Nineteenth Century* (Cambridge: Cambridge University Press, 1987).

Greenaway, J. R., *Drink and British Politics since 1830: A Study in Policy Making* (Basingstoke: Palgrave Macmillan, 2003).

Gutzke, G. W., 'Gender, Class, and Public Drinking in Britain during the First World War', in J. S. Blocker and C. L. Warsh (eds), *The Changing Face of Drink: Substance, Imagery, and Behaviour* (Ottawa: Les Publications Histoire Sociale – Social History Inc., 1997), pp. 291–319.

Louwers, O., and I. Grenade, *Codes et lois du Congo Belge. Textes annotés d'après les rapports du conseil colonial, les instructions officielles et la jurisprudence des tribunaux* [Codes and Laws of Belgian Congo. Annotated Text from the Rapports of the Colonial Council, the Official Instructions and the Legislation of the Tribunals] (Brussels: Weissenbruch, 1923)

Gubin, E., 'Home Sweet Home'. l'Image de la femme au foyer en Belgique et au Canada avant 1914', *Belgisch tijdschrift voor de nieuwste geschiedenis – Revue belge d'histoire contemporaine*, 22: 3–4 (1991), pp. 521–68.

Haine, W. S., *The World of the Paris cafe: Sociability among the French Working Class, 1789–1914* (Baltimore, MD: Johns Hopkins University Press, 1999).

Hall, C., *White, Male and Middle-Class: Explorations in Feminism and History* (Cambridge: Polity, 1992).

Hanlet, C., *Les écrivains Belges contemporains de langue Française: 1800–1946* [Belgian Contemporary Writers in the French Language] (Liège: H. Dessain, 1946).

Hare, E. H., 'The Origin and Spread of Dementia Paralytica', *British Journal of Psychiatry*, 105 (1950), pp. 594–626.

Harris, B., *The Health of the Schoolchild: A History of the School Medical Service in England and Wales* (Buckingham and Philadelphia, PA: Open University Press, 1995).

Harris, R., *Murders and Madness: Medicine, Law and Society in the Fin de Siècle* (Oxford: Oxford University Press, 1989).

Harrison, B., *Drink and the Victorians: the Temperance Question in England, 1815–1872* (Pittsburgh, PA: University of Pittsburgh Press, 1971).

Havelange, C., 'Quelques aspects du discours médical pendant la 2nd moitié du XIXe siècle' [Some Aspects of the Medial Discourse during the Second Half of the NineteenthCentury] *Belgisch tijdschrift voor de nieuwste geschiedenis – Revue belge d'histoire contemporaine*, 16, (1985), pp. 175–99.

—, *Les figures de la guérison, XVIIIe–XIXe siècles. Une histoire sociale et culturelle des professions médicales au pays de Liège* [Figures of Healing in the Eighteenth to Nineteenth Centuries: A Social and Cultural History of the Medical Professions in the Region of Liège] (Liège: Université De Liège, 1990).

—, 'De uitvinding van de wanorde. Het negentiende-eeuwse verbond tussen collectiviteit en gezondheid', [The Invention of Disorder: The Nineteenth Century Connection between Collectivism and Health], in L. Nys, H. De Smaele, J. Tollebeek and K. Wils (eds), *De zieke natie: over de medicalisering van de samenleving, 1860–1914* [The Sick Nation: On the Medicalisation of Society] (Groningen: Historische Uitgeverij, 2002), pp. 74–85.

—, 'La Belgique médico-sociale, l'individu, la société, la race' in G. Kurgan – Van Hentenryk (ed.), *Laboratoires et réseaux de diffusion des idées en Belgique: XIXe–XXe siècles* [Laboratories and Networks of Diffusion of Ideas in Belgium Nineteenth to Twentieth-Centuries] (Brussels: Editions de l' Université de Brussels, 1994), pp. 19–33.

Hayward, S., *French National Cinema* (London, Routledge, 1993).

Hélin, E., 'Reconstituer l'histoire des 'bricteux' saisonniers' [Reconstructing the History of the Seasonal Brickworkers], in A. Morelli (ed.), *Histoire des étrangers et de l'immigration en Belgique de la préhistoire à nos jours* [History of Strangers and of Immigration in Belgium from the Prehistory to our Days] (Brussels: Éditions Vie Ouvrière, 1992), pp. 213–28.

Herbert, E. W. *The Artist and Social Reform. France and Belgium, 1885–1898* (New Haven, CT: Yale University Press, 1961).

Herman, S., 'De grenzen van seksueel geweld. Schuld en schande in Vlaanderen tijdens de 19e eeuw' [The Boundaries of Sexual Violence. Guilt and shame in Flanders during the Nineteenth Century] *Tijdschrift voor sociale Geschiedenis*, 23:1 (2002), pp. 57–80.

Heyselbergs, B., 'Onstaansgeschiedenis van de wet Vandervelde en het impact op het alcohol-gebruik' [History of the Development of the Law Vandervelde and the Impact on the Use of Alcohol] (Student Dissertation, Catholic University Louvain, 1986).

Hirano, N., 'Le retour des immigrés belges à la suite des événements de Lens et Liévin à août-septembre 1892' [The Return of the Belgian Immigrants Following the Events of Llens and at Lleévin in August-September 1892], in *Belgisch tijdschrift voor de nieuwste geschiedenis – Revue belge d'histoire contemporaine*, 37: 3–4 (2007), pp. 307–23.

Hilton, G. W., 'The British Truck System in the Nineteenth Century', *Journal of Political Economy*, 65: 3 (June 1957), pp. 237–56.

Hobsbawm, E. J., *The Age of Capital, 1848–1875* (London: Weidenfeld & Nicolson, 1999).

—, *The Age of Empire, 1875–1914* (London: Abacus, 1994).

Hoegaerts, J., 'Legal or Just? Law, Ethics and the Double Standard in the Nineteenth Century Divorce', *Law and History Review*, 26:2 (Summer 2008), pp. 259–84.

Houtte, J.A., et al (eds), *Algemene geschidenis der Nederlanden deel XI, Van liberal naar social getij*, 1885-1914 (Zeist: W. De Haan, 1961).

Huertas, R., 'Madness and Degeneration, II. Alcoholism and Degeneration', *History of Psychiatry*, 4 (1993), pp. 1–21.

Huizinga, J., 'Herfsttij der middeleeuwen', [The Waning of the Middle Ages] in J. Huizinga, *Verzamelde werken. Deel 3*, ed. L. Brummel (Harlem, NY: H.D. Tjeenk, Willink & Zoon, 1949).

Hunt, G., J. Mellor and J. Turner, 'Wretched, Hatless and Miserably Clad: Women and the Inebriate Reformatories from 1900–1913', *British Journal of Sociology*, 11, (1989) pp. 244–70.

Jacyna, L. S., *Lost Words: Narratives of Language and the Brain, 1825–1926* (Princeton, NJ: Princeton University Press, 2000).

Jaumain, S., 'Les petits commerçants et la frontière entre petite bourgeoisie et classe ouvrière (1880–1914)' [Small Shopkeepers and the Boundary between Petty Bourgoisie and Working Class], in S. Jaumain and G. Kurgan – Van Hentenryk (eds), *Aux frontières des classes moyennes: la petite bourgeoisie Belge avant 1914* [At the Frontiers of the Middle Classes: The Belgian Petty Bourgeoisie before 1914] (Brussels: Éditions De l'Université de Brussels, 1992), pp. 101–9.

—, *Les petits commerçants belges face à la modernité, 1880–1914* [Small Belgian Shopkeepers Face to Face with Modernity] (Brussels: Editions de l'Universite de Brussels, 1995).

Jewitt, C., and R. Oyama, 'Visual Meaning: A Social Semiotic Approach', in T. Van Leeuwenand C. Jewitt(eds) *Handbook of Visual Analysis* (London: Sage, 2003), pp. 134–56.

Johnstone, G., 'From Vice to Disease? The Concepts of Dipsomania and Inebriety, 1860–1908', *Social and Legal Studies*, 5 (1996), pp. 37–56.

Jordanova, L., *Languages of Nature: Critical Essays on Science and Literature* (New Brunswick, NJ: Rutgers University Press, 1986).

—, 'The Social Construction of Medical Knowledge', *Social History of Medicine*, 4 (1995), pp. 361–81.

—, *The Look of the Past. Visual and Material Evidence in Historical Practice* (Cambridge: Cambridge University Press, 2012).

Jorissen, M., *Ethiek ten dienste van de défense sociale: de stellingnamen van regering en parlement tegenover prostitutie, alcoholisme, landloperij en bedelarij (1884–1894)* [Ethics in Service of Social Defence: The Position of Government and Parliament on Prostitution, Alcoholism, Vagrancy and Mendicity] (Student Dissertation, Catholic University Louvain, 1997).

Jowett, G. S., 'The First Motion Picture Audiences', in J. L. Fell (ed.), *Film before Griffith* (Cambridge, MA: University of California Press, 1983),

Kane, A., 'Reconstructing Culture in Historical Explanation: Narratives as Cultural Structure and Practice', *History and Theory*, 39 (October 2000), pp. 311–30.

Kermabon, J., *Pathé: Premier Empire du Cinéma* (Paris: Centre Georges Pompidou. 1994).

Keymolen, D., *Ongewenst seksueel gedrag op de werkplek in het 19de eeuwse België* [Sexual Harassment at Work in Nineteenth-Century Belgium] (Louvain: Hoger Instituut voor de Arbeid, 1990).

Kocka, J., 'The Middle Classes in Europe', *Journal of Modern History*, 67 (December 1995), pp. 783–806.

Gubin, E., 'Les enquêtes sur le travail en Belgique et au Canada a la fin du 19e Siècle'. [Enquiries into Work in Belgium and Canada in the Nineteenth Century], in G. Kurgan – Van Hentenryk (eds), *La question sociale en Belgique et au Canada: XIXe–XXe Siècles* (Brussels: Editions de L'université de Brussels, 1988), pp. 93–122.

Kurgan – Van Hentenryk, G., 'Une classe oubliée: la petite bourgeoisie de 1850 à 1914' [A Forgotten Class; The Pettty Bourgoisie from 1850 to 1840], in S. Jaumain, S. and G. Kurgan – Van Hentenryk (eds), *Aux frontières des classes moyennes: la petite bourgeoisie belge avant 1914* (Brussels: Éditions de l'Université de Brussels, 1992), pp. 15–24.

Labrie, A., *Zuiverheid en decadentie. Over de grenzen van de burgerlijke cultuur in West-Europa. 1870–1914* [Cleanliness and Decadence. On the Boundaries of Bourgeois Culture in Western Europe] (Amsterdam: Bakker, 2001).

Lalouette, J., 'Alcoolisme et classe ouvrière en France aux alentours de 1900', *Cahiers d'Histoire*, 13:1 (1997), pp. 89–107.

Leboucq, G., 'Barella (Hippolyte)', *Biographie nationale*, t.29, supplément t.1er (Brussels: Emile Bruylant, 1967), pp. 202–4.

Leboutte, R., 'A propos de la condition ouvrière en Wallonie, fin 18e – 19e Siècle', in M. Bruwier, and N.Caulier-Mathy(eds), *1886, La Wallonie née de la grève?: colloque organisé a l'Université de Liège les 29 octobre, 14 et 29 novembre 1986* (Brussels: Editions Labor, 1990), pp. 7–24.

Lefebvre, T., 'Les victimes de l'alcoolisme (Pathé 1902)', *Archives. Institut Jean Vigo – Cinémathèque de Toulouse*, 50 (May 1992).

Lesko, D., *James Ensor, The Creative Years* (Princeton, NY: Princeton University Press, 1985).

Levine, H. G., 'The Discovery of Addiction: Changing Conceptions of Habitual Drunkenness in America', *Journal of Studies of Alcoholism*, 23 (1978), pp. 143–74.

—, 'The Vocabulary of Drunkenness', *Journal of Studies on Alcohol*, 42:3 (1981), pp. 1038–51.

Liebman, M., *Les socialistes Belges 1885–1914: La révolte et l'organisation* (Brussels: Editions Vie Ouvriere, 1979).

Liégois, A., 'Triest, Guislain en de Broeders en Zusters van Liefde', in P. Vandermeersch (ed.), *Psychiatrie, godsdienst en gezag: de onstaansgeschiedenis van de psychiatrie in België als paradigma* [Psychiatry, Religion and Power: History of the Develompent of Psychiaty in Belgium as Pardigm] (Louvain: Acco, 1984), pp. 171–203.

Lis, C., and H. Soly, 'Food Consumption in Antwerp Between 1807 and 1859: A Contribution to the Standard of Living Debate,. *Economic History Review*, 30(1977), pp. 460–86.

Lockamper, N., 'Een situatieschets van de anti-alcoholische beweging in het laatste kwart van de 19e en het begin van de 20e eeuw', [A Summary of the Anti-alcohol Movement in the Last Quarter of the Nineteenth and the beginning of the Twentieth Century] (Student Dissertation, Free University Brussels, 1994).

Lorwin, V. 'Belgium, Religion, Class and Language in National Politics', in R. A. Dahl (ed.), *Political Opposition in Western Democracies* (New Haven, CT: Yale University Press, 1960), pp. 147–87.

Luc, A. F., *Le naturalisme Belge* (Brussels: Editions Labor, 1990).

Mackenzie, C., *Psychiatry for the Rich: A History of Ticehurst Private Asylum, 1792–1917* (London: Routledge, 1992).

Madden, J. S., 'Substance Use Disorders. Clinical Section', in G. E. Berrios and R. Porter (eds), *A History of Clinical Psychiatry: The Origin and History of Psychiatric Disorders* (London: Athlone Press, 1995), pp. 656–67.

Marechal, D. (ed.), *Musée d'Art Moderne. Oeuvres choisies* (Brussels: MRBAB, 2001).

Marrus, M. R., 'Social Drinking in the Belle Epoque', *Journal of Social History*, 7:2 (Winter 1974), pp. 120–28.

Matkava, S., 'l'Union des Femmes Belges contre l'Alcoolisme. 1899–1951: de la lutte antialcoolique aux militantisme féministe et pacifiste' [From Anti-alcohol Struggle to Feminist and Pacifist Activism] (Student Dissertation, Free University Brussels, 1998).

Maza, S., 'Stories in History: Cultural Narratives in Recent Works in European History'. *American Historical Review*, 51:5 (December 1996), pp. 1493–515.

Mccandless, P., '"Curses of Civilisation": Insanity and Drunkenness in Victorian Britain', *British Journal of Addiction*, 79 (1984), pp. 49–58.

McClintock, A. *Imperial Leather: Race, Gender, and Sexuality in the Colonial Contest* (Routledge: London, 1995).

Meyers, P., *Het N.P.C. Sint-Alfons door de tijden heen 1843–1993* [The Psychiatrc Hospital St Alfons Through Time] (Ghent, 1993).

Mostra internazionale del nuovo cinema, *Pathé i film* (Pesaro, 1988).

Musschoot, A.-M., *Cyriel Buysse* (Antwerp: Manteau, 1996.)

Nead, L., *Myths of Sexuality: Representations of Women in Victorian Britain* (Oxford: Basil Blackwell, 1988).

Noël, B., *La rebuveuse d'absinthe – autour de l'oeuvre de Félicien Rops* (Sainte Marguerite des Loges: Éditions BVR, 2005).

Nicholls, J., *The Politics of Alcohol: A History of the Drink Question in England* (Manchester: Manchester University Press, 2008).

Nourrisson, D., *Le buveur du XIXe siècle* (Paris: Albin Michel, 1990).

Nye, R., 'Degeneration and the Medical Model of Cultural Crisis in the French Belle Époque', in S. Drescher, D.Sabeanand, and A. Sharlin (eds), *Political Symbolism in Modern Europe: Essays in Honor of George L. Mosse* (New Brunswick, NY: Transaction Books, 1982), pp. 19–41.

—, *Crime, Madness and Politics in Modern France: The Medical Concept of National Decline* (Princeton, NJ: Princeton University Press, 1984)

—, 'The Evolution of the Concept of Medicalisation in the Late 20th Century', *Journal of the History of Behavioral Sciences*, 29:2 (2003), pp. 115–29.

Nys, L., '"De grote school van de natie": Legerartsen over drankmisbruik en geslachtsziekten in het Belgische leger (ca. 1850–1950)' [Army Doctors on Alcohol Abuse and Venereal Diseases in the Belgian Army], *Bijdragen en mededelingen tot the geschiedenis der nederlanden*, 65:2 (2000), pp. 392–425.

—, 'De metamorfose van Clio Medica. Evolutie en huidige stand van het medisch-historisch onderzoek' [Evolution and Actual Condition of Medical Historical Research], *Mededelingenblad van de Belgische Vereniging voor Nieuwste Geschiedenis*, 23:1 (2001), pp. 9–15.

—, '"Groene toverdrank of gebottelde epilepsie?" Absint in België omstreeks 1900', [Green Magic Potion of Epilepsy in a Bottle? Absinthe in Belgium around 1900] *Tijdschrift voor sociale geschiedenis*, 17:4 (2001), pp. 411–36. Reprinted in J. Tollebeek, J. Van Paemel and K. Wils (eds), *Degeneratie in België 1860–1940: een geschiedenis van ideeën en praktijken* (Louvain: Louvain University Press, 2003), pp. 155–82.

—, '"De ruiters van de Apocalyps": alcoholisme, tuberculose, syphilis en degeneratie in medisch België. 1870–1940', *Tijdschift voor Geschiedenis*, 115:1 (2002), pp. 26–46. Reprinted in J. Tollebeek, J. Van Paemel and K. Wils (eds), *Degeneratie in België 1860–1940: een geschiedenis van ideeën en praktijken* (Louvain: Louvain University Press 2003), pp. 11–42.

—, '"Nationale plagen. Hygiënisten over het maatschappelijk lichaam"' [National Plagues. Hygiensts on the Social Body], in L. Nys, H. De Smaele, J. Tollebeek and K. Wils (eds), *De zieke natie: over de medicalisering van de samenleving, 1860–1914* (Groningen: Historische Uitgeverij, 2002), pp. 220–41.

—, *Moderation as a Medical Moral. The Invention of the Hygienic Body in Belgium ca. 1840–1914*. Unpublished Paper. Anglo-Dutch-German Workshop: Patients' Body Perceptions, Warwick, 11–13 July 2003.

Oris, M. 'Hygiène publique et médicalisation dans une cité industrielle. Seraing au XIXe siècle et au début du XXe siècle', *Revue Belge de philologie et histoire*, 73 (1995), pp. 983–1009.

Pasture, P., 'Views from Abroad: Foreign Historians on a Small State by the North Sea. With Reflections on Historical Writing in Belgium and Elsewhere', *Belgisch tijdschrift voor de nieuwste geschiedenis – Revue belge d'histoire contemporaine*, 35:4 (2005), pp. 413–33.

Paul, H. W., *Bacchic Medicine: Wine and Alcohol Therapies from Napoleon to the French Paradox* (Amsterdam: Rodopi, 2001).

Penn-Hilden, P., 'The Rhetoric and Iconography of Reform: Women Coal Miners in Belgium, 1840–1914', *Historical Journal*, 34:2 (1991), pp. 411–36.

—, *Women, Work, and Politics: Belgium, 1830–1914* (Oxford: Clarendon Press, 1993).

Pick, D., *Faces of Degeneration: a European Disorder, c. 1848–c. 1918* (Cambridge: Cambridge University Press, 1989).

Pirenne, H., *Histoire De Belgique. Vol.VII. De la révolution de 1830 à la guerre de 1914* (Brussels: H. Lamertin, 1932).

Pirlot, F., 'l'Alcoolisme en Belgique de 1830 à 1950. Mythe et réalité.' (Student Dissertation, University of Liège, 1993).

Polasky, J. L, *The Democratic Socialism of Emile Vandervelde: Between Reform and Revolution* (Oxford: Berg, 1995).

Pollock, G., 'Artists Mythologies and Media Genius: Madness and Art History, in *Screen* 21 (1980), pp. 57–96, on p. 66.

Poovey, M., *Uneven Developments: The Ideological Work of Gender in Mid-Victorian England* (Chicago, IL: University Of Chicago Press, 1988).

—, *Making a Social Body: British Cultural Formation 1830–1864* (Chicago, IL: University of Chicago Press, 1995).

—, 'Reading History in Literature: Speculation and Virtue in Our Mutual Friend', in J. Smarr (ed.), *Historical Criticism and the Challenge of Theory* (Urbana, IL: University of Illinois Press, 1993), pp. 42–80.

Porter, R., 'The Drinking Man's Disease: The "Pre-history" of Alcoholism in Georgian Britain', *British Journal of Addiction*, 80 (1985) pp. 385–96.

Porter, D., '"Enemies of the Race": Biologism, Environmentalism, and Public Health in Edwardian England', *Victorian Studies*, 34:2 (Winter 1991), pp.159–78.

Preiswerk, F., 'Auguste Forel (1848–1931): Un projet de régénération sociale, morale et raciale', *Annuelles – Revue d'histoire contemporaine*, 2 (1991) pp. 25–50.

Prestwich, P. E., *Drink and the Politics of Social Reform: Antialcoholism in France since 1870* (Palo Alto: Society for the Promotion of Science and Scholarship, 1988).

—, 'Family Strategies and Medical Power: "Voluntary" Committal in a Parisian Asylum, 1876–1914' *Journal of Social History*, 27 (1993), pp. 798–819.

—, 'Female Alcoholism in Paris, 1870–1920.The Response of Psychiatrists and Families', *History of Psychiatry*, 14:3 (2003), pp. 321–36.

—, 'Le rôle des infirmiers et infirmières psychiatriques à la fin du 19 siècle: garder, soigner, innover?' [The Role of Psychiatric Nurses at the end of the 19th century. Keeping, Caring, Innovating?], *Soins Psychiatrie.* 137 (March 1992), pp 43–7.

—, 'Sources for Research on the History of Alcohol in France since 1850'. *Social History of Alcohol Review*, 14 Xix (Spring 1989), pp. 9–13.

—, 'Temperance in France: The Curious Case of Absinthe', *Historical Reflections/Réflections Historiques*, 6:2 (1979), pp. 301–20.

—, 'Drinkers, Drunkards, and Degenerates: The Alcoholic Population of a Parisian Asylum', *Social History/Histoire Sociale*, 27:53–4 (1994), pp. 321–35.

Pruitt, A. A., 'Approaches to Alcoholism in Mid-Victorian England', *Clio Medica*, 9:2 (1974), pp. 93–102.

Puissant, J., 'Le bon ouvrier, mythe ou réalité du XIXe siècle. De l'utilité d'une biographie. J. F. J. Dauby (1824–1899)'[The Good Worker, Mythe or Reality of the NineteenthCentury.

On the Usefulness of Biography: J. F. J. Dauby (1824–1899)] *Revue belge de philologie et d'histoire*, 56:4 (1978), pp. 878–929.

Quétel, C., and J. Y. Simon, 'L'aliénation alcoolique en France (XIXe et 1ère moitié du XXe Siècle) [Alcoholic Insanity in France], *Histoire, Economie, Société*, 7:4 (1988), pp. 507–33.

Quétel, C., *History of Syphilis* (Cambridge: Polity Press, 1990).

Radkau, J., 'The Neurasthenic Experience in Imperial Germany: Expeditions into Patient Records and Side – looks upon General History', in M. Gijswijt-Hofstra andR. Porter(eds), *Cultures of Neurasthenia from Beard to the First World War* (Amsterdam; New York: Rodopi, 2001), pp. 199–217.

Reynebeau, M., *Een geschiedenis Van België* (Tielt: Lannoo, 2003).

Rioux, J. P., *La révolution industrielle, 1780–1880* (Paris: Editions Du Seuil: 1971).

Risse, G. B., and J. H. Warner, 'Reconstructing Clinical Activities: Patient Records in Medical History', *Social History of Medicine*, 5 (2004), p. 183–205.

Roberts, J. S., *Drink, Temperance and the Working Class in Nineteenth Century Germany* (Boston, MA: Allen & Unwin, 1984).

Roberts, J. S., 'Drink and Industrial Work Discipline In 19th Century Germany', *Journal Of Social History*, 15:1 (Autumn, 1981), pp. 25–38.

Robinson, D., 'Influence du Cinema Français sur le Marché Londonien', in J. A. Gill,

M. Langy (eds), *Les vingt premières années du cinema Francais, Actes du colloque international de la Sorbonne Nouvelle 4, 5 et 6 novembre 1993* [The Twenty First Years of French Cinema] (Paris: Presses de la Sorbonne nouvelle, 1995), pp. 337–50.

Rousseaux, J. P., 'Alcoolisme et co-alcoolisme dans l'Assommoir d'Emile Zola', in J.-P. Roussaux, B. Faoro-Kreit, D. Hers (eds), *L'Alcoolique en famille: dimensions*

familiales des alcoolismes et implications thérapeutiques, [Alcoholics in the Family: Familial Dimensions of Alcoholism and Therapeutical Implications] (Brussels: De Boeck and Larcier, 2000), pp. 143–8.

Rousseaux, X., 'C'est arrive près de chez vous/Het geweld van België. La violence est-elle un objet d' histoire des Belges?' [Is Violence an Object of History of the Belgians?], in G. Kurgan – Van Henterijk (ed.), *Un pays si tranquille: la violence en Belgique au XIXe siècle* [Such a Quiet Country: Violence in Belgium in the NineteenthCentury] (Brussels: Editions de l'Université de Brussels, 1999), pp. 9–40.

Sadoul, G., *Histoire générale du cinéma* (Paris: Denoel, 1973).

Schepers, R., 'Een wereld van belangen. Artsen en de ontwikkelingen van de openbare gezondheidszorg' [A World of Interests. Physicians and the Developments in Public Health], in L. Nys, H, De Smaele, J. Tollebeek and K. Wils (eds), *De zieke natie: over de medicalisering van de samenleving, 1860–1914* (Groningen: Historische Uitgeverij, 2002), pp. 200–18.

Scholliers, P., *Arm en rijk aan tafel: tweehonderd jaar eetcultuur in België* [Rich and Poor at the Table: Two Hundred Years of Food Culture in Belgium] (Berchem: EPO, 1993).

—, 'The Medical Discourse and the Drunkard's Stereotyping in Belgium, 1840–1919', in A. Fenton (ed.), *Order and Disorder. The Health Implications of Eating and Drinking in the Nineteenth and Twentieth Centuries* (East Linton: Tuckwell Press, 2000), pp. 227–39.

—, 'Meals, Food Narratives and Sentiments of Belonging in Past and Present', in Scholliers, P. (ed.), *Food, Drink and Identity. Cooking Eating and Drinking in Europe since the Middle Ages (*London: Berg Publishers, 2001), pp. 3–20.

—, 'Een vijand die men kennen moet. Jenever in België in de 19de en vroege 20e Eeuw' [An Enemy One Needs to Know. Gin in Belgium in the Nineteenth and the Early Twentieth Century] in E. Van Schoonenberghe (ed.), *Jenever in de Lage Landen* (Antwerp: Stichtig Kunstboek, 2004.) pp. 138–77.

—, *Food Culture in Belgium* (Westport, CT: Greenwood Press, 2009).

Scott, J. W., 'Gender: A Useful Category of Historical Analysis', *American Historical Review*, 81 (1986), pp. 1053–75.

Sevenois, D., *De anti-alcoholproblematiek van het einde van de 19de eeuw tot het begin van de 20ste eeuw en de rol van de medische professie hierin.* [The Anti-Alcohol Question at the end of the Nineteenth and the beginning of the Twentieth Century and the Role of the Medical Profession] (Student Dissertation, Vrije Universite Brussels, 2006).

Seyn, E. M. H., *Dictionnaire des Eécrivains Belges. Bio-bibliographie. Tome II* (Bruges: Editions Excelsior, 1930), pp. 2095–6.

Shorter, E., *A History of Psychiatry: From the Era of the Asylum to the Age of Prozac* (New York: Wiley, 1997).

Simons, T., 'Het Volksgeluk: geïllustreerd maandblad tegen alcoolism (1889–1914): het Belgische alcoholprobleem en haar bestrijding' [The Happiness of the People: Illustrated Monthy Journal Against Alcoholim] (Student Dissertation: Catholic University Louvain, 2004).

Small, H., '"In the Guise of Science": Literature and the Rhetoric of 19th Century English Psychiatry', *History of the Human Sciences*, 7 (February 1994), pp. 27–55.

Smith, R., *Trial by Medicine: Insanity and Responsibility in Victorian Trials* (Edinburgh: Edinburgh University Press, 1981).

Soloway, R., 'Counting the Degenerates: The Statistics of Race Deterioration in Edwardian England', *Journal of Contemporary History*, 17:1 (1982), pp. 137–64.

Sournia, J. C., *Histoire de l'Alcoolisme* (Paris: Flammarion, 1986).

Stark, D. E., 'Charles De Groux et le réalisme social dans la peinture Belge', in J. Dewilde, J.M. Duvosquel, and A.M. Meessen-Doneux (eds), *Charles Degroux, 1825–1870 et le réalisme en Belgique* (GhentGhent: Snoeck-Ducaju & Zoon, 1995).

Starks, M., *Cocaine fiends and Reefer Madness: An Illustrated History of Drugs in the Movies* (New York ; London: Cornwall Books, 1982).

Steverlynck, C., *Kleine martelaars: een historisch document over misbruikte kinderen, kindermishandeling, incest en prostitutie* [A Historical Document about Child Abuse, Incest and Prostitution] (Antwerp: Icarus, 1997).

Stockman, 'Life within the walls of the Guislain Institute in Ghent (1850–1950)', in L. Gloeiand J. Vijselaar, *Proceedings of the 1st European Congress on the History of Psychiatry and Mental Health Care, 's-Hertogenbosch, The Netherlands, 24–26 October 1990* (Rotterdam: Erasmus Publishing, 1993), pp. 194–203.

Strikwerda, C., 'If All of Europe were Belgium: Lessons in Politics and Globalization from One Country', *Belgisch tijdschrift voor de nieuwste geschiedenis – Revue belge d'histoire contemporaine*, 35:4 (2005), pp. 503–22.

Swinbourne, A., *James Ensor* (New York: Museum of Modern Art, 2009), p. 84.

Thomas, B., *Cross-Examinations of Law and Literature: Cooper, Hawthorne, Stowe and Melville*, (Cambridge: Cambridge University Press, 1987).

Thompson, E. P., *The Making of the English Working Class* (Harmondsworth: Penguin, 1986).

Timmerman, M., 'De sociale ernst van het alkoholisme en de mobilisatie voor de drankbestrijding, vanaf het laatste kwart van de 19de eeuw' [The Social Seriousness of Alcoholism and the Mobilisation for the Temperance Movment in the Last Quarter of the Nineteenth Century (Student Disseration, University Ghent, 1981)

Todts, H., D. Cardijn-Oomenand N. Monteneye, *Het volk ten voete uit. Naturalisme in België en Europa* [Naturalism in Belgium and Europe](Ghent: Ludion, 1996).

Todts, H., *James Ensor. Schilderijen en tekeningen uit de verzameling van het Koninklijk Museum voor Schone Kunsten Antwerpen* [Paintings and Drawings from the Collection of the Royal Museum of Fine Arts Antwerp] (Schoten: BAI, 2008).

Tollebeek, J., 'Degeneratie, moderniteit en culturele verandering. Een Belgisch perspectief' [Degeneration, Modernity and Cultural Change. A Belgian Perspective], in J. Tollebeek, J. Van Paemel and K. Wils (eds), *Degeneratie in België 1860–1940: een geschiedenis van ideeën en praktijken* (Louvain: Louvain University Press, 2003), pp. 299–320.

Tosh, J., *The Pursuit of History* (New York: Longman, 1999).

Trolli. G., *Exposé de la législation sanitaire du Congo belge et du Ruanda-Urundi* [Account of the Sanitary Legislation of the Belgian Congo and of Ruanda-Urundi] (Brussels: Ferd. Larcier, 1938).

Turner, V., 'Social Drama's and Stories about Them', *Critical Inquiry*, 7:1 (Autumn 1982), pp. 141–68.

Upstone, R., and C. Holden, *George Cruikshank's The Worship of Bacchus in Focus* (London: Tate Publishing, 2001).

Valverde, M., *Diseases of the Will: Alcohol and the Dilemmas of Freedom* (Cambridge: Cambridge University Press, 1998).

—, 'Slavery from Within: The Intervention of Alcoholism and the Question of Free Will', *Social History*, 12:3 (1997), pp. 251–68.

van Bork, G. J., and P. J. Verkruijsse(eds), *De Nederlandse en Vlaamse auteurs van middeleeuwen tot heden met inbegrip van de Friese auteurs* (De Haan: Weesp 1985).

Van Bouchaute, S., 'Grenzeloos drinken? De enscenering van de herberg en het drinken in de beeldende kunst en literatuur tijdens de lange zestiende eeuw' [The Representation of the Inn and Drinking in Art and Literature during het Long Nineteenth Century], in D. J. Baetens and D. Jacobs, *De kunst van het drinkien. Herberg- en drinkscenes in de Belgische schilderkunst* (Hasselt: Van Der Wiele, 2011), pp. 11–31.

Vandecaveye, H., 'Het proletariërslied, Een sociaal-kulturele verschijningsvorm van de socialistische arbeidersvereniging' [The Proletarian Song. A Social and Cultural Manifestation of the Socialist Workers' Movement], *Belgisch tijdschrift voor de nieuwste geschiedenis – Revue belge d'histoire contemporaine*, 6:2 (1980), pp. 171–202.

Van Den Abeele, V., 'Het sociaal-geografisch profiel van de opgenomen krankzinnigen en het dagelijks leven in twee Gentse mannengestichten, 1857–1900' [The Social and Geographical Profile of Admitted Mental Patients and Daily Life in Two Ghent Male Institutions] (Student dissertation, University Ghent , 1999).

Vanden Borre, S., 'Union et fraternité. Verenigingen van Belgische migranten in Roubaix in de tweede helft van de negentiende eeuw' [Organizations of Belgian Migrants in Roubaix in the Second Half of the Ninettenth Century] *Belgisch tijdschrift voor nieuwste geschiedenis— Revue belge d'histoire contemporaine*, 39: 3–4 (2009), pp. 369–404.

Van De Kerckhove, M., 'Discours juridique et discours psychiatrique. Aux sources de la loi de la défense sociale' [Legal and Political Discourses. To the Roots of the Law of Social Defense] *Droit et Société*, 3 (1986), pp. 279–302.

—, L'Organisation d'asiles spéciaux pour aliénés dangereux' [Organization of Special Institutions for Dangerous Mental Patients], in F. Tulkens (ed.), *Généalogie de la défense sociale en Belgique (1880–1914)* (Brussels: E. Story-Scientia, 1988).

Van De Merwe, J., *Gij zijt kanalje, heeft men ons verweten! Het proletariërslied in Nederland en Vlaanderen* [The Proletariat Song in the Netherlands and Flanders] (Antwerp, Utrecht: A. W. Bruna & Zoon, 1974).

Van den Berg, M., *De volkssage in de provincie Antwerpen in de 19de en 20ste eeuw* (Ghent: Koninklijke academie voor Nederlandse taal – en letterkunde, 1993).

Van den Eeckhout, P., '"Facing History": Verslag van een Colloquium over de Relatie tussen Literatuur en Geschiedenis', *Belgisch tijdschrift voor de nieuwste geschiedenis – Revue belge d'histoire contemporaine*, 28: 1–2 (1998), pp. 279–85.

—, 'The Quest for Social History in Belgium (1848–1998)', *Archif für Sozialgeschichte* 40, (2000), pp. 321–36.

—, 'Eten en gegeten worden. Historici en consumptiegeschiedenis in België (19e–20e eeuw)' [Historians and Comsumption History in Belgium] *Tijdschrift voor sociale geschiedenis*, 28 (2002), pp. 373–90.

Van den Eeckhout, P., and G. Vanthemsche (eds), *Bronnen voor de studie van het hedendaagse België, 19e–20e eeuw* [Sources for the Study of Contemporary Belgium in the Nineteenth and Twentieth Centuries] (Brussels: Koninklijke commissie voor geschiedenis, 2009).

Van den Eeckhout, P., and P. Scholliers, 'De hoofdelijke voedselconsumptie in België, 1831–1939' [Individual Food Consumption in Belgium] *Tijdschrift voor sociale geschiedenis*, 9 (1983), pp. 274–301.

—, 'Social History in Belgium: Old Habits and New Perspectives', *Tijdschrift voor sociale geschiedenis*, 23:2 (1997), pp. 147–81.

Van De Perre, S., 'Noble drinking: Wine consumption in Belgium, 1930–1914', in P. Janssens and S. Zeischka, *The Dining Nobility: From the Burgundian Dukes to the Belgian Royalty* (Brussels: VUB Press, 2008), pp. 60–80.

van der Stel, J. C., *Drinken, drank en dronkenschap: vijf eeuwen drankbestrijding en alcoholhulpverlening in Nederland* [Five Centuries Temperance Movment and Alcohol Assistance in the Netherlands] (Hilversum: Verloren, 1995).

Van Dijk, P., and H. Winterwerp, *Volksgeneeskunst in Nederland en Vlaanderen* [Folk Medicine in the Netherlands and Flanders] (Deventer: Ankh-Hermes, 1981).

Vanfraechem, S., *Een sfeer om haring the braden: arbeidsverhoudingen in de haven van Antwerpen* [Worker's relationships in the Antwerp Harbour] (Ghent: Academia Press, 2005).

Van Hageland, A., *Hendrik Conscience en ons volksleven* (Aartselaar: Vlaams Boekenfonds, 1984).

Vanhaute, E., *Heiboeren. Bevolking, arbeid en inkomen in de 19de-eeuwse Kempen* [Population, Poverty and Income of the Nineteenth-Century Campine] (Brussels: VUB press, 1992).

Vanheste, B., 'Een tweede eeuw voor Streuvels? Gedachten over eeliteratuursociologisch programma' [A Second Century for Steuvels? Thoughts about a Literary Sociological Programme of Study], in P. Thomas (ed.), *Een tweede eeuw? Jaarboek I van het Stijn Streuvelsgenootschap* (Tielt: Lannoo, 1995), pp. 13–30.

Van Isacker, K., *De Antwerpse dokwerker, 1830–1940* (Antwerp: De Nederlandsche boekhandel, 1963).

—, *Mijn land in de kering: 1830–1980* (Antwerp: De Nederlandsche boekhandel, 1978).

Vanoverschelde, V., 'Tot herstel der krankheid van mijn zwakke geest is nodig. De psychiatrische praktijk in het Sint-Jozefshuis en het Maison de santé te Gent door de Zusters van Liefde en Jozef Guislain (1808–1860)' [Psychiatric Practice in Ghent by the Sisters of Charity and Joseph Guislain] (Student Dissertation, University of Ghent, 2008).

Van Outrive, L., Y. Cartuyvels and P. Posniers, *Les polices en Belgique: histoire socio-politique du système policier de 1794 à nos Jours (*Brussels: Editions Vie Ouvrière, 1991).

Van Parijs, J., *Het leven, niets dan het leven: Cyriel Buysse en zijn tijd* (Antwerp: Houtekiet, 2007).

Van Reybrouck, D., *Congo, een geschiedenis* (Amsterdam: De Bezige Bij, 2010)

Van Waesberghe, W., 'Het Belgische krankzinnigenbeleid in de XIXe eeuw' [The Belgian Mental Health Policies of the Nineteenth Century] *Annales de la Société belge d'histoire des hôpitaux et de la santé publique*, 22 (1984), pp. 69–96.

Velle, K., 'Statistiek en sociale politiek: de medische statistiek en het gezondheidsbeleid in België in de 19e eeuw', *Belgisch tijdschrift voor de nieuwste geschiedenis – Revue belge d'histoire contemporaine*, 16:1–2 (1985), pp. 213–42.

—, 'Medikalisering in Belgie in historisch perspektief, een inleiding', *Belgisch tijdschrift voor de nieuwste geschiedenis – Revue belge d'histoire contemporaine*, 64:2 (1986), pp. 266–85.

—, 'De syphiliskwestie in België in de 19e en het begin van de 20e eeuw', *Tijdschrift voor sociale wetenschappen*, 4 (1987), 331–63.

—, *De nieuwe biechtvaders: de sociale geschiedenis van de arts in België* [The New Confessors: Social History of the Phycisian in Belgium] (Louvain: Kritak, 1991)

—, 'Medisch onderwijs en de professie: de gerechtelijke geneeskunde in België in de 19de eeuw', [Medical Education and the Profession: Legal Medicine in Belgium in the Nineteenth Century] *Gewina*, 16:3 (1993), pp. 171–86.

—, 'De misdaad als kwaal. Het succes van de criminele antropologie' [Crime as Disease. The Success of Criminal Anthropolgy] in L. Nys, H. De Smaele, J. Tollebeek and K. Wils (eds), *De zieke natie: over de medicalisering van de samenleving, 1860–1914* (Groningen: Historische Uitgeverij, 2002), pp. 332–54.

—, 'Het beeld van de magistratuur van de Belle Epoque tot na de Eerste Wereldoorlog. Casus: Raymond de Ryckere (1862–1918)' [The Image of the Magistrature from the Belle Epoque to after the First World War. Case Study: Raymond de Ryckere] in F. Daelemans, M. Lebert, E. Bodart, L. Honnoré and J. Houssiau (eds), *Image et imagination. Recueil d'articles offert à André Vanrie à l'occasion de son septantième anniversaire. Archives et Bibliothèques de Belgique*, 91, special issue (Brussels: Bibliothèque Royale de Belgique, 2010) pp. 483–518.

Verboven, H., 'Jenever en fiscaliteit', in E. Van Schoonenberghe (ed), *Jenever in de Lage Landen* (Antwerp: Stichtig Kunstboek, 2004.) pp. 179–89.

Verherie, I., 'Ontspanningsleven van Brugse arbeiders (1890–1921)' [Recreation among Brugge Workers] (Student Dissertation, University Ghent, 1998).

Vincent, J. J., *Naslagwerk over de Vlaamse film* [Reference of Flemish Film] (Brussel: C.I.A.M. 2000).

Vloeberg, S., *Tot we barsten. Een impressie van het banket in de 19e eeuw in drie Belgische steden: Leuven, Mechelen en Diest* [The Banquet in the Nineteenth Century in Three Belgian cities] (Student Dissertation, Katholieke Universiteit Catholic University Louvain, 1991).

Vogt, I., 'Alkoholkonsum, Industrialisierung und Klassenkonflikt', [Alcoholscomsumption, Industrialisation and Class Conflict], in G. Vögler and K. von Welck (eds), *Rausch und Realität: Drogen im Kulturvergleich, Vol. 1* (Reinbek: Rowohlt Verlag, 1982), pp. 202–11.

Vreckem Paul, H. S., *De invloed van het Franse naturalisme in het werk van Cyriel Buysse* [The Influence of French Naturalism on het Work of Cyriel Buysse] (Brussel, Tijdschrift van de Vrije Universiteit Brussel, 1968).

Walkowitz, J., *Prostitution and Victorian Society: Women, Class and the State* (Cambridge: Cambridge University Press, 1982).

Walkowitz, J. R., *City of Dreadful Delight: Narratives of Sexual Danger in Late-Victorian London* (Chicago, IL: University of Chicago Press, 1992).

Willis, J., *Potent Brews, A Social History of Alcohol in East Africa, 1850–1999* (Nairobi: British Institute of East Africa, 2002).

Wils, K., *De omweg van de wetenschap: het positivisme en de Belgische en Nederlandse intellectuele cultuur, 1845–1914* [Postivism in Belgian and Dutch Intellectual Culture] (Amsterdam: Amsterdam University Press, 2005).

Warner, J. H., 'Psychological Theory and Therapeutic Explanation in the 1860's: the British Debate on the Medical Use of Alcohol', *Bulletin of the History of Medicine*, 54 (1980), pp. 235–57.

Weesmaals L., *De relatie tussen het antialcoholistisch vrouwelijk activisme en het feminisme in het fin de siècle in België* [The Relationship between Female Anti-alcohol Activism and Feminism] (Student Dissertation, University Ghent 2008).

Willekens, E., and G. Degroote, *Hendrik Conscience en zijn tijd* (Antwerp: Stichting Mercator-Plantijn, 1983).

Willekens, E., *Hendrik Conscience 1812–1883* (Brussels, 1961).

—, *Hij leerde zijn volk lezen: profiel van Hendrik Conscience 1812–1883.* [He Taught his People How to Read. Profile of Hendrik Conscience] (Antwerp: Esco, 1982).

Willems, N., 'La Loi Vandervelde et ses antécédents' (Student Dissertation, Free University Brussels, 1971).

Williams, A. L., *Republic of Images: A History of French Filmmaking* (Cambridge, MA: Harvard University Press, 1992).

Williams, R., *The Long Revolution* (London: Hogarth Press, 1961).

—, *Keywords: A Vocabulary of Culture and Society* (London: Fontana, 1988).

Willis, J., *Potent Brews, A Social History of Alcohol in East Africa, 1850–1999* (Nairobi: British Institute of East Africa, 2002).

Witte, E., 'Electorale agenten aan de vooravond van de partijformaties', [Electoral Agents at the Wake of Party Formations] *Belgisch tijdschrift voor nieuwste geschiedenis – Revue belge d'histoire contemporaine*, 1:2 (1969), pp. 216–53.

Witte, E., Craeybeckx, J., and Meynen, A., *Politieke Geschiedenis van Belgie: van 1830 tot heden* (Antwerp: Standaard, 1990).

Woiak.D. J. 'Drunkenness, Degeneration, and Eugenics in Britain, 1900–1914' (PhD Dissertation, University of Toronto, 1998).

Woestenborghs, B., 'Les travailleurs saisonniers flamands en France de 1870 à 1970', [Flemish Seasonal workers in France], in A. Morelli (ed.), *Les émigrants Belges. Réfugiés de guerre, émigrés économiques, réfugiés politiques ayant quitté nos régions du XVième siècle à nos jours* (Brussels: Éditions Vie Ouvrière, 1998), pp. 205–12.

Wouters, H., *Documenten betreffende de geschiedenis der arbeidersbeweging (1831–1853)* [Documents Concerning het History of the Woker's Movement] (Louvain: Editions Nauwelaerts, 1963).

—, *Documenten betreffende de geschiedenis der arbeidersbeweging (1853–1865).* (Louvain: Editions Nauwelaerts, 1966).

—, *Documenten betreffende de geschiedenis der arbeidersbeweging ten tijde van de Ie Internationale (1866–1880)* (Louvain: Editions Nauvelaerts. 1970).

Wright, D., 'Discussion point. Getting out of the Asylum: Understanding the Confinement of the Insane in the Nineteenth Century', *Social History of Medicine*, 10 (1997), pp. 137–55.

Zolberg, A., 'The Making of Flemings and Walloons: Belgium 1830–1914', *Journal of Interdisciplinary History*, 5 (1974), pp. 179–235.

INDEX